Everyday Matters in Science and Mathematics

Studies of Complex Classroom Events

Matters in Science
Mathematics

x Classroom Events

classroom events |

pbk. : alk. paper)
thodology.
—Study and teaching
ching (Elementary)—Methodology—
and teaching (Elementary)—

2004015839

are printed on acid-free
and durability.

n

This book was typeset in 10.5/13 pt. Goudy Old Style, Bold, and Italic.
The heads were typeset in Goudy Old Style, Bold, and Bold Italic.

Lawrence Erlbaum Associates, Inc., Publishers
10 Industrial Avenue
Mahwah, New Jersey 07430
www.erlbaum.com

Cover design by Kathryn Houghtaling Lacey

Library of Congress Cataloging-in-Publication Data

Everyday matters in science and mathematics : studies of comple
edited by Ricardo Nemirovsky . . . [et al.].
    p.   cm.
  Includes bibliographical references and index.
  ISBN 0-8058-4722-7 (alk. paper)—ISBN 0-8058-4723-5
  1. Mathematics—Study and teaching (Elementary)—M
2. Mathematics—Curricula—Evaluation.   3. Mathematic
(Elementary)—Case studies.   4. Science—Study and te
5. Science—Curricula—Evaluation.   6. Science—Stud
Case studies.   I. Nemirovsky, Ricardo, 1951-

  QA11.2.E945   2005
  372.7—dc22

Books published by Lawrence Erlbaum Associates
paper, and their bindings are chosen for strength

Printed in the United States of America
10 9 8 7 6 5 4 3 2 1

Contents

Preface

This book results from a multiyear collaboration made possible by the National Center for Improving Student Learning and Achievement housed at the Wisconsin Center for Educational Research, University of Wisconsin, Madison. This collaboration focused on investigating the nature of learning in science and mathematics classrooms and on ways to design classrooms that foster rich understanding of these domains. The specific contributions in this volume were first presented at a seminar in Ashland, Massachusetts, sponsored by the Center in November 2000 entitled, "Case Studies and Instructional Design."

The aim of this book is to reexamine the dichotomy between the "everyday" and the "disciplinary" that has dominated much of educational thinking as well as to explore alternatives to this opposition from points of view grounded in the close examination of complex classroom events. Traditionally in the context of schooling, everyday knowledge and practices are seen in opposition to disciplinary knowledge and practices. In this book we make the case that the teaching and learning of science and mathematics builds on students' everyday experience and knowledge in all their manifold forms. The chapters in this book explore this thesis from various angles. They capture the voices of students, teachers, and curriculum developers as they wrestle with the complexities of their encounters with everyday and disciplinary matters. This book will be of interest to those—researchers, teacher educators, practitioners, and policymakers—who are interested in research that is grounded in close analysis of classroom events, student thinking, and teacher practice.

The book is organized in three sections, each with a particular lens: (1) the experiences of students in encounters with what we call "everyday matters of a discipline"; (2) the actions of teachers as they create classroom encounters with everyday matters of a discipline; and (3) the concerns of curriculum designers, including teachers, as they design activities intended to focus on everyday matters of a discipline.

The first section of the book addresses a number of provocative questions about what is entailed in becoming a participant in the "everyday matters of scientific or mathematical disciplines." The main question addressed is: How do students experience or make sense of the problem or environment set before them? What do learning environments become *for* them? The analyses focus on the varied and complex ways in which students encounter the occasions that have been designed to bring them into contact with disciplinary ideas and practices.

In "'Why would Run be in Speed?' Artifacts and Situated Actions in a Curricular Plan," Stephen Monk explores the varied ways in which a class of third and fourth graders grappled generatively with the inherent ambiguity of language and symbol use as they investigated ways of describing their own motion along a 10-foot straight line.

In "Mathematical Places," Ricardo Nemirovsky elaborates a perspective on symbolizing as a process of inhabiting symbolic places that embrace both the symbol user and the world in which he or she lives. The discussion of symbolic places leads into an analysis of how two high school students experienced two mathematical places—"a graphical place" and "an algebraic place"—as they worked to find a quadratic function to describe the motion of a toy car driven by a "line becomes motion" computer interface.

In "Developing Concepts of Justification and Proof in a Sixth-Grade Classrom," Carrie Valentine, Thomas Carpenter, and Margaret Pligge present a case study of a sixth-grade classroom engaged in developing concepts of mathematical justification and proof in the context of investigating the commutative property of multiplication. The analysis focuses on the students' efforts, in concert with their teacher, to establish norms for what counts as justification within mathematics.

In "Everyday and Scientific: Rethinking Dichotomies in Modes of Thinking in Science Learning," Beth Warren, Mark Ogonowski, and Suzanne Pothier question the strong tendency to view modes of thought in terms of binary oppositions. Focusing on episodes in which a class of first and second graders worked at describing the motion of a toy car as it rolled down a ramp, the authors show how the children's accounts of their experiences running down hills were not mere replications of the "everyday," but instead newly interpreted, in-the-present encounters, shaped by emerging intentions and ideas.

The second section discusses what it is that experienced teachers do before, during, and after a lesson to manage the complexity that is inherent in any given classroom encounter with disciplinary ideas. How do they negotiate the uncertain waters of everyday and disciplinary matters? Each of the chapters in this section attempts to address these and related issues from unique yet complementary angles. In tandem, these chapters explore fundamental issues related to where the responsibility and authority for learning resides in complex classroom events.

In "The Mathematics Behind the Graph: Discussions of Data," Kay Mc-Clain argues that it is the teacher's responsibility to negotiate classroom discussions so that they stay focused on mathematical ideas in ways productive for learning. To demonstrate what this means, McClain presents a case study of the instructional decisions she—as the classroom teacher—made to ensure that a whole-class discussion among eighth graders about their analyses of bivariate data remained focused on McClain's mathematical agenda.

In recent years, the scope of what is taught in elementary mathematics has broadened to include inquiry into the nature of mathematical concepts and operations, and the articulation, explanation, and justification of alternative strategies for solving mathematical problems. Ellice Ann Forman and Ellen Ansell address this issue in "Creating Mathematics Stories: Learning to Explain in a Third-Grade Classroom." They describe how one third-grade teacher, Mrs. Porter, designed and negotiated pedagogical encounters between the important social norms of mutual respect and clarity of communication and sociomathematical norms for evaluating and justifying mathematical explanations.

Finally, Maria Blanton and James Kaput take up the question of how teachers can leverage the "everyday matters of a discipline" and the "disciplinary matters of the everyday" to support students' algebraic reasoning. In "Instructional Contexts That Support Students' Transitions From Arithmetic to Algebraic Reasoning: Elements of Task and Culture," they explore two basic questions: (1) What types of tasks might teachers select or develop to coordinate students' everyday experiences with number and arithmetic operations and mathematical ideas that are recognized as "algebraic" by the discipline?; (2) How should these tasks be integrated into the life of the classroom?

The third section includes four chapters exploring the various considerations with which curriculum designers are concerned as they work to develop mathematics and science curriculum that attempts to connect with everyday matters. The chapters raise a set of questions about four key considerations of curriculum developers: (1) their sense of what students are likely to bring to the class, (2) their proximity to the students, (3) their own conceptions about the discipline, and (4) the limits and possibilities of the classroom. The chapters come at these questions from differing perspectives and approach curriculum on differing scales.

In "Constructing a Learning Environment That Promotes Reinvention," Els Feijs describes a cycle of curriculum development as a set of stages: the establishment of an underlying learning trajectory, initial materials development, classroom observations, analysis of findings, and curriculum refinements, which results in both a final product and an improved hypothetical learning trajectory.

In "Involving Students in Realistic Scientific Practice: Strategies for Laying Epistemological Groundwork," Jennifer Cartier, Cynthia Passmore, Jim Stewart, and John Willauer describe the implementation of a curriculum unit designed to articulate and investigate their underlying design principle that the primary goal of science education is to develop students' understanding of and participation in the *practices* of particular scientific disciplines, rather than in any particular content area.

In "'What are we going to do next?': Lesson Planning as a Resource for Teaching," Ann Rosebery explores the complexity of planning a single lesson with an experienced teacher as she draws upon her theory of learning and teaching, her knowledge of her students, her knowledge of the subject matter, and her instructional objectives to create scenarios of how the lesson will unfold, preparing herself for the inevitable and surprising negotiations of meaning that will occur in the next day's class.

Finally, in "Exploration Zones: A Framework for Describing the Emergent Structure of Learning Activities," Bruce Sherin, Flávio Azevedo, and Andy diSessa present a language and framework for describing the rich set of possible directions a lesson may take—which they conceptualize as "exploration zones"—as it is co-created by curriculum developers, teachers, and students.

ACKNOWLEDGMENTS

The authors thank Tom Carpenter and Tom Romberg, who directed NCISLA at different points in its history, for their support for this volume. We also wish to thank Susan R. Goldman and one anonymous reviewer who reviewed the chapters and provided valuable feedback. Our editor, Naomi Silverman, was extremely helpful in guiding us to the completion of the book. Finally, we appreciate the thought and care that Cara DiMattia and Darrell Earnest took in organizing and ensuring the success of the seminar in Ashland.

Introduction

Over the last 15 years a shift has taken place in the field of educational research moving away from formal, structural models of learning toward emphasizing its situated nature and the sociocultural bases of teaching and learning (Lave, 1988; Lave & Wenger, 1991; Rogoff, 1990; Suchman, 1987; Wertsch, 1991). An emerging trend in the study of learning is the fine-grained examination of selected classroom episodes, not to replace the work on general theoretical frameworks but to ground them in actual complex events. This trend is stimulated by at least two forces: (1) the increasing awareness that formal theories can be useful guides but are always partial and provisional in how they disclose classroom experiences, and (2) the widespread availability of video and audio equipment that enables effortless recording and study of classroom interactions. These two forces have reoriented the field by allowing researchers and teachers to look at learning starting with complex classroom events rather than formal theories of learning.

This reorientation means that researchers and teachers can now encounter the complexity of learning and teaching as lived, human meaning-making experiences. Immersion in this complexity compels us to rethink our own assumptions about the dichotomies that have traditionally organized the field's thinking about learning. Further, it has important implications for how we view the relationship between theory and practice in understanding teaching and learning. On the one hand this shift brings researchers and educators into full contact with countless nuances and subtle dynamics taking place in the actual interactions between students and teachers. Whereas on the other hand it elicits considerable skepticism with respect to grand narratives and universal theories that not long ago were common paradigms in educational research. As studies become more local and context-bound, the connections between them are themselves subjects of interpretation.

Inscribed in this context, the aim of this book is to reexamine the dichotomy between the everyday and the disciplinary, as well as to explore alternatives to this opposition from points of view grounded in the close examination of complex classroom events. In the field of education research, the term "everyday" often connotes, among other things, "commonplace," "simple," or "prosaic." It is frequently associated with intuitive, or even immature or mistaken conceptions of phenomena, and is contrasted with "disciplinary," "sophisticated," "expert," or "analytic" as qualities of reasoning involved in learning complex subject matter such as science and mathematics. Indeed, from some points of view, the goal of education is to fix or correct the misguided "everyday" understandings of scientific or mathematical phenomena that students are said to develop through their everyday experiences (Champagne, Klopfer, & Anderson, 1980; Clement, 1982; McCloskey, Caramazza, & Green, 1980; McDermott, Rosenquist, & van Zee, 1987; Trowbridge & McDermott, 1981; Viennot, 1979; see also Smith, diSessa, & Roschelle, 1993 for a critique of the "misconceptions" tradition).

In this book, we argue counter to this view and instead make the case that students' everyday experience and knowledge in all their manifold forms matter crucially in learning science and mathematics. Like others before us (Hymes, 1996; Goody, 1977; Latour, 1986), we oppose the long-standing tendency in Western thinking to dichotomize kinds of meaning or modes of thought:

> the division of societies or modes of thought into advanced and primitive, domesticated or savage, open or closed, is essentially to make use of a folk-taxonomy by which we bring order and understanding into a complex universe. But the order is illusory, the meaning superficial. As in the case of other binary systems, the categorisation is often value-laden and ethnocentric. (Goody, 1997, p. 36)

Anthropologists like Goody and Hymes made clear how evaluation is built into these binary frameworks, in which one term of the pair—advanced, domesticated, disciplinary, expert, analytic—is meant to reflect a cognitive ideal involving *more* information, *more* complexity, and *more* precision (Hymes, 1996). We propose a different way of thinking about "everyday" and "disciplinary" experience, one that seeks to dismantle the tendency toward dichotomies in order to shed new light and open new questions on learning and teaching as human meaning-making experiences.

There are different ways of questioning a dichotomy. One is to argue that the opposite poles are not static, rigid, predefined, and so forth. In our case this would amount to saying that what different people recognize as "everyday" and "disciplinary" changes with their circumstances and their use; what counts as everyday once might be seen as disciplinary a moment later. Another argument would be that the poles of the dichotomy are not defined in opposition to each other. There could be, for example, ways of knowing that are at the same time everyday and disciplinary. When a dichotomy is seen as encompassing a hierarchical line of progress, such as progressing from everyday to disciplinary knowledge, another form of questioning is to deny that there is any simple way of depicting advancement from one to the other.

The contributions in this book adopt different approaches to such questioning. To conceptualize these different approaches it is useful to introduce two notions: (1) the everyday matters of a discipline, and (2) classroom episodes as gathering places in which various encounters occur.

THE EVERYDAY MATTERS OF A DISCIPLINE

Becoming an insider in a discipline like science or mathematics means becoming intimately familiar with—that is, having everyday knowledge of—the objects, events, symbols, stories, tools, ideas, and jargons that make up its sociohistorical tradition. Because we do not have a shared term for referencing what matters in a discipline, we will refer to these as the "everyday matters of a discipline." If one wishes to practice chemistry, second-nature familiarity with the periodic table of elements is a sine qua non (literally, "without which not"). In the field of electronics, knowing one's way around oscilloscopes is essential. Likewise, to earn a membership card in linguistics one must be fluent with a host of specialized meanings (e.g., syntax, signifier, conversational turn, register). The process by which particular everyday matters become defined as central to and commonplace in the lives of the practitioners of a given discipline is a social–historical–institutional process of considerable complexity, imbued with debate, traditions, hallmark events, commitments, investments, and much more (Biagioli, 1999; Galison, 1997; Latour, 1987). Moreover, the everyday matters of a discipline continue to change as long as the discipline is practiced; they evolve as specialized branches emerge and struggle to become part of the core or separate themselves to constitute new disciplines (e.g., ecology, molecular biology, biophysics).

The everyday matters of a discipline are central to worldviews endorsed by disciplinary communities and lead their members to recognize connections, experiences, and memberships. Members of a discipline distinguish between the everyday matters required for practitioners and those that are important for "everyone." Those matters deemed important for the general culture tend to be pushed into the public school agenda in the form of curricular guidelines, assessment instruments, teacher professional development, and so forth. Recent efforts at local, state, and national levels to redefine science and mathematics education according to disciplinary standards and frameworks bear witness to this tendency (AAAS, 1993; NCTM, 2000; NRC, 1996). These efforts are often highly politicized and even volatile, reflecting the lack of consensus that exists even within disciplines regarding what everyone needs to know.

CLASSROOM EPISODES AS GATHERING PLACES IN WHICH VARIOUS ENCOUNTERS OCCUR

In the classroom, teachers are responsible for teaching the everyday matters of a discipline to students who are often seen as having little or no previous relevant experience. To address this, teachers carefully plan lessons in which their students will meet or engage with select everyday matters from the point of view of the discipline, in which students come into contact with a text, tool, idea, or technique in a partially or entirely new light. Lessons are deliberately designed and managed as occasions for students to work with select everyday matters of a discipline, where "to work with" can take countless forms: to talk about, to play with, to try out, to figure out, or to argue with.

Despite teachers' best efforts, these interactions often turn out to be more like encounters than meetings, that is, they can be experienced as unexpected or even bewildering events by students and teachers alike. Sometimes the hoped-for meeting between students and discipline does not happen at all because the student is never aware of the everyday matter she was intended to meet. For example, she counts all the possible combinations of four coin tosses and never feels the "need" to develop the combinatorial ideas that were the lesson's focus. At other times, students and teacher end up working with everyday matters of a discipline that were not the intended ones, for example, the planned lesson on probability ends up becoming a discussion about conversions between decimals, fractions, and percentages. And, of course, every encounter is subject to interpretation because different observers and participants may have different ideas as to whether any contact between students and discipline actually took place (e.g., Did the teacher simply "cover" the material or did the students "engage" with it? Were the students engaging with art or botany as they produced detailed drawings of plants?).

It is our contention that such classroom encounters constitute "gathering places" for the everyday and the unfamiliar, the ordinary and the extraordinary, the fluent and the novice (cf. Latour's [1986] notion of "a common place" as a meeting ground for things normally viewed as incommensurable, e.g., fiction and nature, cities and heavens, etc.). How does this range of experiences come together? Is the process of becoming fluent with the everyday matters of a discipline a matter of gradual extension of the familiar? Does it entail seeing the ordinary as extraordinary, the familiar as strange? Can it involve a far-reaching break with the familiar and an abrupt dive into foreign territory?

These ideas of the "everyday matters of a discipline" and of the "classroom episodes as gathering places in which various encounters occur" help us re-examine the traditional dichotomy of the everyday and the disciplinary because they move us away from defining them in opposition to each other, from seeing them as rigid givens, and from expecting an easy recognition of progress from one to the other in any actual classroom interaction.

REFERENCES

American Association for the Advancement of Science/Project 2061. (1993). *Benchmarks for science literacy.* New York: Oxford University Press.

Biagioli, M. (Ed.). (1999) *The science studies reader.* New York: Routledge.

Champagne, A., Klopfer, L., & Anderson, J. (1980). Factors influencing the learning of classical mechanics. *American Journal of Physics, 48,* 1074–1079.

Clement, J. (1982). Students' preconceptions in introductory mechanics. *American Journal of Physics, 50,* 66–71.

Galison, P. (1997). *Image and logic: A material culture of microphysics.* Chicago: University of Chicago Press.

Goody, J. (1977). *The domestication of the savage mind.* New York: Cambridge University Press.

Hymes, D. (1996). *Ethnography, linguistics, narrative inequality: Toward an understanding of voice.* Bristol, PA: Taylor and Francis.

Latour, B. (1986). Visualization and cognition: Thinking with eyes and hands. In H. Kuclick (Ed.), *Knowledge and society: Studies in the sociology of culture past and present,* 6, 1–40. Greenwich, CT: JAI Press.

Latour, B. (1987). *Science in action.* Cambridge, MA: Harvard University Press.

Lave, J. (1988). *Cognition in practice.* Cambridge, UK: Cambridge University Press.

Lave, J., & Wenger, E. (1991). *Situated learning:* Legitimate peripheral participation. Cambridge, England: Cambridge University Press.

McCloskey, M., Caramazza, A., and Green, B. (1980). Curvilinear motion in the absence of external forces: Naïve beliefs about the motion of objects. *Science, 210,* 1139–1141.

McDermott, L., Rosenquist, M., & van Zee, E. (1987). Student difficulties in connecting graphs and physics: Examples from kinematics. *American Journal of Physics, 55,* 503–513.

The National Council of Teachers of Mathematics. (2000). *Principles and standards for school mathematics*. Reston, VA: The National Council of Teachers of Mathematics, Inc.

National Research Council. (1996). *National science education standards*. Washington DC: National Academy Press.

Rogoff, B. (1990). *Apprenticeship in thinking*. New York: Oxford University Press.

Smith, J. P., diSessa, A., & Roschelle, J. (1993). Misconceptions reconceived: A constructivist analysis of knowledge in transition. *The Journal of the Learning Sciences*, 3(2), 115–163.

Suchman, L. (1987). *Plans and situated actions*. New York: Cambridge University Press.

Trowbridge, D., & McDermott, L. (1981). Investigation of student understanding of the concept of acceleration in one dimension. *American Journal of Physics*, 49, 242–253.

Viennot, L. (1979). Spontaneous reasoning in elementary dynamics. *European Journal of Science Education*, 1, 205–221.

Wertsch, J. V. (1991). *Voices of the mind: A sociocultural approach to mediated action*. Cambridge, MA: Harvard University Press.

I
Experiences of Students in Encounters With Everyday Matters of Science and Mathematics

Introduction to Part I

In the book Introduction, we argued against a view that separates "everyday" and "disciplinary" matters into distinctly different, even opposed, forms of knowing. We argued instead that learning means becoming intimately familiar with the objects, events, symbols, stories, tools, ideas, and social languages that constitute disciplinary traditions, which continually and dynamically evolve as specialized subdisciplines emerge. Learning, we suggested, entails developing everyday knowledge of a discipline, a complex extension—along a continuum of possible relationships from complementary to conflictual—of what one already knows and knows how to do. In this way, we aim to dissolve the dichotomous view of everyday and disciplinary knowledge and knowing that has dominated the field's thinking about learning, and to offer an alternative view that better reflects the elasticity of human sense-making.

The chapters in this section both pose and raise a number of provocative questions about what is entailed in becoming a participant in the "everyday" matters of scientific or mathematical disciplines. They work from the assumption that "everyday" indexes the richness of the lives that people lead, what they are fluent in across domains of experience, what they care about, rather than a realm of experience apart from disciplinary knowing. In particular, they focus our attention on the diverse ways in which learners (and teachers) encounter the occasions designed to bring them into contact with the everyday matters of a discipline. In the same vein, they do not view a learning environment as a set of tools and activities that are given, but one in which what counts as significant emerges dynamically—not linearly—in interaction, as participants engage with each other and with the tools, ideas, symbols, discourses, and materials that are brought forth. In light of this set of assumptions, a main question raised in these chapters is: How do students *experience or make sense* of the problem or environment set before them? What do learning environments become *for* them?

1

"Why Would Run Be in Speed?" Artifacts and Situated Actions in a Curricular Plan

Stephen Monk
University of Washington

This chapter explores the implications for curriculum designers, teachers, and students of a basic fact of human communication: that words and symbols do not necessarily convey our meanings and intentions to others. It is based on an analysis of a brief moment in a classroom conversation among a group of third- and fourth-grade students who were designing a chart to describe their own motion along a 10-foot straight line. This conversation took place during a series of lessons the author helped develop as a member of a research team conducting a curricular design study around the mathematics of motion. The students in the class were designing the chart as a means of directing someone else to walk along such a line according to their directions. In the process they were discovering that words placed in a chart meant different things to the various members of the class and that their intentions did not necessarily convert into the actions of others. Nonetheless, we see in the analysis of this conversation that, in and around their struggles to get one another to understand their meanings, these students were slowly beginning to build a collective world of meaning that included their motion, their charts, and their words in which there was enough commonality among their understandings to begin to communicate certain aspects of their motion to another.

A further reflection on this conversation shows that although it was undeniably conditioned by the curricular plan the session was based on, the connections between the conversation and the plan were far less direct or predictable than one might expect. A curriculum designer, like the children, proceeds from intentions and meanings he or she wishes to share with a class and, just like the children, must cope with the consequences of the ambiguities of the meanings of words and symbols, the complexities of the phenomena being considered, and the realities of any attempt to influence the actions and understandings of others. An examination of these two worlds of activity—of the students and a designer—suggests an analogy that is instructive in considering a critical question that emerges from a study of this classroom conversation: How can we describe the way in which curriculum planning shapes the events and learning in a classroom, once we acknowledge how indirect and unpredictable the effects of such an effort are? After presenting an analysis of the classroom conversation, I explore this question, guided in part by the analogy between these two situations, of children working to communicate about motion and a curriculum designer planning lessons.

In analyzing the meaning-making processes around the classroom conversation, this chapter adopts a social interactionist point of view toward the way meaning is attached to symbols—one that eschews two traditional assumptions about the relationship between symbols and their meanings (Blumer, 1969; Cobb, 1999; Cobb & Bauersfeld, 1995). Under one traditional assumption, meaning is taken to be intrinsic to the symbol itself, as simply part of its makeup, available to anyone who attends to it. A chair is a chair, a tree is a tree, and a number is a number. A person who does not see this either needs training or is, somehow, resistant or confused. Under the other traditional assumption, meaning is taken as coming primarily from the psychological processes of the individual. The child has a particular conception of fraction or the concept of speed. If it is not adequate or correct, then it must be changed, often by being exposed for its inconsistency with the way the world really is. In the social interactionist point of view, meanings are seen as "social products, as creations that are formed in and through the defining activities of people as they interact" (Blumer, 1969, p. 5). Such a view does not necessarily exclude the qualities or features of things in the world or individual psychological processes, but does not acknowledge them as primary, determining, or sufficient.

Taking a social interactionist point of view opens the question of how to view the social world in which these meanings are being made. Such a world has many layers and facets, including its social norms, daily routines, physical arrangements, group values, and shared mathematical ideas. Genuine questions exist as to how these are linked and how, if at all, they are open to outside influence—from a teacher or curriculum designer, for example. The point of view taken here is that the classroom is a community made up of the teacher and students all busily interacting with one another as they work toward shared, although often shifting, goals, through an enormous variety of practices—of solving problems together, looking words up in the dictionary, doing arithmetic exercises, and questioning one another's assertions. That is, the classroom is viewed as a community of practice (Wenger, 1998). In this particular series of lessons, the class is viewed as a community around practices of designing representations. This is similar to the approach taken in other studies of children inventing representations (diSessa, Hammer, Sherin, & Kolpakowski, 1991; Lehrer, Schauble, Carpenter, & Penner, 2000), and it is related to the point of view taken in the studies by Lampert (1990) and Cobb and his colleagues (Cobb, 1999; Cobb, Boufi, McClain, & Whitenack, 1997; Yackel & Cobb, 1996) in which classrooms are viewed as communities around practices of mathematical argumentation and symbolization.

BACKGROUND OF THE DATA

The data for this chapter come from a single lesson that took place in the course of a classroom study conducted by Ann Rosebery, Beth Warren, Cynthia Ballenger, and me, in collaboration with the classroom teacher, Mary DiSchino. Ms. DiSchino (Ms. D) is a highly experienced teacher who has participated in a variety of teacher professional development research projects, including the Cambridge Teacher Research Seminar of the Chèche Konnen Center and the Moon Group (Duckworth, 1987). She has also documented her professional experiences in a number of presentations and papers (DiSchino, 1987, 1998).

The classroom phase of the study was a design experiment, investigating classroom learning of the relations between distance, speed, and time primarily through the development of a variety of representations of motion. There were 20 lessons in the series which took place at approximately 1-week intervals between February and June, 1998 (allowing for vacations, testing, and so on). Each lesson lasted between 45 and 60 minutes and was videotaped. One or two of the four research team members involved in the study was present at each lesson, sometimes working with the children and sometimes taking notes. At weekly meetings involving Ms. D and the researchers, the previous lesson was reviewed (often using videotape), the children's learning and mathematical issues behind it discussed, and the next lesson planned, at least in a general way. I must emphasize, however, that in spite of the intensity of this collaboration, Ms. D was chiefly responsible for the design of these lessons.

The class was in an alternative public school in Cambridge, Massachusetts, with a very diverse group of students. Of the 24 children in the class, 14 were girls and 10 were boys. Thirteen of the children were of color. Five children who spoke Haitian Creole as a first language had started in the Haitian Creole Bilingual program in the school and were being "transitioned" into English-speaking classes during that school year. Twelve of the children received free or reduced lunch.

THE OVERALL GOAL AND LEARNING TRAJECTORY OF THE LESSONS

The goal of the series of lessons, as articulated by Ms. D and often echoed by the children, was that they would learn to communicate about motion along a straight line, especially about distance, speed, and time. This goal was made operational by the challenge: *How can you take a trip along a straight line and then describe how you moved so that someone else who is only given your description can re-create your trip?*

The overall structure of the 20 lessons was that they consisted of repeated rounds of activity in which pairs of children would work to create and represent a trip, and then have another pair of children test their representation by reenacting it. The class used a progression of six different representational forms in these lessons, moving from informal forms that included words and pictures to conventional forms, such as tables and graphs of distance versus time.

At first the trips and the descriptions made by the children were highly fanciful and focused on styles of movement, such as hopping, running, falling down, and "walking the dog." They included actual characters, such as rock-stars, who had motivations for their motion such as running away from their fans. These features dropped away as the representations became more conventional, but they never disappeared completely. They indicate a general playfulness and creativity brought to these lessons by the children and encouraged by Ms. D that was an important factor in the overall dynamic of the classroom.

Each round of activity, which was determined by a particular representational form and could last several lessons, had the same overall structure: Ms. D would propose a new form of representation, and the class would discuss how they would use it and how it might be customized to their needs. Thus, for example, they discussed labels for column headings in a chart and subsequently in a table of values. Later on, they spent several lessons discussing how distance should be denoted so that it was standardized and replicable from one trip to another. After that, the children would work in pairs to invent a trip and represent it and then swap their representations with another pair to be enacted, thus testing the effectiveness of their representation. This would be followed by a whole-class discussion of how this worked, what was confusing, and what was difficult. Then there was either another round using the same kind of representation, or Ms. D would introduce a new form. Ms. D generally opened the lessons by asking the children to recall what had happened in the previous class that was important and how this all related to the overall goal of the lessons.

THE DATA OF THE PRESENT STUDY

This chapter's data are taken from the third in the series of twenty lessons. It begins just after the class has finished using words and pictures to communicate about their trips and have had a discussion of "what worked and what didn't work" in their use of this form. Now Ms. D wants to move in the direction of more formal and symbolic representations of motion. This will also involve placing constraints on the kinds of trips the children invent and the aspects of motion upon which they focus. She has devised an informal chart they will use to do this (Fig. 1.1). In this chart, each trip is to be made up of three segments, each of which has instructions for the mover that include a type of movement (e.g., walking, running, jumping, crawling, hopping) along with information such as speed and distance. She begins to present this chart to the children in an open-ended and exploratory way.

Things to do	
#1	
#2	
#3	

FIG. 1.1. Outline of chart.

The data cover approximately 13 minutes of classroom conversation divided into two episodes. In Episode 1, which lasts ten minutes, Ms. D first presents the general idea of the chart and the children explore many possibilities for how it might be related to the trips they have been taking and their past experience of motion. These data serve primarily to set the background for the conversation in Episode 2 and to open issues that are examined further in the analysis of that episode. Because the conversation in Episode 1 is exploratory and somewhat diffuse, it is presented in the form of a narrative outline with occasional quotes. In Episode 2, which lasts just over 3 minutes, the children discuss how the instructions for a particular trip should be placed in the chart and explore the meanings of the words used in the column labels of the chart and their instructions to the person taking the trip. The data of this episode are presented in the form of a detailed transcript. Each episode is further divided into segments for the sake of comprehensibility, with the data of each segment followed by initial comments or "interpretive notes" intended to highlight aspects of the conversation that will be further analyzed in a discussion at the end of the episode.

Episode 1—*Designing the chart together.*

Episode 1.1. *Introducing the chart: "Things to do," "Walk," and "Movement."* Ms. D introduces this part of the lesson by telling the children that they will use charts to communicate about motion. She reminds them that they have been using a chart, as a class, to keep a daily record of the temperature outdoors. She reiterates that the purpose of this activity is to learn to communicate about trips, making the point that "Charts are more efficient," and that they will be easier and less confusing to understand than the words and pictures they have been using.

She makes the beginnings of a chart on the chalkboard as in Fig. 1.1, and as she does this, she says:

> "I'm going to put. . . 'Things to do.' Then I'm going to number it: 1st thing to do, 2nd thing to do. . . . Then we're going to figure out what's the thing you wanted done in the walk. What's the one kind of thing all of you told your receiver [the person who is to enact the given trip] to do?"

When a child answers "walk," she makes a second vertical line to create a second column and labels it "Walk."

She follows this by asking, "What's another thing you told people to do?" When Jimmy answers "move," Ms. D seems puzzled and asks him what he means by this. Many children respond at the same time, talking over one another. One child says "run," but Jimmy's answer to this is that "Everyone didn't run." Another child says, "Like you put your hands in the air." Ms. D asks Jimmy to help her understand what he means; she walks across the front of the space and asks him: "Is this moving?" His reply is, "I mean like *actually* moving." Ms. D asks the other children to help by suggesting other words they could put in the next column. They make suggestions like "run," "strut," "hopping," and "movement."

Interpretive Notes:

a. Ms. D's opening move is to ask the children: "What's the thing you wanted done in the walk? What's the one kind of thing all of you told your receiver to do?" But this immediately opens up the many ways in which her questions can be interpreted and reveals the inherently ambiguous nature of language. The first child responds with "walk," which Ms. D has sometimes used for what is called a "trip" in this class (as in "Then we're going to figure out what's the thing you wanted done in the walk."). But it has also been used by the children in their instructions to describe a particular way of moving. The phrase "one kind of thing" also opens up several possibilities as to what kinds of distinctions are to be made. It is possible that what is being asked for here is a general quality that is common to all the instructions. But when pressed, most of the children give particular kinds of movement—run, strut, hop—although it is not true that any one of these was common to all instructions.

b. Jimmy's suggestion that "move" be added to the chart is of this first kind of possibility. All of the instructions require that the person "move," whereas, as Jimmy says, "Everyone didn't run." But Jimmy is also making a point of a different kind here. As he says in his response to Ms. D, he means "actually moving," instead of, for instance, "Like you put your hands in the air," as is offered by another child. Jimmy is looking for a category that not only includes kinds of motion like run and walk, but also captures their quality of movement from one place to another—in which there is physical displacement of the mover.

Episode 1.2. *Three more column labels: "Speed," "Distance," and "Kind of Step."* Now Ms. D takes another tack by saying: "OK. Watch me. Watch. Here I am." And, as she says this, she walks slowly across the front of the space, pauses, and then moves back across the space in a broad imitation of a person running. She says, "This is movement," and asks the children: "OK. What is the difference in those two kinds of movement?" Jimmy responds by saying, "Faster and slower." And Elaine says, "Fast and slow." Ms. D acknowledges this and says: "And, fast and slow . . . is a way of expressing what? When your car goes fast or your car goes slow, you measure the what it goes at . . . ?"

When Juanita says "speed," and another child repeats this, Ms. D makes a new column and labels it "Speed." She says: "OK. So, that was very important. So we said to the person that they had to walk or they had to run. That was the speed."

When Ms. D asks for another word of this kind, a child says "distance." Ms. D then makes a new column with "Distance" as its heading. Now we see on the board a chart like the one in Fig. 1.2.

Now Ms. D looks back at the chart and column headings that they have created and raises a question as to whether the heading "Walk" is a good one. When the children respond with suggestions like "Fast and slow," which suggests that they do not understand her question, she erases the word "Walk," and

Things to do	Walk	Speed	Dist-ance
#1			
#2			
#3			

FIG. 1.2. Chart with headings.

replaces it by "Kind of Step." She reviews the column headings by saying: "We have Kind of Step. We have Speed. We have Distance."

Interpretive Notes:

a. We see, on the basis of these first two segments, the exploratory and tentative nature of this activity. Ms. D has proposed the outlines of a chart, but has intentionally left many choices open to the children. They respond by drawing on their diverse experiences to make suggestions. As they do so, she needs to make sense of what they have said while she takes into account the future requirements that the chart must meet.

b. Here she presses harder than earlier for a single term ("speed") that refers to the potential entries in a column. Again, we see the complexities of these issues. Most of us, reading this description, would agree that "Speed" is somehow the preferred label over "slow/fast?" But why is this so? Is it *only* convention—or are there underlying mathematical and linguistic issues here?

c. In her intention to highlight speed as an attribute of movement, Ms. D has walked back and forth across the room, first moving slowly and then moving fast. She emphasizes the contrast even further by walking in one direction and (mock) running in the other, while using the words "walk" and "run." Quite apart from her intentions, however, a child in the class could surmise that the point she is making is to establish a pairing that "run goes with fast" and "walk goes with slow."

Episode 1.3. *Two more columns: "Pause" and "How many."* Ms. D now remarks that they still do not have enough column headings to include all of their instructions, and reminds them of instructions that include things like "turn around." A child suggests they have also used "fall down." Together, she and the children arrive at the label "Pause," which is proposed by one of the children.

Ms. D suggests they may need even more columns, making room for it on the chalkboard and asking: "OK? OK. Anything else that you gave instructions for in your walk—that would help make it clear to someone who read your instructions?" Sonja raises her hand and says: "Kind of like numbering or something. Cuz you said, like 'Walk 4 steps.'" Jimmy quickly responds that this is the same as Distance, saying, "Well, if you take 5 steps, you're sort of taking like . . . 5 feet." Sonja responds to Jimmy with "No, it's like numbering, you **told** people to do that," to which he responds with "Don't you tell people about distance?" Ms. D suggests that a column heading that would go with Sonja's suggestion is "How many?" Other children make comments supporting Jimmy or Sonja. When Ms. D asks the class for an indication of agreement or disagreement with these two views, she gets a mixed response and decides to take a vote. The consensus is strongly for "Distance."

Interpretive Notes:

a. A complicated issue has emerged between Sonja and Jimmy. To Sonja, the instruction "Walk 4 steps" contains some new information that is not included in the term "Distance," which is already on the chart. Perhaps her statement "No, it's like numbering, you **told** people to do that" means that she sees the instruction as close to the way one moves along in a board game, which is different from a sense she might have that distance is something one measures with a ruler, using standard units of measurement.

b. We also see here a first instance of Sonja and Jimmy disagreeing with one another, with other children taking sides in their disagreement. This alerts us to the possibility that these two articulate and forceful children will become class spokespersons who give voice to issues and concerns more generally shared in the class. By encountering one another, such spokespersons can also serve to clarify such issues and concerns. The danger is that they may take over more of this functioning than is warranted.

Episode 1.4. *The class works on two examples together.* Now Ms. D and the class have the chart in Fig. 1.3 in front of them and she asks the students, "Are we all set then?" One girl, Irene, says that she is "confused." Ms. D responds with the suggestion that they work together on an example of how they will use the chart to give instructions. She begins by suggesting the single instruction: "Walk three steps." When she receives little response from the class, Ms. D writes three instructions on the chalkboard and asks the children to read each instruction and enter it into the chart. The instructions are:

Things to do	Kind of Step	Speed	Dist-ance	Pause
#1				
#2				
#3				

FIG. 1.3. Chart with new headings.

    Walk 3 steps   Stop for count of 2   Run to the end

Without much discussion or difference of opinion, the children enter this set of instructions into the chart as is in Fig. 1.4. Ms. D's responses suggest that she is comfortable with this set of entries.

Next, Ms. D suggests that they do another example together and elicits from the children the following set of instructions:

Things to do	Kind of Step	Speed	Dist-ance	Pause
#1	Walk		3	
#2				Count to 2
#3		Run	End	

FIG. 1.4. Chart with entries.

    Walk 2 steps   Run 3 steps   Powerwalk[1] to the end

As with the first set of instructions, the children enter these instructions into the chart with little comment or difficulty. When Ms. D asks Annie how to enter "Powerwalk to the end" into the chart, Annie first seems to hesitate and then responds in a very soft voice. Before Ms. D can ask her to repeat her answer, another child says loudly that Powerwalk should be entered in "Kind of Step," which is where Ms. D places it,[2] as in Fig. 1.5.

---

[1]"Powerwalk" was a term familiar to the children, but not to Ms. D or me. It is apparently a form of walking used in exercise classes in which one walks very fast while moving one's arms and legs in an exaggerated fashion.

[2]It is interesting in this connection that upon studying the videotape very closely, one sees that Annie's softly spoken suggestion is that the word "power" be placed in the Speed column, with the "walk" part of "powerwalk" to be placed in the "Kind of Step" column.

As Ms. D enters Powerwalk in the Kind of Step column, Sonja raises her hand and says: "Well, I have a question." Ms. D asks her to put her question off for a few moments while the class decides where "to the end" should be entered into the chart. When they agree that it belongs in the "Distance" column, she turns to Sonja and asks: "OK, now, before you go off, let's have your question, Sonja."

Things to do	Kind of Step	Speed	Distance	Pause
#1	Walk		2	
#2		Run	3	
#3	Power-walk		End	

FIG. 1.5. Chart with "powerwalk".

Interpretive Notes:

a. The set of instructions given by the children in the second example is the first time they have actually created instructions for a trip to be used in the chart. In doing this, they have closely followed the first set of instructions given by Ms. D, replacing "Walk 3 steps" by "Walk 2 steps," "Count to 2" by "Run 3 steps," and "Run to the end" by "Powerwalk to the end." Significantly, they have included no instruction that parallels "Count to 2." In effect, they have narrowed the kinds of instructions to be given for a trip to those that consist of ways of "actually moving" (in Jimmy's phrase), "walk," "run," and "powerwalk," together with a distance to be moved. As part of the process of agreeing on how to use their chart, the children have constrained the range of possible trips to be taken and the way they are to be described.

b. In both of these examples, there is a basic consensus about the entries, including the placement of Run in Speed.

Discussion:

The children and Ms. D are developing a new technology—the chart. This is somewhat unfamiliar to them, in general, and completely so in this specific case, which is far more complicated than the uses they have put charts to in the past. By the word "technology," I want to suggest that a chart is something to be used to interact with the world in particular ways, just as an X-ray machine, a highway map, or an e-mail program is. For most adults in our culture, a chart has built into it its own logic and structure, with rows and columns and a vast amount of implicit knowledge around it acquired with use. This implicit knowledge includes our expectation of how column labels work and the particular uses of language that go along with it. As complex as this knowledge is, few of us have any sense or recollection of what is involved in becoming able to use a chart. It is likely, on the other hand, that there is an enormous range among the children in this class as to what they bring to the use of charts. There is a genuine question, then, as to what it will take for children this young to come to be to able to use them.

To get a sense of how this activity might be experienced by the children, imagine a situation in which they are developing a chart to describe a simpler, more tangible world. Suppose that, instead of proposing a chart for describing motion, Ms. D had asked the children to use a chart to describe the things in various places in their classroom, as is suggested in Fig. 1.6. Just as Jimmy makes a basic distinction that the person "must actually be moving," a child in this case might make the distinction that the objects to be classified must "actually belong in the room." Thus a child's shoe might not be included because it belongs to one of them, not to the room, and will

Where?	Seats	Size	Color
Front			
Middle			
Back			

FIG. 1.6. Places in our classroom.

not always be in the room. When asked to list some categories of things in the room, a child might reply with "seats" which has some of the same ambiguity as the word "walk" does. Is a "seat" any place one can sit down, including a big pillow on the floor and perhaps even the floor itself? Or is a seat a particular kind of furniture made of wood, with a back, and so forth—in other words, a chair? Then imagine that the teacher points to two objects, a board eraser and her desk, and asks the children: "What is the difference between these two things?" Many children would probably give answers like big and small, but there are many other distinctions that could be made between them: one is made of wood and the other of cloth, one is hard and the other is soft, and so on. In fact, this pair of objects could easily be used to illustrate an endless number of different distinctions.

The point I wish to make with the example of a chart of the things in the room, is that the world to be described by the chart does not have its own existence and natural order that is separate from the activity of designing a chart to describe it. This world of things in the room is created and organized in the act of defining a chart to describe it. One group of children and their teacher could outline one world (where a child's shoe is included and a desk and board eraser illustrate a distinction as to size), and another group of children and their teacher could outline another world (where a child's shoe in not included and where a desk and a board eraser indicate "hardness"). What is true of tangible objects in a room is true—and more so—of people moving along a straight line. The world of possible motions to be considered as relevant and the characteristics of these motions to be taken as significant and then grouped are not at all obvious or given. The same is true of charts, with their columns, rows, and labels. The world of motion that is to be the object of study in this classroom and the charts that will be used to describe it reflexively constitute one another (Cobb & Bauersfeld, 1995). An understanding of this world and the technology used to describe it can only co-evolve together.[3]

Even as these children simultaneously learn about the world of motion and about charts, it is important to note here that significant mathematical issues are beginning to come into play. Using this chart can be viewed as an early step toward the mathematization of motion, the formation of abstract and manipulable quantities that can be assigned to any instance of motion, whether it is an electron moving in its orbit or a child moving along a straight line. The key issue in this episode, the naming and use of the columns in the chart, is closely linked to issues surrounding the central mathematical concept of a variable. This is already evident in the two columns called "Distance," and "Speed." The idea is that a frame can be placed around any instance of motion in socially agreed-upon ways to allow us to talk about *the* distance covered over any given time interval, or *the* speed of the object at any given point in the trip. This assignment of numerical values is supposed to be abstract in that it does not depend on particulars of the motion (the child is running hard, or fast; the rocket is still propelled by its booster and turning slowly), and it is supposed to be objective and neutral in the sense that any two observers could agree on the specific value of the quantity to be assigned at any point in the trip.

Episode 2. "Why would Run be in Speed?"
When the class has agreed that "to the end" belongs in Distance in the second example, Ms. D turns to Sonja and says: "OK, now, before you go off, let's have your question, Sonja."

---

[3]Terms like "co-evolution" and "reflexively constituted" carry with them an unfortunate connotation, that there are two distinct worlds, one of motion and the other of symbols, and that the goal of these lessons is that the children learn to correctly "map" the elements of one world onto the elements of the other. In order to avoid this connotation, and to explore much more deeply than is done here, the way in which symbols come to have meaning, Nemirovsky and colleagues proposed the concept of fusion, to mean "acting, talking, and gesturing without distinguishing between symbols and referents, while being aware of the illusion [that they are the same]" (Nemirovsky & Monk, 2000).

Episode 2.1

1	*Sonja:*	Um (.) Why would Run be in Speed? Why wouldn't it be in Kind of Step?
2	*Ms. D:*	OK. // That's a good question.
3	*Jimmy:*	//Run isn't stepping.
4	*Child⁴:*	It means speed.
5	*Sonja:*	//powerwalk
6	*Ms. D:*	Does anyone want to answer Sonja's question? Sonja? Can anyone answer Sonja's question? //I don't think there's any one answer.
7	*Boy:*	//Sonja
8	*Boy1:*	(*sotto voce*) Jimmy.
9	*Boy2:*	(*sotto voce*) Answer, Jimmy.
10	*Jimmy:*	Well, um, because run–ning is not a kind—you're not step–ping⁵
11	*Sonja:*	//Yeah you are.
12	*Boy:*	No you're not.
13	*Boy:*	Yeah, but you ( ) **fast.**
14	*Child:*	You're stepping fast.
15	*Sonja:*	I know but step—just the same as powerwalking, you're stepping—
16	*Child1:*	Alright, alright.
17	*Child2:*	No you're not. No you're not.

The children erupt with a flood of opinions, noises, cross-talk.

18	*Ms. D:*	If you want to help Sonja, raise your hand.
19	*Ronald:*	Alright (2) And anyways, when you're running, it's also speed.
20	*Girl:*	Because you're going fast, not as fast as powerwalk.

---

⁴On the day of this particular lesson, there was no video operator. Consequently, the video camera was left in place and not focused at the various parts of the room as the speaker changed. In addition, the lighting conditions were poor. Thus, it is not possible to tell which student is speaking at any given time, except for those students who were in the narrow range of the lens and a few, such as Sonja and Jimmy, who speak very emphatically and clearly. The unidentified speakers are therefore referred to as "Child," "Boy," or "Girl."

⁵In listening to the videotape, it is quite plain that Jimmy says the word "step–ping" in a way that emphasizes the marked cadence of the kind of motion in contrast to running, in which the motion is smoother.

21	Child:	Powerwalk—
22	Boy:	Powerwalk is faster than walking, too
23	Child:	// not unless you're—
24	Child:	You can't really—You can't really be—

Interpretive Notes:

a. By asking "Why *would* Run be *in* Speed?," Sonja seems to be not only asking a question, but also making the assertion that there is something to think about here. Her use of the subjunctive case suggests that placing Run in Speed is only one possible choice. Her use of the word *in* suggests that she thinks of Speed as being a place (a column) or a category, or a set of things.

b. Jimmy's response to Sonja is about the words "run" and "kind of step." Like Sonja, Jimmy is arguing *against* a pairing of the term run with the term used in a column heading. She does not want to pair run and speed and he does not want to pair run and kind of step. To some extent, the difference between them is about how one views the act of running: Which is its most salient feature, the rate at which one moves or the physical movement itself?

c. In line 4, Child says that "It [run] means speed." This is a very natural, even a compelling, statement to make. Not only do we run in order to go fast, but also, in Episode 1.2, Ms. D used the close connection between running and "fast" (in contrast to walking and "slow") in order to illustrate the distinction slow versus fast, captured in the label "Speed." An experienced user of charts is likely to feel that Run belongs in Kind of Step. (At first, I, myself, had not imagined that any other choice was possible.) But a genuine question does arise as to why this is true: Why does Run *not* belong in Speed? Among the points one might make is that placing a word in a column is not so much about literal meanings of column headings, as Child may be suggesting, as it is about membership in a category, as Sonja may be suggesting. In addition, the three instructions are so closely parallel that one wants to treat them in a "consistent" manner, which leads in this case, for most experienced users of this kind of chart, to putting them in the Kind of Step column. But these reasons, which are largely implicit, are the result of using charts and having experiences of the same kind the children are engaged in here.

d. In line 11, Sonja bluntly counters Jimmy's statement by asserting that one does step when running. And she is just as bluntly countered by Boy in line 12. This is followed by two children who say, in lines 13–14, "Yeah, but you ( ) fast" and "You're stepping fast." These statements tend to move the discussion beyond the dichotomous issue of where to place Run to a broader examination of combinations of aspects of running, one of which is that when one runs, one moves fast. This is also true of Ronald's statement in line 19 ("And anyways, when you're running, it's also speed,"), where he uses the word "also" to suggest that in giving directions to someone else, the word "run" can function in more than one way. Regardless of whether or not it involves taking steps, it does indicate that one should move fast. Like many of the statements in this episode, Ronald's statement is at least as important for the claims it makes about the possible bases for making choices in the design of the chart as it is for the particular choice it supports. He is saying that regardless of where in the chart one wants to put the word "run," the word itself carries implications of several different kinds.

e. At this point, in line 15, Sonja succeeds in bringing the term "powerwalking" into the discussion. Her doing so potentially has a broad impact on the conversation. It links the two other terms used to describe motion in this trip—walking and running—in that powerwalking involves stepping, in the same way walking does, and it also carries a suggestion of speed, as running does. Introducing this term is also a way of raising the possibility of considering all three instructions for the trip at the same time, which is a different approach than those who have spoken thus far appear to have taken.

f. Following Ronald's remark and Sonja's introduction of powerwalking, other children begin, in lines 20 and 22, to make more explicit comparisons among the speeds suggested by running and powerwalking. This is a movement toward viewing the entries in the Speed column as indicating the relative speed of the mover, using the words "walk," "run," and "powerwalk" to indicate degrees of going fast or slow.

g. Although I have focused my comments on the way in which the children are building their understandings of the chart and the world of motion it refers to, it should also be pointed out that the dynamic of the classroom conversation has undergone a radical shift. As is readily apparent from watching the videotape, the energy level has increased greatly at the same time that the centrality of Ms. D's role has diminished. The children are talking directly to one another, taking on one another's points of view, and building on what others have to say.

Episode 2.2

25   Ms. D: Do you think there's a difference between Kind of Step and Speed?

26   Children: Yes.

27	Girl:	When you walk—then you **can** do that
28	Ms. D:	What do you think that difference is?
29	Girl:	If you can walk—then you can actually
30	Child:	//Because when it's speed . . .
31	Ms. D:	One at a time, please.
32	Karen:	In walking, f'rinstance, if you did power—power-walking you can count your steps and how many you're taking, whereas in running you can't really do that, because—
33	Child:	Because you could ( ) it would take an hour.
34	Sonja:	Because how come someone says, "Run three steps?"
35	Child:	Because we know we're taking three steps.
36	Child1:	Yeah!
37	Child2:	Running
38	Child3:	//**Listen**!
39	Girl:	You pick up speed when you run.
40	Boy:	Kind of Step. That does not mean—And speed. Run. That means run, means you go f-a-a-st.

Many voices erupt again. More talk about powerwalking. Much talking back and forth.

41	Child:	Powerwalking is walking fast.
42	Child:	I don't think powerwalking is so fast.
43	Irene:	Running is a kind of speeeed.
44	Girl:	If you run, that means—you could call it like (1.5) you (1.5) you wouldn't . . .
45	Child:	OK, OK, I get that!!
46	Child:	Big deal, then. So you're ( )

Interpretive Notes:

a. Ms. D opens by suggesting that the children consider the nature of the column labels, Kind of Step and Speed. But after a few exchanges the children have returned to the issues they were previously concerned with, the relationships between walk and speed and between walk and powerwalk.

b. Karen's statement in line 32 is another example of how utterances in this conversation can have implications on many levels. She is supporting Jimmy's claim that Run does not belong in Kind of Step and basing her argument on the practical entailments of the word "step." But within her statement is the suggestion that they might not be able to agree on *the* meaning of "run" and "step." She is proposing that they widen the basis for making such decisions to operational considerations, to include the practical difficulty of counting the steps of someone who is running. In this she is supported by another child in line 33.

    c. Sonja's counter to Karen's claim ("Because how come someone says, 'Run three steps?'") is an appeal to the notion that the things they are talking about, including the instructions, must make sense in some way. After all, the conversation has gone on for quite a while and has been about a real and imaginable world. If the instruction to "Run three steps" makes sense, then counting the number of steps must be a legitimate thing to do and steps must be a part of running.

    d. Sonja's statement is responded to by Child in line 35, who says: "Because we know we're taking three steps." Perhaps this is a way of interrupting or disallowing the inference Sonja is making from the fact of the instruction having been given to the nature of the terms in the instructions. Certainly, it opens up the question of whether such inferences can be made.

    e. In lines 39–40, a girl and a boy go back to the issue of the Speed column and its entries by saying: "You pick up speed when you run" and "And speed. Run. That means run, means you go f-a-a-st." This is followed by two children in lines 41–42 who say: "Powerwalking is walking fast.", "I don't think powerwalking is so fast." This is capped by Irene's statement in line 43, "Running is a kind of speeeed." This indicates that the children are once again considering the notion of relative speeds and how they should be marked. How should powerwalking be used as an indicator of how fast a mover should move? Is powerwalking very fast or isn't it? Irene's statement is the first use of the expression "*kind* of speed," which sets up a parallel between the two column headings "Kind of Step" and "Speed" and points to an issue they have been implicitly dealing with. It also suggests that speed is a category of "kinds," or types, rather than a quality, as "fast" is.

Episode 2.3

47	Ms. D:	OK, Sonja //Irene just said "Running is a kind of speed."
48	Child:	//Well, it is a kind of walking
49	Boy:	//I know it's a kind of speed.
50	Ms. D:	Are you trying to say that walking is a kind of speed as well?
51	Jason:	No it's not. Not unless you're powerwalking.
52	Child:	Yes, yes, you are—
53	Girl:	Yes, you actually—speed.

54   *Ms. D:*   Listen to Sonja's words. Sonja, why don't you say those words. Let's see if we can think about them. No one is saying either is right or wrong.

55   *Sonja:*   If run was a speed, then walk would be a speed.

56   *Ms. D:*   I want you to think about what Sonja said, she just said, Carlos, if running is a speed—then walking is a kind of speed also   //Now, just think of that.

57   *Karen:*   //Well, yeah...

58   *Girl:*   It **is** a kind of speed.

59   *Ms. D:*   And then, I also want you to think about kind of step. Some people in their directions wrote "Jump." Is jumping a kind of step? // Some people said hop.

60   *Child:*   //Well, yeah, yeah...

Interpretive Notes:

a. Ms. D opens by echoing Irene's statement that "Running is a kind of speed," and then asks her question of Sonja. However, one cannot tell from the videotape where Ms. D has gotten the idea that the statement "walking is a kind of speed" has been made or implied by Sonja. Because there has been so much cross-talk, we do not know if Sonja has actually made this statement and Ms. D has heard her and wants to broadcast it to the rest of the class, or whether Sonja has said something else and Ms. D has inferred this. It may also be that, upon hearing Irene's statement, Ms. D has begun to see a clearer connection among Sonja's utterances and those of other children than she had seen earlier.

b. In line 55, Sonja immediately takes up and amplifies the idea beneath Ms. D's question by saying: "If run was a speed, then walk would be a speed." This indicates, first, that Ms. D's statement is very in much in tune with what she is thinking. But Sonja's statement also differs from Ms. D's in two important respects. Unlike Ms. D's statement, it is in the subjunctive case, as her statement in line 1 (in Episode 2.1) was, thus reemphasizing the need for consideration among alternatives. It is also more explicitly in the form of an *If...then* proposition, challenging her classmates by saying, in effect: "If you believe that Run belongs in speed, then you will also need to believe that Walk belongs in speed."

c. It seems likely that Sonja's intention is to make a new argument against placing Run in the Speed column. It is to have the form known in mathematics and logic as "proof by contradiction." In it, she is saying that "If we allow Run to be in Speed, then we must also place Walk in Speed. But we have already agreed to place Walk in Kind of step. Therefore, we cannot place Run in Speed." Her argument is first countered by Jason in line 51, who simply states that walking is not a kind of speed, "unless you are powerwalking." This is very much in keeping with the commonsense notion that one only "has speed" when one is going fast. But this argument does not directly address the main point Sonja is making, which is about logical connections among the various entries they make in the chart and not about one particular entry or another.

d. The response by Girl in line 58 builds on Irene's statement in line 43 and directly challenges Jason's assertion that one only "has speed" when one is going fast. Thus the discussion about the chart, its labels and entries, has opened up an important issue within the mathematics of motion for exploration among these children: "Does 'speed' connote a general quality of motion that has various levels or degrees, or does it connote a particular level of this quality?" But it is also true that Girl has effectively countered Sonja's argument against putting Run in Speed and that she has done this by extending the view increasingly held by the children in the class—that the entries in the Speed column should give relative speeds, and that they can do so by using words like "walk" and "run." The effect of Girl's statement is, possibly, to make this more explicit. From this point of view, one could say that because "powerwalk" has also been suggested for this purpose, a new way of using the columns of the chart is now moving into the foreground: In the Speed column, one puts words that tell how fast the person should move. To do this, one uses words like "run," "walk," and "powerwalk." This is a response to Sonja's question, of "Why would Run be in speed?" that says, in effect, that we *should* put Run in speed, although this means that we should also put Walk and Powerwalk there. Although it is counter to what some may expect in using such a chart, it is consistent and coherent and perhaps reflects a growing sense of speed as a category and, therefore, as a quantity used to describe motion.

Postscript:

This conversation, which took place in session #3, was the beginning of a series of activities with the charts that lasted late into session #5, when the class took up the issue of the various ways distance can be marked on a trip. Among the activities around the charts were two rounds in which pairs of children designed and represented trips using charts, and exchanged them with other pairs to be tried out. Each of these rounds was followed by a whole-class discussion of the particulars of their charts and of the issues surrounding these charts. In session #4, Ms. D read the story of the Tortoise and the Hare to the class as a way of grounding a discussion of the notion of speed and how we talk about going fast or slow. Throughout these discussions, which were increasingly broadly based, the children repeatedly brought up such issues as: Does any kind of movement, even walking and spinning, have speed? Does speed mean fast? What is the relationship between walk, run, and powerwalk? Increasingly, these terms became descriptions of a kind of step and not markers of speed. The children also went back over the meaning of "movement" and what it implies, as well as the terms used for column headings, Distance and Kind of Step (which became "Kind of movement"). Whatever else took place in the two episodes analyzed here, it can be safely stated that they framed the key issues of a very fruitful series of conversations.

Discussion:

The overall goal of these lessons is that the children learn to communicate about motion along a straight line. As can be seen from the interpretive notes, this goal depends intricately on a number of related goals. The children must grapple with basic physical and mathematical ideas such as speed and how it is used as an attribute of motion and they must come to share as a group meanings and usages, not only of words, but also of the chart as a means for describing motion. Since these subgoals are so complex and present so many difficulties for students, the standard approach in mathematics education has been to treat them separately and to work with students on one and then another. One of the questions researchers and curriculum designers regularly struggle with is about the *order* in which these subgoals should be addressed. Should students learn to use charts in simple situations and then apply what they know to complex phenomena such as motion, or should students first have a solid understanding of a conceptual domain like motion as a basis for developing their abilities to use representations in the domain? In these episodes, we see the children working simultaneously toward all these goals, with the interrelatedness and complexity of these goals presenting interesting possibilities for learning.

In and around the intense discussion of the word "run" and the nature of this form of motion, the wider issue has arisen of the meaning of speed as an attribute of motion and how it might be marked. This is not the direct result of any one claim or argument, but of an examination of the particular set of instructions the children created in modifying the first set of instructions and the outline of a chart provided by Ms. D. The instructions "Walk 2 steps," "Run 3 steps," and "Powerwalk to the end" are not only nicely parallel in their linguistic form, but they also contain the three terms "walk," "run," and "powerwalk," which can be played off against one another. Even Sonja, the child who seems the most aware of these instructions as a set and who challenges her classmates to consider them in this way, does not anticipate all of the ramifications of examining these words. Because each of these words can be seen as indicating how fast or slow one moves, "walk" can be viewed as a kind of speed, so that all three words can be placed in the Speed column. Perhaps the most important point to be made about this conversation is that these children were able to take up Sonja's challenge and explore the complex issues brought up by these instructions, the words used in them, and the words used in the column labels.

That the goals of these lessons are deeply intertwined is seen in the way that every utterance operates on several levels, that every statement has its subtexts. When Jimmy claims that "because run–ning is not a kind—you're not step–ping," he is not simply making an argument for placing Run in the Speed column. He is opening the enormous issue of the meanings of the words used in the instructions and column labels and in lived experience. This is an issue that other children take up in their own way, such as when Ronald points to the possibility that words can have several meanings by saying, "When you're running, it's *also* speed," or as when Karen wants to interpret "Kind of Step" a bit more loosely and not place Run in Kind of Step, not because one does not step when running, but because of the practical difficulties of counting the steps of someone running. In a similar manner, Sonja's use of "powerwalk" as a middle term between "walk" and "run" would not have been as effective as it was, if she had not been able to slowly bring these three words into the foreground as a set—to be used to tease out the possible meanings and entailments among them.

Words and their meanings are at the center of this conversation, and, although some words begin to take on specialized meanings, their everyday use continues to influence the conversation. The word "run" is interrogated as to whether it points more strongly to a particular way of moving one's body or a rate of movement. In the ensuing discussion, the question comes up as to whether or not the steps of a runner can be counted. Eventually, the group considers using the terms "walk," "run," and "powerwalk" to indicate speed. But this is difficult for many of the children who feel that speed always connotes going fast, whereas walking means going slowly. The word "powerwalk," which originally gets its meaning from the particular world of exercise classes, comes to play a role in this conversation that is reminiscent of the specialized role technical terms often play in mathematical conversations in that they lead students to question what they see and think: Is a square a rectangle? Does a circle have sides? Is zero a number?

The other main focus of the children's work is the chart, which functions in this conversation in distinct but crucial ways, as both means and end. Although they never arrive at a complete and settled set of understandings and agreements about the chart and its use, the children seem to feel there is enough there for them to talk about at any given time. And the resulting conversations seem sufficiently focused for shared use and ways of talking to begin to emerge from them. On a practical level, the chart serves here as a specific and concrete focal point for the exploration of meanings. It does this by requiring that certain choices be made—"Should Run be in Speed—or shouldn't it?" "Does Distance include '4 steps'?" These choices themselves may not be critical in the end, but they focus the conversation in ways that are more productive than abstract and general questions like: "What do we mean by 'run'?" or "Does 'Distance' tell how far one is to go?" A chart is a way of organizing how one sees a trip and, as such, it is a hybrid meaning-making space, where the meanings of words, the requirements of communication about physical phenomena, and the use of cultural forms overlap and inter-penetrate one another. To the extent that these conversations result in shared understandings, the chart is an artifact of their work, a product that emerges from a process, which also serves as a carrier of the group's understandings that emerge from it. That the children use this chart with increasing ease not only makes their subsequent conversations more productive, but also is a sign of their accomplishments as a group.

The chart also operates in this activity in a practical way that has a hidden, but considerable impact on the students. As they participate in this far-ranging conversation, these children know that they are about to work with their partners to design a trip and use the chart to give directions to another pair so that they will be able to enact the trip as it was designed. This provides an important source of motivation for the children to try to get things right, which means here to try to be certain that their understanding of how to use the chart has as much in common with their classmates' understanding as is possible. Even if a child were not particularly given to explorations of the term "powerwalk," there is good reason here to figure out how others understand various ways of moving and how these ways should be placed in the chart. Once involved in these issues, it is difficult to avoid the issues that surround the chart, such as what the meanings and entailments are of words like "powerwalk," "run," and "speed."

There are many sources of energy in this classroom conversation, including the overlapping roles played by the chart. Another source of energy is the game-like quality of the working out of the column labels and the way in which the two sets of instructions should be placed in the chart. Related to this game-like quality is the more general quality of openness and shared excitement of exploring meanings of everyday experiences and words in this peculiar task of putting instructions in a chart. This juxtaposition of the everyday and the technical has the effect of bringing the richness of the children's enormous background of experience of motion to a demanding task in school, while it is a means for encountering familiar words and phenomena in a new and strange way. This is what lies behind the fact that so many of the children's utterances have an element of surprise—for themselves and for others. Has Jimmy ever argued that running does not involve stepping? Has anyone ever had to respond to a claim such as his? Has Irene ever had to state so emphatically and with so much effect that "Running is a kind of speeeed?"

I have tried to show that, rather than being a conversation in which they move, more or less directly, more or less certainly, toward the commonly agreed-upon use of this kind of chart as a means of describing motion, these children are inventing a world made up of many interacting layers of meaning and understanding. In the process of this conversation, they take on such matters and issues as: What will the *stuff*—the kinds of motion—of this world be? What will be the meanings of key words that refer to that stuff, and what issues will underlie our discussions about these meanings? How do we use this form, called a chart, for communicating about motion? How free are we to make up our own rules and understandings about this form for our use? What can we base our claims about motion, words, and the chart on, as we try to get others to see our point of view? None of these issues precedes the others. All arise all at once. This inevitably results in a diffuse and unpredictable process. Yet these third- and fourth-grade children are able to productively engage in this process of world-making and they seem to be thriving while doing so. This is in spite of the fact that they are, in effect, building a boat while sailing in it.

CURRICULAR DESIGN AND CLASSROOM ACTIVITY AS PLAN AND SITUATED ACTION

> As common-sense constructs, plans are a constituent of practical action, but they are constituent as an artifact of our reasoning about action, not as the generative mechanism of action. Our imagined projections and our retrospective reconstructions are the principal means by which we catch hold of situated action and reason about it. (Suchman, 1987, p. 39)

In the ordinary sense, lesson planning is taken to be a task in which one designs a series of activities for a class in such a way that particular behaviors and interactions occur, which, in turn, give rise to specific meanings and understandings among the students. But what if events and interactions cannot be guided or constrained in the manner one hopes for? In what ways will the children's understandings be influenced by the lesson? How can the designer's intentions be realized? Suchman's tantalizing suggestion was that even if a plan does not generate actions, even if there is no direct connection between plan and events, there is still an important value in the process that led to the plan. This value lies in the reasoning that takes place through "imagined projections," both before and after the events. Rather than shaping events themselves, the plan is a "means by which we catch hold of" the events for the sake of this reasoning. But what does this mean in terms of the real work of a designer of classroom activities? In what ways do prospective and retrospective reasoning about classroom events have an impact on the designer, the events in the classroom, and on the understandings of the children themselves? How does the designer come to be more effective in planning lessons, so that his or her meanings and intentions are more likely to be taken up by children? I wish to explore such questions that arise from Suchman's suggestion, as it applies to the design of classroom activities of the kind exemplified by Ms. D's class, particularly in these episodes.

Little of what is significant in the conversation in these episodes is the direct result of planning. Nor could it have been. The plan for the lesson called for Ms. D to lay out the general form of the chart and give the example of a trip the chart could be used to define. Then the children would develop the chart further by using it to describe this trip and possibly creating and working with a second trip. But, so much of what then took place was due to the choice of the three instructions for a trip the children contributed and the way they dovetailed into Ms. D's illustration of the distinction between "slow" and "fast," that one could not reasonably predict that a similar conversation would take place with a similar class at another time. Even more striking is the way the trajectory of the episode hangs on the particular and peculiar relationship between the two most common means of locomotion, walk and run, and the serendipitous term, powerwalk. But even if one had predicted something like these instructions with their implications, how could one have anticipated the responses of these particular people, with their own individual and collective concerns and styles, and the way these played such a crucial role in shaping this conversation? If one were to try this lesson in another class, who would be the "Jimmy" and the "Sonja," and how would one get two students to play off one another in such a way as to propel the conversation as these two did and, at the same time, make it possible for an "Irene," a "Ronald," and a "Karen" to enter in their ways?

Then there is Ms. D and the particular role she played in this episode. There are many ways she has shaped this conversation, but it can even be argued that the details of her influence are a consequence of this moment, of this particular situation. If we imagined Ms. D conducting the same lesson with an identical class at a later time, it is difficult to believe that events would flow in the same manner, because an even slightly different conversation among the students could evoke very different responses from Ms. D and, as the teacher, she has an enormous effect on the class. Furthermore, Ms. D would have changed as a result of her experience in this session, bringing in yet another unpredictable factor.

But the unpredictability of this particular conversation is not itself a singular event—it is inherent in such events. It is the result of the sheer diversity of the ways children understand things, hear one another, and experience the world. This is made more extreme in a classroom such as this in which the goal is communication on a topic such as motion, to which people bring such rich and varied experiential resources and on which there is such heterogeneity of background understandings of language, physical phenomena, and cultural forms as we see here. Not only does each child have his or her own meanings for terms like "Kind of Step" and "Speed," but these differences also are confounded by the diversity of ways of looking at motion and differences in ideas about how the column labels in a chart operate. The lack of shared understandings and expectations about motion and charts requires that the children be fully involved in making both suggestions and choices from their own experience, which inevitably leads to a vast array of possible trajectories for the lesson.

This high level of unpredictability in the relationship between classroom plan and events suggests the need for an approach to lesson planning beyond the implicit default assumption that the task of lesson planning is to guide or shape particular behaviors, interactions, and meanings. In a paper based on a case of a conversation between a student and an interviewer around a graph of motion, Nemirovsky and Monk (2000) documented the fundamentally unpredictable nature of the interactions among students and adults around symbols and events and discussed its implications for the design of classroom materials. They developed their ideas around the example of an architect who is designing a house and whose task is to make spaces for the occupants to use in their own way, but who does not know who its occupants will be or how they will use it. In the case of curricular design, they argued that artifacts such as graphs and charts can never determine how students use and understand them, but instead, only make possible an endless variety of trajectories of meaning-making. In the light of the indeterminacy of meaning-making processes, they argued that the task of curriculum design in situations involving this process is one of "the creation of artifacts (i.e., description of activities, documentation of students' ideas, manipulatives, software environments, etc.) intended to open up domains of contact between teachers, students, and practices that are historically situated within the broad culture" (Nemirovsky & Monk, 2000, p. 234). As the means of opening up such domains of contact, they highlighted three key aspects of the curricular design task, which correspond to three aspects of the architect's task. These are the design of: (1) *resources*, both experiential and material, that are the stuff of such contact; (2) *boundaries* that determine which of the range of possible resources are to be brought into the domain of contact; and (3) *encounters* in which classroom members with their individual histories and experiences come into contact with one another and with culturally based practices. In effect, what Nemirovsky and Monk proposed is a shift in the focus of curricular and lesson planning, from specific events, interactions, and meanings to the environment of a classroom activity and the encounters that will take place within it.

In spite of the unpredictability of classroom events, planning still involves careful reasoning and decision making. Even if the designer knows that a plan can lead to an enormous range of possible outcomes, including the surprising turn that could not possibly have been anticipated, it is still necessary to think through what can happen and how likely it is, how the many combinations will play out, and what the probable effects of the various scenarios will be. This is planning *for* uncertainty instead of planning *against* or *around* uncertainty. In a paper based on the evidence of a planning session involving Ms. D and other members of the design team several weeks after the session considered here, Ann Rosebery documents and analyzes the process by which Ms. D begins with a proposed scenario in which the children will first work with the distinction between a trip that is fast and one that is slow (Rosebery, chap. 10, this volume). The context of the classroom conversation is to be based on the familiar story of Hansel and Gretel. Her first idea is that, because children have such a strong kinesthetic sense of speed, the class will go out into the school yard and pairs of children will enact a race in which Hansel and Gretel are running from the Witch. By imagining how such an event would be experienced, she becomes concerned that the activity will be so engrossing for the children, as first-person actors, that they will be unable to get a larger view of it, to discuss it as an event in which important distinctions about motion can be made. She then proposes an alternative activity to take place in the classroom in which the children will enact the race, moving two fingers of one hand, as if they are Hansel's legs and two fingers of the other hand as if they are Gretel's.

As Ms. D develops this scene and must make decisions about the mix of whole-class conversations and work in pairs, she considers the experience of particular children in the class, how they have participated in previous activities around motion and how they are likely to respond to the planned activities. All of these decisions involve a careful sorting and balancing of long- and short-term goals, an exploration of her own understanding of motion and how she came into it through activities built around a ball rolling down a ramp, as well as a consideration of the capacities and likely responses of individual children and the class as a whole. As Rosebery makes clear, all of this reasoning takes place within a lived-in space of an imaginary classroom in which Ms. D envisions the classroom, "populating it with specific ideas, questions, activities, personalities, materials, experiences and memories" (Rosebery, chap. 10, this volume). Her description of this process illuminates what Suchman (1987) meant by reasoning through the "imagined projection" of planned events. A similar process lay behind the plan for the lesson being considered here. The crucial issue there was how the children might bring their diverse experiences of giving and following instructions for trips to the activity of designing a chart. How would they respond to the general form of a chart as a means of describing this kind of motion? To what extent would various strategies for leading or scaffolding the way they use the chart be helpful and to what extent would it get in the way? Once any examples of describing a trip through such a chart had been agreed upon, how would various children carry this experience forward as they went to work in pairs?

Reflection and analysis on the events of a lesson such as this, once it has taken place, is a critical means by which the resources for reasoning about future lessons are developed. This is the role of what Suchman called "retro-spective reconstructions," as a means of reasoning about action. Regardless of what one knows about motion and children's sense-making processes around it, and regardless of how experienced one is in designing and reflecting on classroom activities around motion, there is always something new or deeper to be learned by carefully reconstructing and exploring the meaning of events in a past lesson. This is illustrated by what one learns by the close analysis of the episodes being considered here. For instance, it is widely understood that children have rich understandings about motion based on their experiences and on their general intellectual development. We see in these episodes how deeply their understanding is entangled with their use of everyday language to describe it. Nonetheless, their use of such language can be used as an important resource in building a sense of speed as a variable quality, as something a moving object has more or less of. Similar inferences can be made about the ways in which a cultural form like a chart can be used as a medium for meaning-making and communication. By carefully observing how children begin to use such a form, we become aware of the implicit understandings behind its use and how such use shapes the way we see phenomena. What we discover in these episodes is a particular example of how children can come to be users of such a form when it serves them as a tool for reasoning and a medium for sharing their meanings and intentions. We also see how the struggle to communicate to others contributes to the building of a community in which their meanings can be understood and, at the same time, helps to grapple with deeper issues within the notion of speed as an attribute of motion.

It was pointed out in the analysis of the classroom episodes how, although the conversation was always in terms of the specific details of the particular trip and one particular column label or another, the children were also grappling at the same time with more general issues. Thus, even as the conversation focused on whether or not Run should be in the Speed column, the wider issue of the nature of speed as an attribute of motion, which an object has more or less of, was also opened up. The reasoning processes of the designer have the same quality of sliding easily between the specific and the general. In planning a lesson, one is always planning for particular children with their own collective and individual histories. But doing so continually calls upon what one knows about children in general. Retrospective analysis of a classroom situation always starts with the particular conversation, but the very notion of analysis contains an assumption that the particular is being joined with what one knows in general. In all these cases of reasoning, whether on the part of a child or a designer, thinking moves so fluidly between the particular and the general that the distinction is difficult to maintain.

The observation just made, about how the children's thinking processes are both specific and general and how this is also true of a designer, points to an analogy between these two situations that is both surprising and instructive. In both situations, we have an individual who is filled with meanings and intentions that he or she wishes to express within a classroom in which the shared understandings and expectations do not support such expression. In both situations, the individual learns through an iterative process of expressing his or her self and taking in the responses of the classroom group. In both situations, there are parallel and interactive processes of the development of understanding, one in the individual and another in the collective. These are processes of *co-emergence* of shared meanings between the individual and group. It is not simply a matter of the group coming around to one individual's meanings or of any individual needing to adopt the meanings of the group.

The parallel between the two situations, of designer and individual child, provides a means by which we can elaborate and better understand the role of the lesson plan in the design process. It thereby gives insight into what Suchman (1987) meant by saying that "plans are a constituent of practical action, but they are constituent as an artifact of our reasoning about action, not as the generative mechanism of action" (p. 39). As has already been shown about the role of the chart in the two episodes, the plan is both a site and a tool for meaning-making processes, as well as a product that carries the results of these processes. As it begins to emerge in the work of the designer, the plan is a hybrid meaning-making space in which the designer is able to reason about the flow of activities in terms of particular children's responses to the task, the concrete objects and materials at hand, as well as the mathematical ideas that are emerging. Just as the chart imposes on the children the need to decide on a single label for each column and thereby focuses their interactions, the emerging lesson plan requires that the designer think through the likely consequences of any particular instruction in terms of its possible effects on the class—"What will be the immediate effect of asking the children to give labels to these columns; how much specific guidance will they need?" As a product, the lesson plan serves the designer chiefly as a lens through which to see the lesson based upon it. It is a particular way of framing and taking in the many layers of meaning in this complex phenomenon. It serves in this way as the basis for the retrospective reasoning about the lesson that is a crucial step in his or her own learning process.

The lesson plan also serves in a manner that does not have a direct coun-terpart in the situation of the child in Ms. D's class. It is the means of communication between the designer and the teacher, who plays a critical role in the enactment of the plan. As Nemirovsky and Monk pointed out, "It is the teacher who deals with the unexpected and unintended approaches emerging in the midst of students' symbolizing. The teacher, like a sailor piloting a boat, makes decisions in response to both the issues coming forth in the classroom and her own sense of direction and priorities" (Nemirovsky & Monk, 2000, p. 214). We see this in these episodes when, for example, Ms. D substitutes "Kind of Step" for "Walk," or presses Jimmy for what he means by "move," or takes whatever Sonja said in Episode 2.3 and broadcasts it as: "Are you trying to say, that walking is a kind of speed?" Ms. D played a dual role in this design project as key member of the design team and as classroom teacher, but this is only a concrete version of a relationship that always exists in some form or other—the teacher and the designer are always collaborators in the use of a curricular plan. But just as the chart cannot communicate all of its meanings and information to a child who was not in on the process of developing it, the plan of a lesson cannot directly communicate to a teacher all that went into it. A lesson plan serves as the starting point for the teacher's own planning, which must be carried out in very much the same way as the designer's planning. This is illustrated by the fact that, even though Ms. D was a member of the planning team for these lessons, she always took the results of the planning sessions and made her own lesson plans from them. It is also the reason why, in the case of a published curriculum like "Investigations in Number, Data, and Space" (Russell, Tierney, & Mokros, 1994), which was a source of this present curricular plan, the material is addressed to the teacher and, in addition to lesson plans, supplies "Teacher notes," illustrated by classroom vignettes and student work as well as commentaries on the underlying mathematical ideas.

This section opened with a question about the role of lesson planning in the learning that takes place in a classroom and in the work of the designer. My response began with the suggestion that a revision is needed in the way the task of planning activities in a classroom such as Ms. D's is conceptualized. Rather than seeking to evoke and guide particular behaviors, interactions, and resultant meanings on the part of the students, an approach that focuses on the classroom mathematical environment in which certain kinds of encounters among the students are likely to take place is a more realistic and productive one. Within such an approach to curricular design, the process of planning a particular lesson can be seen as having two distinct kinds of effects—one immediate and direct, the other long-term and indirect. The immediate effect of curricular design is through the particular ways in which a lesson plan organizes the classroom environment and the encounters within it, with the outcome depending, to an extent, on the thoughtfulness and care of the designer's reasoning process as it is carried out in what Suchman (1987) called "imaginative projection." This has been elaborated in the present situation primarily through reference to the study by Rosebery of a lesson-planning session carried out by the planning team that included Ms. D. The role of the lesson plan here is as a product of the planning process that communicates the designer's intentions to the teacher. In this, it is only a starting point for the teacher's own planning. The long-term and indirect effects of curricular design are through the overall iterative process that includes not only the planning of individual lessons, but also the observation and analysis of past lessons, as it is carried out in what Suchman called "retrospective reconstructions." This kind of reasoning is exemplified by the analysis of the episodes provided in this chapter. The role of the lesson plan here is as a site and a tool for the designer's reasoning processes, and as a product that carries the results of this reasoning from one session to another. What Suchman suggested, in effect, is that the lesson plan is an artifact of these reasoning processes which can operate in significant ways, and that, although the immediate effects of curricular design may be less than a designer hopes for—although the lesson plan may not serve as "the generative mechanism of action"—the overall long-term process of curricular design does have a considerable effect on the students' learning through its effects on the designer.

We see, then, that the process of planning a particular lesson is at the intersection of two distinct learning processes, one involving the students in the class and the other involving the designer. There are important similarities between these two learning processes, in that each begins with an actor—a student or a designer—filled with intentions and meanings that he or she wishes to share within a classroom situation. In both cases, this can only take place in the long run, through an iterative process in which this person expresses his or her own meanings and intentions and receives the responses of others. In both cases, the reasoning that is carried out is both specific and general. A written artifact is central to each of these processes, the chart in the case of the students and the lesson plan in the case of the designer. In the course of this process, individuals learn to express themselves in ways that others in the classroom can take in, while the classroom community develops more effective means for communicating what the individuals within it, including the teacher, wish to express.

CONCLUSION

This chapter consists of descriptions and examinations of two quite different situations, one of a classroom conversation and the other of a curriculum designer planning a lesson. The presentation of both situations was initially occasioned by the fact that the analysis of the first gave rise to significant questions about the second. As our study of the second situation has proceeded, the similarities between the two have become increasingly clear and have led to the juxtaposition of these two strikingly different, but analogous, situations. Among the points and issues that can be grasped more deeply as a result of this juxtaposition are: the iterative and gradual nature of learning through experience—as, in Dewey's phrase, "trying and undergoing"; the co-emergence of individual and collective meanings, understandings, and expectations within a community; the fluid exchange between thinking about a particular situation and thinking about such situations more generally; and the use of written artifacts in these reasoning processes. There is a further important benefit that derives from this juxtaposition: As designers, researchers, and teachers, we habitually see the first of these situations, that of the child in a classroom, from the outside, and we habitually experience the second of these situations, that of a lesson planner, from the inside. This parallel and its resultant resonances not only enable us to get inside the experience of the child, but they also help us see our own actions as designers from the outside, leading to a fuller view of ourselves as designers, engaged in a process of learning.

ACKNOWLEDGMENTS

The author was supported for much of the writing of this chapter by a grant from the National Science Foundation, #DUE-9653068. The classroom study on which it is based was funded by U.S. Department of Education, Office of Educational Research and Improvement, Cooperative Agreement No. R305A60007-98 to the National Center for Improving Student Learning and Achievement in Mathematics and Science, University of Wisconsin, Madison and the National Science Foundation, ESI 9555712. The data presented, the statements made, and the views expressed are solely the responsibility of the author. No endorsement by the funding agencies should be inferred.

REFERENCES

Blumer, H. (1969). *Symbolic interactionism*. Englewood Cliffs, NJ: Prentice-Hall.

Cobb, P. (1999). Individual and collective mathematical development: The case of statistical data analysis. *Mathematical Thinking and Learning, 1*, 5–43. Hillsdale, NJ: Lawrence Erlbaum Associates.

Cobb, P., & Bauersfeld, H. (1995). *The emergence of mathematical meaning: Interaction in classroom cultures*. Hillsdale, NJ: Lawrence Erlbaum Associates.

Cobb, P., Boufi, A., McClain, K., & Whitenack, J. (1997). Reflective discourse and collective reflection. *Journal for Research in Mathematics Education, 28*, 258–277.

DiSchino, M. (1987). The many phases of growth: One teacher's experience of learning. *Journal of Teaching and Learning, 1*(3), 12–28.

DiSchino, M. (1998). "Why do bees sting and why do they die afterward?" In A. Rosebery & B. Warren (Eds.), *Boats, balloons, and classroom video: Science teaching as inquiry* (pp. 109–133). Portsmouth, NH: Heinemann.

DiSessa, A., Hammer, D., Sherin, B., & Kolpakowski, T. (1991). Inventing graphing: Meta-representational expertise in children. *Journal of Mathematical Behavior, 10*, 117–160.

Duckworth, E. (1987). *The having of wonderful ideas*. New York: Teachers College Press.

Lampert, M. (1990). When the problem is not the question and the solution is not the answer: Mathematical knowing and teaching. *American Educational Research Journal, 27*, 29–63.

Lehrer, R., Schauble, L., Carpenter, S., & Penner, D. (2000). The inter-related development of inscriptions and conceptual understanding. In P. Cobb, E. Yackel, & K. McClain (Eds.), *Symbolizing and communicating in mathematics classrooms: Perspectives on discourse, tools, and instructional design* (pp. 325–360). Mahwah, NJ: Lawrence Erlbaum Associates.

Nemirovsky, R., & Monk, S. (2000). "If you look at it the other way . . .": An exploration into the nature of symbolizing. In P. Cobb, E. Yackel, & K. McClain (Eds.), *Symbolizing and communicating in mathematics classrooms* (pp. 177–221). Mahwah, NJ: Lawrence Erlbaum Associates.

Russell, S., Tierney, C., & Mokros, J. (1994). *Investigations in number, data, and space*. Palo Alto, CA: Dale Seymour Publications.

Suchman, L. (1987). *Plans and situated actions: The problem of human machine communication*. New York: Cambridge University Press.

Wenger, E. (1998). *Communities of practice: Learning, meaning, and identity*. Cambridge, UK: Cambridge University Press.

Yackel, E., & Cobb, P. (1996). Sociomathematical norms, argumentation, and autonomy in mathematics. *Journal for Research in Mathematics Education, 27*, 458–477.

2

Mathematical Places

Ricardo Nemirovsky
TERC

Written numbers and equations, drawings of graphs and geometrical diagrams, and many other symbols are pervasive signs of mathematical activity, both in mathematical teaching and learning as well as in professional work. These symbolic expressions are often seen as external representations of mental ones (Dufour-Janvier, Bednarz, & Belanger, 1987; Goldin & Shteingold, 2001; Kaput, 1998). Whatever the differences between mental and physical objects, the assumption is that of a causal resemblance between the symbols written on different surfaces and the mental images of those who understand them, so that the former ones are an "external" version of the "internal" ones and vice versa. By means of internalizing and externalizing, what is outside goes inside and what is inside goes outside. Whereas external representations—those marks on paper or computer screens that can be moved and looked on—can be observed directly, the internal or mental ones have to be inferred from what the symbolizer says or does. In this chapter we lend support to an alternative point of view: Using mathematical representations is not a matter of holding correspondences between an outside and an inside, but of inhabiting symbolic places that embrace both the symbol-user and the world in which he or she lives.

A recurrent topic in mathematics education is the creation, use, and roles of multiple representations, such as graphs, number tables, and equations. It is not uncommon among mathematics educators to think there must be a common core knowledge that is expressed differently in each particular representation (Even, 1998). Because multiplicity of representations for a given mathematical idea is the norm, rather than the exception, the question arises of how they relate to each other. Janvier talked about these relationships as "translations," resembling how statements in one language are translated into another (Janvier, 1987). Other authors (English, 1997; Presmeg, 1998) studied the relationships among multiple representations by focusing on the ideas of analogy and metaphor. Analogies and metaphors are conceived as mental structures interrelating a "source" and a "target" or allowing us to see one thing as another.

> An obvious example of reasoning by analogy in mathematics learning lies in children's interpretation of concrete and pictorial/diagrammatic representations. These external representations act as the source for the learning of the target concept, as indicated in the base-ten block representation of the numeral 3231 [shown in a figure]. (English, 1997, p. 5)

> "A conceptual metaphor allows us to reason about one kind of object as if it were another. For instance, we may think of numbers as points on a straight line." (Bazzini, 2001, p. 261)

Over the last 10 years, two strands of ideas have influenced research on this topic: embodied cognition and semiotics. Lakoff and Nunez (1997) identified the metaphorical power to interrelate ideas expressed with different representational systems as stemming from our everyday activity structured by the body:

> Our everyday conceptual system and capacity for reason is grounded in the human body, brain, and everyday experience. Basic mathematical concepts are expert versions of everyday human concepts. As we saw, our basic mathematical ideas are metaphorically grounded in everyday experience and make use of our commonplace conceptual system. (p. 84)

Ernest (2002) argued that semiotics can offer a synthesis integrating the psychological and the social aspects of mathematical activity, so that the "personal appropriation of signs" and the "patterns of sign use and production" can be drawn together. Some semiotics-oriented studies tend to rely on the formal analysis of signs (Duval, 2001) whereas others bring to prominence the sociocultural context of use (Morgan, 2002; Radford, 2003).

In this chapter we talk about multiple representations in terms of symbolic places one inhabits, so that that one juxtaposes symbolic places in the ways that we juxtapose, say, different rooms of a house we live in by preserving their different identities and sorts of things one does in each of them, while also having a sense that they all are part of the same house. These ideas are rooted in our past work related to Winnicot's theory of "transitional space" (Nemirovsky &

Noble, 1997) and to the notion of "lived-in space" (Nemirovsky, Tierney, & Wright, 1998); in this chapter we attempt to build on these by elaborating on the common notion of place.

Our everyday sense of place is an insightful background to overcome the dichotomy opposing the realms of the physical and the mental because we commonly understand that two people can be next to each other but in very different places, that places are not habitually lived in terms of objective and subjective sides, and that one's life history and circumstances are crucial to what place one is in. This richness is likely to be behind the current upsurge of interest in the philosophy and ethnography of place (Casey, 1993, 1997; Light & Smith, 1998; Malpas, 1999; O'Neill, 2001; Relph, 1976; Seamon, 1979; Seamon & Mugerauer, 2000). What does it mean to be somewhere? What is entailed in being at a place? What is that we call "a place"? These are the type of questions that the next section elaborates on. Grounded in this context, we will also immerse ourselves in issues such as: What kind of place is a mathematics classroom? How does each student's "being there" participate in the life of the class? How is it possible to be at a symbolic place, that is, a place manifested in and by symbolic expressions? What kinds of places are suitable to live in with mathematical entities?

After the ensuing section devoted to the notion of place and symbolic place as they come into view from everyday life, we introduce the methodology and the context of annotated classroom episodes, which will provide concrete examples of mathematical places as experienced by two high school students— Cora and Beatriz. We selected two episodes, the first analyzed in the section entitled "A Graphical Place" and the second discussed in the section "An Algebraic Place." These episodes allow us to trace how Cora and Beatriz came to inhabit a graphical and an algebraic place.

IN PLACE

I am my body; but I am also my habitual surrounding. This is demonstrated by the laceration, the division with myself that accompanies exile from my home.

(Marcel, 1952, p. 201)

Questions about place are complex, so we need to sort out and choose entry points. Let us start with this one: How is "being at a place" similar and different from "being in a situation" and "being at a location"?

Place and situation are often interchangeable in common language. One might say, for instance, "I wouldn't like to be in her place," meaning not the room she is in but the situation with which she is dealing. Conversely, we could refer to being at an enjoyable place, such as a peaceful hiking trail, as a desirable situation, although this usage appears to be less common. People are frequently described as "being in" feeling states, which are crucial qualities of situations (e.g., "he is in love"). On the other hand, there are distinctive aspects between place and situation. A hint at these is the phrase we wrote a few lines above: "meaning not the room she is in." What does lead us to perceive a room as a place but not *necessarily* as a situation? One central element in addressing this question stems from the fact that a room has a physical extension whereas a situation might not. In a place one can perceive and point out "heres" and "theres" that are associated with particular physical locations. In a place one can gesture here or there, in *this* drawer, next to *that* tree, and so on and physically point at those "spots," whereas one can talk about a situation, about this pressure, that event without them being definitely located somewhere.

On the other hand, we would not treat place and location as equivalent. We will make distinctive use of place and location to be able to point out several aspects central to our analysis. A postal address, a pair latitude/longitude, or a reference object (e.g., "under the table") are some of the ways to indicate locations. But two people—or the same person at different times—can be at the same location while in different places. The same location, say a certain park, can be for someone a workplace and for someone else a playground. Places are "for" someone, whereas locations can be determined regardless of whoever is there, why they are there, or what they are doing there.

As a first approximation, we will describe "being in a place"[1] as that experience that combines the qualities of situation and location. Being in a place means at once being situated and located. In spite of being a commonplace, sometimes we feel amazed at how elements of location attach themselves to the situation lived there. Consider, for instance, Penelope Lively's (2001) account of this autobiographical event:

One weekend in 1956 I visited my father in London. I was then living and working in Oxford. On the Sunday evening he drove me to Paddington to catch the train back. He was rather silent, as though something were on his mind. As we waited at a traffic light on Kensington

---

[1]We do not distinguish between "place" and "being in a place" because a place is constituted by and through what it is like to be in it.

Gore (I know which one, to this day), he spoke, abruptly: "There's something I've been meaning to say to you. Isn't it about time you were thinking of getting married?"

I was twenty-three. I had a job, so was financially independent. I remember being startled—this seemed an injunction from another time. (p. 171)

Lively's parenthetical remark, noting that more than 40 years later she can still tell in which corner of London she and her father were at that moment, reflects a feeling of surprise at preserving what seem to be random contingencies. Far from being a curiosity, we take such merging of situation and location as a major trait of what being at a place, or what a place itself, is. Although everyday language extends the use of "place" to experiences that are just situated or located, we will call in this chapter for their mutual presence in the constitution of place. We begin to unfold this notion by commenting on three aspects: orientation, placing, and juxtaposition.

Orientation

A deceptively simple answer to the question of where one is, is the following: wherever one's body is. This response is deceptively simple because, as opposed to the where of an inert object, it is impossible to strictly confine the where of a lived body, be it of a human being or of any living organism. A lived body is in part always outside of itself: in the things one is paying attention to, in the places one has been at, in the materials one touches, in the other bodies that speak to us, and so forth.

We have said that in contrast to locations, places are always "for" someone. Here we want to add a complementary facet: places come to be "by way of" a lived body. There are no places for an inert object because places are constituted by the living bodies for which the place is. The body's constitution of place entails countless aspects, such as being far/close, being inside/outside, and orientation. Here we discuss the latter.

Faced with the question of where someone is, there is no limit to the degree of specification one could provide. One can say that he is in the house, but also that he is in the living room, sitting next to the big table, facing the window, looking at bills that need to be paid, worrying about when they have to be paid, and so forth. In reality we always assess what information is the most relevant and avoid going into what might be seen as endless superfluous details, but let us note that we customarily distinguish between the place one is in (e.g., a peaceful bench at the park) and what we are going to call one's "orientation" in that place, such as the things one is dealing with, what one is looking at and responding to, how the surroundings look like from where one stands, and so on.[2] The following quote will help us elaborate on the phenomenon of orientation.

> In order to reconstruct the summer of 1914, when the numb fury of verse-making first came over me, all I really need is to visualize a certain pavilion. There the lank, fifteen year-old lad I then was, sought shelter during a thunderstorm, of which there was an inordinate number that July. (...) The storm passed quickly (...) A moment later my first poem began. What touched it off? I think I know. Without any wind blowing, the sheer weight of a raindrop, shining in parasitic luxury on a chordate leaf, caused its tip to dip, and what looked like a globule of quicksilver performed a sudden glissando down the entire vein, and then, having shed its bright load the relieved leaf unbent. Tip, leaf, dip, relief—the instant it all took to happen seemed to me not so much a fraction of time as a fissure in it, a missed heartbeat, which was refunded at once by a patter of rhymes: I say "patter" intentionally, for when a gust of wind did come, the trees would briskly start to drip all together in as crude an imitation of the recent downpour as the stanza I was already muttering resembled the shock of wonder I had experienced when for a moment heart and leaf had been one. (Nabokov, 1966, pp. 215–217)

"When for a moment heart and leaf had been one." This is perhaps the central quality of orientation: We are oriented toward that with which we are one. The idea of oneness helps to highlight the bi-directionality of orientation: one is oriented toward something while at the same time one is being oriented by that something. For this reason we will say that we are oriented toward/ by it.

In being oriented, the place as a whole counts. In Nabokov's example, his being oriented toward/by that "fissure" in time was not merely his looking at an isolated raindrop sliding on a leaf, but the sheltering quality of the pavilion, the storm that had just passed, the bareness of its interior, its being frequented by trespassers, his perennial need for solitude, and many other aspects that our quote has skipped in order to keep it short. Because of this holistic nature of orientation, it seems to us correct to say that being at a place is being oriented, albeit in transient and momentary ways. One's orientation constantly shifts and renews.

Vladimir Nabokov's account of his initiation in verse-making could be a bit misleading for our purposes because to some readers it might suggest that that toward which the person is oriented is something one can point at in a

---

[2]The distinction between the place one is in and one's orientation in that place is context-dependent. What counts as a different orientation might be taken as a different place in another context.

definite fashion (e.g., "Tip, leaf, dip, relief"). Let us question this possibility by reading a different example:

> My sole consolation when I went upstairs for the night was that Mamma would come and kiss me after I was in bed. But this good night lasted for so short a time, she went down again so soon, that the moment in which I heard her climb the stairs, and then caught the sound of her garden dress of blue muslin, from which hung little tassels of plaited straw, rustling along the double-doored corridor, was for me a moment of utmost pain; for it heralded the moment which was bound to follow it, when she would have left me and gone downstairs again. (Proust, 1989, p. 13)

As soon as Marcel Proust heard his mother climbing the stairs, his place suddenly adopted a new orientation. It would be shallow to say that this orientation was simply toward the noises made by his mother's dress.[3] He became oriented toward/by another sleepless night, his father who stayed downstairs and who barely tolerated this ritual of good night, his mother's effort to liberate him from his emotional dependence, the demons that would wake him up in his dreams, the darkness of the night, and so on. All these were part of his frightful orientation.

At times one's being at a place holds more than one orientation at once, which gives one a feeling of tension and instability, like when we are talking to someone but, mindful of the hour, sneak a peek at our watch out of the corner of our eye. Orientations come in infinite varieties. Sometimes they are focused and steady, such as when one is waiting for an opportunity to cross the street; other times they are itinerant and wandering, like when one comes to a new place and looks around before settling for a corner to go to. The body is in a perpetual dance in synchrony with the orientation of the place it is in. Note, for example, how in a conversation when the conversant needs to remember something, a name, say, or to solve some question before continuing, that for a fraction of a second her eyes close or look upward and her hands display a stop gesture, like asking for a little time-out. It is a momentary orientation shift after which she "returns." The perpetual dance of the body orienting itself and its place embodies customary and pervasive distinctions such as being above/below, being next to/on top of, being to the right/to the left, and so on.

Sometimes the body expresses our being somewhere else—maybe because we are silent and not looking at anything in particular around us—prompting someone else to ask us, "Where are you?" We said earlier that living bodies

---

[3] It might be said, as the common expression goes, that he was "paying attention" to his mother's climbing the stairs, but paying attention to is much narrower than being oriented to.

are outside of themselves. Now we can say what part of the outside they are in: the part they are oriented toward and by, that is, the part of the outside they are one with.

PLACE/DWELLING

Some places are different from others because we live in or have lived in them. After being asked where does one live, depending on the circumstances, our response might be to point to a house, a neighborhood, a piece of land, a country, a street, a mountain, a city, a building, and so on. Here we interpret the where of our lives in a broad sense: wherever we feel or have felt at home, which is not only a house, but could also be a workplace, a park, a church, a downtown, and countless other places that have become identified with the life one has lived there. Let us call them "dwellings." How does an initially untried place become a dwelling? This is the question we examine in this section, which, like many other questions we discuss in this introduction, we can only glimpse. We have chosen two entry points into these matters: placing and juxtaposing.

Placing

Some wealthy art collectors have donated their houses to an art museum with the strict condition that everything will remain in place. It is not uncommon for someone to be reluctant to change the location of a familiar object in her home. What is the source of such objects' attachment to their surroundings? It is as if moving certain things breaks their "natural" place, where they "belong" and where they got their proper room. We see as the source of these attachments between a thing and its surrounding, the phenomenon of placing, that is, of making room for something and living with its active and fitting presence there.

During her youth, Virginia Woolf frequently took walks across Kensington Gardens with friends and family members. This is a piece of her description of the gardens:

> There were two gates, one opposite Gloucester Road, the other opposite to Queen's Gate. At each gate sat an old woman. The Queen's Gate old woman was an elongated, emaciated figure with a goat-like face, yellow and pockmarked. She sold nuts and boot-laces, I think. And Kitty Maxse said of her: "Poor things, it's drink that makes them like that". (. . .) The other old

woman was round and squat. To her was attached a whole wobbling balloon of air-ball. She held this billowing, always moving, most desirable mass by one string. They glowed in my eyes always red and purple, like the flower my mother wore; and they were always billowing in the air. For a penny, she would detach one from the bellying soft mass, and I would dance away with it. (Woolf, 1985, p. 75)

Strolling across Kensington Gardens, she placed the two old women at their respective gates, not only because she made room for them there, on the gates she passed through, but also because each woman developed an active and distinctive place in her own life. One as a poor and sick person for whom she felt pity and perhaps aversion, and who others made her see as a by-product of alcoholism. The other as a robust supplier of attractive and colorful balloons she yearned for. It is likely that many other walkers in Kensington Gardens noticed these two women only fleetingly, or not at all, and therefore they did not place them at the gates, although they might have placed there other things, people, or events to which Virginia Woolf was oblivious. Like orientation, placing has a dual directionality: As one places something, it places us. The glowing mass of balloons "always billowing in the air" let her know where she was and sometimes how far she was from getting one of those. And the emaciated woman who sold boot-laces perhaps gave her a sense of how dreadful were other lives luckily distant from her own. Because of this dual directionality, placing composes the identity between a place and one's life at that place.

The ancient "art of memory" in which things are systematically placed in imaginary locations illustrates how placing is a key to making something memorable. The mnemonist studied by Luria (1987), for instance, performed many of his feats by pasting names, images, and symbols on successive houses or stores arranged along his mental image of the Nevsky Avenue continued by a street of another town where he had grown up. Time and again, a past event is placed somewhere and the location becomes a memorial, that is, a place that calls for a certain recollection. Vladimir Nabokov recalls a memorial of this sort that his father conveyed to him:

There was a certain spot in the forest, a footbridge across a brown brook, where my father would piously pause to recall the rare butterfly that, on the seventeenth of August, 1883, his German tutor had netted for him. The thirty-year-old scene would be gone through again. He and his brothers had stopped short in helpless excitement at the sight of the coveted insect poised on a log and moving up and down, as though in alert respiration, its four cherry-red wings with a pavonian eyespot on each. In tense silence, not daring to strike himself, he had handed his net to Herr Rogge, who was groping for it, his eyes fixed on the splendid fly. (Nabokov, 1966, p. 75)

It is often the case that what we place is invisible to others, because only certain backgrounds of life experience make them visible, like in this example written by the author:

> I was biking with Damian along a bike path I frequently go across. For years he had run along this same path to stay fit for the races he participated with his track team. At every turn Damian would comment on how easy or hard the ensuing piece was to run, he pointed at certain trees next to which he would get the displeasing feeling that he had still a long way to go, or at others marking cheering closeness to the end, also at certain big stones that would show how many miles he had run so far. I felt that Damian was showing me a bike path I had never seen before.

Damian had placed along the bike path numerous and detailed indications of what running through it felt like to him. At the same time, these invisible (to others) markers placed him along past and upcoming lived moments of his own run.

Juxtaposing

We can exemplify the process of juxtaposition, and the role that it has for a new place to become a dwelling, through the description a colleague, Teresa Lara-Meloy, wrote of two trips she had made to Tucson, Arizona, and how they left in her distinct images of the city. This is the first one:

> The first time I went to Tucson, for a wedding, I took a cab from the airport to a hotel and met my friends. We spent most of the weekend at the hotel where the wedding was celebrated. The following day, one of my friends, a local, drove us tourists around the city. As he took us around, I was fascinated with the fact that this town reminded of my hometown, Tehuacan. There were mountains in every direction; the desert flora is strikingly similar, too. Even the plants and the streets are named in Spanish. I spent time admiring similarities in landscape but I was left with a vague idea of Tucson. Actually, I felt that every road was indistinguishable from the next because of the interminable miles of strip-malls and fast-food joints. I knew places in the city, like the resort where we stayed, the park where we had a barbeque, the Desert Museum somewhere outside of the city, and the store where I bought Mexican candy but I had no idea how close or far these things were in relation to each other, nor where they were located around the city.

There are several elements in this description that characterize many first encounters with a place. On the one hand there is an initial sense of the landscape: mountains in every direction, certain colors and luminosity of the soil and the sky, architectural styles, urban profiles, miles of strip malls and fast-food joints, and so forth. On the other hand there is a close-up memory of a few places she stayed or stopped at, like the resort or the candy store. These places felt like isolated, sharply drawn, and well-illuminated spots in the midst of a large undifferentiated mass of streets, buildings, people, and other urban elements. Each one of these places remained aloof surrounded by a vast space of Tucsonian landscape. Virginia Woolf (1985) thought that childhood memories are made of crisp, strange, and profoundly meaningful scenes "surrounded by a vast space" (p. 79). Perhaps our first encounters with a place re-create some of the qualities of childhood memories.

This is Teresa's description of another trip to Tucson:

> My last trip to Tucson was different, though. I rented a car. Each time I left the house I needed to know where I was going to and how I was going to get there. The act of driving itself was determinant in giving me a sense of where things were, how far away in space and time they were in relation to each other, and routes for getting from one place to another. Towards the end I didn't even need the map anymore. The Tucson I discovered from driving around is extensively different than the one I had experienced while in the passenger seat. A final experience was significant to me. Flying out of Tucson I was able to recognize landmarks and streets. I could even find places that I intended to visit the next time, even though I hadn't been there. It was as if the paper map and my experience in the city were blending into each other as I saw Tucson from the plane.

During this last trip, Teresa Lara-Meloy developed a connectedness between places in Tucson that had been absent before. Borrowing a concept taken from Poulet (1977), we can say that she began to juxtapose the places she stayed at or stopped by. Juxtaposing not by making them physically contiguous, but by exploring and establishing ways to go from one to the other and to imagine both of them at once. Juxtaposing criss-crosses that vast undifferentiated space enclosing each secluded place, opening little veins through which different places can communicate with each other. Juxtaposing results from mindful local travel. Mindful in the sense of the traveler being oriented towards the ways she traverses ("on the driver seat," as Teresa said), and local in that the traveling remains within the contours of the emerging dwelling. Because the juxtaposing is in her experience of the city, which included reading its map, as her plane took off she could see a Tucson in which places and relating ways were located and situated by her memory of them, some of them pointing at unknown spots she might visit next time.

Juxtaposing does not eliminate discontinuities and disjointedness. Sometimes places get juxtaposed by an impassable gap. Like a collage that puts dissimilar things next to each other and that derives its appeal precisely from the contiguity of its disparities, juxtaposing incorporates also fissures between places:

> The Church! Homely and familiar, cheek by jowl in the Rue Saint-Hilaire, upon which its north door opened, with its two neighbors, Mme. Laiseau's house and M. Rapin's pharmacy, against which its walls rested without interspace (...) There existed, nonetheless, between

> the Church and everything in Combray that was not the church a clear line of demarcation which my mind has never succeeded in crossing. In vain might Mme Laiseau deck her window-sills with fuchsias, which developed the bad habit (. . .) [of cooling] their purple, congested cheeks against the dark front of the church, to me such conduct sanctified the fuchsias not at all; between the flowers and the blackened stone against which they leaned, if my eyes could discern no gap, my mind preserved the impression of an abyss. (Proust, 1989, p. 67)

As we travel mindfully and locally, what we juxtapose are not only different places but also the same places seen from different sides and times, like in this example of the steeple of Saint-Hilaire:

> It was the steeple of Saint-Hilaire that shaped and crowned and consecrated every occupation, every hour of the day, every view of the town. (. . .) And in the evening, when I came in from my walk and thought of the approaching moment when I must say good night to my mother and see her no more, the steeple was by contrast soft and gentle, there at the close of the day, (. . .); while the cries of birds that wheeled around it seemed to intensify its silence, to elongate its spire still further, and to invest it with some quality beyond the power of words.

> Even when our errands lay in places behind the church, from which it could not be seen, the view seemed always to have been composed with reference to the steeple. Which would loom up here and there among the houses, and was perhaps even more affecting when it appeared thus without the church. (Proust, 1989, pp. 69–70)

By juxtaposing different orientations, we develop the "it" toward/by which we orient ourselves, such as the steeple of Saint-Hilaire. Each orientation discloses certain aspects of it, successively revealing what it is for us. Both placing and juxtaposing evoke images of an organic growth, like a tree bifurcating ever more with new and thinner branches that would in time hold their own region. This is how we cultivate places to let them become dwellings. And because of the identity between a place and our life in that place, cultivating places is also cultivating ourselves.

SYMBOLIC PLACES

Maps posted to orient visitors are ubiquitous. Many of them have the customary "You are here" label, as in Fig. 2.1.

Where is that "here"? It is a here that is at once on the map itself and wherever the map has been posted. This dual location makes it significant and motivates us to look for it (for we already know that we are "here," in front of the map). Note that it is we ("you") who are in both at once. Being in the map *as well as* wherever our feet stand makes of the map a symbolic place. Let us characterize a symbolic place as a place in which one experiences a spatial distribution of here and there that are at once in it and in some other

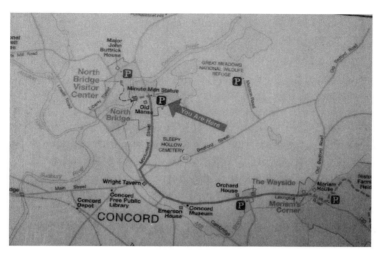

FIG. 2.1. You are here.

"symbolized" place. Being in a symbolic place is being simultaneously in two separated places, which hold common here and there.

How is it possible to be in two places at once without ignoring one of them or feeling split? This is where the phenomenon of fusion comes into play. We have defined fusion as acting, talking, and gesturing without distinguishing between symbols and referents (Nemirovsky & Monk, 2000; Nemirovsky et al., 1998). It is an "as if" phenomenon, like the pretend play in which children and actors engage all the time. It is an attitude we all immerse ourselves in, except when we feel disoriented or we suspect that we are not sharing common interpretations of what is being said or shown, in which case we tend to be explicit about correspondences between symbols and referents. The experience of fusion allows us to sense, or to make-believe, two places as being one place, in which we are and orient ourselves.

There is nothing "intrinsic" that makes a place symbolic. A place is or is not symbolic as a result of how we experience it. Consider this example of a seating arrangement in an old church:

For customary it was, and surely an echo of the ubiquitous earlier practice whereby church seating not only reflected the social structures of the parish but tethered each house to a particular pew or "kneeling". Those parishioners who moved house or left the area relinquished their right to an established position in the church each Sunday. And where you sat indicated your status—gentry at the front, yeomen and husbandmen in the middle, cottagers at the rear. Richard Gough's *The History of the Myddle* (written around 1700) uses the seating plan of his parish church a few miles north of Shrewsbury to give a vivid and discursive account of an entire community in the late seventeenth century, family by family, person by person. Who was married to whom, who lived where and bequeathed what, who was "pilfering, thievish', who "went dayly to the alehouse", who "lived very high and kept a pack of beagles". The church layout becomes in effect a mnemonic system. (Lively, 2001, p. 58)

A visitor unfamiliar with the parish's history and characters might "know" that the seating arrangement "must" reflect social status and interpersonal hierarchies, but this is different from the experience of those acquainted with that history, who fuse the church layout with those who seat or kneel there and with their place in the community—to the point that it becomes a mnemonic system—and for whom the distribution of seats is a symbolic place. It is for the latter that pointing at a group of chairs can be pointing at a dual "here," which is in that spot of the church as well as in the web of relationships enacted by community life. On the other hand, being familiar with what one sees symbolized is not an all-or-nothing affair. Rather, it is partial, evolving, and multifaceted. Let us take as an example this map of railways in greater Tokyo (Fig. 2.2) and a growing acquaintance with a train station:

Before going to Tokyo I knew that I was supposed to stay at a hotel that was close to a train station called Koiwa. I spent a long time on the Internet examining Tokyo's railways maps. The map looked to me like an extended mass of crossing lines with no distinctive landmarks or orientation points. Through a "blind" search I did find Koiwa station. Then I got an idea about

FIG. 2.2. Section of the map of Tokyo railways.

how to get there from the Narita airport, which was noticeable in the map next to the drawing of an airplane. But that was only the beginning. Gradually Koiwa became different from all the other train stations in an increasing number of ways. Unlike other stations, Koiwa does not have an electric escalator to get to the street level, something highly noticeable when you go there loaded with luggage. In addition, the trains coming from Narita airport go through but do not stop in Koiwa, going from Koiwa to Tokyo station costs 210 yens, there is in the station a small restaurant with good croissants, Flower Street (where the hotel was at) comes out right from the station, Koiwa means Little Rock, etc. Now, two months later, if I look at the railway map of Tokyo I can see right away where Koiwa is and how it connects to central Tokyo. However, the left side of the map (opposite to Narita, Koiwa, etc.) still looks to me as a rather amorphous or confusing set of crossing lines.

On many occasions, to the extent that the symbolic place provides means to stimulate the imagination in rich and intense ways, we gain fluency with the symbolized by imagining it. For instance, when we read a novel or watch a movie, the book or the movie theater become symbolic places. This is how Proust described the flight of his imagination during his afternoon readings under a chestnut tree in Combray:

in my state of repose, which (thanks to the enlivening adventures related in my books) sustained, like a hand reposing motionless in a stream of running water, the shock and animation of a torrent of activity. (. . .) for these afternoons were crammed with more dramatic events than occur, often, in a whole lifetime. These were the events taking place in the book I was reading. (. . .) It is in ourselves that they are happening, that they are holding in thrall, as we feverishly turn over the pages of the book, our quickened breath and staring eyes. (Proust, 1989, pp. 90–92)

By living in symbolized places, we can get to know them in ways that are not equivalent to living in places "in reality." "Real" characters, regardless of how much we understand them, always encompass "parts that remains opaque, present a dead weight which our sensibilities have not the strength to lift" (Proust, 1989, p. 91). Besides, the author of a written account

. . . sets free within us all the joys and sorrows of the world, a few of which only we should have to spend years of our actual life in getting to know, and the most intense of which would never be revealed to us because the slow course of their development prevents us from perceiving them. (Proust, 1989, p. 92)

There are infinite examples of symbolized places that can *only* be known by imagining them. For where could one have gone to "really" see the Little Prince watering the flower or the caterpillar advising Alice? One could equally say that the flower and the caterpillar are nowhere or anywhere; they have no definite location; nevertheless, in looking at their textual description or their illustrated portrayal one can naturally say, "Here they are."

FIG. 2.3. Little Prince and Alice with the caterpillar.

These are examples of what we will call "fully fictional" symbolic places, that is, those in which the symbolized place has no locale: it is nowhere, or everywhere, or anywhere. They avoid drifting away by being moored to their symbolic places. The reader might wonder why we talk about symbolizing places that are fully fictional if on the one hand we have said that a place entails both situation and locality, and on the other hand we are now asserting that fully fictional symbolized places have no locale. We attribute to fictional places a quasi-locality—fleeting and wavering for the most part—such as the ones constituted by the drawings included in Fig. 2.3. To the extent that the symbol-users fuse symbols and referents, these fully fictional places admit multiple here and there that are intelligible and vivid to the symbol-users themselves.

Nonfictional symbolic places, such as the map of railways in greater Tokyo, admit numerous common and regularly practiced ways of verifying their "truth": Go there and see. If one follows directions based on the map and it turns out that a certain train station is not there, the map contains a falsehood. These empirical truth-setting ways are not possible in fully fictional symbolic places because for them there is nowhere to go and see. However, there are other nonempirical truth-ascertaining approaches for fully fictional places. For example, how is truthfulness ascertained in literary fiction? How can one know, for instance, what in fact Alice said to the Queen? The ultimate resource for these types of questions is the book, the text written in this case by Lewis Carroll, which has been reproduced word for word thousands of times. One has only to locate the right page and paragraph and then read what Alice actually said to the Queen.

There are also certain kinds of symbolic places, which we will call "mathematical places," that, in spite of being fully fictional, let a truth, of a nonempirical type, be established. In contrast to the literary ones, in a mathematical place inhabited by a member of the community of math-users, books and texts do not have the same status of ultimate sources of evidence. Instead, truth is ascertained by what might be called "rule-following": the idea that anyone who makes certain assumptions and follows certain rules will *necessarily* find out the same truthfulness of certain results. Mathematical rule-following is a complex endeavor not only because what counts as a rule and as rule-following changes with cultural movements and communities of practice, but also because it entails imagining mathematical objects, such as numbers, geometric constructions, and functions, placing them in different symbolic places, juxtaposing different views and different mathematical objects by a sort of "local travel," shifting our orientations, and so forth. Some of these aspects arise in this case study.

We hope to have given a sense of our entry points into the topic of mathematical places. It is time to start all over, but now by closely examining certain events that took place on the fifth of May 1999 just after 8 A.M., in Mr. Barros' classroom at the Jeremiah Burke High School in Boston, Massachusetts.

METHODOLOGY

Levine (1983) introduced the phrase "the explanatory gap" to describe an open range of phenomena for which cognitive science, at least in 1983, did not account: how the world is experienced by human beings. Cognitive scientists have postulated many types of mechanisms for, say, visual perception, but these mechanisms are largely silent when it comes to what it is to be conscious of an object in front of us or attributing meanings to our surrounding space. The literature on the explanatory gap often cites a paper entitled "What is it like to be a bat?" (Nagel, 1970). The question "What is it like?" is a key indicator of the explanatory gap. What is it like to be a student dealing with this or that problem? How do things look and feel to a student? Bridging the explanatory gap entails a richer understanding of what philosophers have called "phenomenality" (Petitot, Varela, Pachoud, & Roy, 1999), of how things appear to someone in this or that situation. Understanding phenomenality is particularly central in education because educators are constantly coping with the need to figure out how things look to their students.

Many scholars have developed empirical approaches to investigating phenomenality, particularly in the areas of anthropology and cultural studies (Geertz, 1973), but also in educational research (Lincoln & Guba, 1985; Spindler & Spindler, 1992). Some medical cases have become famous, like the celebrated studies by Oliver Sacks (1995, 1998) on patients with neurological diseases, because they offer us a glimpse into strange and extraordinary views of the world. Spindler and Spindler (1992) described the standards of good research of this type:

> Observations are contextualized, both in the immediate setting in which behavior and in further contexts beyond that setting. Hypotheses emerge in situ as the study continues in the setting selected for observation. Judgment on what may be significant to study in depth is deferred until the orienting phase of the field study has been completed. Observation is prolonged and repetitive. Chains of events are observed more than once to establish the reliability of the observations.

To realize this research work, we conduct teaching experiments. We now describe the main traits of this process.

Conduction of Teaching Experiments

The teacher comes to the session with ideas about activities and tools to ask the students to work on and with, as well as with goals regarding students' learning. These pre-planned questions and materials are to be used as resources and starting points. The session unfolds as an open-ended conversation and interaction through which the teacher pursues the learning goals for his students. The teacher's ideas, surprises, and uncertainties are fully part of the experiment. As opposed to thinking of the session as a window into unaltered students' thinking, we strive to bring to the surface how students think in this situation with others and with such-and-such tools. We do not conceive of a learning environment as a set of tools and activities that preexist their use by students and are given to them. The learning environment is constituted on an ongoing basis by the students and the teacher/interviewer. There is no way to ascertain what a learning environment is without examining what it is for the student. The relationship that is established between the teacher and the students is crucial. The teacher strives to express to the students through the ongoing interaction that he is trying to genuinely learn from them how things look to them, that this is not about withholding information to test whether they know something he knows, and that he is receptive to their contributions. All the classes are videotaped; when the students work in groups, we choose one group to film. The person behind the camera must understand the complex dynamic of the interaction in order to capture its flow (Hall, 2000).

Analysis of the Teaching Experiment

The analysis here is based on the videotaped sessions and the students' work. The most important and difficult aspect of our approach to interpretation is to see and talk about the films without "diagnostic" attitudes (this is good/bad, this child has such and such misconception, the teacher should have asked something else, this boy has x learning style, these students confuse z with y, and so forth). Avoiding diagnostics demands a great deal of self-awareness. We sense a need to avoid these attitudes because they prevent us from learning anything new; they lead us to repeat ourselves. Diagnosing involves locating the object of analysis in preexisting and often tacit taxonomies (e.g., students' misconceptions, learning styles, etc.) by projecting our assumptions on the data (Lincoln & Guba, 1985); this is particularly inappropriate when we are still learning about the conceptual and empirical issues raised by the research questions. Instead of judging actions and utterances, our interpretive efforts seek to recognize what students experience. We try to make sense of how someone else makes sense and understand something of what it is like to be in someone else's shoes at particular moments in particular contexts. The complex and momentous shift from the diagnostic to the interpretive attitude is related to what Husserl has variously called "epoche," "phenomenological reduction," or "bracketing." We describe bracketing as abstaining from seeing the world in terms of self-standing or absolute things and events, such as mechanisms or causal relationships, to seeing the world in how things and events are experienced by someone.

The analysis proceeds through cycles of examining and interpreting the data, which involves transcribing and writing interpretive notes. Through an iterative process, specific episodes are selected and overarching themes emerge; the themes become more and more connected to strands of literature that are found to be illuminating. Remaining close to the data is of paramount importance because the validity of the results rests on such proximity. As our prior published papers show, such proximity does not impede the articulation of far-reaching interpretations addressing the research questions.

THE CLASS

The chapter is based on the analysis of a session that took place in Apolinario Barros' Algebra I class at the Jeremiah Burke High School in Boston. Mr. Barros taught bilingual classes in Capeverdean Creole, and most of his students had immigrated to the United States from Cape Verde in the previous two years.

The class was using a tool consisting of graphing software and hardware that links a computer to physical devices. The software allows for two representational orientations from which to study the relationships between physical motion and motion graphs. These are referred to as "line becomes motion" (LBM) and "motion becomes line" (MBL). With LBM, a user constructs a graph on a computer, which in turn communicates with a motor that moves the mechanical device based on the graphical specifications. In the other direction (MBL), one moves the motorized devices by hand and the instrument generates graphs of motion in real time.

In this 90-minute session the class was working to find a quadratic function describing the motion of a toy car driven by the LBM interface. The computer screen was covered with a sheet of paper, so that although the students knew that the motion followed a quadratic function, they could only see and measure the physical motion of the cars. The students watched a motion of the toy car and completed a worksheet and discussed results. The worksheet asked students to describe the toy car motion in words, graph it as a position versus time graph, and formulate an equation for the motion.

Throughout the year, students had been working in pairs or groups of three and they did so for this class as well. The class as a whole watched the motion of the red toy car on the track. The car started at one end of the track, moved forward at a decreasing speed until it reached the other end of the track where it changed direction, and then started to move backwards at an increasing speed. Even though there was no explicit reference to the fact that they were observing a quadratic motion, they are likely to have assumed so because they had worked with a quadratic motion in the previous class involving the minicars; in addition, the day's objective written on the chalkboard read: "Students will use minicars to study quadratic functions."

At the beginning of the class Mr. Barros explained the day's assignment:

> Mr. Barros: (....) We are going to show you a movement. We are going to give you more time than we gave you [in a previous session]. If you want to use the stop-watch, I'll give it to you so you use it for you to describe the movement (...).

> Describe the movement of the car—we will show you one
> car only—then you will do a graph and function. (. . .) Can
> we start? Everyone observe just the first time, then I'll give
> you the worksheet for you to work on. [car runs]

When the motion ended, students got up from their seats and began taking measurements using a chronometer. In one of these large informal groups, in which Cora and Beatriz participate, one student starts the timer as the toy car begins moving. He reads out 10 seconds when he sees the car stop at the opposite end of the track before returning: he then reads out 18 seconds for the toy car's way back. The motion is repeated several more times. Someone gives the position of the car just before it turns back (35 cm). Simultaneously, other students are pointing to the location where the car starts and call out the measurement. We cannot tell exactly what Beatriz and Cora are doing or saying at this point. Some students go back to their seats and share this information with the members of their group who had not gone to the front of the class. Several groups start drawing their graphs, using roughly the same coordinate points. All the students who participated in the first large group had the time coordinates 0 (for the beginning of the motion), 10 (for the middle of the trajectory, when the toy car turns back), and 18 (for the end of the motion). The camera pans to several groups, including Cora and Beatriz.

A GRAPHICAL PLACE

2.20 minutes

1. *Beatriz:* This is how it goes, look. [starts drawing, using her pencil very lightly]

2. *Cora:* Just wait a minute and I'll show you how it ends up. It ends up like this. [draws the left side of the graph—from vertex to starting point—and then the right side from the vertex on; Fig. 2.4]

3. *Beatriz:* [After she's finished drawing] It ends up more or less like this. [tracing her parabolic shape]

4. *Cora:* It's the volcano from Fogo [Fig. 2.5]. [Beatriz erases her graph.] It's the volcano from Fogo.

There is more talk about volcanoes from Cape Verde. Cora redraws the vertex of her graph to make it more curvy, as she comments: "I have to make a curve like this because it changes velocity." The camera pans away from Cora and Beatriz. Then it returns.

(commentaries are in italics)

Beatriz and Cora's first approximation to drawing the graph introduces a language, or a way of speaking, that reflects what we call "local travel": going from somewhere to somewhere else within a circumscribed region; a region delimited, in this case, by

FIG. 2.4. Cora's first graph.

the graphical space of their student worksheets: "This is how it goes" [1]. There is a "going" from here to there. At the same time, this "going" leaves a trace that can be seen in "how it ends up" [2] as a finished whole with its own holistic appearance. Such global appearance of the traces left by the "going" elicits multiple memories of familiar images, which resemble it in some way, such as the silhouette of the volcano from Fogo—one of the Cape Verdean islands. Note that so far the graph is referred to in the third person, as an "it" that "goes." There will be moments in which the going becomes a first-person event. From Lines 1 to 4 Cora and Beatriz have placed a parabola in the graphical part of their student sheets. Placing something somewhere is not only allowing it to stay at a certain location but also bringing to this location a whole background of life experience, expressed in this case by evoking the landscape of their native land.

FIG. 2.5. Volcano from Fogo.

5. Cora: This [pointing to bottom right side of the parabola] is seconds, this [Fig. 2.6, moving the pencil along the y-axis] is centimeters. So, it's here [points first to the top of the y-axis, then to the bottom of the y-axis]. It [the car] starts at 38 [points to the y-intercept at −38, meanwhile Beatriz traces the time axis with her pencil]...don't you get it?[4] centimeters, seconds. On the way forward [indicates upward slope of parabola] it goes for 10 seconds, right? Then, it goes for 8 seconds [downward half of parabola]. That's it. So then it goes from here [somewhere in the middle of the x-axis] to here [somewhere near the end of the x-axis] and from here [somewhere near the end of the x-axis] to there [somewhere near the middle of the x-axis], in 20 seconds. So, that's what I said. So, it [the car] comes... That [pointing to vertex] is the stop it makes, you know what I mean? [Beatriz:

---

[4]Cora said, in Capeverdean, "bo també?" (literally: you too?), an expression which is used to mean many different questions. Here, "don't you get it?" seemed to be a proper translation. In other parts of the transcript, the same expression has been translated in different ways.

Description of the motion in Cora's worksheet: The blue car starts on-38 and it goes with a normal speed then it goes to a certain point and it decreases speed, then it goes +35 and it does a little stop and it starts again and it goes backwards with little . speed to a certain point and then it increases speed and it stops on 38 again

FIG. 2.6. Motion story and graph in Cora's worksheet.

mmhmm] Negative [redraws a negative sign near the negative half of the y-axis], positive [makes a plus sign near the upper half of the y-axis], right? [**Beatriz:** yeah] Now, we have to do this [points to the part of the worksheet that asks for an equation] . . .

"This is seconds, this is centimeters," Cora said as she gestured to the horizontal and vertical axes, respectively. Her "this . . ." simultaneous with the motion of her finger constituted a series of pointing acts that were her way to tell Beatriz what aspects of the car's motion are marked where on the student sheet. Such "wheres" include lines that hold either seconds or centimeters. Immediately afterwards, each one of her pointing acts constituted a "here" ("So, it's here") where one can be at by attending to it, the minicars can be at by being at certain position at certain times, and seconds and centimeters can be at by their distance to the origin. Then she proceeds to tell a narrative about the past motion of the minicar that was, simultaneously, a narrative about going across the graphical space. Her narrative fused two goings: the minicar on its track and the pencil tracing the graph. Let's follow Cora's narrative:

It [the car] starts at 38 [points to the y-intercept at –38]

This phenomenon of referring at once to the where of the pencil and of the minicar is what we have more broadly described in previous work as "fusion": talking and acting without distinguishing between symbols and referents (Nemirovsky & Monk, 2000); the start is a location on the track and a point on the graph.

> . . . don't you get it? centimeters, seconds.

While Cora's narrative marked her own bearings in traversing the graphical region, it also had the ostensive purpose of guiding Beatriz into the simultaneous travel of the car on the track and of the pencil on the graph. Throughout their interaction, Cora often assumed the tone of a patronizing guide. Cora punctuated her narrative with questions to Beatriz to verify that she was following her story.

> On the way forward [indicates upward slope of parabola] it goes for 10 seconds, right?

Cora said "forward" while she gestured upward, suggesting how gestures participate in utterances to signal the scope of what is fused: the remembered forward motion of the car on the track and the shape of the graphical trajectory. Her "it" denotes at once the car and the graph that "goes" on the track and on paper. Even though the graph can be traced at any speed, this joint "going" has a duration of 10 seconds that are the seconds one has to wait as one watches the car moving forward as well as the extent of the horizontal width covered by that segment of the graph.

> Then, it goes for 8 seconds [downward half of parabola]. That's it.

As it commonly occurs in English narratives, its phases are coupled by a "then." In this case Cora's "then" is a transition toward a new phase that is backward and downward. Note that her "then" allows for the insertion of discrete discontinuities (from going forward/upward to going backward/downward) in telling events that are continuous (e.g., the curve is drawn continuously, without "jumps") (Nemirovsky, 1996). Narratives are natural ways of accounting for local travel: They are split in successive intervals and have a beginning and an end separating two places linked by the local travel itself. Cora closed her narrative by marking its end: "That's it."

> So then it goes from here [somewhere in the middle of the x-axis] to here [somewhere near the end of the x-axis] and from here [somewhere near the end of the x-axis] to there [somewhere near the middle of the x-axis], in 20 seconds. So, that's what I said. So, it [the car] comes . . .

In this utterance Cora recounts first the movement forward of the minicar by highlighting two "spots" marking the beginning and end of the minicar's travel: "So

*then it goes from here to here." Note her "here's." In saying "from here to here,"
it is not only the minicar that "goes" from one place to another but also, in some
sense, themselves: Cora and possibly Beatriz (to the extent that Beatriz is following
the narrative in the same way). They are wherever they are attending to.*

The second part of Cora's utterance marks the return of the minicar: "and from
here [somewhere near the end of the X-axis] to there [somewhere near the middle of
the X-axis]." Another aspect to note about these here's is that they are not taken to
be places that can hold the body of the entities that are there. Cora's utterance points
at, and gesturally touches, a place that does not literally surround the things that
are located there (the minicars, themselves, etc.). This is a major power of symbolic
places: making room for things, people, and events that are out of proportion with
their physical extension in the symbolic place. There are limits to what a "here" can
encompass in a symbolic place but these limits are visuo-tactile; for instance, one
cannot specifically point at the street one lives on in a map of the whole country,
unless one zooms-in.

Rather than the final stop of the minicar or the last point of the curve, Cora's
closing emphasizes the end of her saying, "So, that's what I said." Cora's narratives
highlight a series of places demarcating a traveling phase. It is like postulating a
succession of train stations so that the trip gets described by the stations it goes to and
the traveling in between them.

> That [pointing to vertex] is the stop it makes, you know what I mean? [Beatriz: mmhmm]

Cora is placing events—the stop at the vertex—on the graph. The vertex is not
only a "then" transitioning between two phases, but also has its own distinctive
event: a fleeting stop. Cora is herself stopping at the vertex to expand on what
happens there.

> Negative [redraws a negative sign near the negative half of the y-axis], positive [makes a plus sign near
> the upper half of the y-axis], right? [Beatriz: yeah]

We do not know what led Cora to emphasize the sign of the vertical axis at this
time. It might have been she noticed that she had overlooked this sign aspect (note
that above she said, "it starts at 38," not ". . . minus 38").

> Now, we have to do this [points to the part of the worksheet that asks for an equation] . . .

Cora feels that this graphing task is done and points at the upper part of the
student sheet to highlight what they should be doing next. She thought it was time to

get outside of the graphical place, to go somewhere else and to do other things they were expected to accomplish.

6. *Beatriz:* Yeah, but first we have to do this [referring to her page].
7. *Cora:* *You* have to do it.
8. *Beatriz:* I can't [do her graph].
9. *Cora:* You do this [pointing to Beatriz's page]
10. *Beatriz:* And it will end up wrong. I'm going to show Mr. Barros and then he'll do it. [Cora starts doing something on her graph.] Oh, Mr. Barros, I can't quite do my [Beatriz erases her graph] . . .

Even though Cora thinks that it is time to start the next task, Beatriz feels that she has not finished the first one. She starts by describing this state of affairs as a collective one ("first we have to do this" [6]), but Cora reacts by stating that it is Beatriz's matter ("You have to do it"). The ensuing exchange (lines 8 to 10) involved at least two issues. The explicit one is Beatriz's lack of confidence in her ability to generate the proper graph ("I can't"); the implicit one is that Beatriz felt a need of more clarity on how to do it or on what the graph meant. Evidence for the second issue is Beatriz's decision to not copy Cora's graph onto her own sheet and instead call for Mr. Barros' help. One way of describing the difference between the ways in which Beatriz and Cora dwelt in the graphical place is in terms of the extent to which they felt "at home" in it. Cora is close to the graphical place; she feels she can move the events and features that she has placed there in a flexible manner, whereas Beatriz is far from it; she feels literally "out of touch" with the details of what is there. Similarly to how two people can reside and mutually interact in the same house but live in the house in markedly different ways, Cora and Beatriz were literally on the same "page" but their experiences in it appeared rather incommensurate.

11. *Mr. Barros:* Your line? Did you put the points?
12. *Beatriz:* Points, I know . . . [she marks over the vertex point on her student sheet and then others] these are where it stops . . .
13. *Mr. Barros:* Plot all your points . . . [**Cora:** But she's said that she has . . . but she'll do it wrong.] Plot all your points, first. [Beatriz marks over her points.] You only have those three points? It's little. You don't have any other points? Do you want us to run the car so that you can obtain some other points?

14. *Beatriz:*   Yeah
15. *Mr. Barros:*   Do you know how? . . . think how you can obtain other
                      points.
16. *Beatriz:*   . . . how to obtain points? [Beatriz looks at her student
                      sheet]
17. *Mr. Barros:*   Here, here . . . [pointing to the tracks]
18. *Cora:*   She knows [the three of them walk toward the tracks]

*Mr. Barros' expectation had been that the students would have collected enough points to trace the graph across them in a relatively accurate way. Upon not seeing enough points marked on Beatriz's graph, he immediately asked her whether all her points had been "put" on the graph. Beatriz called Mr. Barros to help her overcome the alienation she experienced with respect to this graphical task. Mr. Barros' response brought up the issue of the "points," as if Beatriz's difficulties had arisen from the lack of enough points to be able to properly trace the function. This transaction shifted Cora's and Beatriz's attention to the status of the so-called points: What are they? How to obtain them? How many are needed? Beatriz expressed her understanding of what "points" meant: "these [points] are where it stops." Note that a point is an entity on the graph, ideally generated by a single touch of the writing instrument, whereas a stop is an event that takes place on a certain spot on the track; although the stop has a where and a when on the track, it also can be seen as having only a where, a fact that seems to be expressed by the vanishing of time in Beatriz's assertion "these [points] are **where** it stops." Mr. Barros' utterance in [17] had a radical impact on Cora and Beatriz's orientation. From being focused on the graphical place populated by points, stops, shapes, and so on, his "Here, here . . . [pointing to the tracks]" displaced their orientation toward the minicars, there, on the table in front of the class, in the direction of which they started to walk. The classroom has many corners. In this segment Cora and Beatriz had dwelt on the student sheet, within which they struggled to manifest the past motion of the minicar, but the segment ends when Mr. Barros points at another "here" to dwell in for the sake of obtaining more points.*

Discussion

The first ideas we introduced in the transcript annotations were the ones of "local travel" and "placing." To inhabit a new place is often a matter of local travel and placing. One goes around in repeated cycles reaching different corners while gradually accruing a sense of the whole. This local travel is also punctuated by placing things, events, and, more generally, memories in some of these corners. In Lines 1-4 the graph/car "goes" from one corner to another and Beatriz and Cora go with it, occupying different graphical regions and placing across them a curve that keeps a record of their traveled path. Their placing of the graph brought forth some qualities stemming from the act of tracing it ("this is how it goes," "I have to make a curve", etc.) as well as traits for the overall result ("it's the volcano from Fogo"). Local travel and placing are sources of narratives. The sequence of corners one is at successive times, as well as the things one places in them, becomes the sequence of narrated events, out of which emerges a sense for the whole (e.g., "So then it goes from here to here and from here to there, in 20 seconds" [5]).

In our commentary for line [5] we related their utterances to the notion of "fusion": a pervasive trait of dwelling in symbolic places characterized by treating symbols and referents as interchangeable and united, such as in Cora's utterance "It starts at 38 [points to the y-intercept at −38]" in which the "it" is at once the car on the starting position on the track as well as the graph intersecting the y-axis. Line [5] is also an opportunity to note the process of nesting: There are many "wheres" in a place and some of them end up being "inside" others. "This is seconds, this is centimeters" [5] characterizes the graphical place as a whole inside which many different "goings" are possible. The graphical place is in turn inside a student sheet encompassing other places, such as the one with a written story for the motion of the car; and the students themselves were inside a classroom containing many other spaces inhabited by others.

We remarked how Beatriz and Cora dwelled differently in the graphical place, leading us to assert that at times they were "on the same page" but in different places. Cora assumed a guiding role with respect to Beatriz. Whereas Cora expressed easiness navigating the graphical place, Beatriz felt insecure and wanted reassurance from Mr. Barros. Mr. Barros in turn approached Beatriz's graphical place with a different orientation, remarking on the sparseness of only three points. This shift in orientation prompted the three of them to examine the nature and number of "points" and to momentarily go to another place—the track in front of the class—to gather more points in order to obtain a better graph.

The symbolizer's experience in graphical places of the sort inhabited by Cora and Beatriz appears to have some common traits: There is a continuum of paths one can follow and locations one can be at; the different regions are nested within an all-encompassing space with definite attributes ("this is centimeters, this is seconds"), there is an interplay between being in different "heres" and the shape of the overall path, one comes to dwell in it by placing points and curves along multiple local travels, and these points and curves fuse symbols and referents in a unified chain of events amenable to be told by various narratives. Against the background of these commonalties, different symbol-users, or the same ones at different times, orient themselves differently (e.g., oriented toward the overall shape, the number of points, etc.) and come to inhabit it with a varying sense of closeness or alienation, all of which leads the graph-dwellers to adopt different roles in their mutual interaction.

The next section traces Beatriz's and Cora's development of an algebraic place. It will offer us an opportunity to compare that experience with the one described here of a graphical place.

AN ALGEBRAIC PLACE

9:10 minutes

During the time between the end of the "Graphical Place" episode and this one, Cora and Beatriz went to the minicars set up next to the classroom's whiteboard, to collect more "points." Then they returned to their seats and struggled with the fact that the new graph drawn to go through all the points did not look fully symmetrical, as a parabola is supposed to. They ended up accepting this asymmetry because it seemed to be the best they could do, and decided to work on the next task, which is to derive a quadratic equation for the graph. Through the following lines [1] to [4], Cora works toward finding an equation describing the graph. She begins by assuming that each branch of the parabolic graph corresponds to a straight line; therefore she aims at obtaining two linear equations. However, the search for the first y-intercept leads her to rethink what she is doing.

1. *Cora:*   It's...two equations that we have to get from here, from this [Fig. 2.7, C] and this [D]. We have to get this [A] and this [B]...This [A] and this [B]...from here [Bottom of B] to here [Top of B] it's 10. This is Y, right? [writes Y over the graph—highlighted in box]

2. *Cora:*   X, right? [writes X on the right of the graph, not shown]...So, it ends up like this.. um...m equals [writes m on the algebraic area]...X goes up, right? No. Y goes up. Y...is 10 [writes 10 as numerator]. From here [left of A] to here [right of A] it's 1 second, right? [Writes 1 as

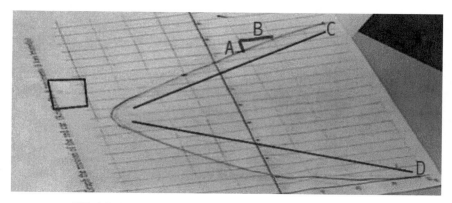

FIG. 2.7. Cora attempts two linear equations to describe her graph.

denominator] Y = mx + b ... 10x + b [as she writes these in
the algebra area] Where does it cross? On which axis? It
doesn't ... [looking for the y-intercept of the second line]

3. *Beatriz:*   Where does it [the line] cross? It *does* cross.

4. *Cora:*   No. This isn't the function. This [points to her paper], I'm
doing is linear. *It* is quadratic.

*The student sheet included a blank space making room for a future algebraic place
that Cora and Beatriz are supposed to create and inhabit. They are getting ready to
do so. Getting ready in this case means finding out elements from the graphical place
that will act as seeds to cultivate the algebraic one; they are performing preparatory
activities to enable themselves to go to the prospective algebraic place with basic
tools to work with. Note how gathering these elements already entails bringing forth
a distinct way of talking, such as the language of X and Y ("This is Y, right? X,
right?"). At the beginning of the "A Graphical Place" section, Cora had talked about
the graphic axes as "this is centimeters, this is seconds." They are now renamed X
and Y, and Cora labels them as such on her student sheet. The graphical place
changes and accommodates itself to reveal what they need for their move to the new
place. This is the beginning of the juxtaposition between both of them: The two places
remain distinct and separate but also next to each other. Together with the talk of X
and Y, a host of ideas and procedures are brought to bear: finding the slope of a line
as a "rise over run" ratio, identifying the crossing point between the line and Y, the
verticalness of Y, and so on. This is an example of the gathering power a symbolic
place can have for the symbol-users. In this case, it gathers notational procedures,
motion stories, points and ordered pairs, and more.*

*Because a single line cannot overlap with the curved graph, Cora begins the task by
looking for two linear equations, one for each branch ("two equations that we have to
get"). Solving first the one corresponding to the downward half, she estimates a slope
of 10, which is the ratio between the segment that "goes up" and the one that goes
sideways. Then she proceeds to look for the y-intercept but she then faces the problem
that the drawn intersection with the vertical axis occurs only for the upward half of
the graph. It is then that she confronts her assumption of double linearity ("This
isn't the function") and recalls that "it is quadratic." Not all that at one time is
gathered in a symbolic place remains there. Cora's "no" in [4] marks her dispensing
of double linearity, letting it be displaced from her student sheet—a displacement
physically enacted by erasing the linear equation from the emerging algebra place.
Cora proceeds to place in it a new entity that she names a "quadratic function."*

5. *Beatriz:*   That's why we have to do that formula that ... X ... Let me
get a sheet of paper. Adilson, can I borrow a paper? [Adilson

Write a quadratic model for the motion of the red car. (Indika funsau kuadratika ki ta reprezenta movimentu di karu brumedju)

_____ .

$Y = ax^2 + bx + c$

FIG. 2.8. Cora writes an algebraic form of the quadratic equation.

gives her a sheet of paper.] It ends up like this, look. [Beatriz starts writing down a formula; she seems to write something like this: $(x + c)( ]$

6. *Cora:*   Quadratic function is how? How is the quadratic function? No! Wait, the quadratic function ... [Beatriz stops writing]

7. *Beatriz:*   Is what?

8. *Cora:*   Is [writing] $y = ax$ squared, right? $+ bx + c$. Ok. [Fig. 2.8]

Beatriz and Cora struggle to recall the notational form of a quadratic equation. Cora briefly looks at Beatriz's writing but quickly rejects it ("no! wait" in [6]) and moves on to her own version of it. She writes $y = ax^2 + bx + c$. Although the camera does not close up on Beatriz's sheet of paper, her hand motion might indicate that she was writing down the root form of a quadratic information: $Y = a(x - x1)(x - x2)$ that Mr. Barros had taught a week before. In [8] Cora places a quadratic equation in the algebraic place. Note how differently the process of placing elements in the graphical or the algebraic place is. In the graphical place it makes a substantial difference whether, say, a point or a graph are located in one location or another. The "here" of a thing in the graphical place is situated against a continuum of possible locations across the region already given before the thing is placed there. In an algebraic place, instead, the formula written by Cora on the upper-left corner created a "here" whose location is not particularly consequential: It could also have been written on the opposite side or below. It, however, makes a claim on that spot; from then on pointing at that corner will constitute the subject of definite statement: This is a quadratic function. No other entity is supposed to occupy that space unless the current formula is erased or crossed over; that space has been seized.

9. *Cora:*   Right here we need to get three points. This one [Fig. 2.9, pointing to (15, 0)] that ... No, this one [pointing to (0, -38)] ...

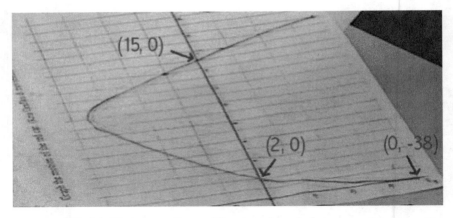

FIG. 2.9. Three points Cora and Beatriz used to calculate an equation.

10.	*Beatriz:*	Look, we can get the one from 2 here [pointing to (2, 0)].
11.	*Cora:*	But remember that . . . it doesn't cross the y-line. It's here that . . . Oh! It's here [pointing to (0, -38)]! OK. I'll get this one [(0, -38)] first, then we get this one here [(2, 0)] . . .
12.	*Beatriz:*	This one [pointing to (0, -38)] is 38, remember?
13.	*Cora:*	38, what?
14.	*Beatriz:*	38.
15.	*Cora:*	Oh, yeah. We'll get the point. That is 38 [pointing to (0, -38)] . . . No! 10, 20 . . . 38 and . . . ah! Y, X, right? [Fig. 2.10, Cora puts x and y as an ordered pair, with y on left and x on right] Y is 38.
16.	*Beatriz:*	[repeating] 38.
17.	*Cora:*	X is 0.
18.	*Beatriz:*	0.
19.	*Cora:*	Yeah.
20.	*Beatriz:*	38 and 0.
21.	*Cora:*	X right here [pointing to (2, 0)] is 1, 2.
22.	*Beatriz:*	Negative 38!
23.	*Cora:*	Oh, good girl! [In Fig. 2.10, Cora adds a negative to 38.]

As soon as the form of the quadratic equation is settled for Cora, she said: "We need to get three points" [9]: getting three points is a step toward getting the number values of a, b, and c. It is one of the things one does with quadratic functions. Although

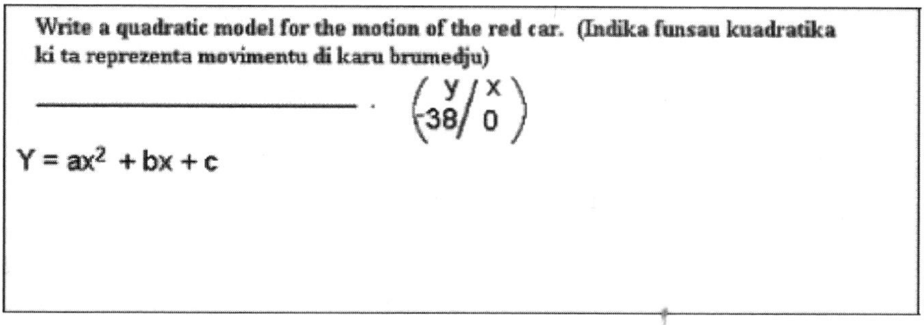

Write a quadratic model for the motion of the red car. (Indika funsau kuadratika ki ta reprezenta movimentu di karu brumedju)

$$\text{_____} \quad . \quad \left(\begin{array}{c|c} y & x \\ \hline -38 & 0 \end{array} \right)$$

$$Y = ax^2 + bx + c$$

FIG. 2.10. The first ordered pair to work on.

any three points will do it, Cora is selective: She looks for points that intersect the Y- and the X-axis because they simplify the subsequent process. Following a procedure is not only executing a sequence of actions but also adapting them to the current circumstances: The choice of points depends on the particular graph at hand. Beatriz suggests "getting" (2, 0) but Cora is keen on first using (0, −38). Note Cora's utterance in [11]: "I'll get this one [(0, −38)] first, then we get this one [(2, 0)] here." The action of taking (0, −38) is hers ("I") whereas the getting (2, 0) is theirs ("we"). On the same symbolic place different actions can be enacted, and they are owned by those who want to enact them. The same points that get selected on the graph become also expressed next to the equation. Each point develops a double existence: It is in two different locations at the same time, each reflecting distinct forms. (38/0) symbolized the corresponding point on the graph. In addition to the two places—the graphical and the algebraic ones—being juxtaposed next to each other, certain components placed in one of them symbolize components in the other one. The two places are both related at once by juxtaposition and symbolizing.

24. *Beatriz:* No . . . listen now . . . do you know what formula is easier . . . [inaudible]

25. *Cora:* It won't do because it crossed . . . both cross on Y . . . for example, it's only 1 point that crosses Y [Cora points to (0, -38) on her graph]. That's why it won't do, and we have to use that other point . . . [correcting herself] that other formula. Because if it were like this [draws another parabolic shape that appears to have the vertex on the y-intercept] . . . We'd get from here [origin] to here [positive x], and from here [origin] to there [negative x]. But only it does not pass [cross] . . .

In [24] Beatriz is likely to have referred to her root form of the equation (although we cannot see her student sheet). Cora, however, interprets that Beatriz is pointing out a linear equation, possibly because the root form does not include an X squared. Cora then argues that a pair of linear equations, which is what she had started with, does not work because there is only one y-intercept. Cora suggests that it might work only if the vertex crossed the Y-axis because, we interpret, then the two lines would have a common single y-intercept on the vertex. This is an example of how a symbolic place is always for someone. Cora and Beatriz are pointing to the same marks on the same page, but as they do so they inhabit places that are different in some ways. For Beatriz, her formula is one way of defining a quadratic equation, which conveys its own consequences (e.g., the point (2, 0) is a good choice); for Cora that same formula is a mistaken one that "won't do." From the perspective of Beatriz, what Cora said in [25] probably did not make sense.

Cora and Beatriz briefly talk about which points to choose. Cora points at (2,0), (15, 0), and then focuses again on the initial one (0, -38).

26. Cora: this is Y...this is C! Y-intercept, understand? [**Beatriz:** mmhmm] That's the one that we wanted. Now, we have to do this one here [(2, 0)]. We do it the way I am saying. For example...we'll do it, then I'll show you. Let's take 3 points, then I'll show you. Because the other one confuses me.

27. Beatriz: For me it's this one that confuses me [They laugh].

Having selected three points, Cora grapples with how to use them to find out the constants a, b, and c of the quadratic equation. She starts by recognizing that (0, -38) is C. This productive result reaffirms her own sense that she is on the right path and she asks Beatriz to go along with her: "then I'll show you." Sensing that this difference between how they want to proceed stems from their two distinct formulas, Cora says "the other one confuses me," and Beatriz responds that "this one [y = ax^2 + bx + c]" confuses her. Note that the root form does not explicitly include the y-intercept: It has to be derived. Each formulaic expression calls for different points to be chosen. However, Cora misunderstands Beatriz's idea and thinks that Beatriz will change her mind after being shown the procedure successfully completed.

28. Cora: Y is 0, X is 2. [Fig. 2.11, writes numbers on worksheet]
29. Beatriz: Which...where and where did you get it?
30. Cora: Here [pointing to (2, 0)].
31. Beatriz: Oh, 0 and 2?

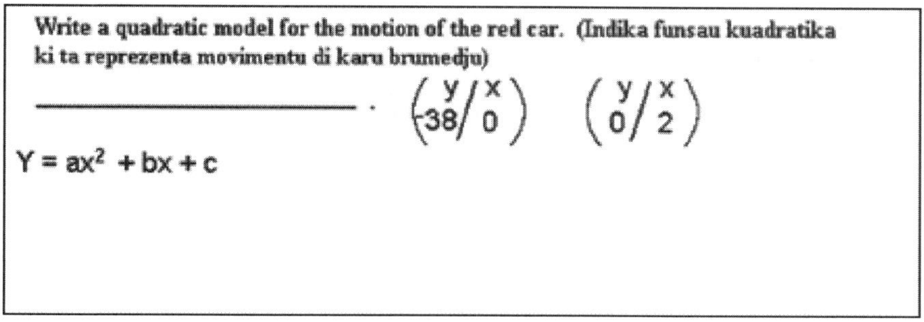

Write a quadratic model for the motion of the red car. (Indika funsau kuadratika ki ta reprezenta movimentu di karu brumedju)

$$\underline{\hspace{5cm}} \cdot \quad \left(\overset{y}{\underset{-38}{}} \Big/ \overset{x}{\underset{0}{}}\right) \quad \left(\overset{y}{\underset{0}{}} \Big/ \overset{x}{\underset{2}{}}\right)$$

$$Y = ax^2 + bx + c$$

FIG. 2.11. Adding a second ordered pair.

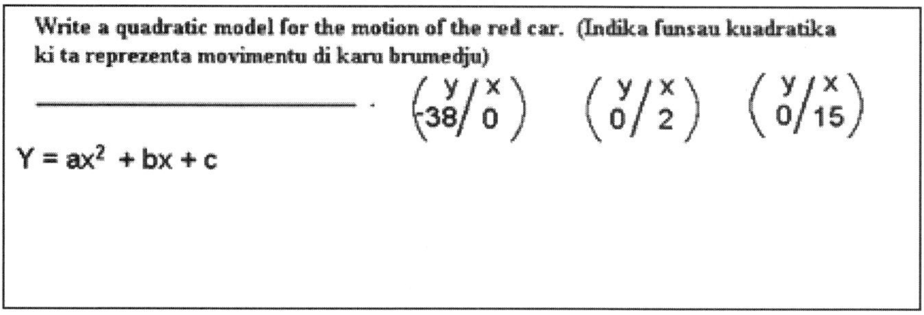

Write a quadratic model for the motion of the red car. (Indika funsau kuadratika ki ta reprezenta movimentu di karu brumedju)

$$\underline{\hspace{5cm}} \cdot \quad \left(\overset{y}{\underset{-38}{}} \Big/ \overset{x}{\underset{0}{}}\right) \quad \left(\overset{y}{\underset{0}{}} \Big/ \overset{x}{\underset{2}{}}\right) \quad \left(\overset{y}{\underset{0}{}} \Big/ \overset{x}{\underset{15}{}}\right)$$

$$Y = ax^2 + bx + c$$

FIG. 2.12. Adding the third ordered pair.

32. *Cora:*   Mmhmm. Y is 0 [writes zero as in Fig. 2.12]...right here [pointing to (15, 0)] it's 15, right? Yeah...15.
33. *Beatriz:*   Which one did you take?
34. *Cora:*   This one [points to (15, 0) off screen]. (...)

Mr. Barros tells the class that they have 15 more minutes before presenting to the class.

35. *Beatriz:*   We took three points...
36. *Cora:*   Yeah, three points.

The points have been "taken" from the graph and became newly noticeable somewhere else as ordered pairs. Cora has placed on her algebraic place three ordered pairs that symbolize three chosen points in the graphical place; she was now getting ready to act on them. Beatriz on the other hand, is following Cora's actions, trying to grasp where they are going. In the next segment their focus will be on transformations

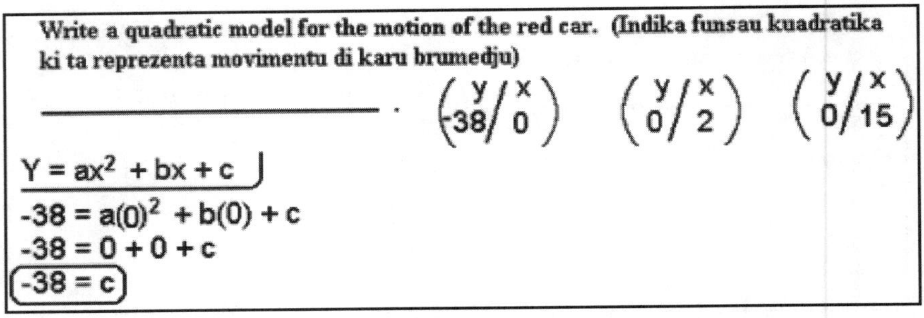

Write a quadratic model for the motion of the red car. (Indika funsau kuadratika
ki ta reprezenta movimentu di karu brumedju)

$$\left(\begin{array}{c} y / x \\ -38 / \ 0 \end{array}\right) \quad \left(\begin{array}{c} y / x \\ 0 / \ 2 \end{array}\right) \quad \left(\begin{array}{c} y / x \\ 0 / 15 \end{array}\right)$$

$Y = ax^2 + bx + c$

$-38 = a(0)^2 + b(0) + c$

$-38 = 0 + 0 + c$

$-38 = c$

FIG. 2.13. Calculating the value of c.

within the algebraic place, as opposed to its juxtaposing/symbolizing the graphical place by means of "taking" points and placing them anew.

37.   *Beatriz:*   'c' we already found.
37.   *Cora:*   No!...wait! We have to show [our work]...that we saw...you know what I mean? For example, we do like this, right here we put Y is equal to 38 [writes equations in Fig. 2.13] equals 'a'...X is 0...squared, plus 'b'...X is 0, plus 'c'. It leads to minus...
39.   *Beatriz:*   It's not 38. It's *negative* 38!
40.   *Cora:*   Same thing.
41.   *Beatriz:*   M-mm [negative] No. 38 is 38 and -38 is -38.
42.   *Cora:*   It leads to negative 38 is equal to 'c' [Fig. 2.13]. We've found 'c'. There it is [draws a border around $-38 = C$]. We've already found 'c'.

Beatriz starts in [37] by asserting that C had been found. Cora responds by saying that they need to show how C had been found. Cora seems to say that it is not enough to know C's value; finding it is different from just knowing it because finding it entails tracing a path that gets one to its value. Cora is voicing a standard practice in mathematics classrooms. What she does first is to draw a line under the quadratic formula to make room for a new self-contained process. Beatriz assumes [see 39] a role as critical companion that she will express throughout this episode; in other words, she points out inconsistencies and mistakes in Cora's derivations. It is only after making explicit the notational chain of steps that Cora concludes: "We've already found 'c'" [in 42]. The value of 'c' has now a definite location: "there it is." To get to this location one is supposed to follow three steps marked by successive lines on paper. This sequence abides algebraic rules and expresses a type of determinism: C's value is, and can only be, -38. The necessity of each step conveys the ultimate

Write a quadratic model for the motion of the red car. (Indika funsau kuadratika ki ta reprezenta movimentu di karu brumedju)

$$\left(\begin{array}{c} y/x \\ -38/\ 0 \end{array}\right) \quad \left(\begin{array}{c} y/x \\ 0/\ 2 \end{array}\right) \quad \left(\begin{array}{c} y/x \\ 0/15 \end{array}\right)$$

$Y = ax^2 + bx + c$	$0 = a(2)^2 + b(2) - 38$
$-38 = a(0)^2 + b(0) + c$	$0 = 4a + 2b - 38$
$-38 = 0 + 0 + c$	$0 - 38 = 4a + 2b$
$\boxed{-38 = c}$	$-38 = 4a + 2b$

FIG. 2.14. Deriving a relationship between a and b.

validity of the result. This is a type of determinism that connects paths with points of arrival: If the path and one's path-following are correct, one will get to whatever truly is there. In a stable physical place, as well as in this algebraic place, there is a sense of determinacy and reality given by the fact that what one encounters at the end is not subject to the will of the symbolizer: It is what is really there and in some sense had been there even before her arrival; their experience is that $C = -38$ was found, not invented. On the other hand, they are enacting a kind of local travel that is different from the local travel across a graphical place leaving continuous traces behind. In that case, the going from here to there went along empirical observations of the car's motion, whereas now the local travel is a discrete sequence of steps, each one attaining legitimacy by conforming to tacit rules and carrying the symbolizer toward desired points of arrival. In the local travel at the graphical place, the result was not the last point of the drawn curve but its overall shape. In this algebraic place the last step is the actual outcome; the intermediate steps prove its truth but the end result can be detached from them.

43. Cora: Then, let's go. [Fig. 2.14] Y right here is 0 [for the point (0,2), she writes 0 =]. 'a' [she writes 0=a]. . . X right here is 2. 'b' right here . . . plus . . . no, minus 38 [Cora completes first line]. That comes out to [writing the second line] 0 . . . 2 times 2 is what? [laughs] Four. 4a plus 2b minus 38. It comes out to [writing the third line] $0 - 38 = 4a + 2b$. It comes out to [writing the last line] $-38 = 4a + 2b$.

44. Beatriz: Did you say 'c' is equal to 0?

45. Cora: 'c' is equal to minus 38, negative 38. There it is [Fig. 2.15, points to $-38 = C$; see arrow]. You substitute these here [points to $-38 / 0$] for these here [points to column on the left]. For example, minus 38 I put here [-38 in circle] . . . 'a'. You substitute each point. Then, after you go and do the math and we'll find the equation.

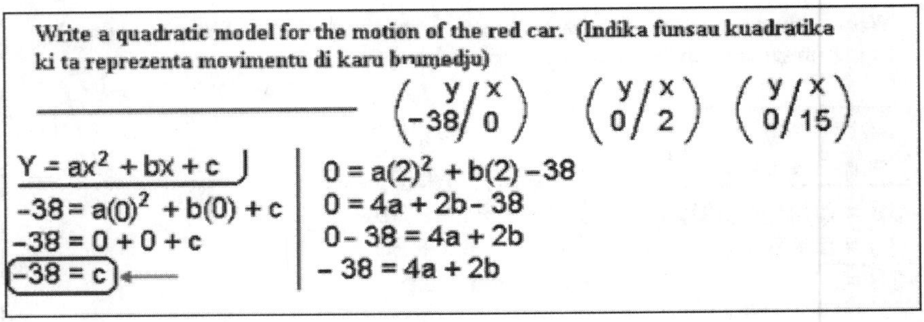

Write a quadratic model for the motion of the red car. (Indika funsau kuadratika ki ta reprezenta movimentu di karu brumedju)

$$\begin{pmatrix} y/x \\ -38/0 \end{pmatrix} \quad \begin{pmatrix} y/x \\ 0/2 \end{pmatrix} \quad \begin{pmatrix} y/x \\ 0/15 \end{pmatrix}$$

$Y = ax^2 + bx + c$

$-38 = a(0)^2 + b(0) + c$

$-38 = 0 + 0 + c$

$-38 = c$

$0 = a(2)^2 + b(2) - 38$

$0 = 4a + 2b - 38$

$0 - 38 = 4a + 2b$

$-38 = 4a + 2b$

FIG. 2.15. Cora explains how the value of c is derived.

After concluding that C is −38. Cora says "let's go." She expresses a sense of local travel as trail making: gradually new steps and intermediate arrival points populate the blank region of the algebraic place. In [43] Cora derived an equation for 'a' and 'b' using the values of the second point that had been "taken" from the graph. She made a mistake with the sign of 38, which will later be corrected by Beatriz. Note in [43] how Cora began a new line on paper by saying "it comes out to"; in [38] and [42] she marked the transition to a new line on paper by saying "it leads to"; in all cases she uttered the transition to a new line with words that emphasize that a new line is derived from the previous one. This is a different transition from the usual one that we all use in narratives (i.e., "and then"), which indicates temporal contiguity without suggesting a necessity for a new phase to follow the previous one.

Each notational step made by Cora expressed a local validity (e.g., that the point was located at X = 2 was implicated in the first line that replaced X by 2) as well as a holistic sense of direction: Each step participated in the movement from the algebraic form of the quadratic equation and the set of chosen points to the values of the 'a', 'b', and 'c'. Cora's grasping of such a sense of direction is expressed in [45]: "You substitute each point. Then, after you go and do the math and we'll find the equation." In both physical and symbolic places to know where one is requires both, following local steps as well as maintaining a sense of overarching direction. The sequence of notational steps conforms to a direction toward uncovering the coefficients, and grasping the overall direction is as vital as making sure that each step is lawful. In [43] Cora is immersed in executing a series of local steps; in [45], on the other hand, she is stepping back and reviewing a global sense of direction. Her talk suggests a type of nesting woven in the algebraic place: All the local derivations are nested within the large one: "You substitute each point. Then, after you go and do the math and we'll find the equation."

Write a quadratic model for the motion of the red car. (Indika funsau kuadratika ki ta reprezenta movimentu di karu brumedju)

$$\left(\begin{array}{c|c} y & x \\ -38 & 0 \end{array}\right) \quad \left(\begin{array}{c|c} y & x \\ 0 & 2 \end{array}\right) \quad \left(\begin{array}{c|c} y & x \\ 0 & 15 \end{array}\right)$$

$Y = ax^2 + bx + c$	$0 = a(2)^2 + b(2) - 38$	$0 = a(15)^2 + b(15) - 38$
$-38 = a(0)^2 + b(0) + c$	$0 = 4a + 2b - 38$	$0 = 225a + 15b - 38$
$-38 = 0 + 0 + c$	$0 - 38 = 4a + 2b$	$0 - 38 = 225a + 15b - 38$
$\boxed{-38 = c}$	$\boxed{-}38 = 4a + 2b$	$\boxed{-}38 = 225a + 15b$

FIG. 2.16. Deriving a second relationship between a and b.

46. *Cora:*   Oh, right now, it's this [points to 0 / 15)] that we are sub-
             stituting.

Cora works on the third column shown in Fig. 2.16. Beatriz brings a graphic calculator to compute the square of 15. Cora looks for another piece of paper.

47. *Cora:*   OK, I've found that. C is equal to −38. [She seems to
             be writing C = −38 on a new piece of paper.] [inaudible].
             What do I find now?

48. *Beatriz:* Cora, you, if you, if 38 passes to here [points at −38; see
             third lines, center and right columns, Fig. 2.16], doesn't it
             turn positive? If negative 38 passes to the first side doesn't
             it turn positive?

49. *Cora:*   Oh yeah! I just remembered. Yeah.

Cora changes − to + for the signs marked with squares in Fig. 2.16. They disagree about a certain sign in Fig. 2.16, which we cannot follow because the camera does not show what they point at.

Cora had reached a certain "stage" in her path. It was a time to look back and reassess what to do next ("What do I find now?" [47]). Beatriz's critique of a past step concerning the sign of 38 interrupted Cora's getting ready for what comes next and moved them to review past work. Beatriz was attentive to each step made by Cora and noted a violation of a rule in not "turning" 38 positive when it "passes to here [the left side of the equal sign]" [48]. Cora immediately felt herself "remembering." It is as if her mistake had been a matter of forgetting something. To perform an algebraic operation, one has to keep in mind possible pitfalls that have to be avoided, such as forgetting to reverse signs when a term switches sides; a moment of "distraction" is

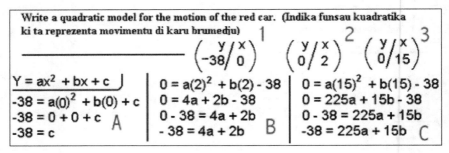

Write a quadratic model for the motion of the red car. (Indika funsau kuadratika
ki ta reprezenta movimentu di karu brumedju)

$$\left(\frac{y\,/\,x}{-38\,/\,0}\right)^{1} \quad \left(\frac{y\,/\,x}{0\,/\,2}\right)^{2} \quad \left(\frac{y\,/\,x}{0\,/\,15}\right)^{3}$$

$Y = ax^2 + bx + c$	$0 = a(2)^2 + b(2) - 38$	$0 = a(15)^2 + b(15) - 38$
$-38 = a(0)^2 + b(0) + c$	$0 = 4a + 2b - 38$	$0 = 225a + 15b - 38$
$-38 = 0 + 0 + c$ A	$0 - 38 = 4a + 2b$	$0 - 38 = 225a + 15b$
$-38 = c$	$-38 = 4a + 2b$ B	$-38 = 225a + 15b$ C

FIG. 2.17. This for this and this for this.

*enough to end us up in a wrong place, and then realizing that one has been mistaken
is experienced as an act of remembering. Cora's feeling of remembrance is also an
indication that she is not changing the sign merely because Beatriz is saying she should,
but because of a personal source of conviction. This is another element that provides
a feel of reality to the algebraic place: Unless one is inadvertently misinterpreting
directions, such as the one about sign reversal, one is bound to arrive at the directed
result; this shows again a difference between how they had inhabited their graphical
place and this one. Instead of focusing on going along empirical results (i.e., "points"
observed on the track), in this algebraic place they are following a sequence of steps
enabled by logical necessity. The computation of 15 squared marked the moment in
which the calculator was incorporated by Beatriz and Cora as an accessory to their
algebraic place.*

Cora continues writing on the new piece of paper the equations for 'a' and
'b' that remain to be solved (i.e., $38 = 4a + 2b$ and $38 = 225a + 15b$). Cora
and Beatriz briefly talk about what to do with these pair of equations and Cora
begins to operate on them to eliminate 'b'. But then Beatriz returns to the
equations portrayed in Fig. 2.17:

50.   *Beatriz:*   Look, let me look at one thing. You have three operations
here [Fig. 2.17], right?

51.   *Cora:*   M-hmm. This one [Fig. 2.17, A] is for 'c', I substituted this
[Fig. 2.17, 1] first, this [Fig. 2.17, 2] for this [B], this [3] for
this [C].

52.   *Beatriz:*   This for this, this for this [waving her hand all Figure
17]... where are you looking?

53.   *Cora:*   Look. I substituted this [Fig. 2.17, 3] for this [C]. And I put
zero for Y.

54. *Beatriz:*   I already understood this!
55. *Cora:*   So! This [Fig. 2.17, 3] is for this [C].
56. *Beatriz:*   Where are their values?
57. *Cora:*   No. I haven't found them. I'm going to finish this. [Cora points to the new page she had started to write on.]
58. *Beatriz:*   [after 11 seconds] Are you doing elimination?
59. *Cora:*   Yeah. Then I'll do substitution.

Rather than letting Cora continue to eliminate 'b', Beatriz wants to review the whole process. She feels exasperated. While she kept track of individual steps (e.g., [39]), Beatriz felt at a loss regarding the whole. The same symbolic place in which Cora felt at home and within which Cora felt capable of moving in and out of nested views, was for Beatriz a disjoint accumulation of facts and derivations. It is perhaps analogous to riding in a car driven by someone familiar with a neighborhood that is unknown to us. Every corner and block we go through makes sense; and yet, we feel that we do not know where we are or how to get to the destination. Cora tries to address Beatriz's request by gesturing overarching motions across corners on the page, pointing at each ordered pair and then to its corresponding algebraic substitution ("this for this. . . " [51]), but that only added to Beatriz's disorientation ("this for this. . . where are you looking?" [52]). Cora reacted by being more specific in her pointing acts: "Look, I substituted this [the 15 in the third ordered pair] for this. And I put zero for Y" [53]. But Cora's pointing failed to add anything new for Beatriz ("I already understood this!" [54]). She wanted to understand what these substitutions were part of: where they were coming from and leading to. Being somewhere is also being on one's way to be somewhere else, and lacking the latter amounts to feeling disoriented. Orientation entails such personal sense of past and future. These transactions suggest what a mathematical explanation often is. On the background of a symbolic place, sequences of pointing acts highlight movements between different spots striving to address immediate concerns (e.g., is this movement lawful?) as well as an overarching sense of direction. An explanation may fail by being too local or too broad; searching for a mutually satisfactory zooming in or out onto the symbolic place often repairs these failures. Such repair was attempted by Beatriz's question in [56]: "Where are their values?," in other words, how are all these substitutions going to get us to the searched values? Cora clarifies that she had not found them yet, and pointed at the elimination/substitutions about to take place in the additional sheet. Note in [58] how Beatriz looks for a proper naming to place Cora's derivations as part of a whole.

Discussion

Our first commentary alluded to the "gathering" of elements in a place. Cora and Beatriz worked to gather in the graphical place elements that would be suitable to be placed in the new algebraic place. This gathering involved also a distinct way of talking (e.g., what used to be "centimeters" is now called "Y"). They worked to juxtapose both places. Juxtaposing meant not only to make the graphical and algebraic places contiguous, next to each other, but also to move elements from one to the other and to let them influence each other in terms of ways of talking and things to do. The prospective algebraic place brought to the graphical place, in addition to the language of the X's and Y's, the search of suitable points to become ordered pairs. Beatriz and Cora strived to implement different functional forms and this led them to press for different ways to proceed. However, they both came to dwell on Cora's student sheet with the implication that Cora led the decision-making process. Some of the elements gathered in the graphical place came to be symbolized in the algebraic place, such as the three chosen points [(0, -38); (2, 0); and (15, 0)] symbolized in the algebraic place as ordered pairs. In this example, what we mean by "symbolizing" is that the ordered pairs *were* actual points on the graph: Points and ordered pairs developed a common identity and Cora or Beatriz could point at them in either the graphical or algebraic places. We are then outlining the difference between juxtaposing and symbolizing. The two places were juxtaposed by being next to each other and by mutually influencing what Cora and Beatriz did in them (e.g., look for points where the curve crosses the axes) and the way they talked (e.g., "X" instead of "centimeters"). On the other hand, some gathered elements, such as the three chosen points, got to be symbolized by being in the two places at once.

Cora started to inhabit the algebraic place by movements of placing and displacing. She first placed a linear equation building toward a double linearity, but soon she displaced it and called for a quadratic equation instead. Along the way we have found important differences between the graphical and the algebraic place. In the graphical place going from one corner to another left a continuous trace and what they wound up "finding" was, rather than a set of values amenable to being detached from how they were obtained, an overall shape that "ends up being" self-contained. Whereas placing an entity in the graphical place entailed marking a location along an already defined continuum of possible locations, placing in the algebraic place involved seizing rather arbitrary spots for the new item. Local travel in the algebraic place took on distinctive qualities. Cora moved in discrete steps reflected by successive lines on paper, each line being a "step" in the problem-solving process. Every single step is a choice made among the domain of possibilities offered by a set of "lawful" moves. It is also a choice guided by a sought-out result. The legitimacy of any single step is conferred by its compliance with permissible transformations, and its fruitfulness is assessed by how much closer it gets to a desired outcome. They are nested within broader movements in pursuit of desired outcomes; they get embedded in an overall sense of movement toward a sought-after destination. These broad movements hinge on critical bifurcations and junctions, such as the set of three chosen ordered points constituting a three-branch bifurcation as shown in Fig. 2.14, which, in addition, joined two of these bifurcated paths (the ones departing from 0/2 and 0/15) toward getting the values of 'a' and 'b'. We remarked how similar the experience of such local travel is to the one commonly pursued in physical places. Bifurcations and junctions are critical moments—moments when one is prone to getting off-course by absent-mindedness—that call for enacting a specific "direction" which must be compliant with conventional rules and fit an overall sense of direction toward the anticipated destination. As in following directions to going somewhere, unless one commits mistakes in direction-following, one finds whatever is in fact there, which appears to be equally accessible to anyone else pursuing the same sequence of directions. Whereas local travel in the algebraic place led to a necessary consequence that "comes out," tracing in the graphical place had to primarily be faithful to the students' *empirical* observations of the cars' motion. In the algebraic place logical necessity was paramount; in the graphical place empirical results constituted the leading edge.

There were important differences in how Cora and Beatriz inhabited the algebraic place emerging in Cora's sheet. A place is *for* someone. Whereas Cora wanted to place in the algebraic place a quadratic equation of the form $ax^2 + bx + c$, Beatriz would have preferred to place another form of it, possibly the root form $a(x - x1)(x - x2)$. Cora conducted her local travel, as Teresa Lara-Meloy said for her second trip to Tucson, "in the driver seat." She felt at home in it by being able to embed each local "step" in an overarching sense of direction. Beatriz judged the validity of individual steps at different times, but she missed a sense of direction that she attempted to achieve in [55]. Beatriz was attentive to transitions and turns; she noticed several mistakes in direction-following that prompted Cora to "remember" them correctly; but she also felt disoriented and in need of grasping where individual steps were leading them.

CONCLUSIONS

In this chapter we attempted to contribute toward a point of view according to which using mathematical representations is not a matter of holding correspondences between external symbolic marks and internal mental models, but of inhabiting symbolic places that embrace the symbol-user and the world in which he or she lives. Framing symbol use as an interaction between two separate realms, mental and physical, creates a conceptual rift that is not easily healed. Once we separate these realms we cannot unite them again, regardless of how extensively we elaborate on their intimate relationships. Seeing students as carriers of invisible mental entities who manipulate external representations restricts our ability to grasp the students' experiences, which are not formed by mechanisms that need to be fixed but by complex ways of being and coping that may be enriched.

The everyday notion of place provided us with a background from which to build. We characterized being at a place as being located and situated at once. Intertwining location and situation prevents us from identifying place with just its location (e.g., a street address) or with a situation that could happen anywhere. In the same way that in common language we understand that two people can be next to each other and yet in different places, we say that a place is *for* someone. Places are constituted by living bodies that inhabit them. We focused on two aspects of being at a place: orientation and dwelling. In coming to dwell somewhere, we identified two main activities: placing and juxtaposing, both emerging from repeated "local travel" in and around the dwelling. We wanted both placing and juxtaposing to evoke images of an organic growth, like a tree bifurcating ever more with new and thinner branches that would in time hold their own region. This is how we cultivate places to let them become dwellings. And because of the identity between a place and our life in that place, cultivating places is also cultivating ourselves.

We introduced the idea of "symbolic place" as one in which in which one experiences a spatial distribution of here and there that are at once in the surroundings one can look and point at, as well as in some other symbolized place. Being in a symbolic place is being simultaneously in two separated places, which hold common here and there. There are certain kinds of symbolic places, which we have called "mathematical places," that, in spite of being fully fictional let a truth of a nonempirical type be established. Truth in them is ascertained by what might be called "rule-following": the idea that anyone who makes certain assumptions and follows certain rules will *necessarily* find out the same truthfulness of certain results. Mathematical rule-following is a complex endeavor not only because what counts as rule and rule-following changes with cultural movements and communities of practice, but also because it entails imagining mathematical objects, such as numbers, geometric constructions, and functions, placing them in different symbolic places, juxtaposing different views and different mathematical objects by a sort of "local travel," shifting our orientations, and so forth.

We pursued this notion of mathematical place by tracing the utterances and actions of Cora and Beatriz. The chosen segments focused on their inhabiting two symbolic places that we have referred to as "graphical" and "algebraic" places. In the graphical place we discussed their efforts to place in it a graph portraying the motion of a toy car on a track set in front of the class. Such placing entailed a form of local travel through which the students delineated trajectories that were at once in the graphical place and on the physical track. Although the local travel in the graphical place unfolded over time, the students strove also to appraise the resulting shape of the graph as a whole. Cora and Beatriz inhabited the graphical place, located in Cora's page, in very different ways. Beatriz did not feel at home in it; she asked Mr. Barros to help her develop her own graphical place. Mr. Barros' suggestion led them to revisit the cars to "collect more points." They reoriented themselves toward the physical cars. The analysis of what they did there could have been an example of juxtaposing two places: the graphical and the cars. However, we preferred to skip this segment and to center on Cora's and Beatriz's process of juxtaposing their graphical and their algebraic places.

The juxtaposition between the graphical and algebraic places entailed not only choosing suitable points or segments to be brought from one to the other, but also adopting distinctive ways of talking and notating the graph (e.g., "this is X"). The gathered elements brought to the algebraic place developed a common identity across both places, and therefore they constituted a symbolic relationship: The same ordered pairs could be pointed out as locations in both, the graphical and algebraic places.

We have noticed important differences between the graphical and algebraic places inhabited by Cora and Beatriz. For example, in the graphical place locations were distributed across a continuum so that whatever is placed means by virtue of being located within that continuum; in the algebraic place elements are placed by "seizing" a discrete spot which from then on is devoted to "housing" it—unless it gets displaced. Furthermore, whereas Cora and Beatriz's local travel in the graphical place aimed at making proper room for empirical measurements of the physical movement of the cars, in the algebraic place their local travel was a search for number values along the paths of logical necessity and rule-following. There were also marked differences in how Cora and Beatriz inhabited the graphical and algebraic places, which evokes again the notion that two people can be next to each other—on the same page in this case—and yet in very different places.

ACKNOWLEDGMENTS

The work reflected in this chapter has been supported by the "Math in Motion" project, funded by the National Science Foundation, Grant REC-0087573. All opinions and analysis expressed herein are those of the author and do not necessarily represent the position or policies of the funding agency. Apolinario Barros has always been an inspiring teacher and colleague whose contributions and ideas are present here in countless ways. Teresa Lara-Meloy has been closely involved in all the stages of data collection, transcription, and initial data analysis. The author wishes to thank the feedback on previous drafts provided by Tracy Noble, Jesse Solomon, Beth Warren, and Tracey Wright.

REFERENCES

Bazzini, L. (2001). From grounding metaphors to technological devices: A call for legitimacy in school mathematics. *Educational Studies in Mathematics*, 47(3), 259–271.

Casey, E. (1993). *Getting back into place. Toward a renewed understanding of the place-world*. Bloomington, IN: Indiana University Press.

Casey, E. (1997). *The fate of place. A philosophical history*. Berkeley, CA: University of California Press.

Dufour-Janvier, B., Bednarz, N., & Belanger, M. (1987). Pedagogical considerations concerning the problem of representation. In C. Janvier (Ed.), *Problems of representation in the teaching and learning of mathematics* (pp. 109–122). Hillsdale, NJ: Lawrence Erlbaum Associates.

Duval, R. (2001). *The cognitive analysis of problems of comprehension in the learning of mathematics*. Paper presented at the PME Discussion group: Semiotics in mathematics education research, Utrecht, NL.

English, L. D. (1997). Analogies, metaphors, and images: Vehicles for mathematical reasoning. In L. D. English (Ed.), *Mathematical reasoning: Analogies, metaphors, and images* (pp. 3–18). Mahwah, NJ: Lawrence Erlbaum Associates.

Ernest, P. (2002). *A semiotic perspective of mathematical activity*. Paper presented at the PME Discussion group: Semiotics in mathematics education research, Utrecht, NL.

Even, R. (1998). Factors involved in linking representations of functions. *Journal of Mathematical Behavior*, 17(1), 105–121.

Geertz, C. (1973). *The Interpretation of cultures*. New York: Basic Books.

Goldin, G., & Shteingold, N. (2001). Systems of representations and the development of mathematical concepts. In A. A. Cuoco & F. R. Curcio (Eds.), *The roles of representations in school mathematics* (pp. 1–23). Reston, VA: National Council of Teachers of Mathematics.

Hall, R. (2000). Video Recording as Theory. In A. A. Kelly & R. A. Lesh (Eds.), *Handbook of research design in math and science education*. Mahwah, NJ: Lawrence Erlbaum Associates.

Janvier, C. (1987). Translation processes in mathematics education. In C. Janvier (Ed.), *Problems of representation in the teaching and learning of mathematics*. Hillsdale, NJ: Lawrence Erlbaum Associates.

Kaput, J. (1998). Representations, inscriptions, descriptions and learning: A kaleidoscope of windows. *Journal of Mathematical Behavior, 17*(2), 265–281.

Lakoff, G., & Nunez, R. E. (1997). The metaphorical structure of mathematics: Sketching out cognitive foundations for a mind-based mathematics. In L. D. English (Ed.), *Mathematical reasoning: Analogies, metaphors, and images* (pp. 21–89). Mahwah, NJ: Lawrence Erlbaum Associates.

Levine, J. (1983). Materialism and qualia: The explanatory gap. *Pacific Philosophical Quarterly, 64*, 354–361.

Light, A., & Smith, J. M. (Eds.). (1998). *Philosophies of place*. Lanham, MD: Rowman & Littlefield.

Lincoln, Y. S., & Guba, E. G. (1985). *Naturalistic inquiry*. Beverly Hills, CA: Sage.

Lively, P. (2001). *A house unlocked*. New York: Grove Press.

Luria, A. R. (1987). *The mind of a mnemonist. A little book about a vast memory*. Cambridge, MA: Harvard University Press.

Malpas, J. E. (1999). *Place and experience. A philosophical topography*. Cambridge, UK: Cambridge University Press.

Marcel, G. (1952). *Metaphysical journal; translated by Bernard Wall*. London: Rocklife.

Morgan, C. (2002). *What does social semiotics have to offer mathematics education research?* Paper presented at the PME Discussion group: Semiotics in mathematics education research, Utrecht, NL.

Nabokov, V. (1966). *Speak, memory*. New York: Putnam.

Nagel, T. (1970). What is it like to be a bat? *Philosophical Review, 79*, 394–403.

Nemirovsky, R. (1996). Mathematical narratives. In N. Bednarz, C. Kieran & L. Lee (Eds.), *Approaches to algebra: Perspectives for research and teaching* (pp. 197–223). Dordrecht, The Netherlands: Kluwer Academic.

Nemirovsky, R., & Monk, S. (2000). "If you look at it the other way…": An exploration into the nature of symbolizing. In P. Cobb, E. Yackel & K. McClain (Eds.), *Symbolizing and communicating in mathematics classrooms: Perspectives on discourse, tools, and instructional design* (pp. 177–221). Hillsdale, NJ: Lawrence Erlbaum.

Nemirovsky, R., & Noble, T. (1997). Mathematical visualization and the place where we live. *Educational Studies of Mathematics, 33*(2), 99–131.

Nemirovsky, R., Tierney, C., & Wright, T. (1998). Body motion and graphing. *Cognition and Instruction, 16*(2), 119–172.

O'Neill, M. E. (2001). Corporeal experience: A haptic way of knowing. *Journal of Architectural Education, 55*(5), 3–12.

Petitot, J., Varela, F. V., Pachoud, B., & Roy, J.-M. (Eds.). (1999). *Naturalizing Phenomenology. Issues in contemporary phenomenology and cognitive science*. Stanford, CA: Stanford University Press.

Poulet, G. (1977). *Proustian Space*. Baltimore: Johns Hopkins University Press.

Presmeg, N. C. (1998). Metaphoric and metonymic signification in mathematics. *Journal of Mathematical Behavior, 17*(1), 25–32.

Proust, M. (1989). *Swann's Way*. New York: Vintage Books.

Radford, L. (2003). Gestures, speech, and the sprouting of signs: A semiotic-cultural approach to students' types of generalization. *Mathematical Thinking and Learning*, 5(1), 37–70.

Relph, E. (1976). *Place and placelessness*. London: Pion.

Sacks, O. (1998). *The man who mistook his wife for a hat and other clinical tales*. New York: Simon & Schuster.

Sacks, O. W. (1995). *An anthropologist on Mars: Seven paradoxical tales*. New York: Knopf.

Seamon, D. (1979). *A geography of the lifeworld*. London: Croom Helm.

Seamon, D., & Mugerauer, R. (Eds.). (2000). *Dwelling, place, and environment*. Malabar, FL: Krieger.

Spindler, G., & Spindler, L. (1992). Cultural process and ethnography: An anthropological perspective. In M. D. LeCompte, W. L. Millroy, & J. Preissle (Eds.), *The handbook of qualitaive research in education* (pp. 53–92). New York: Academic Press.

Woolf, V. (1985). A sketch of the past. In J. Schulkind (Ed.), *Moments of being*. New York: Harcourt, Brace.

3

Developing Concepts of Justification and Proof in a Sixth-Grade Classroom

Carrie Valentine
Madison Public Schools

Thomas P. Carpenter
Margaret Pligge
University of Wisconsin

This chapter presents a case of the students and teacher in a sixth-grade classroom engaged in developing concepts of justification and proof. Specifically, the case focuses on the evolution of how the students in the class justified their conjectures about the commutative property of multiplication. The case examines tasks and interactions in which the students and teacher jointly developed socio-mathematical norms for what would count as justification and considers the reflexive relation between the classroom culture in which these norms evolved and the conceptions of individual students who participated in constructing them.

BACKGROUND

Debates about the goals for the mathematics curriculum have often revolved around the relative importance of process and content. These debates concern whether it is more important for students to do mathematics—that is,

exercise the processes used by mathematicians to develop and justify mathematical principles—or whether instead they should acquire the products of
those disciplines—the facts, concepts, and procedures that represent the hall-
marks of mathematical and scientific knowledge. This is a false dichotomy.
Students cannot understand mathematics unless they acquire and employ the
forms of argument used to justify mathematical propositions, and they cannot
appreciate the power of these forms of thinking unless they are deployed in
learning important mathematical ideas. Justification and proof are applied in
the service of learning important mathematics, and they are a critical part of
the mathematics that students should learn.

Reasoning and proof is one of the primary strands of The National Council
of Teachers of Mathematics (2000) *Principles and Standards for School Mathematics*, which recommends that students at all grade levels should recognize
reasoning and proof as fundamental aspects of mathematics and be engaged
in developing and evaluating mathematical arguments and proofs. Ball and
Bass (2000) argued that:

> [T]he *reasoning of justification* (emphasis in the original) [is central to] the construction of
> mathematical knowledge. Recognizing the role of such reasoning to investigate claims provides
> a medium for inspecting and verifying representations and solutions produced individually
> and in class. It suggests the need for the development of classroom participation structures
> and intellectual and social norms that would enable students to reach sound mathematical
> conclusions that are neither idiosyncratic("this makes sense to me") nor rooted in assumptions
> of others' authority ("the book says so"). (p. 219)

This chapter provides a glimpse of how participation structures and intellectual and social norms evolved in one classroom as students negotiated what
counted as valid justification that the commutative property of multiplication
was true for all whole numbers.

Socio-mathematical Norms

Cobb and Yackel (1996) asserted that students' learning in classrooms is
impacted by collective classroom processes including social norms, sociomathematical norms, and classroom mathematical practices. They described
these social processes as reflexively related to the beliefs and conceptions of
the individuals in the classroom. Social norms, socio-mathematical norms,
and classroom mathematical practices affect the beliefs and conceptions of
individual students. In turn, the developing conceptions and beliefs of the
individual contribute to the evolution of the larger classroom processes.

Yackel and Cobb (1996) defined socio-mathematical norms as "normative understandings of what counts as mathematically different, mathematically sophisticated, mathematically efficient, and mathematically elegant" (p. 461). They also suggested that socio-mathematical norms include what counts as an acceptable mathematical explanation and justification. It is this last norm that we focused on in this case study.

Developing understanding of the norms for proof by having students present and compare alternative arguments provides different challenges than comparing different answers or alternative strategies. When students use incorrect strategies to solve a problem, the strategies generally result in incorrect answers. If other students have different answers, there is some basis for questioning the validity of a given strategy. Alternative justifications, on the other hand, may, and often do, result in the same conclusion. In the particular case discussed in this chapter, almost all students were convinced that multiplication was commutative, but most of them thought that the property could be proved by providing examples illustrating that switching the order of the numbers in a multiplication problem resulted in the same answer.

Similarly, when students use a variety of strategies representing different levels of abstraction and efficiency, the strategies can be compared. Although it is not trivial to establish norms for what counts as a better or more efficient strategy, it is quite different from establishing norms for justification. General arguments may not readily appear easier or more efficient. If one considers trying all numbers, it certainly is more efficient to use some alternative form of proof, but if students do not readily understand the general proof it may not be compelling to them. Learning to appreciate the need for general forms of proof represents a version of the learning paradox (Bereiter, 1985). It is difficult to recognize the need for more general forms of argument unless one already sees the limits of examples and has some inclination to seek out more general forms of justification. In other words, the argument for more general forms of justification depends on the presumption that a general justification is needed.

Forms of Justification and Proof

For the purpose of this chapter, we use Balacheff's (1988) distinctions between forms of justification and proof which provide appropriate labels for the kinds of argument that occur in elementary classroom communities where notions of justification and proof are evolving. Balacheff distinguished "justification" from "proof" and "mathematical proof." He specified justification as discourse that aims to establish for another individual the validity of a statement, proof as an explanation that is accepted by a community at a given time, and mathematical proof as proof accepted by a community of mathematicians. It is reasonable that a classroom community of elementary students and their teacher studying mathematics will have different requirements for acceptable proof than mathematicians. In negotiating norms for what counts as a proof in an elementary class, it is not, however, the case that anything goes. In the class in this case, we see the students negotiating the norms for what counts as a legitimate proof.

Sowder and Harel (1998) defined three proof scheme categories: (1) externally based proof, (2) empirical proof, and (3) analytical proof. The three proof schemes are useful labels for discussion of students' justifications and proof. The proof schemes are grouped according to the source of the students' reasoning. Externally based proof schemes are justifications that students use or accept as proof that reside in a source other than their own reasoning. The outside source may be an authority such as a teacher, textbook, a ritual form of argument, or a meaningless manipulation of symbols. Students who make their justifications by offering examples are using empirical examples-based proof schemes. Examples illuminate an idea and can lead to higher levels of justification. However, justification based on examples can be misleading. When students rely on empirical examples, they do not consider all cases, which is necessary for more principled generalization. Analytic proof schemes include students' justifications that involve reasoning oriented toward showing that a claim is true for all cases.

From the beginning of the year, the teacher in this case had not accepted externally based arguments. When students presented them, she pressed them to provide reasons to support their claims. As a consequence, students abandoned externally based arguments early in the year, but empirical proof offers one kind of support for a claim, and it can be more difficult to help students see the limits of this form of argument. Recent studies have shown, however, that even at the elementary level students can begin to develop an appreciation of the need for more general forms of argument.

Related Studies

Maher and Martino (1996) and Lehrer, Kemeny, Gance, and Curtis (1996) studied the development of arguments that elementary students used to convince each other that they had found all possible cases of certain types of geometric shapes. Although children's initial attempts to argue that they had found all the cases were not systematic, their arguments became more refined as they attempted to construct more general forms of argument that they had indeed found all the possibilities. These justifications dealt with situations that students needed to systematically analyze and organize. They are somewhat different from the justification required in the current case in which students are asked to provide a convincing argument that a proposition, the commutative property of multiplication, is true over an infinite collection of numbers.

Bastable and Schifter (1998) described a third-grade classroom in which students were engaged in a struggle to develop a general argument that is similar to the one portrayed in the study reported in this chapter. In this third-grade class, students observed, questioned, and challenged each other to generalize the commutative property of multiplication. The questions asked and their justifications arose naturally from a solution to a story problem. Students worked for several weeks to convince each other that the commutative property works for all numbers. The students first used pairs of numbers 3×4 and 4×3 and their products to justify their reasoning. Because one student remained unconvinced, another student modeled the product of 4×3 with a four-by-three array of linking cubes. As in the current study, another student then demonstrated the commutative property by turning the array on its side, thus showing the relationship 3×4 was the same as 4×3. He then rotated the array on its side to show the commutative relationship. Students moved beyond the problem context to discuss the structure of the commutative property when one student questioned, "Does that always work?" It took several weeks of exploration for the students to become convinced that multiplication was always commutative (for whole numbers).

Justifying Commutativity

There are a number of issues that arise in considering how to justify that the commutative property of multiplication is true for all numbers. If one stays entirely within the symbolic system of number and number operations, the commutative property is one of the axioms of the system that cannot be derived from more basic properties. However, by considering a basic model of multiplication, such as an array or area representation, it is possible to generate a general argument that multiplication is commutative. Most elementary students, however, have not mastered a notational system that they can use to represent a general n-by-m array. Therefore, they are stuck with particular cases. Nevertheless, although they may use a particular array, they can generate an argument that is general. Although they have used a specific array, say 3-by-5, they can argue that the transformation of the array could be applied to any array of any size.

Another limitation of this argument is that demonstrations using arrays only support the conclusion that multiplication is commutative for whole numbers, but the general form of the argument can be applied to rectangular regions representing any real number. It is doubtful that many students in the class recognized the limitation of the representation they used or thought about how it might be extended beyond whole numbers, but one student did extend the array model to rectangular regions.

The use of the array model in students' arguments depends on several fundamental assumptions. One is that multiplication can be represented by an array. Arrays are not natural models for children unless they are representing problems that are naturally portrayed by array, such as rows of chairs or muffins in a muffin tin. Children do not generally use arrays to represent the most common types of multiplication problems involving n sets with m elements in each set (Carpenter, Ansell, Fennema, Franke, & Weisbeck, 1993). But it is not readily obvious from a set model that multiplication is commutative, and it takes some insight to figure out that m sets with n elements in each set represent the same total number of elements as n sets with m elements in each set. Array models provide a much more accessible demonstration that multiplication is commutative, and for that reason array models for multiplication are, for the most part, a product of school instruction. By the time students in this class were addressing the issue of whether multiplication was commutative, the array had been established as a model for multiplication of whole numbers.

Another fundamental assumption is that rotating an array does not change the number of elements in the array. Piaget's (1965) conservation studies show that this is not an entirely trivial assumption by demonstrating that young children do not recognize that the number of elements in a set remains constant when the sets are transformed in various ways. By the sixth grade, however, most students do conserve number, and whether the number of elements in the array changed when the array was rotated was not an issue for the students in this study. Although the students in this study were not plagued by the question of whether the rotations of the arrays would change the number of elements in the array, they also did not identify conservation of number as a fundamental assumption upon which their argument depended. In other words, they did not specifically construct a system of proof based on a clearly specified set of axioms. This is a limitation, but it seems to be a reasonable limitation for students beginning to engage in general argument.

OVERVIEW OF THE CASE

The goal of the instruction illustrated in this case was to help students to move from using examples to justify propositions about number and number operations to using more general forms of justification that apply to all numbers. During the five classes discussed in this case, the students worked on and discussed problems that drew on the commutative property of multiplication. In the next-to-last case they explicitly attempted to prove the commutative property for multiplication of whole numbers. This entailed representing multiplication as an array that can be rotated to show that the operation is commutative. But rotating a given array just illustrates a specific case, and in order to produce a general proof, students had to argue that the model they had used to illustrate commutativity applied to multiplication of any two numbers. Actually, the array model they employed only applies to whole numbers, but the model can be generalized, as one student did in the final interview.

PRINCIPLES OF INSTRUCTIONAL DESIGN
ILLUSTRATED BY THIS CASE

One goal of this chapter is to illustrate how classroom interaction can support the development of students' use of fundamental forms of mathematical argument, but we also have a broader purpose: to show, in action, basic principles of instructional design that support the development of this form of argumentation. This instruction in this case is based on five basic assumptions about instruction:

- Students are responsible not only for their own learning but also for the learning of the group. They have an obligation to explain their ideas so that other students can understand them. They have an obligation to seek to understand the thinking of other students and to ask questions if they do not understand what another student has said. In this case we see one student, Daniel, playing a key role both in modeling a general justification strategy and in questioning other students to establish norms for justification of conjectures that applies to all (whole) numbers.
- Students have the opportunity to discuss alternative arguments and strategies, but the purpose of sharing arguments or strategies is not just to give students an opportunity to participate and make their answers public. Discussion of students' arguments or strategies serves explicit goals.

Purposes for discussing alternative arguments and strategies include: developing norms for what counts as an acceptable justification or explanation, drawing connections among strategies that represent different levels of abstraction, developing norms for distinguishing more efficient or more sophisticated strategies, and providing support for students to adopt more efficient strategies. This case focuses on developing norms for justification and proof.

- Discussion is anchored in specific tasks. Tasks provide a context and focus for discussion. The nature of a task significantly influences what students attend to and the nature of their arguments and explanations. As the tasks vary between episodes in this case, we see different features of argument emerging.

- Tasks and norms for class interactions are designed to provide a window on students' mathematical thinking. The tasks and norms in this class require students to explain the reasons for their responses.

- The teacher and students negotiate norms for articulating and justifying mathematical statements. What counts as valid justification is a specific focus of discussion.

THE CONTEXT FOR THE CASE

The data for this case are drawn from a school year of classroom discussions that involved generating and justifying generalizations about number and operations on numbers. The case focuses on five classroom discussions about commutativity from the first semester of the school year. They provide evidence of the kinds of justifications the students used and how it changed over time. All five episodes were audiotaped, and field notes were taken by a graduate student who, throughout the year, observed the discussions involving the generation and justification of conjectures about basic number concepts. Students' written work in preparation for each discussion was collected, and the teacher kept a journal during the year documenting her thoughts about the development of the students' thinking and reflecting on her questioning. An end-of-year individual interview with each student provided additional data about the notions of proof individual students had gained over the course of the school year.

The subjects for the case consisted of the teacher, Carrie Valentine, and her 22 sixth-grade students. The school served a predominately middle to upper-middle class neighborhood with approximately one-fourth of the population receiving free or reduced lunch. Thirteen of the students in the class were

Caucasian, one was Hispanic, four were African-American, and four were Asian. Two students received ESL services and five students received LD services. This class was not tracked, and the students stayed together as a cohort for all academic classes.

Ms. V was participating in a research–professional development project studying the development of students' algebraic reasoning, and it was her first year explicitly engaging students in discussions about generalization, justification, and proof. For the previous ten years, she had been working with the Cognitively Guided Instruction project and had well-established norms for engaging students in talking about their mathematical ideas, but she had limited experience in selecting tasks and focusing discussion to draw out the central ideas involved in justifying generalizations like the commutative property of multiplication.

Building a Community of Learners

One of Ms. V's primary goals for the school year was "to build a community of learners where students would be given significant opportunity to take charge of their learning." This entailed creating a classroom community in which honest, respectful mathematical talk could occur and students were likely to propose conjectures and challenge each other's ideas. Creating this kind of environment posed a number of challenges. Many of the students reported having little prior experience reasoning or talking about mathematics in the elementary grades. They described their previous mathematics as repeated practice of procedures taught to them by teachers, parents, and tutors. Even the pullout enrichment program had consisted almost entirely of learning procedures. Furthermore, keeping all of the students together in a heterogeneous group conflicted with school norms of tracking for mathematics instruction.

Class norms for discussion were made explicit as needed. Occasionally a student, a group of students, or Ms. V would make a suggestion for a desired behavior. Ms. V would ask the class to consider the suggestion and decide on its efficacy. For example, she wondered out loud why students addressed her when answering a classmate's question and why they mostly looked to her for answers. Ms. V asked individual students to address the class or classmate when commenting or questioning each other's reasoning. By the time of the case episodes, students were beginning to talk directly to each other about mathematics during class discussions, and they had learned that they needed to be ready to explain their reasoning to their peers.

Ms. V used revoicing to focus the class on individual students' reasoning and to compare and contrast different perspectives. Early in the year she modeled responding to the students' ideas with questions like: "Is that always true for all numbers?" "Why does that work?" "How do you know?" As the year progressed, these questions became norms for discussions involving justification. In the episodes included in this case, we see the class assuming increasing responsibility for conducting the discussions.

Ms. V began the year by challenging the students' thinking about commonly held notions in an effort to establish norms for mathematical reasoning. For example, the students suggested that when multiplying numbers that end in zero, you just take off the zeros, multiply, and add the zeros back on. Ms. V wanted the students to clearly describe the procedure in precise mathematical language and explain why the method worked. She wrote their steps as stated on the board and they became very animated when she wrote, "+ 0" for "add zero" and didn't place a zero at the end of the product. To justify the method, the majority of the students said their teachers had taught them the "dropping common zeros" trick and argued that it always worked. They seemed to think that because a teacher had told them this trick always worked, they could use "the teacher" as their reasoning about why the method worked.

Algebra Day

Although students were expected to explain and justify their thinking in all mathematical activities, one day a week, designated as "algebra day," focused particularly on tasks that often led to the generation and justification of conjectures about properties of numbers and operations on numbers. A typical algebra day began with students working individually, in pairs, or in small groups on true–false or open number sentences posed on the chalkboard. Students explained their reasoning about the number sentences. This occasionally led to conjecture making. The conjectures served as material for follow-up discussion and justification of the conjectures.

THE COMMUTATIVE CASE

This chapter focuses on a series of class discussions about the commutative property of multiplication. The class discussed the topic on five occasions. Each time the topic was introduced in a different way, either by a true–false or open number sentence that led to a discussion about conjectures made by the students. The students developed their own ideas about acceptable justifications during each session.

October 5, 1998

Early in October, Ms. V posed the first problem that directly addressed the general idea of commutativity. She asked the class to write whether they thought $\square \times \Delta = \Delta \times \square$ was always true and to explain their thinking. Seven students could not say whether the open number sentence was always true. Five students wrote numbers in the sentence to show that the equality was true (e.g., $3 \times 5 = 5 \times 3$), and one student added, "because it will always be the same sum." Nine students wrote that the number was always true, but their responses focused on the value of the numbers or statements about the order of the numbers. Abby's response was typical: "It is always true because the product will be the same no matter the order of the numbers." Karl wrote, "The numbers still have the same value when they switch." Brenda wrote, "Because there is the same number and shape on each side of the $=$ sign." Only one student, Daniel, offered a general argument to support his reasoning: "This is true because if you have an array with $\square$ rows and Δ columns it doesn't matter if you count by rows or columns the total is still the same."

October 14, 1998

About 10 days after the written assignment, Ms. V gave the class an assignment to write true, false, or open number sentences for the rest of the class to solve. After the students had each written several number sentences, Ms. V chose Billie's number sentence, $5 \times 7 = 7 \times 5$, for discussion.

Ms. V: What are we going to do with this? Are we going to solve it? Jordan, what are we going to do with a sentence like that?

Jordan: We're gonna take 5×7 and multiply and take 7×5 and multiply and see if they come out the same.

Ms. V: And, what do you think?

Jordan: I think it is true because you can take any numbers and switch it around whichever way you want. But you can't switch the operations. [pause] They will equal the same thing.

Arial: Well. You can just look at it and say it is true. Because the numbers are the same, the digits are the same on each side: 7 and 5 on the left and 7 and 5 on the right. So, it would be the same and it's true.

Nicole: The values of the numbers stay the same no matter how you switch on either side.

Ms. V: The values of the numbers stay the same no matter how you switch on either side. Is that always true?

Class: No.

Nicole: But it has to be for multiplication or addition.

Ms. V: That's true for multiplication? Is that always true for multiplication, Lisa? Is it always true that 5×7 is always equal to 7×5?

Lisa: Yes.

Ms. V: So, how do you know?...<laughter>...What's the matter, Billie?

Billie: (A little impatiently) I think we're getting a little weird.

Ms. V: Why is that always true?

Billie: Because they both equal 35.

Karl: If I can use the board I'll tell you.

Ms. V: Can you tell me what to put on the board?

Karl: Five seven times. And 7 five times. If you add them up they both equal 35. This is the reason.

Ms. V wrote on the board: 5 5 5 5 5 5   7 7 7 7 7

Almost all the students were convinced that multiplication was commutative. However, although they were convinced themselves, they had not established norms for what counts as justification, and many of the students had difficulty figuring out what Ms. V was getting at when she asked how they knew that it was always true, as illustrated by Billie's comment about "getting weird." At that point, Daniel proposed a justification that multiplication was commutative that potentially represented a first step toward establishing norms for justification.

Daniel: I have a different reason that doesn't just say it is true. You can put a dot array. 5 rows of 7 or 7 rows of 5.

Daniel drew the arrays in Fig. 3.1 on the board. He explained that in the first case there were 7 rows and 5 columns and in the second there were 5 rows and 7 columns.

Daniel: Notice there are still only 35 dots in the array.

Daniel used the array to justify why switching numbers for this sentence was true. This is the same general argument that he proposed on October 5.

The task the students were given involved specific numbers, so they were not obligated to come up with a general argument that applied beyond the given example. They had, however, begun to discuss proving conjectures. Most of the students had not yet accepted that more

FIG. 3.1. Daniel's dot array.

general forms of justification were needed to prove a conjecture was true and had limited understanding of what was required for such a proof. Daniel, on the other hand, recognized that the other students were simply asserting that the conjecture was true without offering any real justification. "I have a different reason *that doesn't just say it is true* (emphasis added)." Daniel proposed a specific example using the same numbers that Karl used, but by showing how the 5-by-7 array could be rotated to a 7-by-5 array, he illustrated the general form of an argument that could apply to any whole numbers.

This type of use of an example based on specific numbers is what Kaput and Blanton (2001) referred to as "the algebraic use of numbers" and Fujii and Stephens (2001) called using "quasi-variables." Although Daniel used specific numbers, the specific numbers were not important. An underlying mathematical relationship was illustrated by the example that would be the same whatever whole numbers were used. The generality of the argument illustrated in the specific example became an explicit topic of discussion in a subsequent lesson in December. At this point, however, and in the following lesson, few of the students recognized the generality of the argument that Daniel had proposed or really engaged with issues regarding the norms for justification that his argument raised.

November 11

About a month after the last discussion of commutativity, Ms. V asked the students to determine what number could replace n to make the following number sentence true: $325 \times 6 = n \times 325$. Only Daniel explained the array model in his written response. Thirteen students wrote that the numbers must be the same because the equal sign means "the same as." These students explained in a variety of ways that both numbers should be represented on both sides of the equal sign. One proposed that "If you take 325 from both sides you only have 6 and n. So n equals 6." Three students explained that the products would be the same if n was 6. One student thought that n should be the product of 325×6. She still interpreted the equal sign to mean, "the answer comes next." Because of the large numbers involved, none of the students actually carried out the calculation.

In the class discussion that followed, many students still had difficulty articulating a conjecture about commutativity, and many provided ambiguous explanations about why n = 6. A number of students gave responses similar to Abby, who responded: "N equals 6, because you have one 325 on each side of the equal sign and since both sides are equal, the other number on each side would be equal to each other." These students never mentioned switching the order of the numbers or the operation of multiplication.

For many of these students, the equality of the two sides of the equation was the prominent feature of the number sentence that they attended to. This is clearly illustrated in Karl's response: "I think it is 6 because the two 325's are the same and so that means that the 6, the n has to be 6 if they are going to be the same thing. We can use the conjecture from up there" (pointing to the conjecture "A number is equal to itself, x = x" on the conjecture board). When asked directly whether the order of numbers could be switched for all operations, virtually all students did acknowledge that commutativity only applied to addition and multiplication, but at this point many of their explanations and justifications were not clearly focused.

Daniel, the one student who had provided a principled explanation for his response, explained that with an array with 325 dots in 6 rows and an array with 6 dots in 325 columns you are counting the same number of dots. Ms. V ask the class to look at 3×5 and 5×3 arrays. Aaron noticed that it is switched around, and Billie said you can count rows or columns. By the end of the session, Aaron, Billie, Joel, and several other students had demonstrated some understanding of Daniel's array model, but it was questionable whether they could apply it to larger numbers or more general cases. Furthermore, the argument was only applied to a specific case, and even Daniel had not publicly argued for a general proof of the commutative property of multiplication. That is the task addressed in the next episode.

December 9

In early December Ms. V gave assignments to small groups of students to write on one of three different tasks. Each group had a large sheet of grid paper to present their solution to the entire class. One group was asked to decide whether the statement $124 \times 396 = 396 \times 124$ was true or false, to write a conjecture for equations like this, and to justify that the conjecture was true for all numbers. The group included Jordan and Arial. The other students participating in the following interaction were not part of this group. The group wrote, "The conjecture for multiplication and addition is that it does not matter which order the numbers are in. The answer will always equal the same thing." This group then drew two arrays of fifteen dots (Fig. 3.2). They named their conjecture the Order of Multiplication.

FIG. 3.2. Arrays showing that $3 \times 5 = 5 \times 3$.

Norms for discussion had evolved so that students now called on each other without Ms. V's intervention and continued discussion until no more questions were asked.

Jordan: Here it is 3×5 (pointing to the array) and here it is 5×3.

Daniel: It does prove that 3×5 equals 15 and so does 5×3 equal 15. But does it prove for every number you can do that?

Jordan: Yes.

Arial: It was just an example. It could have been 2×4 and it would have been 8.

Jordan: I could give another example. See this [pointing to the dot arrangement] is six. Here this is 3×5 and this is 5×3.

Ms. V: Jordan, what do you think Daniel's question is?

Jordan: How does this prove that it would work for any problem?

Ms. V: OK, that's the problem.

Arial: I can say now why it proved it. Because that's 5 and that's 3. So it shows that if you switch the numbers around you would have the same answer, Even though you could have different like numbers like 4: what I mean by different numbers is not like 3 and 6 and 3 and 5. But I mean like 2 and 6 and 6 and 2. . . . But . . . well . . . it's just showing that you can flip them around.

Daniel: But then again, I can see why it works. I know it works. Actually, I am not sure why it works. I don't see why another one up there would help. I can see why . . . I just don't see any proof.

Arial: There are a billion possibilities. Like 10 and 20 and 20 and 10 numbers. It is the picture that changes. Well, there would be more dots.

Karl: With any number, you can just turn it. Like if you make a dot array and you just turn it. It's *always* gonna have the same number of dots, no matter what.

Arial: Yeah.

Daniel: That's a little better. It's just that I didn't want more and more examples.

Abby: Well, Daniel, you can spend a lot of time trying a lot of examples and then you think you know it would work for any numbers.

Daniel: I know. But then again there are an infinite amount of numbers so it shouldn't matter. You need to show that it always works.

Ms. V: Did you accept Karl's explanation?

Daniel: I accepted Karl's explanation.

Jordan: Take any group of dots...and flip it on its side. It will be the same number of dots!

Jordan and his partners used an array model to demonstrate that the order of numbers could be switched, but their model only illustrated a specific case. They did not take the further step of arguing that the process they had demonstrated could be applied to any number (at least any whole number). Daniel insisted on a new level of justification. He stated explicitly that numerous examples would not yield a proof. Jordan's suggestion that the array could be turned and not change the number of dots did not satisfy Daniel. He probed until Karl explicitly stated that the process could be applied to any number. Jordan's final statement also acknowledged the necessity of making a general argument that applied beyond the specific case being illustrated. Arial, on the other hand, continued to talk about switching the numbers around, and in the next episode it became clear that she still had a superficial conception of commutativity.

In this episode, the students assumed almost complete responsibility for class discussion. Ms. V's voice was seldom heard. She only interjected to clarify that the group had actually reached some consensus about making an argument about the generality of the proof. Although Ms. V did not guide the discussion, it remained focused on establishing norms for justification. Daniel played a key role in this discussion, actually assuming the role that one might expect of the teacher. He explicitly pressed the other students to show that the argument they were using generalized to all whole numbers, saying that he did not think one more example would help. Rather than simply stating the generalization himself, he asked a question of the other students to get them to articulate the principle. There are possibly alternative interpretations of Daniel's participation in this last exchange. It might be proposed that Daniel was pursuing a question jointly with his classmates. But looking back through all the episodes and drawing on yearlong observations of Daniel's interactions in the class, it appears clear to us that Daniel recognized the generality of the argument using arrays and that the uncertainty he expressed in this exchange was a way of formulating questions to engage other students in negotiating norms for justification. Thus, we conclude that Daniel actually understood the answers to the questions he posed and that his way of interacting was evidence of his feeling of responsibility for participating in the group to collectively establish norms for justification.

January 21, 1999

The students had worked in small groups on the previous day on four tasks evaluating equations. One task indirectly addressed their understanding of commutativity of multiplication using multidigit numbers. This task asked the students to decide whether $37 \times 54 = 57 \times 34$ was a true or false number sentence. Students who held superficial notions of commutativity might think that switching the numbers in the one's places would not make a difference. If students decided that sentence was true, they were to explain why it was true. If they decided it was false, they were to tell how they could make it a true number sentence.

Six students wrote that the equation was true because the numbers were just switched. Of the students who initially answered false, five found the partial products that would differ without computation. The rest of the students who answered false computed the answer for each expression to answer the question. No students used an array as a way to represent the problem.

The following protocol begins with a student explaining why she thought the answer was true.

Brenda: This number sentence is true because if you look at the 37×54 the 37 is 3 more than the 34 in 57×34. But then the 54 in 37×54 is three less than 57 in 57×34. So in 37×54 it is just like saying plus 3 from 57×34 and minus 3 from 57×34.

Ms. V: So [pause] it is true? You're saying it is true because there are 3 more here from the 37 (pointing to the 37×54) and 3 more here from the 57 (pointing to the 34×57). So they are kind of the same on both sides?

Brenda: Yes.

Ms. V: So your saying that's true?

Lisa: I think it is false. Brenda, I think your reasoning is very good except for the fact that 30×4 is different from 50×4. I know it is 37 ... I did it both ways ... But if you got it lined up for the computation ...

Lisa listed the two partial products to each multiplication that were different, and Ms. V wrote them on the board.

$$37 \times 54 = 57 \times 34$$

$$50 \times 7 = 350 \quad 30 \times 7 = 210$$

$$30 \times 4 = 120 \quad 50 \times 4 = 200$$

Myra: You don't really need the 50×30.
Billie: 50×30 and 30×50 is the same thing. You only need to pay attention to the [pause] there is something else missing.
Ms. V: You said something else is missing?
Myra: You don't have to worry about the 7×4 and the 4×7 are the same.

Ms. V added the two missing partial products to what was already on the board.

Nicole: I changed my answer because 54×3 is greater than 34×3.
Ms. V: You have a different way of saying why it is false?
Nicole: Yes.
Ms. V: Before we do that, do these parts all have to be done to do multiplication (pointing to the four partial products on the board)? (Yes's and no's) These parts are the same (pointing to 50×30 and 30×50 and to 7×4 and 4×7). So the only parts to look at are the different parts?

. . .

Ms. V: (Returning to address Nicole's earlier response) You think it is false because 54×3 is greater than 34×3. Where did the 3 come from?
Nicole: They both have a difference of three.

After some discussion, it emerged that Nicole was thinking of the problem as $34 \times 54 + 3 \times 54 = 34 \times 54 + 3 \times 34$.

Arial continued to struggle with this problem. There are several potential explanations for the misconception shown in the following exchange. She might have a limited understanding of commutativity rooted in symbolic form so that she does not recognize that the changes in this problem actually result in different numbers being multiplied. Ariel's comments seem to suggest, however, that much of her difficulty lies in not understanding how the distributive property applies to the multiplication of two-digit numbers. She appears to presume that $37 \times 54 = 30 \times 50 + 7 \times 4$, because those are the only partial products she mentions. Although some of her conclusions about this problem were wrong, it is worth noting that she did recognize that a single counter-example would invalidate the general principle she was trying to apply to the problem, which suggests that she had a reasonably good grasp of the role of counter-example in mathematical argument.

> *Arial:* One of our conjectures is wrong. When I looked at it, I said it was true cause 7×4 and 4×7 and 30×50 and 50×30. Then that conjecture (referring to $a \times b = b \times a$) is not clear. It has to have an exception that it doesn't work for a double-digit number.
>
> *Billie:* That conjecture is still right ... All the a's have to be the same number.
>
> *Mary:* I think "a" has to equal "a". If you had a number sentence.

Ms. V wrote $(30 + 7) \times (50 + 4) = (50 + 7) \times (30 + 4)$ on the board and noted the relation with the partial products already written on the board.

> *Billie:* There is more to a multiplication problem. It is not just 30×50 and 7×4 ... There is also 30×4 and 50×7.
>
> *Arial:* I know I am wrong. But that means the conjecture is wrong.

At this point the period ended so that there was no time to bring closure to the discussion.

INDIVIDUAL INTERVIEWS

In the third week of May, five months after the last discussion about the commutative property, students were individually interviewed on a number of tasks, three of which dealt specifically with the commutative property. In one task, students were asked to prove the conjecture $a \times b = b \times a$. Then the students were shown the following three ways other children had proven this conjecture, which correspond to Sowder and Harel's (1998) proof schemes.

1. *External Proof*
   Stacey said, "It always works, you can always switch the order when you multiply, it doesn't matter which one comes first."
2. *Empirical Proof*
   Rico said this: "Look 5 times 4 that is 20 and 4 times 5, that is also 20. I spent a lot of time proving this one. I used my calculator and did 50 different ones; Like I did 45×53 and I got the same thing as 53×45. It will always work.
3. *Analytical Proof*
   Audrey made an arrangement with blocks. She said, "See here is 7 times 3, 7 groups of 3, look I can just turn it and it is 3 times 7, 3 groups of 7. I didn't add any blocks or take any away so of course it is the same number both ways. You could do this for any number, it would always work."

For this task, students were asked: "Who do you think did the best job of proving this conjecture? Why?" The results are shown in Table 3.1.

Many students used an empirical proof scheme for their own proof. However, when given proofs of other students to examine, more than three-fourths chose the analytical proof as the best way to prove the conjecture. One student, Karl, produced a more general model than had been used in the class by drawing a box to represent the array for his proof that $a \times b = b \times a$. When

TABLE 3.1
**Number of Students Using Each Proof Scheme to Generate a
Proof and Select the Best Proof for $a \times b = b \times a$ (N = 19)**

Proof Scheme	Student-Generated Proof	Student's Answer to Whom Did the Best Job of Proving This Conjecture
1 *External*—restate rule, describes the situation.	3	2
2 *Empirical*—one or several examples are given.	9	2
3 *Analytic*—student draws an array or explains an array.	7	15

asked why he used a box, he explained that the box better represented the situation than dots because dots would mean a "certain number," and the box would work better for all situations. In fact, he actually wrote variables instead of numbers on the sides of his box. Furthermore, the area representation that Karl used extends the array model to accommodate fractions, although we cannot be sure that Karl recognized that feature of his representation.

In the third task, students were asked to decide whether $38 \times 27 = 28 \times 37$ was true or false and to explain their reasoning. Out of 12 who said the statement was false, only four had complete reasoning that involved analyzing the partial products for differences. The other eight students that said the statement was false had incomplete reasoning, but only two of these students computed the product to justify their thinking. In January, seven of the students computed the product of a similar problem to justify their thinking.

DESIGN PRINCIPLES REVISITED

To conclude, we revisit the five principles of instructional design that were outlined at the beginning of the chapter.

- Students were responsible not only for their own learning but also for the learning of the group. The evidence for this design principle is most clearly seen in Daniel's participation in the group. As early as the first episode, he demonstrated understanding of a general argument to justify the commutative property of multiplication, but in all the episodes he participated at a level that is consistent with the task and norms accepted by the other students. He pushed the agenda forward, but he was sensitive to what other students said and appeared to understand. He appeared to see a role for himself in negotiating with the other students to establish norms for justification. In the fourth episode, rather than simply stating what was missing in the justification presented by Jordan and Ariel, Daniel asked questions that drew out the general principles and engaged other students in formulating norms for justification of a general principle that applied to all numbers.

  One might ask how the norms might have developed if Daniel had not been in the class. In an earlier case study of Ms. V (Carpenter et al., 1999), another student played the same role that Daniel did in this study. This suggests that perhaps an important goal of instruction should be to create an environment in which students like Daniel have opportunity to contribute. Ms. V and one colleague resisted the school norms to homogeneously group students for mathematics instruction. Daniel's participation in this class illustrates the contribution that students can make to one another's learning and the potential benefits of having a heterogeneous mix of students.

- Students discussed alternative arguments for a purpose. In this case the purpose was to establish norms for justification and proof.
- Discussion was anchored in specific tasks, and the nature of a task significantly influenced what students attended to and the nature of their arguments and explanations. In each of the episodes, quite different tasks provided a focus to the discussion. In the second episode, the task involved a single case with relatively small numbers, and many of the students were able to avoid dealing with general principles. In the third episode the numbers were larger, which encouraged the students to think more in terms of general arguments rather than carry out the calculation. But because the task involved a specific case, the students' arguments were limited to the specific case and they did not have to recognize that their justification could be extended beyond that specific case. In the fourth episode, the task puts students in a position to argue the general case, and they were faced with arguing that their argument were generalizable.
- Tasks and norms for class interactions provided a window on students' mathematical thinking. The tasks and norms in this class required students to explain the reasons for their responses. This allowed Ms. V to recognize the limits of students' arguments and adapt subsequent tasks so that they challenged the students to address issues that they had not addressed or had demonstrated a limited understanding of in earlier sessions. Even after students had arrived at a general justification for commutativity of multiplication, Ms. V selected a task for the fifth episode that challenged students' conceptions of commutativity, and she found out that some students' thinking about commutativity was fragile and limited. In this and previous episodes, we see that the students were not reluctant to speak out about their potential misconceptions even if they conflicted with the emerging conceptions.
- Ms. V and students negotiated norms for articulating and justifying mathematical statements, and the students assumed a prominent role in this negotiation. This is most clearly seen in the fourth episode, in which Daniel questioned another students' explanation to bring out the necessity of framing the argument so that it applied to all (whole) numbers.

These principles clearly are not independent, and they are grounded in a particular vision of instruction and what is important for students to learn. Collectively they were instrumental in providing an environment in which students and teacher together explored the nature of mathematical argument.

ACKNOWLEDGMENTS

The research and preparation of this chapter was supported in part by a grant from the Department of Education Office of Educational Research and Improvement to the National Center for Improving Student Learning and Achievement in Mathematics and Science (R305A60007). The opinions expressed in this paper do not necessarily reflect the position, policy, or endorsement of the Department of Education, OERI, or the National Center.

REFERENCES

Balacheff, N. (1988). Aspects of proof in pupils' practice of school mathematics. In D. Pimm (Ed.), *Mathematics, teachers, and children* (pp. 216–230). London: Hodder & Stoughton.

Ball, D. L., & Bass, H. (2000). Making believe: The collective construction of public mathematical knowledge in the elementary classroom. In D. Phillips (Ed.), Yearbook of the National Society for the Study of Education, *Constructivism in education* (pp. 193–224). Chicago: University of Chicago Press.

Bastable, B., & Schifter, D. (1998). Classroom stories: Examples of elementary students engaged in early algebra. In J. Kaput (Ed.), *Early algebra*. Dartmouth, MA: Unpublished manuscript.

Bereiter, C. (1985). Toward a solution of the learning paradox. *Review of Educational Research, 55*, 201–226.

Carpenter, T. P., Ansell, E., Franke, M. L., Fennema, E., & Weisbeck, L. (1993). Models of problem solving: A study of kindergarten children's problem-solving processes. *Journal for Research in Mathematics Education, 24*, 428–441.

Carpenter, T. P. et al. (1999). An Analysis of Student Construction of Ratio and Proportion Understanding. Paper presented at the annual meeting of the American Educational Research Association, Montreal.

Cobb, P., & Yackel, E. (1996). Constructivist, emergent, and sociocultural perspectives in the context of developmental research. *Educational Psychologist, 31*, 175–190.

Fujii, T., & Stephens, M. (2001). Fostering an understanding of algebraic generalization through numerical expressions: The role of quasi-variables. *Proceedings of the 12th ICMI study conference: The future of the teaching and learning of algebra*. Melbourne, Australia.

Kaput, J., & Blanton, M. (2001). Algebrafying the elementary mathematics experience Part I: Transforming task structures. *Proceedings of the 12th ICMI study conference: The future of the teaching and learning of algebra*. Melbourne, Australia.

Lehrer, R., Kemeny, V., Gance, S., & Curtis, C. (1996). Children model the structure of space: From cereal boxes to epistemology. Paper presented at the annual meeting of the American Educational Research Association, New York.

Maher, C., & Martino, A. (1996). The development of the idea of mathematical proof: A 5-year case study. *Journal for the Research of Mathematics Education, 20*(1), 41–51.

National Council of Teachers of Mathematics. (2000). *Principles and standards for school mathematics*. Reston, VA: National Council of Teachers of Mathematics.

Piaget, J. (1965). *The child's conception of number*. New York: Norton.

Sowder, L., & Harel, G. (1998). Types of students' justifications. *Mathematics Teacher, 91*(8), 670–675. [Focus Issue on the Role of Proof throughout the Mathematics Curriculum].

Yackel, E., & Cobb, P. (1996). Socio-mathematical norms, argumentation, and autonomy in mathematics. *Journal for Research in Mathematics Education, 27*, 458–477.

4

"Everyday" and "Scientific": Rethinking Dichotomies in Modes of Thinking in Science Learning

Beth Warren
Mark Ogonowski
Chèche Konnen Center, TERC

Suzanne Pothier
Martin Luther King, Jr. Open School
and Chèche Konnen Center

When we use the term "everyday" as a qualifier of our experience (as in "everyday experience"), we usually intend to convey an idea of our experience as concrete, familiar, commonplace, informal. Use of this term often implies a contrast with another form of experience characterized as scientific, precise, complex, formal. This trade in mutually exclusive contrasts for modes of thinking or kinds of meaning is a distinctive and long-standing tradition in Western thinking (Hymes, 1996; Goody, 1977; Lave, 1988; Leacock, 1972). It is one that has reverberated across many domains of inquiry and has assumed a similar, binary form: scientific versus everyday; abstract versus concrete; complex versus simple; analytic versus intuitive; decontextualized versus contextualized; advanced versus primitive; domesticated versus savage; theoretical versus practical; examined versus unexamined. Evaluation is built into these dichotomies, that is, in how we use them to organize experience. The left-hand term of each pair is the more highly valued, reflecting a cognitive ideal involving *more* information, complexity, precision, analysis, and generality (Hymes, 1996; Lave, 1988; Leacock, 1972). Although these categories may be useful to us as we try to orient ourselves amid the disorder and uncertainty of life, Goody (1977) reminds us that this division into contrasting modes of thought is the product of "a folk-taxonomy by which we bring order and understanding into a complex universe. But the order is illusory, the meaning superficial" (p. 36).

Not surprisingly, the field of science education research has not been immune from this tradition of thought. Indeed, the whole question of the value or function of "everyday experience" in learning science—to take but one example, how laypersons experience the world and how the discipline of physics conceptualizes the world—has been a focus of continuing debate. Roughly speaking, the field divides itself into two camps: those for whom the sciences represent worlds largely *discontinuous* with ordinary, everyday experience, and those for whom the relationship between scientific understanding and everyday experience is fundamentally *continuous*.

The discontinuity tradition is represented in much of the work on student misconceptions (McCloskey, Caramazza, & Green, 1980; McDermott, Rosenquist, & van Zee, 1987; Viennot, 1979) and studies of instructional congruence (O. Lee & Fradd, 1996; O. Lee, Fradd, & Sutman, 1995). This tradition locates one major source of discontinuity in students' encounters with the physical and social world of everyday experience and interaction. It holds that students' everyday ideas are often wrong, strongly held, difficult to change, and interfere with learning. From a discontinuity point of view, the goal of education is to replace, repair, or fix students' wrong ideas and ways of knowing with correct ideas through a variety of instructional means.

An argument against the claims of misconceptionists and others who view "everyday experience" as a source of trouble was mounted in a paper by Smith, diSessa, and Roschelle (1993; see also diSessa, 1993; diSessa, Hammer, Sherin, & Kolpakowski, 1991; Minstrell, 1989). The core of their argument is that the framing assumptions of misconceptions research, which stress discontinuity between students and experts (e.g., scientists and mathematicians), conflict with the basic premise of constructivism, namely, that students build more advanced understandings from prior understandings. Building on diSessa's "knowledge-in-pieces" framework, Smith et al. (1993) offered an alternative view that takes up students' prior knowledge and experience as resources in developing mature understanding in physics. In support of this, they identified important dimensions of continuity between students' ideas and those of experts where misconceptions research has identified discontinuities.

Our intention here is not to do an exhaustive review or analysis of this debate, only to point to some of the implications of each tradition with regard to matters of learning and teaching. These two traditions proceed according to quite different assumptions. The main point of contention is whether students' ways of conceptualizing, representing, and evaluating their lived experience should be viewed and treated as errors that impede learning or as generative resources in learning new ideas and traditions of inquiry. Our particular concern is with the implications of these two views with respect to children who are not experiencing academic success, typically children from low-income, historically underserved communities.

In the discontinuity view, children from historically underserved communities may appear especially disadvantaged because their "everyday" experiences and ways of knowing/talking/valuing are viewed as being the furthest from those traditionally valued in models of Western science or in national standards. Studies of instructional congruence (Lee & Fradd, 1996; Lee, Fradd, & Sutman, 1995), for example, focus on what the authors define as "incompatibility" between habits of mind as well as language and other interactional practices (e.g., deference to authority) they identify as characteristic of students from certain language-minority groups (e.g., Haitian-Creole and Spanish-speaking communities) and those valued in national science standards. They suggest that these putative habits of mind and interactional practices can impede students' learning in science. On this view, then, much of what these children bring in the way of culturally-based linguistic, intellectual, and experiential resources is not likely to be recognized or tapped as an intellectual resource in science learning and teaching.[1]

---

[1]We contrast the idea of cultural resources being deeply related intellectually to disciplinary content and practice with what we consider to be a shallow interpretation. The latter can be seen in instructional moves that introduce everyday experiences such as cooking rice and beans as a familiar context in a discussion of phase transitions, or that make note of the use of the Celsius scale in students' native countries in a discussion of temperature measurement scales. There is nothing wrong with these moves in and of themselves. But, often, they are not connected in any deep way with the core conceptual content or thinking practices of the domain. They thus come to represent the totality of what is seen as culturally grounded, to the exclusion of sense-making practices and understandings that in fact resonate deeply with those of scientific disciplines. They, in short, reduce culture to a referential function rather than seeing it dynamically as lived human experience within and across varied communities of practice (Gonzalez, 1999; Ingold, 1994; C. Lee, 2002; Moll, 2000; Rogoff, 2003), that is, as the acquisition throughout the life course of varied repertoires of cultural knowledge and performance capacities (Erickson, 2002).

Research in the continuity tradition takes a different view. Studies in this tradition have documented the various ways in which the experiences, ideas, and ways of talking and knowing of children from groups historically placed at risk are productively related to those characteristic of scientific communities (Ballenger, 1997, 2000; Conant, Rosebery, Warren, & Hudicourt-Barnes, 2001; Gee & Clinton, 2000; Hudicourt-Barnes, 2003; Michaels & Sohmer, 2000; Rosebery & Warren, 1999; Rosebery, Warren, Ballenger, & Ogonowski, in press; Warren, Ogonowski, & Pothier, 2000; Warren, Pothier, Rosebery & Ogonowski, 2003; Warren, Ballenger, Ogonowski, Rosebery, & Hudicourt-Barnes, 2001; Warren & Rosebery, 1996). In each of these cases, children's inventive use of narrative, animated modes of argumentation, dynamic ways of imagining themselves into physical phenomena, among other sense-making resources, have repeatedly challenged teachers and researchers to examine their own, often limited and limiting, assumptions about what constitutes productive reasoning and deep understanding in the sciences. Thus, unlike the discontinuity tradition, this way of approaching learning and teaching challenges teachers and researchers alike to assume that children are always connecting in some important way to the discipline and to learn to see these connections in the unfolding life of the classroom, no matter how far what children say and do may initially appear from the teachers' or researchers' expectations and understandings.

We are, without question, sympathetic to the continuity side of the argument (see, for example, Warren et al., 2001), which as pursued by diSessa and colleagues (1993; diSessa et al., 1991; Smith et al., 1993) is concerned fundamentally with "uncovering children's competence" and exploring ways in which such competence can be supported to promote development of robust understanding of the physical world. This perspective emphasizes both the heterogeneity and generativity in what children know and know how to do in relation to scientific ideas and practices of representation. It views scientific knowledge as growing out of experience, as a refinement, not a replacement, of experience. In our view, the idea of "uncovering children's competence" is central to the goal of creating classroom communities in which all children learn deeply and from each other (Brookline Teacher Research Seminar, 2004; C. Lee, 1993, 2000; Warren et al., 2001). It entails openness to the many and varied sense-making resources that children bring from their lives outside of school and ongoing analysis of the generative ways in which these intersect with disciplinary ideas and meaning-making practices.

Within a continuity perspective, children's everyday experience is cultivated as an intellectually rich substrate for learning and development. In this chapter we are interested in understanding the relationship between children's experience in the physical world and newly encountered scientific ideas, specifically, how children's "everyday experience" functions in relation to core disciplinary ideas and meaning-making practices in Newtonian physics. The study presented in this chapter explores how young children—first and second graders—used their "everyday experience" of downhill motion in understanding the behavior of toy cars and Newtonian ideas of force and motion. What kind of thing are these "everyday experiences"? How do they function as representations of emergent meaning in the children's inquiries? We use the term representation cautiously here. Our intention is not to suggest that children's accounts of their experience are mere redescriptions of a corresponding lived, past experience. Rather, we wish to suggest that their representations of their experiences running or riding bicycles down hills actually bring to life what did not fully exist before. In this sense, children's accounts of their everyday experience are not acts of replication or recall but acts of creative analysis, in which familiar events and objects are recast, ordinary meanings are subverted, and new possibilities for seeing and understanding are opened up (Rosebery et al., in press).

To begin, we present some background on the context of the study, then an analysis of two classroom episodes, followed by a discussion of the implications of this study for ways of thinking about the relationship of everyday experience and scientific ideas in children's learning in science.

THE STUDY

Background

The study took place in a combined first- and second-grade classroom in which students from diverse socioeconomic, ethnic, and language backgrounds investigated motion down an incline. The children's inquiry was part of a larger investigation of Newtonian ideas designed by their teacher, Suzanne Pothier, and the other authors who are members of the Chèche Konnen Center. The investigation as a whole was motivated by Ms. Pothier's own experience as a member of the Chèche Konnen teacher research seminar. In the seminar, she, other teachers, and Chèche Konnen staff investigated Newton's Laws as learners (see Warren & Ogonowski, 1998; Warren, Ogonowski, & Pothier, 2000). In parallel, we analyzed the talk and activity of children who initially puzzled us, either because they said something that was incomprehensible to us or approached the topic from an unexpected place (Ballenger, 1999; Ballenger & Rosebery, 2003; Brookline Teacher Research Seminar, 2004; Gallas, 1994). Ms. Pothier was especially committed to learning to see the intellectual strengths and traditions of all her students, in particular those from lives distant from her own, and how these connected with scientific traditions of meaning-making. With this commitment in mind, she set out to explore what her first and second graders might be able to understand about accelerated motion and gravity, phenomena typically thought to be beyond the grasp of young children, and how they might approach making sense of these ideas.

Reviewing the district's approved curriculum unit (Education Development Center, 1997), Ms. Pothier decided to refocus it with an emphasis on ideas of motion and force. She organized the children's investigation around visible (e.g., pushes and pulls) and invisible forces (e.g., gravity). The children began in January by exploring pushes and pulls that they could observe or feel directly, for example, experimenting with ways to get a toy car moving from rest, and pulling first one, then two, then three boxes of copier paper. During their initial exploration of toy cars, one boy noticed that at times the car seemed to "move by itself," as when it rolled down his arm. This kind of motion, "moving by itself," became the subject of intense investigation over many months. The children experimented with toy cars on ramps, slid down a giant slide in the playground outside school, drew representations of changes in speed they perceived in a toy car as it rolled down a short ramp, constructed stories and cartoons of the car's trip down the ramp as well as their own trip down a giant slide, and in the waning days of the school year explored gravity as a possible cause of the changes in speed that they and toy cars experience as they each move down an incline.

About two months into the investigation, Ms. Pothier introduced the children to Sir Isaac Newton and some of his ideas about motion. Drawing from his First and Second Laws, she presented a formulation that expressed what is arguably the core principle of the Second Law in a nonmathematized form:

Isaac Newton looked for:

➤ A change in the speed of an object
➤ A change in the direction the object is moving

If Newton saw one or both of these changes, he said there has to be something forcing that to happen.

The class discussed how this idea related to their experiences working with visible forces. They then engaged in several months of activity investigating accelerated motion due to gravity. Ms. Pothier's goals for her students' learning were twofold: (1) that they come to see that an object moving down an incline is always increasing its speed, and (2) that they understand that gravity is the force that causes this continuous change in speed. Our focus in this chapter is on classes related to the first goal.

Ms. Pothier's intention was to put Newton's perspective on the kind of motion they would be investigating out on the table as a perspective to think with, probe, interrogate. This move derived from her own experience in the Chèche Konnen seminar, where Newtonian ideas were taken up in just this way, as an object of inquiry rather than as laws to be unquestioningly applied in solving problems (Rosebery et al., in press; Warren & Ogonowski, 2001) or as universal principles to be discovered. This investigation was also an experiment of sorts, insofar as Ms. Pothier was interested in seeing how her first and second graders would take up Newton's ideas about motion in light of their own lived experience.

We next present an analysis of two episodes from the class's investigation. The focal episodes are drawn from two consecutive classes beginning with the first time the children worked at exploring Newtonian ideas and motion due to gravity by observing changes in the speed of a toy car as it rolled down a short ramp. We focus on the talk and activity of three children—Letisha and Stacey in the first episode and Elton in the second. In both of these episodes, the children invoke aspects of "everyday experience" as they explore the toy car's motion. To show the kind of understandings the children developed over the course of their investigation, we then summarize later classes in the study, during which the children experienced this type of motion numerous times and in numerous contexts, both as observers and participants.

Letisha and Stacey

On the first day of interest, Ms. Pothier asked the children to work in pairs to observe a toy Hot Wheels™ car as it moved down a short (approximately 2-foot) ramp set at a predetermined steepness. Their instructions were to do four runs of the car down the ramp, note any changes in speed they observed, and then create a story of the car's trip, which they would later share with the whole class.

As the children observed the toy car's very brief trip, they noticed various aspects of its motion, often indexing changes in its speed to particular places on the ramp. Some noted that the car "started off slow" at the top and then got fast; a few pointed to specific places on the ramp where the car went the "fastest," including, but not always, the end. Many identified a particular place along the ramp where the car "got faster," although the actual place varied from one pair of children to another as well as across runs of a given car; some children used Post-it notes to label the spot on the ramp where they thought this change occurred in a given run. Thus the children seemed to notice discrete moments of change from one speed "state" to another (i.e., from relatively slow to faster), as if there were *a* change in speed to be observed or a series of discrete changes (i.e., it got faster here and here)—a perfectly sensible perception given the task ("look for changes in speed"), the brief duration (approximately 2 seconds) of the car's run, and the inherent difficulty of directly observing a continuously changing quantity.

Even at this early point in the investigation, however, some students sensed that the car's speed might be changing more continuously or, at least, at multiple points during its descent. And some went beyond the given task to explore, in a way influenced by the circulation of Newtonian ideas, what might be "forcing" any observed changes in speed. Both of these ways of seeing motion on the ramp were present in the work of Letisha and Stacey, on whom we first focus.

Immediately after an initial run of the car, Stacey noticed that the car "went slow" near the top, "then it started going down and faster." At the same time, she perceived the car "going faster . . . up to about here," as she ran her finger from the start of the ramp to its midpoint. She summarized her observations as follows:

> 1. *Stacey:*   So I saw this change in speed. They all—[the car rolls down the ramp] like that one got fast about here [1/3 of the way down] and some got fast about here [1/4 of the way down] and one got fast here [2/3 of the way down].

Stacey saw the car's motion in various ways. She described it gaining speed as it went down ("then it started going down and faster"). In her description, she emphasized how the car's motion is both *going* down and faster, at the same time. She placed them in some kind of contingent relationship, without yet specifying its exact nature; for example, "going down" might entail "going faster" or they may simply happen together. At the same time, she described the car's motion as changing speed at distinct, albeit different, locations during various runs ("I saw *this* change in speed."). Change of speed in this light is not so much continuous as discrete. In addition, she described the car's motion as gaining speed, then leveling out ("going faster up to about here"), presumably at some constant speed. The variability in Stacey's accounts does not reflect confusion; rather, each account is a possible and reasonable way of "seeing" the toy car's downhill motion.

At this point, Letisha introduced a new motion, pushing the car quickly down the ramp with her hand, not letting go. This motion contrasted sharply with the seemingly unaided motion of the car on previous runs.

2. *Letisha:* You can't just go like [*moves car swiftly down ramp holding it the whole way*] with your hand-force.

3. *Stacey:* I know yeah, cuz it doesn't go like [*moves car swiftly down ramp as L did*] like that. It just—you can't—it doesn't go like that [*repeats motion*] it can't—it goes slower and slo—and then faster then faster and faster and faster [*lets car run down ramp on its own*].

Letisha's manipulation seemed to foreground for Stacey the shape of the car's trip as a whole. Agreeing with Letisha, she emphatically described the car's motion as progressively going faster and faster—in contrast with a fast and possibly unchanging speed under the control of one's "hand-force," as Letisha called it. "Hand-force" was a linguistic invention based in the class's earlier work with visible forces, to which they also gave names such as "arm-force" (i.e., in relation to a procedure they used to pull increasing numbers of boxes filled with equal amounts of copier paper).

We note a few qualities of the girls' accounts in lines 2–3. First, note how Letisha, in producing this new hand-forced motion, marked it as different from the car's unaided motion and, strikingly, as a violation of a previous pattern of motion (line 2, "*you can't* just go like . . . with your hand force"). Grammatically, the combination of the impersonal "you" and the modal "can't" delimit, in a generalized way, what is possible here and what is not under the given set of circumstances. In a related way, Stacey followed by saying that "it *doesn't* go like that," which acknowledges the reality that only certain things can happen here, but without committing fully to the generalized claim that Letisha put forward. Although different in force and scope, these two accounts are nonetheless fundamentally related in the way they construct what is possible and what is not in the world of the ramp.

Second, and in a related move, note how in her account Stacey shifted from the past tense ("got fast") in line 1 to the present ("it goes slower and then faster . . . ") in line 3 to describe the car's change in speed, which accompanied her imitation of Letisha's hand-forced motion. This shift in tense foregrounds the change in speed as ongoing, not located in a single moment of change that takes place and then ends, but accumulating all the time. Like the characterizations of the hand-forced motion above, this way of describing the car's motion also emphasizes the generalized nature of this pattern, across time and place.

Third, note the pattern of repetition—"and then faster then faster and faster and faster"—Stacey used to describe the car's change in speed. The words themselves seem to speed up as they accumulate and as Stacey shifts from "*then* faster" to "*and* faster." This shift in markers from "then," which retains some quality of specific location and time, to "and," which is more general and not tied to a specific idea of time and place, seems to foreground Stacey's sense of the car's change in speed as being ongoing and progressive. It is interesting, perhaps, that as she began her account in line 3, she did the same sort of thing with "slower" and then quickly self-corrected. It is as if the idea of speed changing progressively—as contrasted with Letisha's hand-forced motion—now shaped what it is possible to see on the ramp. Letisha's action and way of accounting for the car's motion seems to have brought this realization into focus, namely, that the downhill motion of the toy car involves a progressive increase in speed over the whole length of the trip, a motion completely unlike that of hand-forced motion.

From here, Letisha, with Stacey joining in, embarked on a further, rather expansive exploration of the ramp and motion down an incline. Her approach was at once analytical and exploratory, combining a playful, imaginative attitude toward the material scene with a dogged concern to understand changes in motion in terms of the force(s) that might be causing them, as expressed in the formulation of Newton's ideas with which the class was presented. We note parenthetically that the children were only required to identify changes in speed, not to speculate on the possible force or forces that might be causing those changes. We pick up their interaction approximately 4 minutes after the introduction of the hand-forced motion.

31. *Letisha:*   right, like with a real car what would happen was, well there's like a um like this thing that you like can turn–like can turn the wheels of the car and I mean there's like a wheel in the car that it can turn the car [*she slightly turns car at top of ramp, then lets go leaving car at top edge*]

32. *Stacey:*   =yeah [*she picks up car and looks at its underside*]

33. *Letisha:*   =or keep it straight. So (for a) turn(ed) car that's a ch— that's (just) forcing the car to change.

Just prior to this, Stacey had used Letisha's hand-forced motion, zooming the car down the ramp under the constant control of her hand, to show how it differed from the car rolling down the ramp on its own. Without hand-force, the car veered somewhat. Noticing this, Letisha invoked the motion of "a real car," in particular, the way in which a steering wheel functions to turn a car or keep it straight. She then began to draw out the implication of this observation, beginning this move in line 33 with "so. . .". Bumping up a register, she analyzed the event of "a turned car" in light of the Newtonian-inspired language circulating in the class: "so (for a) turn(ed) car, *that's* just *forcing* the car *to change*." Working creatively with this way of conceptualizing motion, Letisha forged a new object, "a turn(ed) car." This new entity fused the real car she was imagining, the toy car that veered on the ramp, and really any other "turned car" imaginable. In this way, Letisha made these instances of turning into a general case of change of motion, one that could be ana-lyzed in a certain—that is, Newtonian—way. Let's look more closely at what she did.

We can see in Letisha's utterance the trace of her way of thinking. Note how in mid-utterance she interrupted herself—"so (for a) turn(ed) car that's a ch—." Presumably, she was about to say something like "that's a change in speed or direction," drawing on the formulation offered by Ms. Pothier. The presence of such a change would therefore imply the operation of a force or "something forcing that to happen." We suggest that Letisha interrupted her own train of thought at this point because she had already identified the change in motion in the object she had created, "a turned car." She "recognized" in this moment that the way this discourse functioned meant that she now had to infer a forcing mechanism, not the change in motion—in this case, the steer-ing wheel as the something "that's just forcing the car to change." Indeed, in her analysis she unpacked the very nominalization she had constructed, making the action that is being explained explicit as well (*"that's* just *forcing the car to change"*), as if she was exploring for herself how this way of talking—or way of seeing motion—actually worked. In other words, Letisha was not speaking *through* Newton so much as *with* Newton, populating his ideas with her own intentions and accent (Bakhtin, 1981) and exploring the possibili-ties of this way of conceptualizing, representing, and evaluating the world of motion.

The object Letisha constructed, "a turned car," transformed the event or action of "turning" into a nominalization of the sort that has been identified as central to the character of scientific discourses (Gee, 1990; Halliday & Martin, 1993; Lemke, 1990; Myers, 1985). In the sciences, nominalizations are important for various reasons, including their status as fact (presumed to be taken for granted) and the way in which they can organize the distribution and redistribution of information in a clause or organize other nominalizations within a classificatory system or other meanings within an unfolding argument (Halliday & Martin, 1993). We see Letisha working with a prototype of this way of using language. She created the nominalization, "a turned car," out of a felt need for this kind of generalized object, the need for which presumably emerged out of her insistent exploration of the language of force and motion put forward by Ms. Pothier. In this way, Letisha constructed a particular kind of object, one that identified a category of motion ("change in motion") that could then be subjected to a certain kind of analysis.

In Letisha's way of seeing, an ordinary, everyday steering wheel became subject to a different kind of analysis—it was no longer just a steering mechanism. It became as well a force, something that causes a change in a car's direction. As such, this everyday object and event also functioned as a generative tool for thinking and for provoking puzzlement—what forcing mechanism in or about the toy car might have caused it to veer or to change speed? Letisha's insight spurred Stacey's curiosity as well. In line 22, she took hold of the car and inspected its underside, presumably looking for some way to explain the car's behavior, absent a steering wheel. Thus, in Letisha's hands—understood both literally in terms of the actions she performed and figuratively in terms of the way she took hold intellectually of the challenge of a Newtonian perspective— ordinarily unlinked objects and events all became part of the same coherent world of ideas linking force and change in motion.

In the next segment, we see Letisha exploring this way of seeing motion further. Stacey had just given the car a push down the ramp, guided it back up the ramp, let it go so that it rolled back down, guided it back up again, let it go, then given it a push up the ramp. Letisha picked up on this new pattern of motion, lifting the ramp into a horizontal position in order to arrest the toy car's downward motion.

36. *Letisha:* wait *[S takes car off ramp]* I need to like hold on to it like *[she takes car back]* ( ) like this sometimes *[S releases car down ramp]* sometimes you go like that *[L lifts ramp to horizontal position, car continues to roll on ramp and on to rug]*

37. *Stacey:* =oh

38. *Letisha:* =the car won't stop

39. *Stacey:* yeah like this *[she places car at top, holding it, then releases it]*

40. *Letisha:* =sometimes it will like this *[L raises ramp to horizontal and car stops about midway]*

41. *Stacey:* yeah, //and sometimes [*gently lowering bottom of ramp so it slants again*] it won't stop
42. *Letisha:* //if you like tip it, if you ( )

In this scene, Letisha induced a stop in the car's motion by manipulating the ramp from a downward orientation to a horizontal one. Interestingly, this followed directly on her speculation about a "real car's" steering wheel causing changes in direction. She knew the toy car does not have the resources of a real car: steering wheels, brakes, and the like. But she also knew that whenever a car undergoes a change in motion, some force has acted to cause that change. Here she seemed to be exploring the ramp as a possible force that can cause a change in the car's motion, specifically to make it stop. Thus her meditations on the ways in which the motion of "a real car" may be changed created new possibilities for making present what was absent in the architecture of the toy car—a brake—through direct manipulation of the ramp. Through her action of leveling the ramp (line 36) and then tipping it (line 42), she explored the ramp as a possible force, bringing to life new ways of seeing it in relation to the toy car's motion.

Stacey was drawn into the possibilities created by Letisha's improvisational manipulation of the ramp. She, too, began to perform and interpret actions on it. In the following segment, Stacey reversed the slant of the ramp, from downward to upward during the car's run.

43. *Stacey:* ok [*she lets car run down as L maintains horizontal*] put it up—put it up like that [*she raises bottom end of ramp so slant is reversed*] and see what happens [*L raises bottom of ramp*] no no keep it down [*L lowers bottom end of ramp*] and when it gets [*S releases car and L reverses slant on ramp, car rolls back*] see it goes back [*L returns ramp to original position, S releases car down ramp*] and it doesn't stop, it just goes back
44. *Letisha:* That's because when—when you go up [*hits rug with hand*]
45. *Stacey:* =yeah
46. *Letisha:* you gonna have to come right back down [*she sweeps her arm over and down*]
47. *Stacey:* yeah when you go up [*she slants ramp at a greater angle, bottom now the top, facing L, moves car up ramp*] and you—when you go up and it's—when a toy car goes up [*S guides car up ramp, then down*] then without an extra push [*S guides car up ramp, then down*] it can't stay going up, right?

In line 43, Stacey explored what would happen when the slant was reversed ("put it up like that and see what happens"). Then, when the car rolled back, she was not at all surprised ("*see*, it goes back and it doesn't stop"). Although Stacey seems to have anticipated this outcome, it also struck her with new meaning in the contrast it made with Letisha's horizontally positioned ramp, which effected a stop in the car's motion. Letisha immediately offered an account of this particular pattern of motion with an analysis which, in her use of the second person pronoun "you," merged the motion of the toy car with a larger universe of objects or persons that can undergo the same motion and obey the same imperative, lines 44–46: "that's because when you go up, you gonna have to come right back down." Agreeing, Stacey then suggested in line 47 that "without an extra push, it can't stay going up . . . ". As she spoke, she moved the car under control of her hand up and then down the ramp, as if to suggest the need of a continuous push or force to keep the car "going up." In their actions and interpretations throughout this episode, both girls intently explored the central mystery of the car's downhill motion: the absence of a visible force that can explain various patterns of change in the car's speed.

Like Letisha, Stacey linked the language of force ("without an extra push") to a change in motion (from going down, which it will do in the absence of an intervening push, to going up). Indeed, her language—"without an extra push, it can't stay going up"—reflects her growing appreciation for this way of seeing motion. First, it underscores the loss of upward motion resulting from the absence of an added force (". . . it *can't stay* going up"). Second, Stacey framed this absent "extra push" as a force that, implicitly, can work against whatever is making the car change its motion from going up to going down, as she said, to "*stay* going up." There is a certain inventiveness in Stacey's use of language here ("can't *stay going up*"), which may be read as awkwardness, but which, we suggest, reflects instead her emerging sense of the necessary relationship between force and change in motion. The insights of both girls seem anchored in their sense of how things go in the everyday world and in Newton's world, and in their efforts in the here-and-now to work out new possible meanings for previously familiar, ordinary events. The "familiar" has become intriguingly "strange," and at the same time accessible to analysis.

Agreeing, Letisha then likened these cases of motion to a baby carriage on a hill.

48. *Letisha:* mmhmm, like when a baby carriage is up on a hill, you need to turn on the brakes [*L places car part way up on ramp, as if up on a hill, and holds it there*] so it can stop

49. *Stacey:*   =yeah yeah
50. *Letisha:*   =so it won't li—like move
51. *Stacey:*   cuz if a toy car stops, like this *[she re-creates uphill ramp, holds car on ramp]* it's—if it stops *[she moves car to a position on the ramp about halfway up, then releases it, it rolls down]* then it's gonna move right back cuz it doesn't have any control, right?
52. *Letisha:*   Mmhmm

In this segment, Letisha and Stacey collaborated on the creation of an imagined scene in which baby carriages on hills and toy cars on ramps illuminated the case of stopping as a change in their otherwise inevitable downward motion. Both girls moved the car on the ramp in synchrony with their talk, as if they were thinking with and through the physical environment of the ramp and car. Indeed their respective actions—Letisha held the car partway up on the ramp and Stacey moved it halfway up the ramp and then released it—together form a whole for the situation they were exploring: the presence and absence of a force to counter the descent of the car or baby carriage.

We can see in the structure of Letisha's language how she was seeing the car's motion in terms of the relationship linking changes in motion, including stopping, to the action of a force. Note, for instance, how she connected stopping ("so it can stop") with a change in motion ("so it won't like move") through use of parallel structures; in this way, she equated "stopping" with the negation of the baby carriage/toy car's downward state of motion—from "moving" to "not moving," in other words. Likewise, we can see Stacey elaborating Letisha's earlier law-like pronouncement (lines 44–46, "when you go up you gonna have to come right back down") with a mechanism of presence or absence of control: line 51, "cuz if a toy car stops [on a ramp] [letting go] then it's gonna move right back down cuz it doesn't have any control, right?" The toy car, unlike real cars and baby carriages, does not contain the means to control its motion or, implicitly, to counter the otherwise inevitable downward motion on a ramp. In these children's hands and mind's eye, real cars and baby carriages have the power to illuminate something important about toy cars and vice versa. In this world of ideas about motion and force that they were exploring, brakes on baby carriages function much as hands do in controlling the downhill motion of a toy car; both are seen as potential forces that change the motion of the vehicle's descent from moving to not moving.

Throughout this episode, Letisha and Stacey brought together the world of the ramp and the "everyday" world of real cars and baby carriages. They used familiar objects and events analytically in their playful and speculative investigation of the ramp. They worked improvisationally, recasting objects (e.g., a turned car, baby carriages as toy cars) and unfolding events (e.g., downward motion turned into stopping), opening up new paths as they explored the possible meaning of Newton's ideas in relation to their lived experience of motion on and beyond the short ramp and toy car in front of them. As they did so, they both inhabited the world of the ramp and toy car—creating new scenes, experimenting with new actions within it—and treated it as an object of analysis in its own right, as a world of motions and, especially, changes in motion that in theory could be accounted for, even if the precise mechanism seemed, for the moment, not obvious.

Elton

Two days later in a whole-class discussion, the children shared their accounts of changes in the toy car's speed. They related the motion of the toy car to their own bodily experiences running down ramps and hills. In relation to those experiences, they built descriptions of patterns of change in the toy car's speed over the course of its trip. We focus on the contributions of a second grader, Elton.

The first episode occurred about 17 minutes into the approximately 40-minute class. After one pair of students described how they thought their car "started to get faster" in the middle and reached its full speed near the end of the ramp, Elton suggested that the car's motion down the ramp is "sort of the same thing" as running down the ramp at the back of their school:

1. *Elton:* Um putting the car um down the ramp is sort of the same //(thing)
2. *SP:* //I can't hear you
3. *Elton:* putting the car down down the ramp [*points to another child's ramp with left hand*] is sort of the same as you running down the ramp [*makes quick waving motion with same hand*] because (.) (not only) if you're in a car you go down a ramp [*quickly angles left hand from left to right*] you could feel how it's going faster but also when you run down the ramp you could feel getting—when you're running faster [*walks fingers of right hand at a descending angle from right to left*] ( ) (getting faster) [*arcs left hand right to left at eye level*]

4. *SP:*   So you've noticed your experience running down a ramp. How many people have run down a ramp outside, you know the ramp to go to the playground? *[many hands go up]* So tell us again what you've noticed Elton.

5. *Elton:* Um if a—if a car—if a car could get faster going down a ramp *[angles right hand down from right to left]* you could because um um when you get down and down *[repeats gesture]* it makes your legs go faster *[revolves hands in a rolling motion]* //um

6. *SP:*   //Mmm. What did other people notice when you're running down a ramp? Do you go faster when you're running down a ramp?

Let's focus on what Elton did here. Like Letisha, Elton brought together varied contexts of motion, proposing that they are "sort of the same": the toy car on the ramp, a person in a real car, and his own experience running down a ramp (lines 1 & 3). He then went on to show how. He imagined himself into a real car, going down a ramp in some unspecified time and place (line 3: "if you're in a car, you go down a ramp"). Imagining himself in such a car, he can "*feel* how it's going faster." At the same time, he narrated his experience of running down the ramp (line 6: "but also when you run down the ramp"), presumably the very one at the back of his school that he has run down many times before. For both the real car and his running, Elton imagined himself into these scenes, emphasizing the *feeling* one has in the midst of going down. He used the conditional "could" emphatically, which underscores the sense of his having discovered a similarity in the two cases: the *feeling* one has as the car one is in or one's body *goes* or *gets faster*. In other words, "could" conditions the experience of *feeling* one's speed increase, rather than the possibility of increasing speed: This feeling of one's speed increasing is *evidence* for the ongoing increase in speed, what one would feel in such situations, the very same feeling of increasing speed. The fact of increasing speed itself Elton here took as given.

As he spoke, Elton experienced the motion in his arms and hands. He performed this relationship of going down and going faster with gestures of his hands and fingers, his left and right hands becoming at once inclines and objects gaining speed. These performed gestures linked both lived and imagined experience; both were brought to life in the unified motion of his hands. We draw attention to this because in this way of using his body, we see Elton both imagining these scenes through his body—"feeling" what it is like to go down in a car and as he runs—and thinking with his body about what makes them similar—the resulting change in speed. Like Letisha and Stacey, he was both inside and outside these scenes, inhabiting them and also evaluating them. He saw them as part of an encompassing relation, continuous change in speed: going or running faster the farther down one gets on a ramp. What Elton noticed and explained, as Letisha had when she connected baby carriages on hills with toy cars on ramps, is that these two events are in some important sense part of the same *family* of motion (Wittgenstein, 1953).

Asked to repeat what he noticed, Elton (line 5) further elaborated the similarity in these motions: you *could* get faster just like a car *could* because going "...down and down...makes your legs go faster." The "coulds" in this case again seem to us to be functioning as they did before, not so much to mark a conditional status as emphatically to mark the similarity he is noticing— getting faster—which he then went on to link to the experience of "going down and down." Something about his sense of the car's experience helped him to see running down a ramp in a new light and vice versa, a light that seems influenced by the circulation of Newtonian ideas, albeit more implicitly than in Letisha's case. Both the car and his running became yoked together as experiences of "going down and down," which "make(s) your legs go faster." Indeed, in this moment, real cars, toy cars, and bodies running were folded into one image, as Elton simultaneously rolled his hands one over the other in a gesture that fused both wheels turning and legs churning. His hand motion synthesized these experiences into the same pattern of downhill motion.

In Elton's hands, these two worlds—the toy car on the ramp and his body running down a ramp—interpenetrated in a way that made the familiar experience of running down a hill seem strange in the light of new, emergent possibilities of meaning, new ways of seeing. Surely Elton already knew in some sense that as he ran down a ramp he got faster. But here, like Letisha, he seemed to experience it in a new way, to be exploring it from a new perspective, to be noticing new aspects (Wittgenstein, 1953). Indeed, Elton's way of bringing these two instances of motion together seems to have illuminated for him something about the experience of going "down and down" in relation to "going faster." This comes through in the way he explicitly linked the experience of covering distance on the ramp ("when you get down and down") with increasing speed ("it makes your legs go faster"). He seems to have developed a feel for how this kind of trip unfolds, as one involving some ongoing sort of change as one goes "down and down," and a feel for what "go faster" means in these two now fully linked situations. Like Letisha and Stacey in the previous class, Elton explored the ramp as a place in which to bring together various situations and to bring to life new ways of seeing these, that is, as belonging to the same family of motion, in which both cars and people get faster and faster as they progress down an incline.

Synopsis of Subsequent Investigation

Spurred on by the generativity in Elton's contribution, Ms. Pothier elicited other children's experiences with motion down a ramp. Their accounts of these experiences turned out to be richly varied. Like Elton's, these accounts did not merely replicate the given of their prior experience but created new possibilities for noticing connections between aspects of change in the speed of their bodies and the toy car, among them: a pattern of increasing speed from slow to fast to faster, which one boy described as a reversible pattern of walking, jogging, and running, depending on whether you were going down or coming off the ramp; the effort they needed to exert to slow themselves down as they neared the bottom of a ramp; and the difficulty of stopping at the bottom.

Under Ms. Pothier's guidance, the children built on their initial intuitions and insights to investigate more closely the toy car's downhill motion and analogous motions of their bodies. In their initial explorations, a few students noticed that speed was related to the force of impact when the car collided with some other, fixed object (e.g., a ruler, one's hand). Ms. Pothier built on these noticings to create a systematic and publicly shared way to assess the car's changing speed, which she called a "speed test." She introduced a much longer ($\sim 7'$) ramp to allow for a longer trip and easier comparison of speeds, and attached a length of Hot Wheels™ track to the ramp to better control the car's motion. She had the children hold a small wooden block at successive locations on the ramp—initially near the top, middle, and bottom—to stop the car's motion. The children worked with this "block test" in whole-group and small-group contexts for several classes. We briefly describe their work in order to give some flavor of how this investigation continued to take shape and how the children's understanding of the toy car's motion continued to develop.

The "block test" allowed the students to collect multiple kinds of data on the car's speed. Besides being able to feel differences in the force of impact as they moved the block to successively lower locations on the ramp, they were able to observe how the block and their fingers responded to the car's impact and to notice differences in the sound made by the impact. They easily associated relative changes in each effect to corresponding changes in the car's speed. Alicia, for example, said, "I think it's [the car] sort of the fastest down here [near bottom of ramp], because it's knocking (the block) all the way down to the end... Right at the beginning it was only knocking my finger a little bit forward." They brought strong intuitions that the force of impact increases with speed. In these ways, the block test provided the students with a perceptual practice for "highlighting" (Goodwin, 1994) the car's speed at different points in kinesthetic, visual, and audible form. It helped to make visible and specify their emerging intuition that the car's speed was increasing positively and continuously as it traveled down the ramp.

What sense did the students make of their encounters with the block test? In practice, the block test yielded a series of successive "snapshots" of the car's instantaneous speed at three or more discrete points during the car's trip. During the first of many classes organized around the use of the block test and interpretation of its results, one boy, Ken, commented on his experience holding the block at successive positions. He focused especially on the impact at the bottom, which was visibly greater than at the other positions as the car knocked the block out from under his finger and sent it a short distance across the rug. Ms. Pothier asked Ken to report on his experience:

Ken: I sort of felt when the car hit it, I sort of felt the um block go up a little and hit my other finger and um I think that—I think that means that the more the car goes down the track [*dragging his finger down the track from about 2/3 of the way down the track to near the end*] the more it gets faster.

Here Ken, in an echo of Elton's "going down and down," interpreted the block test results to mean that the car's speed increases continuously as a function of the distance it travels down the ramp: "I think that means that the more the car goes down the track, the more it gets faster." As he spoke, he dragged his finger from an area between the middle and bottom test locations down to the third and final spot, to emphasize the car's motion as an *ongoing* process of "get(ting) faster." Merging car and body in this way, Ken extrapolated from the three discrete data points used to perform the block test to fill in the positions between those points with a continuous series of incremental speed changes, as he would have observed had the class applied a series of block tests to the whole length of the ramp.

The students worked with the block test as well as other speed tests for several weeks to refine their sense of how the car moved on the ramp. At the end of this sequence of classes, many of the children gave evidence that they were thinking of the car's motion down the ramp in terms of continuously and positively increasing speed. In a discussion they had toward the end of May, the students shared their views of the car's motion down the ramp. Here is a sample of what they said:

"...the more the car goes down the track, the more it gets faster." [Bill]

"We discussed [in their partner work] that it was fastest at the end, because the speed builds up at each place." [Juan]

"At the beginning it [the car] is just getting speed, in the middle it can still get speed because it has more time, but at the end there's no time left to get more speed." [Tina]

"I think it [the car's speed] builds up at each place. It goes up from the beginning to the end." [Gregory]

The children came to see the car's speed as continuously and positively changing. These students, like Ken before them, suggested that "getting faster" is a *function* of aspects of its ongoing motion (e.g., how far down the ramp the car travels, how long it has been moving, successive positions). Their accounts constituted for them a new language for describing downhill motion, a new way of seeing what literally cannot be seen. In this sense, these later accounts of downhill motion seem as much a *model* of a kind of motion as they are inferences based in their observations and experiences. Having established this pattern of motion for the car on the ramp, Ms. Pothier and the children went on to explore it further in light of Newton's ideas. They grappled with gravity as the force responsible for the car's downward acceleration.

DISCUSSION

We opened this chapter by questioning the value of a dichotomous view of modes of thought in the study of human experience and learning. In such treatments, the mode of "everyday thinking or experience" is viewed negatively, as lacking the logic, rigor, abstractness, power, and precision of the more highly valued mode of "scientific thinking." In one of the more trenchant critiques of this tradition, Lave (1988) argued that "everyday thinking and experience" is for the most part viewed residually, in contrast with "scientific modes of thought," rather than as a phenomenon in its own right. It is also understood as largely static, residing in one's past, rather than being constructed in the present as an immediate relation between persons acting and the social world within which they live.

In this study, we have taken the dichotomy of "everyday experience" and "scientific thinking and knowing" to be problematic. In the traditional contrast, "everyday experience" is viewed negatively, as a residual, static storehouse of past, fully digested encounters not possessing analytic power. Through our analyses of the activity and talk of Letisha, Stacey, and Elton, we have sought to show that these children's accounts of their experiences in the world were not mere replications of those experiences, but instead newly interpreted, in-the-present encounters, shaped by emerging insights, experiences, and intentions. Indeed, through their actions—both physical and analytic—in and on the world of the toy car and ramp, these children generated various possibilities of meaning for motion down an incline. In the process, they subverted the ordinary meaning of their life experience (e.g., real cars, baby carriages, hills, and ramps); they recast objects and unfolding events in new terms, creating new possibilities for analysis and understanding (e.g., a car's steering wheel as a force causing a change in motion, one's body on a ramp experiencing the same pattern of motion as a car on a hill); they played with outcomes, creating new structures for comparison across many situations of motion (e.g., comparing different orientations of the ramp) and populating Newton's ideas in varied ways (e.g., seeing change in motion as encompassing many possibilities, including an increase in speed, a negation of motion as in a stop, a change in direction from up to down, increasing speed as a function of distance traveled).

The putative distinction between "everyday" and "scientific" comes apart, in our view, in the face of accounts such as those presented here that detail the complex ways in which the children brought into contact the world of their lived experience, the world of the ramp, and the world of Newtonian ideas. Bakhtin (1981) called this process of bringing different perspectives into contact "interanimation," which is rooted in the fundamentally heteroglossic nature of language. This means that within a given national language (e.g., English), there are always many different ways of speaking, each reflecting different ways of conceptualizing, representing, and evaluating the world.

> (A)ll languages of heteroglossia...are specific points of view on the world, forms for conceptualizing the world in words, specific world views, each characterized by its own objects, meanings and values. (Bakhtin, 1981, p. 292)

Newtonian physics is thus a language in this sense, a specific way of conceptualizing, representing, and evaluating the world. Likewise, our everyday ways of talking about cars, brakes, and steering wheels is a language in this sense. Bakhtin (1981) illustrated this point with an admittedly oversimplified image of a hypothetical peasant:

> Thus an illiterate peasant, miles away from any urban center, naively immersed in an unmoving and for him unshakable everyday world, nevertheless lived in several language systems: he prayed to God in one language (Church Slavonic), sang songs in another, spoke to his family in a third and, when he began to dictate petitions to the local authorities through a scribe, he tried speaking yet a fourth language (the official–literate language, "paper" language). All these are *different languages*... But these languages were not dialogically coordinated in the linguistic consciousness of the peasant; he passed from one to the other without thinking, automatically: each was indisputably in its own place, and the place of each was indisputable. He was not yet able to regard one language (and the verbal world corresponding to it) through the eyes of another language (that is, the language of everyday life and the everyday world with the language of prayer or song, of vice versa). (Bakhtin, 1981, p. 296)

This image is oversimplified in that a total absence of dialogic coordination in the linguistic consciousness of the peasant is not really possible. For Bakhtin, dialogism is the necessary condition of language use and meaning in a world dominated by heteroglossia. It indexes the ways in which languages are always already in contact, attracting accents and meanings from each other in ways that may be complementary, contradictory, revelatory, and so on. Bakhtin helps us see the nature of this "dialogized heteroglossia" (Morson & Emerson, 1990), again through the experience of his peasant.

> As soon as a critical interanimation of languages began to occur in the consciousness of our peasant, as soon as it became clear that these were not only various different languages but even internally variegated languages, that the ideological systems and approaches to the world that were indissolubly connected with these languages contradicted each other and in no way could live in peace and quiet with one another—then the inviolability and predetermined quality of these languages came to an end, and the necessity of actively choosing one's orientation among them began. (Bakhtin, 1981, p. 296)

Let us focus on this idea of interanimation, specifically, how it relates to the learning of Letisha, Stacey, and Elton. As a word, "interanimation" is not especially felicitous. It is not as well-known a term as some others found in Bakhtin's corpus to which, as we explained above, it is fundamentally related (e.g. dialogic, heteroglossia). Yet in its main parts it conveys a great deal: first, the kernel of "animation," which suggests bringing to life or filling with life, and second, the prefix "inter," which suggests between-ness or mutuality. When Letisha forged "a turned car" as a new object for analysis, she was operating at the boundary of the mundane world of real cars and steering wheels and the specialized world of Newtonian ideas. She brought to life a new object subject to a specific form of analysis. At the same time, she explored this Newtonian way of conceptualizing, representing, and evaluating the world for its analytic potential. She was in both of these senses actively orienting herself among these various languages, inhabiting as well as evaluating them. Elton did this as well, as he noticed and analyzed how a toy car's motion on a ramp and his own motion running down a hill were similarly patterned.

As we are using it, interanimation means bringing into contact realms of experience and ideas, ways of making sense of the world that are not normally in contact (e.g., baby carriages and Newton's Laws) or that are viewed as not capable of productive contact (e.g., as in the dichotomies formulated around modes of thinking discussed at the outset of this chapter). Through a process of interanimation, meanings that are otherwise taken for granted as understood (e.g., Goody's folk taxonomies), whether one's lived experience with downhill motion or a scientific law, are destabilized. In these encounters, the engaged realms of experience and ideas become objects of inquiry *for* each other, as they did for Letisha, Stacey, and Elton. In such a process of critical interanimation, new possibilities of meaning, new objects, new ways of seeing, new questions, new ways of bringing order into the complexity of experience are brought to life.

Interanimation, therefore, denotes a process whereby a person comes to regard one way of conceptualizing, representing, and evaluating the world through the eyes of another, each characterized by its own objects, meanings, and values. As such, it resists the strong temptation to dichotomize modes of thinking or being. As human beings, we inhabit many such ways of seeing, talking, acting, reading, writing, and valuing as we go about our daily lives. In the sciences, as in any academic domain, learners are asked, usually not explicitly, to orient themselves actively among varied—sometimes conflict-ing, sometimes complementary—ways of conceptualizing, representing, and evaluating the world and the possibilities these present for making sense of the world. Interanimation thus involves what we view as a creative struggle—the active coordination of different ways of seeing, talking, valuing in the course of learning in a domain such as physics. In the study reported here, children actively coordinated their "familiar, everyday experience" with downhill mo-tion and "unfamiliar, scientific ideas" in the context of inquiry into the motion of a toy car rolling down a ramp. In their efforts to coordinate these worlds, real cars, bodies running, toy cars, baby carriages, hills, ramps, brakes, hands, and scientific ideas about motion served as sources of insight for each other, with perspectives, questions, and details from each giving shape to the emer-gent ways in which the children conceptualized, represented, and evaluated the nature of motion down an incline. As their work attests, the presumed boundary between "everyday experience" and "disciplinary ideas" blurred as the children both inhabited and analyzed the hybrid worlds they had created, opening up new paths to meaning and new ways of seeing in the process.

We conclude by reflecting further on Letisha and drawing out some of the wider implications of this study, as we see them. Letisha was repeating second grade the year of this study. Overall, she was not seen by the school as a "strong" student. She is African American, from a working class household. She had been identified by institutional practices as needing special attention for what were deemed "language difficulties," an all-too-frequent classification of African American children from low-income or working class households. We noted in the introduction that from a discontinuity point of view, children from historically underserved communities may be especially disadvantaged because their "everyday" experiences and ways with words are viewed as being the furthest from—or incompatible with—those conventionally valued in science (O. Lee & Fradd, 1996; O. Lee, Fradd, & Sutman, 1995). We might wonder, then, how Letisha's expansive way of thinking about downhill motion might be understood by teachers and researchers inclined to see learning through the lens of traditional dichotomies? Indeed, in presentations we have made of the Letisha and Stacey episode, some in the audience have valued the contributions of Stacey and Letisha quite differently. Some have, for example, viewed Stacey as being explicitly focused on the task at hand (a positive feature) and Letisha as going outside the boundaries of the task (a negative feature). Some have suggested that Stacey was working with "more abstract" concepts than Letisha, an interpretation entirely unsupported in the analysis presented here. Interpretations like these can have very large, enduring consequences for children, for how they are taught, how they are perceived, and how they perceive themselves as learners and thinkers, especially if their sense-making efforts are repeatedly judged as not centrally relevant to the academic matters at hand.

Our analysis of Letisha's work in the focal episode leads, without question, in another direction. But we—the authors of this chapter, both teacher and researchers—had to work at learning to see and hear the intellectual substance in Letisha's talk; our understanding did not come automatically. Both Ms. Pothier and the researchers, all Euro-American with advanced education degrees, found Letisha hard to understand initially; we found it difficult to follow her reasoning. She often seemed to be answering a different question from the one asked. However, rather than assuming that the problem resided in Letisha—in something about the way she thought or spoke, in some deficit in her background of life experience, or in the incompatibility of her ways of knowing with those valued in the sciences—we assumed that the problem resided in *our* norms of interpretation, in *our* assumptions and expectations regarding what counted as a meaningful response to the teacher's questions; in other words, in our own trained inability to see and hear the intellectual substance of Letisha's discourse.

We began at this point to examine Letisha's classroom talk closely, as well as our responses to it, by studying videotapes and transcripts from the unfolding investigation. The more we focused on the sense she was making and its potentially deep connections to the scientific matters at hand and the more we opened our assumptions of what counts as scientific to scrutiny, the clearer Letisha came into view as a big, rather than muddled, thinker, as a child who went at questions from an integrated, often speculative, "big idea" perspective in order to make sense of the relations among ideas, objects, and events she encountered in her life and in school. Letisha engaged with ideas she encountered in school through what we now understand to be a process of critical interanimation, analyzing and exploring their potential meaning across the many settings of her life, which initially had confused us; she worked at seeing one way of conceptualizing the world through the eyes of another. With this view of Letisha in hand, we became able to see and hear her as a child who sought to be engaged intellectually with the large questions and conceptual frameworks of the domain of study. Ms. Pothier who, prior to our investigation of Letisha's sense-making was concerned about what she was actually understanding, tended to ask her increasingly narrower questions to assess what she knew or did not know, shifted her way of engaging with Letisha. She now elicited more expansive comment from her, as she did with other students she saw as academically competent. As a result, Ms. Pothier also had more access to Letisha's thinking and concerns. As Letisha expressed her ideas more expansively, she also opened up for others—the teacher, other students, the researchers—perspectives on the subject matter of profound significance to the discipline. We see in detail how she did this for Stacey, who, we note, was by all conventional measures an academically successful student.

Thus, the question of the intellectual value of "everyday experience" and "everyday ways of knowing or talking" is not merely a theoretical matter. How we, as researchers and teachers, view the sense-making resources that children bring from their backgrounds of life experience will have very real consequences for how children are able to participate in science. As we have tried to show, Letisha brought various realms of experience and ideas into critical interanimation. She sought out the connections between these and sought to see them as part of an encompassing view of the physical world of motion. The "everyday" world of her experience, far from being a barrier to understanding Newton's ideas, was a profoundly generative source of objects, events, questions, insights, and construals, which she constructed as part of her encounter with the toy car on the ramp and Newtonian ideas. At the same time, she literally and figuratively took hold of Newtonian ideas as a way to recast the objects and events of her lived experience. She populated these ideas with meaning and intention, creatively inventing ways of talking about motion and ways of "forcing" a change in motion. In so doing, she explored the power of these ideas to explain various experiences of motion. Stacey and Elton explored the toy car's motion on the ramp in similar ways. For her part, Ms. Pothier encouraged the expansive and analytic orientation the children took to their lived experience and Newton's ideas in their study of the physics of motion. She did not bracket their experience as a mere preface to the main work, but engaged it as a central object of inquiry on the same plane with Newton's ideas.

The task learners face is to populate new ideas they encounter with their own intentions and accents, while also coming to grips with the contextual overtones—situated meanings and uses—with which they are already saturated, such as those valued in the discipline (Bakhtin, 1981). This process of appropriation involves the active coordination of multiple ways of conceptualizing, representing, and evaluating the world. It underlies what we recognize as learning. In probing meaning in and across varied contexts, perspectives, objects, events, and ideas, the children in this study began to appropriate Newton's ideas in just this way. Neither Newton's ideas nor their lived experience uniquely disciplined their perception. Rather, their understanding and questions emerged in the interanimation between these, proof of which are the hybrid worlds they created on the ramp, living in them as well as standing outside them in order to populate them with meaning.

ACKNOWLEDGMENTS

The research reported here was supported by grants from the National Science Foundation (REC-0106194, ESI-9555712), the U.S. Department of Education, Office of Educational Research and Improvement (Cooperative Agreement No. R305A60007-98 and R306A60001-96), and the Spencer Foundation. The data presented, statements made, and views expressed are solely the responsibility of the authors. No endorsement by the sponsoring organizations should be inferred.

The authors thank Gary Goldstein and Tracy Noble for the ideas and insights they contributed to the early stages of this analysis. We also thank Cindy Ballenger, Folashade Cromwell, Ann Rosebery, and Jesse Solomon for their very helpful comments on earlier drafts. Lastly, we wish to acknowledge the children, who contributed much more than they know to our thinking about science, children, discourse, culture, learning, and teaching.

REFERENCES

Bakhtin, M. M. (1981). *The dialogic imagination: Four essays*. Austin, TX: University of Texas Press.

Ballenger, C. (1997). Social identities, moral narratives, scientific argumentation: Science talk in a bilingual classroom. *Language and Education, 11*(1), 1–14.

Ballenger, C. (1999). *Teaching other people's children: Literacy and learning in a bilingual classroom*. New York: Teachers College Press.

Ballenger, C. (2000). Bilingual in two senses. In Z. Beykont (Ed.), *Lifting every voice: Pedagogy and the politics of bilingualism* (pp. 95–112). Cambridge, MA: Harvard Education Publishing Group.

Ballenger, C., & Rosebery, A. (2003). What counts as teacher research? Continuing the conversation. *Teachers College Record, 105*(2), 297–314.

Brookline Teacher Research Seminar. (2004). *Regarding talk: Teacher research on language and learning*. New York: Teachers College Press.

Conant, F., Rosebery, A., Warren, B., & Hudicourt-Barnes, J. (2001). The sound of drums. In E. McIntyre, A. Rosebery, & N. Gonzalez (Eds.), *Building bridges: Linking home and school* (pp. 51–60). Portsmouth, NH: Heinemann.

diSessa, A. (1993). Toward an epistemology of physics. *Cognition and Instruction, 10*(283), 105–225.

diSessa, A., Hammer, D., Sherin, B., & Kolpakowski, T. (1991). Inventing graphing: Meta-representational expertise in children. *Journal of Mathematical Behavior, 10*, 117–160.

Education Development Center. (1997). *Balls and ramps, an elementary insights hands-on inquiry science curriculum*. Dubuque, IA: Kendall-Hunt.

Erickson, F. (2002). Culture and human development. *Human Development, 45*(4), 299–306.

Gallas, K. (1994). *The languages of learning*. New York: Teachers College Press.

Gee, J. P. (1990). *Social linguistics and literacies: Ideology in discourses*. London: Falmer.

Gee, J. P., & Clinton, K. (2000). An African-American child's "science talk": Co-construction of meaning from the perspective of multiple discourses. In M. Gallego & S. Hollingsworth (Eds.), *Challenging a single standard: Multiple perspectives on literacy*. Norwood, NJ: Lawrence Erlbaum Associates.

Gonzalez, N. (1999). What will we do when culture doesn't exist anymore? *Anthropology and Education Quarterly, 30*(4), 431–435.

Goodwin, C. (1994). Professional vision. *American Anthropologist, 96*(3), 606–633.

Goody, J. (1977). *The domestication of the savage mind*. Cambridge, UK: Cambridge University Press.

Halliday, M. A. K., & Martin, J. R. (1993). *Writing science: Literary and discursive power*. Pittsburgh: University of Pittsburgh Press.

Hudicourt-Barnes, J. (2003). The use of argumentation in Haitian Creole science classrooms. *Harvard Educational Review, 73*(1), 73–93.

Hymes, D. (1996). *Ethnography, linguistics, narrative inequality.* London: Taylor & Francis.

Ingold, T. (1994). Introduction to culture. In T. Ingold (Ed.), *Companion encyclopedia of anthropology* (pp. 329–349). London: Routledge.

Lave, J. (1988). *Cognition in practice.* Cambridge, UK: Cambridge University Press.

Leacock, E. P. (1972). Abstract versus concrete speech: A false dichotomy. In C. Cazden, V. John, & D. Hymes (Eds.), *Functions of language in the classroom* (pp. 111–134). New York: Teachers College Press.

Lee, C. D. (1993). *Signifying as a scaffold for literary interpretation: The pedagogical implications of an African American discourse genre.* Urbana, IL: National Council of Teachers of English.

Lee, C. D. (2000). Signifying in the zone of proximal development. In C. D. Lee & P. Smagorinsky (Eds.), *Vygotskian perspectives on literacy research* (pp. 191–225). Cambridge, UK: Cambridge University Press.

Lee, C. D. (2002). Interrogating race and ethnicity as constructs in the examination of cultural processes in developmental research. *Human Development, 45*(4), 282–290.

Lee, O., & Fradd, S. (1996). Interactional patterns of linguistically diverse students and teachers: Insights for promoting science learning. *Linguistics and Education, 8,* 269–297.

Lee, O., Fradd, S., & Sutman, F. (1995). Science knowledge and cognitive strategy use among culturally and linguistically diverse students. *Journal of Research in Science Teaching, 32*(8), 797–816.

Lemke, J. L. (1990). *Talking science: Language, learning and values.* Norwood, NJ: Ablex.

McCloskey, M., Caramazza, A., & Green, B. (1980). Curvilinear motion in the absence of external forces: Naïve beliefs about the motion of objects. *Science, 210,* 1139–1141.

McDermott, L., Rosenquist, M., & van Zee, E. (1987). Student difficulties in connecting graphs and physics: Examples from kinematics. *American Journal of Physics, 55,* 503–513.

Michaels, S., & Sohmer, R. (2000). Narratives and inscriptions: Cultural tools, power and powerful sensemaking. In B. Cope & M. Kalantzis (Eds.), *Multiliteracies* (pp. 267–288). London: Routledge.

Minstrell, J. (1989). Teaching science for understanding. In L. Resnick & L. Klopfer, (Eds.), *Toward the thinking curriculum: Current cognitive research* (pp. 131–149). Alexandria, VA: Association for Supervision and Curriculum Development.

Moll, L. (2000). Inspired by Vygotsky: Ethnographic experiments in education. In C. D. Lee & P. Smagorinsky (Eds.), *Vygotskian perspectives on literacy research: Constructing meaning through collaborative inquiry* (pp. 256–268). Cambridge, UK: Cambridge University Press.

Morson, G. S., & Emerson, C. (1990). *Mikhail Bakhtin: Creation of a prosaics.* Stanford, CA: Stanford University Press.

Myers, G. (1985). Text as knowledge claims: The social construction of two biologists' articles. *Social Studies of Science, 15,* 593–630.

Rogoff, B. (2003). *The cultural nature of human development.* New York: Oxford University Press.

Rosebery, A. S., & Warren, B. (1999). *Supporting teachers to develop theories of children in the particular.* Paper presented at the Conference on Teacher Change, National Center for Improving Student Learning and Achievement, University of Wisconsin, Madison.

Rosebery, A., Warren, B., Ballenger, C., & Ogonowski, M. (in press). The generative potential of students' everyday knowledge in learning science. In T. Carpenter &

T. Romberg (Eds.), *Mathematics and science matters*. Mahwah, NJ: Lawrence Erlbaum Associates.

Smith, J. P., diSessa, A., & Roschelle, J. (1993). Misconceptions reconceived: A constructivist analysis of knowledge in transition. *The Journal of the Learning Sciences*, *3*(2), 115–163.

Viennot, L. (1979). Spontaneous reasoning in elementary dynamics. *European Journal of Science Education*, *1*, 205–221.

Warren, B., Ballenger, C., Ogonowski, M., Rosebery, A., & Hudicourt-Barnes, J. (2001). Rethinking diversity in learning science: The logic of everyday sense-making. *Journal of Research in Science Teaching*, *38*, 529–552.

Warren, B., & Ogonowski, M. (1998). *From knowledge to knowing: An inquiry into teacher learning in science*. Center for the Development of Teaching Paper Series. Newton, MA: Education Development Center.

Warren, B., & Ogonowski, M. (2001). Embodied imagining: A study of adult learning in physics. Paper presented at the Annual Meeting of the American Educational Research Association, Seattle, April.

Warren, B., Ogonowski, M., & Pothier, S. (2000). Learning to see the world through Newton's Laws. Paper presented at the Annual Meeting of the American Educational Research Association, New Orleans.

Warren, B., Pothier, S., Rosebery, A., & Ogonowski, M. (2003). "It's everywhere on that line!" Children's inquiry into the dialogic nature of meaning. Paper presented at the Annual Meeting of the American Educational Research Association, Chicago.

Warren, B., & Rosebery, A. (1996). "This question is just too, too easy!": Perspectives from the classroom on accountability in science. In L. Schauble & R. Glaser (Eds.), *Innovations in learning: New environments for education* (pp. 97–125). Hillsdale: Lawrence Erlbaum Associates.

Wittgenstein, L. (1953). *Philosophical investigations*. New York: Macmillan.

III
Concerns of Curriculum Designers as They Develop Activities Intended to Focus on Everyday Matters of Science and Mathematics

Introduction to Part II

Regardless of how researchers have portrayed teaching over the years, teachers are intimately acquainted with the dynamic, uncertain aspects of its character. To borrow Lucy Suchman's (1987) evocative metaphor, in order to "navigate" the ever-shifting waters of everyday and disciplinary matters, teachers must draw on a wide range of resources and be ready to improvise as need be.

It is not that teachers necessarily find themselves in uncharted or even unexpected waters. If a teacher is fortunate, she has access to science and mathematics curricula that provide both a sensible path through the ideas and practices of the discipline as well as varied and useful ways to think about teaching and learning, that is, what Shulman (1986) and others have called "pedagogical content knowledge."

Nor is it that she comes to this pedagogical trip unprepared. Unless it is the beginning of the school year, she will most likely have worked hard to get to know her students along a number of dimensions—who they are, what they know, and what they need to learn, among others. And she will use this knowledge, sometimes consciously and sometimes not, to anticipate the various twists and turns a given lesson might take with them as it unfolds. Furthermore, every teacher brings her own individual history with these waters to the teaching event. If she is an experienced teacher, she will likely draw on her memories of earlier trips taken with other students. Her history will also include her own experiences learning in the discipline. For example, she might have memories of a particular childhood experience that inspired in her a lifelong passion for the domain, or a sense, based on her own learning, of activities or connections that may be potentially fruitful for her students.

Teachers who, as Deborah Ball (1997) has written, are both "responsible to the curriculum and responsive to students," know that unpredictability and messiness are part and parcel of the teaching/learning dynamic. Some might even say—on a good day—that this uncertainty is, in large part, what makes teaching exciting, what keeps it fresh.

It is important to note that this uncertainty does not typically lead to chaos. Experienced teachers rarely create random learning encounters for their students. What is it that experienced teachers do before, during, and after a lesson to manage the complexity that is inherent in any given classroom encounter? How do they negotiate the uncertain waters of everyday and disciplinary matters? Each of the chapters in this section attempts to address these and related issues from unique yet complementary angles.

Taken together, these chapters explore fundamental issues related to where the responsibility and authority for learning resides in complex classroom events. And not surprisingly, in doing so they raise as many questions as they answer. This is perhaps one of the perogatives—and consequences—of trying to map terrain that is neither static nor stable. In their chapters, McClain, Forman and Ansell, and Blanton and Kaput raise questions such as:

- In complex classroom events, who decides what is to be learned and how it is to be learned? The teacher? The student(s)?
- What happens when the "agendas" of participants differ?
- How can teachers "prepare" themselves to teach a given lesson?
- What should a teacher do when he or she finds that the goals of a particular lesson conflict with norms of "everyday" practice?
- What opportunities to teach and to learn are lost when complex classroom events are viewed through disciplinary rather than students' perspectives? Can these sources of knowledge be viewed from complementary rather than dichotomous angles?

In short, by adopting the teacher's point of view, these chapters begin to chart the dynamic waters that make up complex classroom events in mathematics and the sciences.

REFERENCES

Ball, D. L. (1997). What do students know? Facing challenges of distance, context, and desire in trying to hear children. In Biddle, T., Good, T., and Goodson, I. (Eds.), *International handbook on teachers and teaching* (Vol. 2, pp. 769–817). Dordrecht, Netherlands: Kluwer Press.

Shulman, L. (1986). Those who understand. Knowledge growth in teaching. *Educational Researcher, 15*(2), 4–14.

Suchman, L. (1987). *Plans and situated actions.* New York: Cambridge University Press.

5

The Mathematics Behind the Graph: Discussions of Data

Kay McClain
Vanderbilt University

A focus on the importance of teachers' content knowledge has spawned a variety of research aimed at highlighting the mathematics that teachers teach (Ball, 1993; Fennema et al., 1996; Grossman, 1990; Grossman, Wilson, & Schulman, 1989; Lampert, 1990; Ma, 1999; McClain, in press, 2002; National Research Council, 2001; Schifter, 1990; Stigler & Hiebert, 1999; Simon, 2000, 1995). In particular, Simon (2000) has called for models of teaching that take account of the diverse and complex issues involved in successfully orchestrating classrooms, including content knowledge. Ball (1993) described balancing the tensions in teaching mathematics as keeping an ear on the students and an eye on the mathematical horizon. Similar characterizations can be found in the work of Lampert (1990) and others (Carpenter & Fennema, 1991; Ma, 1999; McClain, 2002). The commonality of this work is a focus on the importance of a deep understanding of the mathematics that is taught as a necessary condition of effective teaching. This mathematical understanding makes it possible to simultaneously build from students' contributions while staying focused on the mathematical agenda (McClain, 2002). The process of moving between the students' current ways of reasoning and the mathematical agenda is characterized by Simon's (1997) Mathematics Teaching Cycle, which entails the interplay of (1) the teacher's knowledge, (2) a conjectured learning trajectory, and (3) interaction with students. The focus on teachers' knowledge includes not only knowledge of students and their current ways of reasoning, but also knowledge of the patterns and structures of mathematics that are the focus of the students' activity. As a result, the Mathematics Teaching Cycle offers a way to organize the melange of activities to which teachers must attend while they manage their classrooms.

My purpose in this chapter is to build on this literature to highlight the importance of attending to the mathematics that underlies deliberately facilitated whole-class discussions in supporting students' mathematical development. In doing so, I will present an episode taken from an eighth-grade classroom in which my colleagues and I conducted a 12-week classroom design experiment during the fall semester of 1998.[1] During the course of the design experiment, the research team took responsibility for all aspects of the class including the teaching. In particular, I assumed primary responsibility for teaching and am the teacher featured in the episode that is the focus of analysis in this chapter.[2] The goal of the design experiment was to support students' development of ways to reason about bivariate data as they developed statistical understandings related to exploratory data analysis. This design experiment was a follow-up to an earlier classroom design experiment conducted with some of the same students during the fall semester of the previous year. Over the course of the two design experiments, our goal was to investigate ways to proactively support middle school students' development of statistical reasoning. The design experiment conducted with the students as seventh graders focused on univariate data sets and had as its goal supporting students' understanding of the notion of distribution (for a detailed analysis of the seventh-grade classroom design experiment, see Cobb, 1999; McClain, Cobb, & Gravemeijer, 2000). Our goal for the eighth-grade classroom was to build on this earlier work and extend it to bivariate data sets (for a detailed analysis of the eighth-grade classroom design experiment, see Cobb, McClain, & Gravemeijer, 2003; McClain, 2002; McClain & Cobb, 2001).

The particular focus of this analysis is on the importance of the teacher's understanding of the mathematics and how that contributes to effective

---

[1]Members of the research team were Paul Cobb, Kay McClain, Koeno Gravemeijer, Lynn Hodge, Jose Cortina, Maggie McGatha, Carrie Tzou, and Nora Shuart-Farris.

[2]The way that the research team functions while conducting a classroom design experiment involves one team member taking primary responsibility for the teaching. However, on numerous occasions other members contribute to whole-class conversations by asking clarifying questions. In addition, additional members of the research team circulate around the room to monitor students' activity as they work individually or in small groups.

whole-class discussions. I analyze how my understanding of the mathematical intent of both the instructional sequence and the specific task featured in this chapter contributed to a whole-class discussion focused on significant mathematical concepts. Within the analysis, there is an implied relationship between the negotiation of classroom social and sociomathematical norms and the students' mathematical development. The teacher's role in this process is both to continually support the negotiation of norms for productive mathematical argumentation and to ensure that the discussions have mathematical validity with respect to the overarching goals for the sequence of instructional tasks. The image that results is that of the teacher constantly judging the nature and quality of the discussion against the mathematical agenda in order to ensure that the mathematical issues under discussion offer means of supporting the students' development. For this reason, students are selected to share their solutions so that significant mathematical issues can emerge in the course of discussion. This implies a proactive role on the part of the teacher that includes careful monitoring of individual and small-group work so that informed decisions can be made about appropriate next steps. The teacher's goal therefore involves working to understand the varied and diverse solutions that students are developing to solve the task. The information gained from understanding students' solutions is then used as the basis of the teacher's decision-making process in the subsequent whole-class discussion. This understanding of the students' solutions provides the teacher with the ability to orchestrate a whole-class discussion in a manner that simultaneously builds from students' ways of reasoning while supporting the mathematical agenda. This view of whole-class discussion stands in stark contrast to an open-ended session where all students are allowed to share their solutions without concern for potential mathematical contributions.

Although this chapter will focus on only one episode, it is intended to provide a paradigmatic example of a whole-class discussion orchestrated around specific mathematical goals. This model of classroom activity is grounded not only in the premise that the sequence of instructional tasks is developed to support the emergence of a conjectured learning trajectory, but also that the teacher plays a central role in guiding and orchestrating the classroom. In this way, the discussion serves to provide opportunities for students to extend their current understandings as they explore significant mathematical concepts. The teacher's ability to effectively guide and orchestrate mathematical discussions is contingent on a deep understanding of the mathematics that underlies both the task and the sequence. It is on this issue that I focus my analysis.

In the following sections of this chapter, I first outline the intent of the instructional sequence used in the eighth-grade classroom. I then describe the setting. Against this background I present an episode intended to highlight the importance of deliberately facilitated whole-class discussions. I conclude by returning to the conjectured learning trajectory and the importance of the mathematics that guides its emergence in the classroom.

INSTRUCTIONAL SEQUENCE

The particular ways of working in the classroom that my colleagues and I employ fall under the general heading of *design research*. Design research involves cycles of research and development where ongoing classroom-based research feeds back to inform instructional design decisions in a cyclic manner. As part of this process, prior to entering the classroom the research team develops a conjectured learning trajectory that serves to guide the development of the instructional sequence. This trajectory is a conjecture about the path of the mathematical development of the classroom community. It focuses on pivotal mathematical issues that the research team hopes will emerge into classroom mathematical practices (cf. Cobb, Stephan, McClain, & Gravemeijer, 2001). The sequence as it is sketched out prior to entering the classroom is provisional at best and is constantly being revised in light of informal assessments of students' current ways of reasoning. In this way, ongoing, informal analyses serve to ground daily instructional decisions as we work toward a mathematical endpoint (cf. Gravemeijer, 1998).

In planning for the eighth-grade classroom design experiment, it was important for the research team to take the mathematical endpoints of the seventh-grade design experiment as starting points. I should therefore clarify that by the end of the seventh-grade design experiment, almost all of the students could reason multiplicatively about univariate distributions of data (cf. Cobb, 1999; McClain, Cobb, & Gravemeijer, 2000). For example, interviews conducted shortly after the seventh-grade design experiment was completed document that most students could readily interpret graphs of *unequal* data sets organized into equal interval widths (analogue of histograms) and into four equal groups (analogue of box-and-whiskers plots) in terms of trends and patterns in the distribution of the data points.

With regard to the endpoints of the eighth-grade sequence, the research team intended that the students would interpret standard graphs of bivariate data sets such as scatter plots as texts about the situations from which the data were generated (e.g., the number of years of education and salary of a group of males). If this occurred, the students would conjecture that measures of two attributes of a situation that were judged relevant with respect to a question or issue covaried in some way, and that the nature of their relationship could be determined by analyzing the scatter plot. The research team therefore hoped that the students would come to interpret the cloud of dots on a scatter plot as a bivariate distribution.

Our initial goal for the eighth-grade sequence was that the students would come to inscribe two measures of a single case as a dot in two-dimensional space (e.g., years of education and salary). The initial instructional activities therefore involved the students developing their own inscriptions of two sets of measures in order to resolve a question or understand a phenomenon. Although the students developed a number of different types of inscriptions, this first phase of the experiment was relatively unproblematic.

Our instructional intent for the second phase of the design experiment was that the students would come to interpret scatter plots in terms of trends or patterns in how bivariate data were distributed. A computer tool was introduced at this point in the design experiment in order to enable the students to structure and organize bivariate data in a variety ways. In our design efforts, the research team viewed the use of computer tools as an integral aspect of statistical reasoning. This was based on our belief that students would need ways to structure and organize large sets of data in order to facilitate their exploration. The computer tool the research team developed therefore provides a variety of options for structuring bivariate data sets:

1.   *The cross.* This option provided the students with a cross that divided the data display into four cells. The total number of data points in each cell was also shown. They could drag the center of the cross to any location on the display, thereby changing the size of the cells. As they did so, the record of the number of data points in each cell adjusted automatically.

2.   *The grids.* The students could select from a list of grids that ranged in size from 4 × 4 to 10 × 10. The selected grid was then superimposed on the data display and the number of data points in each cell of the grid was shown. This option built on the second tool in which the students had partitioned univariate data sets into groups of data points within equal interval widths.

3.   *Two equal groups.* As with the grids option, this option partitioned the data display into columns or vertical slices that correspond to equal intervals of the independent variable. The minimum number of slices that the students could choose was 4 and the maximum 10. Within each slice, the data points

were partitioned into two equal groups with respect to the dependent variable (i.e., the display shows the median, low, and high values on the dependent variable within each slice). Given the students' prior experience of structuring univariate data sets into two (and four) equal groups, the research team conjectured that they would be able to interpret the display within each slice as signifying a distribution with respect to the dependent variable, and that they might be able to compare the slices to investigate how the distributions within slices varied across the specified intervals for the independent variable.

4. *Four equal groups.* This option is similar to the two equal groups option except that the data points within each slice are partitioned into four equal groups (i.e., the display shows the median, lower, and upper quartiles and the low and high values of the dependent variable within each slice).

Our goal was that the students would use the Grids, Two-Equal-Groups, and Four-Equal-Groups options on the computer tool to structure the data and then reason about the trends or patterns that emerged. The computer tool was intended to support students' emerging mathematical notions while simultaneously providing them with tools for data analysis (cf. Biehler, 1993; Kaput, 1994).

When the students initially worked with this tool, they used the last three of the four options to structure the data into vertical slices and traced lines on the data display to indicate global trends in the data. Further, they could readily describe these trends in terms of the rate of change of one measure with respect to the other. For instance, as the number of years increased, the CO_2 levels increased. At first glance, the students' reasoning might therefore appear to be relatively sophisticated. However, on closer examination, it appeared that the lines the students traced signified a global perceptual pattern in the data display rather than a conjectured covariation relationship about which the data were distributed. For example, they would trace a line through the most densely populated cells of a Grids display or connect the medians of each vertical slice of a Four-Equal-Groups display. From analysis of their explanations, the research team judged that the data did not constitute a bivariate distribution for the students. Instead, the trends they described involved merely collapsing scatter plots into a single line by using a feature of the tool.[3] As the goal was that students might come to view the data in terms of bivariate distributions, the research team worked to support the notion in terms of viewing vertical

---

[3] Patrick Thompson (personal communication, March 2003) makes a distinction between algebraic covariation and statistical covariation. Algebraic covariation involves reading covariations linearly as opposed to coordinating the variation of two attributes (e.g., statistical covariation).

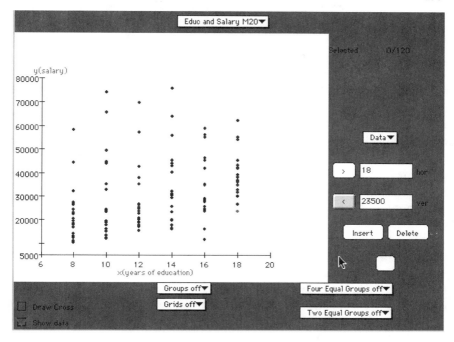

FIG. 5.1. Salary and education data on men.

slices of the graph as univariate distributions instead of viewing the data in terms of global "line fitting." To this end, tasks that were posed to the students during the majority of the class sessions entailed what the research team came to call "stacked data." For instance, the graphs generated by plotting the years of education and salary of a group of males would result in stacks of data points on the corresponding years as shown in Fig. 5.1.

The goal of the research team was that students would come to think of these sequences of stacks or slices in terms of a sequence of univariate distributions. The final phase of the sequence as guided by the conjectured learning trajectory would then involve a transition from stacked data to cloud-like scatter plots.

SETTING

The classroom design experiment that is the focus of this chapter was conducted in a middle school (Grades 5–8) in a large metropolitan school district in the Southeast. The design experiment was conducted over a 14-week period and involved 41 classroom sessions of approximately 40 minutes duration. During the fall of the previous year, the research team had conducted a design experiment in a seventh-grade classroom that focused on the analysis of univariate data. The intent of the research team was to work with the same group of 29 students during the first part of their eighth-grade year to investigate the analysis of bivariate data with a particular emphasis on statistical covariation. However, the eighth-grade mathematics teacher was not convinced that our efforts justified a reduction in her teaching time. The members of the research team were therefore unable to conduct the eighth-grade design experiment during regular mathematics periods and asked for student volunteers to work with us during their afternoon activity period, which occurred during the last 40 minutes of the school day. Of the original 29 students, 8 had transferred to other schools and 4 had other obligations during that time (e.g., practice for the school play or for the school band). Of the remaining 17 students, 16 volunteered to give up their activity period and 11 continued to attend throughout the 14 weeks of the experiment. The five students who dropped out, all of whom were Caucasian, indicated that they were having difficulty completing their homework for other classes and wanted to use the activity period for this purpose. Seven of the 11 students who participated for the entire experiment were African American, three were Caucasian, and one was Asian American. An analysis of interviews conducted with all of the original 29 students at the end of seventh-grade design experiment indicated that these 11 students were reasonably representative of the entire group in terms of the ways in which they reasoned about data.

CLASSROOM ANALYSIS

Over the course of the two design experiments, the students and I (as the classroom teacher) had negotiated norms for argumentation in the setting of classroom discussions. This was viewed as an integral aspect of the work on data analysis and was therefore a focus from our initial introduction to the classroom. As a result, the students were obligated to explain and justify their analyses. In particular, it was insufficient to describe how one used the computer tool to structure the data. The focus of the justifications and explanations were on the backings that substantiated the choice. For instance, if students chose to structure the data using the Four-Equal-Groups option on the tool, it would be necessary to clarify why this way of structuring the data provided the basis for a valid argument. This practice had been established early in the seventh-grade classroom design experiment and came to signify an important aspect of the data analysis process.

Another aspect of the classroom that proved critical in supporting the students' ability to actually engage in the process of data analysis was that of the data creation process (for a detailed analysis of the evolution of the data creation process, see Tzou, 2000). Over the course of the two design experiments, the research team came to appreciate the importance of task analysis contexts for which the students could actually envision someone wanting to examine the results of their analysis. Their conjectures about the utility of their analysis provided not only motivation but also a metric against which to judge the adequacy of their analyses. In other words, would someone outside the classroom find their analysis compelling. In addition, the situations often offered opportunities for exploring other factors and data that might be needed to make a reasoned judgment about the results of the data analysis activity. The students' ability to engage in the activity of data analysis therefore came to depend on the quality of the task selection and the subsequent data creation discussion.

Because the research team made the decision to use archival data during the classroom design experiment, it was important for the students to talk through the design specifications that would generate the measures of the attributes needed to answer the question under investigation. To this end, before the introduction of the data I engaged the students in a discussion of the data creation process. During these discussions, the students would create a list of attributes on which they would want to generate measures in order to answer the question. This was followed by discussions of how to collect the data, what measures would be appropriate, and how to account for differences in data collection procedures. This process proved important in grounding the students' activity in the context of a situation that had real consequences.

As an example, one of the last tasks posed to the students in the eighth-grade sequence challenged them to determine whether or not men make more money than women do. I began the salary task by asking the students if they thought men made more money than women. In response, they engaged in a lively discussion about issues of discrimination and speculated about circumstances that would contribute to inequity in salaries. I then asked the students what information they thought we would need in order to investigate my question. In the ensuing discussion, they clarified that we would need data not just on salaries, but also on other factors that contribute to determining one's pay. As they continued, they pointed to issues of the data creation process that included attention to sampling techniques. I then clarified that the data I had collected was taken from a random sample of Internal Revenue Tax Forms. The students not only questioned the use of Internal Revenue Tax forms as a source of information, but they also pointed to potential problems if a stratified random sample were not used.[4] They were able to articulate the problems inherent in a sample that did not attend to the types of jobs it represented. In particular, they generated a list of professions that could dramatically alter the data if included in only one data set. As the conversation continued, the students also raised a concern about the small sample size. They noted that it was so small that each data value had to represent "millions of people." As a result, they questioned whether their analysis would result in a fair way to make the judgment. After working through these and numerous other issues related to the data creation process, I asked the students to use the data I had available to see if, based in this data, they thought that men made more money than women.

The data as introduced to the students consisted of the number of years of education and the salary for a group of 120 men and a group of 120 women (Figs. 5.1 and 5.2). The intent of the task was to problematize a focus on global trends (e.g., salary increases with years of education). In particular, it would be insufficient to state that an ascending trend occurred in both data sets. An adequate analysis would require that the students tease out the salient aspects of those trends to highlight differences both within and across the data sets. Prior tasks had involved the students in defining aspects of patterns or trends in one data set (e.g., ounces of alcohol and reaction time for a group of people; age and reaction time; year and CO_2 levels). In these earlier instances, the students were able to discern trends and make predictions based on their analysis. However, the research team judged that they were able to do this without attending to the specificity of the trend. For example, students noted that as the years increased, the CO_2 levels continued to increase. They even made predictions about the CO_2 levels in 5 years based on the trend. However, when I tried to focus the students' attention on particular features of the trend, I was often unable to generate a need for such specificity. As a result, the students typically did not see merit in my question. For this reason, the research team decided to create a task where determining the pattern or trend would be insufficient. For example, it would be insufficient to note that as the years of education increased, both the men's and women's salaries

---

[4]The students did not use the language of stratified random sample. However, they did outline the design specifications for such a sample by noting that each sample should contain the same number of people from the same professions, with the same number of years of experience, etc.

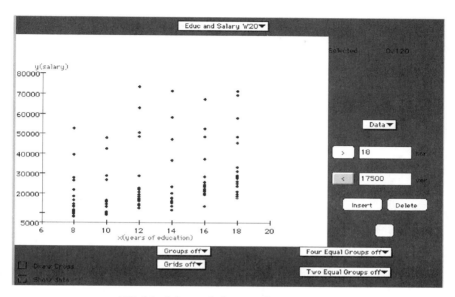

FIG. 5.2. Salary and education data on women.

increased. What would be important would be teasing out the aspects of the trends that allowed them to be compared and contrasted. The research team conjectured that in order to focus on the significant features of the trends, the students would structure the data using the Grids or Equal-Groups options on the computer tool and reason about the changes in the distributions across the stacks. This would require their analyzing the data in two ways—(1) by comparing changes in salary with years of education *within* the data sets and (2) by comparing salary with the same years of education *across* the two data sets.

As the students worked at the computers to analyze the data, I along with other members of the research team monitored their activity in an attempt to plan for the subsequent whole-class discussion. As members of the research team circulated among the groups, we noticed that many of the students initially focused on the extreme data values in each stack as well as the medians. In earlier analyses, the students had often based their analysis on the extreme data values because they wanted to be able to describe the range within which all the data points fell. They used features on the computer tool to "capture" the data set inside the extreme values in order to reason about changes. The research team viewed this way of reasoning as highly problematic in that these values are typically unstable across samples and do not provide a basis for prediction and inference. As a result, the research team worked with the students on issues of sampling where they were asked to note which values they might be able to predict across samples (e.g., the median or the extremes). Our goal was to build an understanding of the stability of the median across samples and a focus on the portion of the data that is clustered around this value. The research team anticipated that this, in turn, would contribute to the students' coming to view data in terms of distributions that built from the median instead of collections of data points that fell between two extreme values. Nonetheless, several of the students still relied on the extreme values as they began in their analyses of the salary data.

However, as the students continued to work on the salary task, several of them began to speak of the extreme values of the stacks as the exceptions (i.e., the people who made atypically high salaries) and focused more on the dense portions of the stacks (i.e., the data clustered around the medians). This way of reasoning can be related to events that transpired during the seventh-grade design experiment. In particular, the metaphor of a "hill" to describe the shape of univariate data sets had emerged shortly after the students began using the computer tool which inscribed univariate data on a line plot (cf. Cobb, 1999; McClain, Cobb, & Gravemeijer, 2000). Students routinely spoke of the "majority" or "most of the data" as being located within the hill. In these conversations, it appeared that these terms signified a qualitative proportion of a data set and thus a qualitative relative frequency. The students were now using this metaphor of a hill as a resource when they analyzed the education/salary data by reading the shape of stacks from Grids or Four-Equal-Groups displays. As they worked, they would trace the shape of the hill in the stacks as shown in Fig. 5.3. For these students, the hills were a signature of the distribution. The research team found this significant because the students and I had previously drawn hills on data sets structured in Four-Equal-Groups to indicate the patterns of relative density in data stacks. Here, the students used this idea to frame their argument. As a result, I decided to highlight these solutions in the subsequent whole-class discussion. My goal was to make the specific characteristics of the distributions of the stacks the focus of analysis. That would allow the students the opportunity to define the characteristics of the trends necessary to make a valid judgment. This would include attention to not only trends within each data set, but also across the two data sets.

It is important to note that all of the students reached the same conclusion as a result of their analysis. They all agreed that based on the data, men made more money than women. However, the norms that had become instantiated

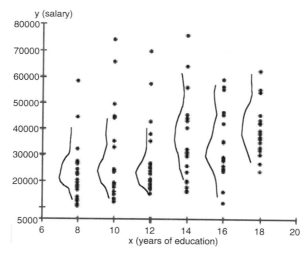

FIG. 5.3. Stacked data with "hills" drawn.

in the classroom mandated that students critique their analyses in whole-class discussion for the purpose of determining their adequacy in justifying the conclusion. For this reason, whole-class discussions were not spent selecting a course of action or a choice. They were instead focused on the specific ways of structuring and organizing the data that would *best* support the conclusion. It was, in fact, not unusual for the students to agree on the outcome of an analysis and still engage in discussions for an entire class period.

I began the whole-class discussion by asking Brad and Mike to share their analysis. They had reasoned about how the data were distributed in the stacks by referring to what they called the "humps." I chose this as the first solution because it offered a way to reason about the distributions by focusing on a perceived perceptual pattern in the univariate distributions or the stacks. This was important in understanding the data as structured with the Two-Equal-Groups or Four-Equal-Groups option. In addition, it built from earlier class sessions in which the students and I had created the hills that underlie the relative density of the stacks.

Brad and Mike began by using a computer projection system to project the data sets onto the whiteboard. They then explained that they had origi-nally begun their analysis by looking at the extreme values in each stack and across the two data sets. However, they continued by noting that they did not find this particularly useful in light of the problem they were investigating. They then noted that they reasoned about the stacks of data by focusing on what they called the "humps." For them, thinking of this metaphor provided an image that identified the cluster or clump of data where "most of the people are." Brad justified their way of organizing the data as follows:

Brad: We were like using the extremes at first like the men's highest and from the women the highest but those don't really matter as much as like the medians and the humps because that's where like most people are, not where like just the exceptions of people who like maybe broke it big or whatever . . . are making that much money, but we like decided to go where most of the people are.

Mike: So we used the humps and we found out the men's salaries are higher than the women's so our conclusion is that men make more.

At this point, the listening students indicated that they both understood and agreed with Brad and Mike's analysis. However, I was surprised that no one questioned Brad and Mike about their use of the term hump.

McClain: Nobody asked them a question and I've never heard anybody use [hump] before but you all seem to know what they are talking about.

In responding, Brad noted that there is usually a hump or cluster in the data around the median and that this is where the majority of the data are located. He then referred to an earlier class discussion in which the students and I had actually drawn distribution curves on several stacks to clarify the shape of the data within the stacks (similar to those shown in Fig. 5.3). As the discussion continued, Brad and Mike used the Two-Equal-Groups option of the computer tool to locate the medians as shown in Figs. 5.4 and 5.5. They then pointed to the data structured in this manner and noted that the humps would be around the median. They could therefore reason about the shape of the data on this basis. In doing so, they noted that the men's salaries were consistently higher than the women's across the years of education. In making this argument, they pointed to the medians of the stacks and noted, "See, you can see where the medians and humps are." In doing so, they were identifying a trend in the humps both within and across the data sets.

My role during this exchange was to make explicit Brad and Mike's way of reasoning. In particular, I wanted to highlight the use of the hump metaphor in characterizing the relative density of the stacks. The goal was for the students to be able to read shape in the graphs. This shape would be the basis for discerning trends and patterns in the data.

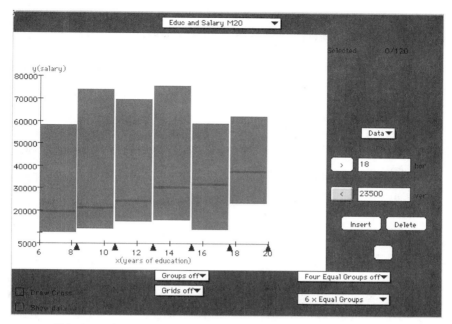

FIG. 5.4. Salary and education data on men structured in two equal groups.

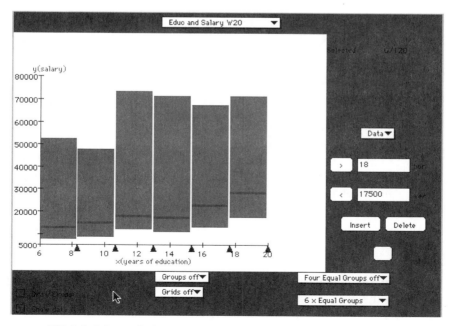

FIG. 5.5. Salary and education data on women structured in two equal groups.

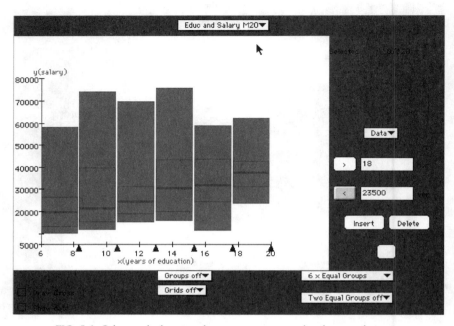

FIG. 5.6. Salary and education data on men structured in four equal groups.

The next student asked to present an analysis was Sue. She had reasoned about the data in a similar manner, but had structured the data sets using the Four-Equal-Groups option on the computer tool (Figs. 5.6 and 5.7) and reasoned about the trends in the middle 50 percent of the stacks. My goal in selecting Sue was to compare and contrast the two ways of reasoning about the data by focusing on the distributions as described by the two structures (e.g., Two-Equal-Groups with a focus on the median and Four-Equal-Groups with a focus on the middle 50 percent).

Sue explained that she focused on the middle 50 percent of the stacks because, "the hump or hill or whatever is in the middle 50 percent." After Sue explained her approach, Val made the following observation.

Val: So you basically did the same way they did by like comparing the medians and groupings and stuff.

I then clarified that Sue had indeed focused on the medians, but had also structured the data stacks into Four-Equal-Groups and had reasoned about trends in the middle 50 percent of the data both within and across the two

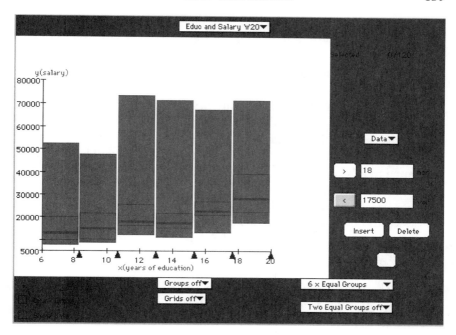

FIG. 5.7. Salary and education data on women structured in four equal groups.

sets of data stacks. My goal was to make explicit the similarities and differences between the two methods by noting that both analyses attended to the relative frequency of the data clustered around the median. This was in keeping with our goal of viewing data structured in this manner, but in different ways. After clarifying that the listening students understood Sue's way of reasoning, I asked the students if they thought this way of organizing the data was useful. They stated it was important to know "what most people are making" and that focusing on the "middle" was a good way to do this.

At this point in the discussion, I built on Sue's presentation by asking the students to describe the trend in each of the two data sets. They agreed that salary increased with years of education for both the men and the women. However, several students noted that the *rate* of increase was greater for the men than the women. They substantiated this observation by using the computer tool to read the shape of the stacks and then contrasted the overall patterns in the two data sets. It is important to stress that in doing so, they were not collapsing the data sets to lines but were instead comparing trends in two bivariate distributions.

The ways of structuring data that were highlighted in this discussion can be contrasted with the alternative that the research team witnessed earlier in the design experiment. The reader will recall that there the students focused on the extreme values of data stacks and seemed to view each stack as an amorphous collection of data points that occupied the space between these values. At that point, the stacks had little structure and were not univariate data distributions. As I have illustrated, it was the use of the hill metaphor as an interpretive resource that enabled the students to view the stacks as a sequence of univariate distributions. This in turn made it possible for them to determine trends and patterns across stacks and thus to view the entire data set as a bivariate distribution.

It is also worth noting that throughout the discussion the students continued to raise questions about the validity of their analyses by making reference to the process that generated the data. In particular, when I asked the students if they thought they could make any predictions about men's and women's salaries for the entire country based on this data, they again raised concerns about the size of the sample and the possibility that the data might be unrepresentative. For example, one student noted that it would be important to make sure that they "weren't all doctors" and another commented that someone like Bill Gates should not be included. They also raised the issue of years of experience in a job and noted that it had not been accounted for in any way. The research team viewed these questions and issues as strong indicators that the students were developing a relatively deep understanding of data creation and its implications for the conclusions that could legitimately be drawn from the subsequent analysis. This is indicated by the manner in which the students were able to step back from their analyses and critique it in light of the appropriateness of the data sampling and collection techniques, and then question the validity of predications and inferences made from such analyses.

DISCUSSION

The reader will recall that the overarching mathematical goal for the design experiment was to support students' ability to reason about data in terms of bivariate distributions. While this goal was viewed as an endpoint to be aimed for, the detailed route to the endpoint was not predetermined. In planning the two instructional sequences, the research team formulated a conjectured learning trajectory that guided the development of both the instructional tasks and the computer tools. However, this trajectory was continually subject to modifications that were informed by ongoing analysis of the students' ways of reasoning. Conjectures inherent in the trajectory about both the course of students' learning and the means of supporting it were therefore tested and revised on an ongoing basis throughout both design experiments.

My decision-making process in the classroom was also informed by the conjectured learning trajectory but constantly being revised and modified in action based on the students' contributions. I was therefore guided by the mathematics while attending to students' emerging ways of understanding (cf. Ball, 1993: Carpenter & Fennema, 1991; Lampert, 1990; Cobb, Yackel, & Wood, 1991; Simon & Schifter, 1991). This required that I not only understand the mathematical goals for each task, but also that I situate those within the broader goals of the instructional sequence. This focus on the overarching mathematical goals guided my interactions with the students in much the same way that Simon (1997) described the Mathematics Teaching Cycle as involving the teacher's knowledge, a conjectured learning trajectory, and interaction with students. I therefore worked to capitalize on the students' contributions to advance the mathematical agenda. In doing so, I took their solutions as points of departure to build toward the envisioned endpoint. For this reason, the students' ways of structuring and organizing the data sets were critical in supporting my ongoing efforts.

An example of this can be seen in the episode in this chapter. My overarching goal was to support students' ability to reason about bivariate distributions. To this end, I wanted them to come to understand the importance of the median as a characteristic of a univariate distribution. For this reason, I focused on those solutions in whole-class discussion that built off of the median in making their argument. My goals and the students' activity were both enabled and constrained by the tools that the students used. These tools included both the tasks and the computer-based tool. The task selection was critical in providing a basis for the students' investigations that would motivate them to want to engage in genuinely analyzing the data for a purpose. The computer-based tool supported this effort by offering them ways to structure and organize the sets of data that would have otherwise been unwieldy. The features that the research team choose to put on the computer-based tool were intended to build from the students' prior activity in the seventh-grade design experiment of analyzing univariate data sets while simultaneously offering the means of supporting shifts in the students' ways of reasoning toward more sophisticated ways of structuring and organizing the data. Because of the norms that became instantiated in the classroom, selecting options for structuring data was only an initial aspect of the analysis. Students had to also understand what the structuring afforded them in terms of supporting their argument. In addition, they had to be able to clarify their intent to other members of the classroom community. For this reason, deliberately facilitated whole-class discussions in which the backing for these ways of reasoning was the focus became an important aspect of the teacher's role. It was therefore critical that I not only understand the diverse ways that the students' reasoned about the task, but I also had to be able to judge their potential worth with respect to my overarching mathematical goals. This had implications for my role while the students worked on their analyses. Instead of working to ensure that students solved the task in similar ways, or came to a predetermined "best" conclusion, my focus was shifted towards understanding the diverse ways in which the students were reasoning so that I could capitalize on their activity in the course of the whole-class discussion. My understanding of their ways of reasoning framed not only my choices for which solutions to highlight in the discussion, but also how to sequence them.

As an example, I chose to ask Brad and Mike to begin the whole-class discussion. I began with a solution which built from the median in a global manner by using perceptual patterns inferred from structuring the data into Two-Equal-Groups. Sue's solution built on this by focusing more squarely on the middle 50 percent of the data as identified by the Four-Equal-Groups feature. Both of these methods were in keeping with the overarching goal of reasoning about bivariate distributions and could be seen as building from each other. For this reason, the discussion offered a mathematical structure that could support shifts in students' ways of reasoning away from a focus on the extreme values toward an understanding of the importance of the median.

In planning for the classroom design experiment, the research team made the a priori conjecture that statistics would serve as an ideal area of mathematical activity in which to explore the role that inscriptions play in enabling students to make profound conceptual reorganizations (cf. Lehrer, Schauble, Carpenter, & Penner, 2000). For this reason, the computer-based tools were designed to build from students' informal ways of organizing data toward conventional graphs (i.e., histograms and box plots). In this episode we see evidence to support this conjecture in that the students' ways of using the computer tool to structure the data to support their analyses served as thinking devices (Wertsch & Toma, 1995) as they reasoned about the adequacy of both their arguments and their ways of structuring and organizing the data.

This provided opportunities to highlight the students' activity in terms of its significance with respect to mathematical agenda while taking their ways of reasoning as starting points for discussion. This deliberately facilitated whole-class discussion can be compared with discussions where all contributions are treated equally. Some have cast the role of the teacher in this era of reform as commensurable with this latter image of the classroom. However, I would argue that although this vision has been propagated by some, it does not offer the "model of teaching" that can best serve students. Instead, the teacher must judge the quality and worth of *all* contributions against the background of the mathematical agenda. For this reason, it is incumbent upon teachers to understand the mathematics that they will teach. Mathematics then becomes the focal point of classroom interactions while taking account of students' diverse ways of reasoning. In these situations, the means of supporting students' learning are critical. This entails instructional materials, tools, and classroom norms. The picture that emerges is that of a complex environment that must be constantly managed so that it offers increased opportunities for student learning.

ACKNOWLEDGMENTS

The research reported in this paper was supported by the National Science Foundation under grant no. REC-0135062 and REC-9814898 and by the Office of Educational Research and Improvement through the National Center under grant no. R305A60007. The opinions do not necessarily reflect the views of either the Foundation or the Center.

REFERENCES

Ball, D. (1993). With an eye on the mathematical horizon: Dilemmas of teaching elementary school mathematics. *The Elementary School Journal, 93*(4), 373–398.

Biehler, R. (1993). Software tools and mathematics education: The case of statistics. In C. Keitel & K. Ruthven (Eds.), *Learning from computers: Mathematics education and technology* (pp. 68–100). Berlin: Springer.

Carpenter, T., & Fennema, E. (1991). Research and cognitively guided instruction. In E. Fennema, T. P. Carpenter, & S. J. Lamon (Eds.), *Integrating research on teaching and learning mathematics* (pp. 1–16). Albany, NY: SUNY Press.

Cobb, P. (1999). Individual and collective mathematical learning: The case of statistical data analysis. *Mathematical Thinking and Learning, 5*–44.

Cobb, P., McClain, K., & Gravemeijer, K. (2003). Learning about statistical covariation. *Cognition and Instruction, 21*, 1–78.

Cobb, P., Stephan, M., McClain, K., & Gravemeijer, K. (2001). Participating in classroom mathematical practices. *Journal for the Learning Sciences, 10*(1&2), 113–164.

Cobb, P., Yackel, E., & Wood, T. (1991). Curriculum and teacher development: Psychological and anthropological perspectives. In E. Fennema, T. P. Carpenter, & S. J. Lamon (Eds.), *Integrating research on teaching and learning mathematics* (pp. 83–120). Albany, NY: SUNY Press.

Fennema, L., Carpenter, T., Franke, M., Levi, M., Jacobs, V., & Empson, S. (1996). A longitudinal study of learning to use children's thinking in mathematics instruction. *Journal for Research in Mathematics Education, 27*(4), 403–434.

Gravemeijer, K. (1998, April). *Developmental research: Fostering a dialectic relation between theory and practice.* Paper presented the Research Presession of the annual meeting of the National Council of Teachers of Mathematics, Washington, DC.

Grossman, P. (1990). *The making of a teacher: Teacher knowledge and teacher education.* New York: Teachers College Press.

Grossman, P., Wilson, S., & Schulman, L. S. (1989). Teachers of substance: Subject matter knowledge for teaching. In M. Reynolds (Ed.), *Knowledge base for the beginning teacher* (pp. 23–36). New York: Pergamon.

Kaput, J. J. (1994). The representational roles of technology in connecting mathematics with authentic experience. In R. Biehler, R. W. Scholz, R. Strasser, & B. Winkelmann (Eds.), *Didactics of mathematics as a scientific discipline* (pp. 379–397). Dordrecht, Netherlands: Kluwer Academic Press.

Konold, C., Pollatsek, A., Well, A., & Gagnon, A. (in press). "Students analyzing data: Research of critical barriers." *Journal of Research in Mathematics Education.*

Lampert, M. (1990). When the problem is not the question and the solution is not the answer: Mathematical knowing and teaching. *American Educational Research Journal, 27*(1), 29–63.

Lehrer, R., Schauble, L., Carpenter, S., & Penner, D. (2000). The inter-related development of inscriptions and conceptual understanding. In P. Cobb, E. Yackel, and K. McClain (Eds.), *Symbolizing and communicating in mathematics classrooms* (pp. 325–360). Mahwah, NJ: Lawrence Erlbaum Associates.

Ma, L. (1999). *Knowing and teaching elementary mathematics: Teachers' understandings of fundamental mathematics in China and the United States.* Mahwah, NJ: Lawrence Erlbaum Associates.

McClain, K. (in press). Supporting preservice teacher change: Understanding place value and multidigit addition and subtraction. *Journal of Mathematical Thinking and Learning.*

McClain, K. (2002). Teacher's and students' understanding: The role of tools and inscriptions in supporting effective communication. *Journal for the Learning Sciences, 11*(2 & 3), 217–249.

McClain, K., & Cobb, P. (2001). Supporting students' ability to reason about data. *Educational Studies in Mathematics, 45*(1-3), 103–129.

McClain, K., Cobb, P., & Gravemeijer, K. (2000). Supporting students' ways of reasoning about data. In M. Burke (Ed.), *Learning mathematics for a new century* (2001 Yearbook of the National Council of Teachers of Mathematics). Reston, VA: NCTM.

National Research Council. (2001). Knowing and learning mathematics for teaching. Proceedings of a workshop. Washington, D.C.: National Academy Press.

Schifter, D. (1990). Mathematics process as mathematics content: A course for teachers. In. G. Booker, P. Cobb, and T. DeMendicuti (Eds.), *Proceedings of the 14th Annual Meeting of the Psychology of Mathematics Education* (pp. 191–198). Mexico City, Mexico.

Simon, M. A. (1997). Developing new models of mathematics teaching: An imperative for research on mathematics teacher development. In E. Fennema & B. Nelson (Eds.), *Mathematics teachers in transition* (pp. 55–86). Hillsdale, NJ: Lawrence Erlbaum Associates.

Simon, M., & Schifter, D. (1991). Towards a constructivist perspective: An intervention study of mathematics teacher development. *Educational Studies in Mathematics, 22,* 309–331.

Tzou, C. T. (2000). Supporting Students' Understanding of the Relationships Between Data Creation and Data Analysis. In P. Cobb (Chair), Supporting the Learning of Classroom Communities: A Case from Middle School Statistics. Symposium conducted at the meeting of the American Educational Research Association, New Orleans.

Wertsch, J., & Toma, C. (1995). Social and cultural dimensions of knowledge. In L. Steffe & J. Gale (Eds.), *Constructivism in Education* (pp. 175–184).

6

Creating Mathematics Stories: Learning to Explain in a Third-Grade Classroom

Ellice Forman
Ellen Ansell
University of Pittsburgh

During the first week of school, Mrs. Porter asked her third-grade students to work independently on the following word problem: "You read for 15 minutes a day. How much time will you have spent reading in one week?" As they solved the problem, she stressed that she was less interested in the accuracy of their answers than in their solution strategies. She made it clear that there were many ways to solve this problem and she was most interested in knowing how each of them came up with their strategies. She said, "I don't want an answer. I want how you figured it out. That's only part of what I want. That's the beginning. I want the whole story." She emphasized that the whole story of their problem solving might include their entire solution path from beginning to end: "And think about how you get started. What would you do first?"

What did it mean to explain your solution to a mathematical word problem in this classroom? That was a question her students would learn to answer in the first few weeks of the school year, and that question is the focus of our chapter. Of course, Mrs. Porter's students were quite familiar with everyday explanations in their families (Beals & Snow, 1994; Callahan, Shrager, & Moore, 1995). In addition, each of them had already experienced several years of schooling where they were frequently asked to answer questions posed to them by an adult (Cazden, 2001). Nevertheless, it is likely that few of them were used to solving mathematics problems in more than one way and justifying their strategy to their classroom community. Thus, Mrs. Porter and her students were faced with a similar puzzle: how to create and maintain classroom norms for acceptable mathematical explanations.

Although the approach to mathematics instruction that Mrs. Porter used did not appear to be typical among teachers in her school (Forman & Ansell, 2001), it seems consistent with the recommendations of leading North American mathematics educators and the National Council of Teachers of Mathematics (NCTM) (Hiebert et al., 1996; NCTM, 2000; Putnam, Lampert, & Peterson, 1990; Yackel & Cobb, 1996). Thus, the challenge Mrs. Porter faced with respect to what constitutes an acceptable mathematical explanation is one with which many teachers are likely to be grappling.

Over the past decade, the study of communication in mathematics classrooms has expanded as more researchers have been studying classrooms that foster meaningful mathematical problem solving. Some ten years ago, Hiebert (1992) found few studies capable of supporting or even illustrating the claim that communication is important in classrooms. He proposed that most mathematics classrooms in North America were designed to foster accuracy and speed in the use of computational algorithms instead of meaningful discussion of and reflection on mathematical problem solving. More recently, Sfard and Kieran (2001) were able to cite several studies of mathematics classrooms in which communication was the focus (e.g., Lampert & Blunk, 1998). Thus, we now have numerous examples of classrooms where students are actively engaged in meaningful discussions of mathematical problem solving.

Changes in classroom communication are just part of an instructional program that transforms a classroom from one that emphasizes speed and accuracy in the use of standard algorithms to one that focuses on problem solving, the fostering of students' invented strategies, and the discussion of those strategies (Hiebert et al., 1996). This shift in instructional focus allows teachers and their students to wonder about the nature of mathematical concepts and operations, to engage in sustained inquiry, and to resolve conflicting interpretations among members of the classroom community. Thus, students could play a more active role in classroom life: asking questions, not merely answering them; explaining and evaluating their solutions and strategies; and collaborating with classmates in problem solving (Hiebert, 1992). Further, classrooms would begin to resemble scientific communities in which the aim of problem solving is to convince an audience of peers of the validity of one's explanations (Bazerman, 1988; Forman & Ansell, 2002; Lampert, 1990; Latour, 1987). Changing classroom practices requires increased attention to discursive processes and the norms that regulate them.

Yackel and Cobb (1996) investigated the norms of mathematical communication in reform-oriented elementary school classrooms. In their work they found it useful to distinguish between social norms and sociomathematical norms. Social norms are those that foster clear, meaningful explanations and thoughtful listening and may be similar in different content domains. In contrast, sociomathematical norms are particular to the domain of mathematics. Sociomathematical norms may promote logical consistency, efficiency, and precision. Yackel and Cobb studied how teachers and students worked together to create and sustain both types of norms in the classroom communities that they studied.

Of course, norms vary according to the community in which they occur. Thus, a sociomathematical norm like efficiency could mean using effective (quick, automatic) procedures for solving problems in one mathematics classroom whereas efficiency could mean something closer to parsimony (explain your strategy in the simplest manner) in another classroom. The former meaning might be promoted in a traditional classroom where accuracy and speed are valued more than sense-making; the latter meaning might be promoted in a reform-oriented classroom where practices that resemble those of professional mathematicians are rewarded (Putman et al., 1990).[1] Therefore, one of our aims in this chapter is to show how norms such as "efficiency" are interpreted in Mrs. Porter's classroom.

A related aim is to understand what it means to tell "the whole story" about your strategy. We have found Hilton's (1990) discursive model of explanation to be useful in understanding the expectation that students need to be articulate communicators. Hilton argued that causal explanations, being part of a conversation, must be interpreted as specific answers to questions posed by listeners to speakers in a given social context: "The verb to explain is a three-place predicate: *Someone* explains *something* to *someone*" (1990, p. 65). As a result, learning to communicate mathematically—either in a classroom,

---

[1] These two definitions of "efficiency" as effective procedures versus parsimony have quite different associations in the philosophy of science. Effective procedures can be modeled by Turing machines that compute without understanding (Audi, 1995). A stark contrast to this view is "Ockham's razor, also called the principle of parsimony, a methodological principle commending a bias toward simplicity in the construction of theories" (Audi, 1995, p. 545). Thus, Turing machines do work without sense-making whereas parsimonious theories do work effectively despite their simple appearance because extraneous information has been deleted by knowledgeable adherents.

workplace, neighborhood, or professional community—requires experience being an active participant in this community by engaging in valued mathematical activities such as explaining strategies efficiently and appropriately for the intended audience.

A DILEMMA OF TEACHING STUDENTS TO EXPLAIN

As investigators have begun to study mathematics classrooms in which communication is a central priority, an important dilemma has emerged. Teachers of communication-rich elementary school classrooms may be faced with a problem enforcing both norms that value students' attempts to use and explain strategies that are meaningful to them and those norms that value some strategies over others due to their reliance on more sophisticated mathematical concepts (Franke & Carey, 1997; O'Connor, 2001). During the early elementary school years, children become increasingly aware of the meaning of social comparisons and judge their own competence by reflecting on the competencies of their classmates (Flavell, Miller, & Miller, 1993). In light of this, teachers may need to be cautious when distinctions are made among different strategies for solving a problem to ensure that students are not discouraged from using less-sophisticated strategies that may be more meaningful to them.

As Franke, Carey, and O'Connor argued, it is important to find ways to help teachers instruct their students about evaluative criteria for strategies without destroying a classroom climate that also fosters mutual respect and clarity of communication. Yackel and Cobb's (1996) distinction between social norms and sociomathematical norms may help us think about this dilemma in a slightly different way. This teaching dilemma seems to be one in which the social norms of mutual respect could contradict the establishment of sociomathematical norms. This situation could occur if students who employ more mathematically concise strategies are encouraged to criticize the more cumbersome strategies of their classmates. We believe that this particular teaching dilemma may be common in classrooms that foster mathematical communication, as other researchers have pointed out.

Hatano and Inagaki and their colleagues (Hatano & Inagaki, 1998; Inagaki, Morita, & Hatano, 1999) argued that Japanese elementary school students frequently evaluate the mathematical sophistication of their classmates' strategies. They stress that this practice relies on a climate of mutual respect and self-examination that enables everyone to focus on the relative merits of different problem-solving strategies without denigrating the worth of the students who used them. They, and others (e.g., Lewis, 1995; Linn, Lewis, Tsuchida, & Songer, 2000; Tobin, Wu, & Davidson, 1989), argued that Japanese educators design preschool and primary school environments so that social norms of mutual respect, self-examination, and collaboration with peers are fostered in a consistent fashion before difficult academic content is introduced. For example, young children spend most of their school day working, eating, and playing in small peer groups. Then, when older elementary school students are asked to work in groups and evaluate each others' problem solving strategies, they are able to focus on the inadequacies of the strategies and not the incompetencies of their classmates. Citing Lewis's research on Japanese preschools and their own experience in classrooms in Japan and the United States, Hatano and Inagaki proposed that "making an error in public would damage American as well as Japanese children's self-esteem unless they are assured and convinced that their classroom constitutes a caring community" (1998, p. 92). Unfortunately, North American preschool and primary school teachers do not spend as much time fostering an atmosphere of mutual respect and cooperative learning as do their Japanese counterparts (Linn et al., 2000). We plan to examine this teaching dilemma by investigating its resolution in three lessons conducted in Mrs. Frances Porter's[2] third-grade classroom.

LEARNING TO EXPLAIN
IN A THIRD-GRADE CLASSROOM

We originally selected Mrs. Porter's classroom for study because she made oral and written communication a priority. For example, in a newsletter sent home to her students' parents, Mrs. Porter wrote, "writing and discussion are essential elements in a successful math program. In order to explain their approaches to solving problems, students must become conscious of their thinking processes. The emphasis shifts from getting the right answer to developing thinking and understanding." She also made communication the principal tool in her assessment practices. In an interview she claimed that communication "helps me to assess what they (her students) understand, and helps me in my ability to help children who don't understand ... When children can articulate what they know and their misconceptions, they are showing me how to teach them."

---

[2]The teacher's and students' names are pseudonyms.

As a classroom teacher, Mrs. Porter often found herself facing dilemmas between competing values and goals inherent in a communication-rich classroom. Thus, we were interested in understanding how she addressed the possible conflict between social and sociomathematical norms in her classroom (cf. Lampert, 1985). The goals of mutual respect and clear meaningful communication, as well as the importance of differentiating between strategies, were part of her explicit teaching philosophy. For example, in a statement that she sent to her students' parents, Mrs. Porter argued that:

> We must believe that all children are able to learn and convey this message to students by continually commenting on the learning that is evident. We must resist the temptation to focus on errors and what children are unable to do. Instead, we must look carefully at what children demonstrate they are able to do and then use our experience and knowledge about the development of mathematical thinking to help them move forward. Children are encouraged to develop and refine algorithms and procedures consistent with their thinking. All workable strategies and algorithms are accepted, but we continually discuss the relative efficiency of strategies and algorithms as we work.

Despite this explicit statement about the need to compare strategies for efficiency, the first author saw few instances of this practice after several months of informal observations in Mrs. Porter's classroom. When this observation was first mentioned to Mrs. Porter, she pointed out the contradiction between the norms of mutual respect, meaningful communication, and efficiency. She worried that some students would feel uncomfortable taking the necessary risks of explaining their thoughts to their classmates if they felt that, in the end, their strategies would be criticized for being deficient. She felt very strongly that students should be encouraged to use any strategy that made sense to them and should not be falsely attracted to strategies that appeared more sophisticated but that they did not understand. After our conversation, Mrs. Porter designed an unusual assignment as a way to resolve this dilemma. This assignment, which we call *strategy choice*, required students to evaluate the strategies used by unknown peers (the work of some of Mrs. Porter's former students). She hoped that her students would feel more comfortable criticizing the strategies of students they did not know than those of their classmates.

The primary aim of this chapter is to depict how the members of Mrs. Porter's third-grade classroom community explored, through individual, small-group, and whole-class discussion, the relative merits of a variety of mathematical explanations for their problem-solving strategies. These discussions served to clarify what adequate mathematical explanations entail in this particular community. A secondary aim is to assess the role of the strategy-choice assignment in the resolution of an important teaching dilemma: the apparent contradiction between social norms of mutual respect (and clear communication) and the sociomathematical norm of efficiency (or parsimony). Before presenting and discussing the strategy-choice task, we provide some general contextual information about our study of Mrs. Porter's classroom.

STUDYING MRS. PORTER'S CLASSROOM

Several months of informal observations gave the first author a sense of the classroom norms and communication practices. Based on this informal information, Mrs. Porter collaborated with the first author in designing a study for the following academic year. The study entailed observations of mathematics instruction for the first four months of that year. This time frame was chosen to enable a research team to record the variety of strategies students used to solve mathematics problems (either alone or in pairs) and to examine how these strategies were explained to their classmates. A team of three ethnographers[3] observed mathematics lessons twice a week from September 3 (the first day of school) until the day before winter vacation, December 17, 1998.[4] Although some instruction in mathematics took place every day, our observations were primarily confined to the two 90-minute blocks of time each week specifically devoted to mathematics. In addition, three interviews with Mrs. Porter[5] elicited information about her teaching philosophy, goals, and practices.

Participants and Instructional Context

Mrs. Porter's third-grade classroom was located in Riverside Academy, Junior School, one of three campuses of an independent school in a medium-sized city in the northeastern part of the United States. Mrs. Porter had been teaching at Riverside Academy (kindergarten, first, and third grade) for over 20 years when we conducted our study. There were 17 students in her classroom (7 girls, 10 boys) between the ages of 8 and 9 years. About half of Mrs. Porter's

---

[3]The ethnographers were: Ellice Forman, Deborah Dobransky-Fasiska, and Jaime Munoz.
[4]The primary data set is comprised of field notes, audiotaped classroom lessons and interviews with the classroom teacher, and classroom artifacts (photocopies of students' mathematical problem solving and answers to open-ended questions).
[5]The formal interviews were conducted in early October and the middle of December, 1999 and in early March, 2000.

students were Euro-American (three girls, seven boys), four children were African American (three girls and one boy), and three students were Asian American (one girl and two boys). Six of her students (two girls, four boys) had siblings enrolled in the school.

Mrs. Porter did not use a formal curriculum in her mathematics instruction. Instead, she relied on her 30 years of teaching young children, her journal, and her personal library of curriculum materials. Her approach to instruction could be characterized as centered on children's learning trajectories—a personal and informal version of more institutionalized approaches such as Cognitive Guided Instruction (CGI) (Carpenter, Fennema, Franke, Levi, & Empson, 1999). She relied on tasks that allowed her students to employ a range of strategies (including using counting as well as standard and invented algorithms) and to experience success in solving the assigned problems.

Many of the typical tasks assigned in Mrs. Porter's classroom involved multidigit arithmetic problems. In these tasks, students were presented with a word problem (e.g., A group of 252 ghosts were needed to haunt 9 cemeteries. How many ghosts went to each cemetery?). After the problem was introduced, students were asked to solve it alone or with a partner while Mrs. Porter circulated around the room to answer questions and to prompt students. Mrs. Porter then orchestrated a whole-class discussion of the strategies the students had used as she elicited and recorded students' strategies on the board.

The following section presents a typical lesson to provide a flavor of the classroom discussions early in the academic year (early September) and to document how the teacher introduced her classroom norms to her students.

Discussion During a Typical Mathematics Lesson

We begin our depiction of this classroom by focusing on the discussion of the reading problem, introduced in the opening of this chapter ("You read for 15 minutes a day. How much time will you have spent reading in one week?"). Mrs. Porter encouraged her students to find their own solution strategy and concentrate on telling the whole story about how they solved the problem. In addition, she indicated that telling the whole story would help her understand their thinking: "I want to know what you think." Thus, she stressed that she was interested in their thinking and that she wanted them to tell her as much as possible about their solution strategies.

As the students worked on this problem, Mrs. Porter answered her students' questions about the problem and how their solutions should be recorded. For example, she told them that they could write their answer in words or in a chart. She reminded them to elaborate their numerical answer with a time unit (hours and minutes). She suggested that they could use tally marks to keep track of the numbers or use a chart to record minutes and days ("It's good to keep track of what things are minutes and what things are days. And make little charts as you go."). Her comments about the acceptable written forms for their solution strategies continued during the whole-class discussion.

To begin the whole-class discussion, Mrs. Porter explained the purpose for asking students to share their strategies:

> You've done what you can then, and when we talk about it, some of the people in the class will teach you. That's what this is all about. This is a class where we all teach each other. Some of you know some things, and others of you know other things . . . And when you explain them, some of the other people who can't do that will learn from you.

In her introductory remarks, Mrs. Porter encouraged her students to see explanations as an important goal of this learning community. She proposed that their explanations should be designed to tell the story of their strategies as clearly and completely as possible. This was important because it fostered learning from each other. Thus, in Mrs. Porter's classroom, public exchanges about private thoughts were highly valued.

Mrs. Porter then called on individual students to explain their solution strategies, which she recorded on a whiteboard for everyone to see. She orchestrated the discussion by repeating, expanding, or reformulating the explanations that she heard. Eleven of the 16 students present that day explained their strategies during this discussion. Three students used multiplicative strategies, one student used a counting strategy, and the other seven students used a variety of additive strategies or strategies that combined additive and multiplicative elements. Almost all of the answers provided were accurate and all but one of the students in the class completed the assignment.

An exchange from the beginning of this lesson appears below. The teacher's turns at talk are marked by FP. In this segment, you can see how Mrs. Porter repeated (turns 2 and 4) and expanded (turn 6) Ophrah's explanation. By expanding and translating Ophrah's previous utterance, Mrs. Porter could be drawing an analogy between the multiplication operation Ophrah had mentioned and addition, which might have been more familiar to some of her classmates. Mrs. Porter referred to Ophrah in turn 6 as "she," indicating that Mrs. Porter was addressing the audience (her classmates) and not Ophrah herself. Thus, Mrs. Porter was not merely repeating Ophrah's explanation for her classmates, she was also implicitly signaling the importance of addressing their needs as an audience.

Turn	Speaker	Utterance
1	Ophrah	15 times 1 equals
2	FP	15 times 1, equals
3	Ophrah	15.
4	FP	15.
5	Ophrah	15 times 2, equals 30.
6	FP	And of course when she's saying 15 times 1 equals 15 it means one 15 is 15 and two fifteens is 30.

In the next segment of transcript, Mrs. Porter helped Lyndsey explain her strategy. In this segment, Mrs. Porter addressed Lyndsey explicitly as her conversational partner (turns 7 and 9) and also addressed her classmates implicitly when she referred to Lyndsey as "she" (turn 11). In addition, Mrs. Porter made explicit Lyndsey's step-by-step thinking processes. It appears from Mrs. Porter's summary in turn 11 that Lyndsey had written a row of five 15's and then moved her finger along the row while successively adding up the numbers (30, 45, 60, 75). Thus, to help Lyndsey's classmates understand her strategy, Mrs. Porter summarized her own impression of that strategy, thereby making Lyndsey's indistinct public communication and private self-communication explicit, verbal, and public.

7	FP	Lyndsey, Lyndsey what did you write?
8	Lyndsey	I wrote uhm, . . . 15 and then, then plus 15 more, 30 plus 15
9	FP	What is it? . . . Did you write the one that's right first. And you said that to yourself, right?
10	Lyndsey	Ya.
11	FP	OK. She said to herself, 15 minutes, plus 15 minutes in her head, would be 30, plus 15 is 45. So, she was kind of adding them up as she went and made the row until she got to 75 minutes. And, that's another thing that people might write down as a way to try it.

Two students in the class, Pulak and Raj, used the standard multiplication algorithm to solve this problem. Mrs. Porter identified their strategies as identical and clarified to the class that their approach was an acceptable way to solve this problem but that it was not the only way. She cautioned the rest of her class to use this algorithm if it makes sense to them but to avoid it if they do not understand it: "That's one way that's possible to do it. Again, if it makes sense, don't try it if it doesn't."

At the end of the class discussion, Mrs. Porter proposed that her students record the strategies of their classmates that made sense to them for future reference:

> Some of you wrote some things down about what other people did. Some of you didn't. I'm not going to make you do it. I'm going to say this to you. When you come to problems that are tricky, if you haven't written down some of this and if you hadn't listened to the things that your classmates are teaching you, you're not going to be learning new things as much.

She also made some further comments on the strategy used by Pulak and Raj, in response to Nathan's remark that he had not understood Pulak's strategy. She again cautioned her students to use the algorithm only if they understand why it works. Nevertheless, she added that the standard algorithm is an efficient (e.g., quick) strategy: "So, it's a really good thing for them to use, cause it's quick. But quick isn't always the best. It's only the best if you understand it. There are other ways that are quick that are good." Thus, using the standard algorithm was associated with a definition of efficiency as speed, not as parsimony during the first week.

Later, during several conversations with members of the research team, Mrs. Porter explained her resistance to teaching her students the standard multiplication algorithm. She argued that she wanted her students to understand that multiplication is a faster strategy for solving some problems than is repeated addition. Yet, without a solid understanding of place value, Mrs. Porter was concerned that her students would learn the standard multiplication algorithm by rote, without appreciating why it works (like a Turing machine). Therefore, she emphasized sense-making over automaticity in the choice of strategies.

In summary, what we can see from these two brief examples from the first week of school is that Mrs. Porter repeated, expanded, clarified, and translated her students' invented strategies for solving a multidigit multiplication problem. She focused on the strategy used more than on the answer obtained and she refrained from explicitly evaluating the answer itself (as is more usual in classrooms). Mrs. Porter addressed her messages both to the student providing the explanation and to their classmates. Furthermore, Mrs. Porter communicated two implicit messages about explanations: that they should fully explain (or tell the complete story of) the solver's strategies (as in Lyndsey's case) and that they should be tailored for the audience's level of comprehension (as in Ophrah's case). In addition, Mrs. Porter identified the standard algorithm as quick but cautioned her students to use it only if they understood it. Finally, in this brief sample of that lesson's discussion, the turn-taking pattern was from the teacher to a single student to the teacher, to the same student, to the teacher, and so on. The other students in the class listened to the exchange but were not speakers. This turn-taking pattern continued throughout this lesson and was a very frequent pattern during whole-class discussion in Mrs. Porter's classroom. This pattern occurred, in part, because her students did not openly evaluate each other's strategies, which could have threatened the social norm of mutual respect.

Thus, we have seen how Mrs. Porter expressed, both explicitly and implicitly, the classroom social norm of clear and comprehensive communication. She told her students to use a variety of recording formats (tally marks, symbols, charts, words, pictures) to convey the whole story of their solution path. In addition, she mentioned the sociomathematical norm of efficiency (as speed) when she discussed the use of the standard algorithm by two students. Nevertheless, she cautioned her students that this quick strategy might be confusing. Finally, we glimpsed a classroom where learning from each other was a valued social norm and thus a shared notion of an adequate explanation was required.

In the following section, we will see how these norms are enacted and elaborated in the context of the discussion of the strategy-choice task. In addition, we will have a chance to see Mrs. Porter's students compare the different strategy options in terms of clarity of communication versus efficiency.

LEARNING TO EXPLAIN DURING THE STRATEGY CHOICE LESSONS

The strategy-choice task was completed in two parts. First, students were presented with a multidigit word problem and five different, but equally accurate, solution strategies. The problem was: "A human brain weighs 3 lbs. If we added together the weight of all of the brains in our class, what would the total be? (The class had 18 students.)" The students were asked to work alone or with a partner to decide which strategy would be the "best" and to explain their choice in writing. A week later, the students and teacher met as a whole class to discuss the reasons for their selections.

In both lessons, two basic reasons emerged for the students' selections of their preferred strategies: (1) clarity of communication and (2) efficiency. The first reason, clarity of communication, seems consistent with the social norm of explaining your thinking clearly and fully so that your audience can grasp your reasoning. The second reason, efficiency, seems consistent with the sociomathematical norm of valuing either speed or parsimony.

Initial Selection and Justification of the Strategy Choices

In the first lesson, Mrs. Porter introduced the strategy-choice task by reminding her students that she frequently displayed their strategies for solving problems on the board. On those occasions, she continued, they might have thought that some strategies were better than others even though all of them were accurate. She then distributed the strategy-choice task and told her students that all of the strategies displayed were correct solutions to the problem. She explained to her students that in this task they needed to decide which strategy was "best" and explain why.

Three of the five strategies explicitly mirrored the problem situation (strategies 1, 2, and 5). Strategies 1 (Fig. 6.1) and 2 (Fig. 6.2) were additive, while the fifth was multiplicative (Fig. 6.3). We will refer to these strategies as

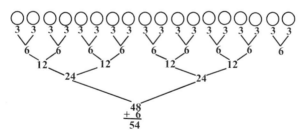

FIG. 6.1. Strategy choice 1.

$$
\begin{array}{ccc}
3\,||| & 3\,||| & 3\,||| \\
3\,||| & 3\,||| & 3\,||| \\
3\,||| & 3\,||| & 3\,||| \\
3\,||| & 3\,||| & 3\,||| \\
3\,||| & 3\,||| & 3\,||| \\
3\,||| & 3\,||| & 3\,||| \\
\end{array}
$$

FIG. 6.2. Strategy choice 2.

3 lbs × 2 = 6	2 brains	3 × 10 = 30 lbs	10 brains
3 × 3 = 9 lbs	3 brains	3 × 11 = 33 lbs	11 brains
3 × 4 = 12 lbs	4 brains	3 × 12 = 36 lbs	12 brains
3 × 5 = 15 lbs	5 brains	3 × 13 = 39 lbs	13 brains
3 × 6 = 18 lbs	6 brains	3 × 14 = 42 lbs	14 brains
3 × 7 = 21 lbs	7 brains	3 × 15 = 45 lbs	15 brains
3 × 8 = 24 lbs	8 brains	3 × 16 = 48 lbs	16 brains
3 × 9 = 27 lbs	9 brains	3 × 17 = 51 lbs	17 brains
		3 × 18 = 54 lbs	18 brains

FIG. 6.3. Strategy choice 5.

"instrumental" using a distinction proposed by Putnam et al. (1990). In their view, instrumental (or practical) approaches to using mathematics are less abstract because "the solution strategy is tied much more closely to the situation of the problem" (p. 105). Strategies 3 (Fig. 6.4) and 4 (Fig. 6.5) required

$$3 \times 10 \text{ Students} = 30 \text{ lbs}$$
$$3 \times 8 \quad \text{Students} = \underline{24}$$
$$54 \text{ lbs}$$

18 × 2 (lbs each) = 36 lbs
36 + 18 (1 more lb each) = 54 lbs

FIG. 6.5. Strategy choice 4.

FIG. 6.4. Strategy choice 3.

greater inference from the problem situation and, thus, would be viewed by Putnam et al. as more abstract. According to Putnam et al., abstract strategies are those that take parts of a problem situation from its context and use mathematical symbols and operations to indicate their quantitative relationships. This is most obvious in strategy 3, in which the weight of a brain (3 lbs.) is treated as merely a mathematical symbol that can be decomposed into numbers $(2 + 1)$ that are easier to multiply.

Most of the students (13 out of 17) chose one of the three instrumental solutions as the "best strategy" because they felt that those explanations would be the easiest to read or understand. (Eight students selected strategy 1, six students selected strategy 2, and three students selected strategy 5. Students were allowed to select more than one "best" strategy.) A review of the students' written justifications for selecting the instrumental strategies demonstrates that many students chose those strategies because of their clarity of communication. They argued that those strategies depicted the whole story of the formats (like charts or tally marks) that communicated the strategy well to a broad audience. For example, Lissa wrote, "I like number one because it has 18 brains on the top and a three under each brain. I also like it because I understood it right away." In a similar fashion, Miranda wrote, "I think number two is the best one because they used three in each group and made three going across and six going down. I like it because it is easy to read." Ophrah had selected both strategies one and five as the best. She justified her choices in the following way: "I like number five because it is easy to understand. I like it also because it has different things on one chart. I understand the way they did it. When there is an equation then an answer then how many there is. I like that one. I like number one because it is a chart and it is easy to understand."

The remaining four students (all male) who chose number 4 as best (no one selected number 3) based their choice on the solution's efficiency (speed or parsimony). For example, Pulak mentioned both speed and parsimony when he wrote, "I think number four is the best way because it's the fastest and it doesn't take up much room and it is a very very easy way to do it." Ethan used a similar justification: "Number 4. Because it takes a short time to know what they're doing. It doesn't take a long time to make it either." The written responses, however, provided us with limited information about students' notions of either clarity or efficiency. The classroom discussion presented a richer picture of their understanding of explanations.

Discussion of the Strategy Choices

One week after the initial task presentation, the whole-class discussion of their strategy preferences took place. This discussion differed from that of more typical problems (as we saw in the September conversation) because in this discussion the authors of the strategies were unknown and the strategies were first examined in a written form. Thus, the strategies were like texts penned by unseen authors and directed to an unknown audience (instead of oral explanations provided by a known author and directed to a familiar audience). In our analysis of the strategy-choice discussion, we highlight the degree to which each student expressed his or her sensitivity to the likely characteristics of the unknown authors and audiences as well as to the attributes of the written strategies. This enables us to evaluate the degree to which Mrs. Porter's students' justifications embodied aspects of the three-part conversational model for explanations proposed by Hilton (1990): speaker (or author); audience; explanation (strategy choice text).

Mrs. Porter began the discussion by returning her students' written work and asking them to look it over. She then opened the discussion with the following comment:

> When you explain why you chose it, what you're really doing is explaining why you think it's the best strategy and what a best strategy is. 'Cause we didn't decide what best means. So part of making this decision is to figure out what does "best" mean. And, some people may think best is one thing and some people might think it's another and that's OK. All of these strategies work. They all work to get the answer.

We present the discussion in three parts: First, we summarize the discussion of the three instrumental strategies (1, 2, and 5) that were selected because they were clearly explained; second, we review the discussion of the one abstract strategy (4) that was selected because it was seen as efficient; and, finally, we describe the end of the discussion in which the students compared and contrasted multiple strategies.

Discussion of the Instrumental Strategies.   The first strategy discussed (1) depicted the 13 brains and then used a doubling tree to keep track of adding the 18 three's. The seven students who spoke in defense of this strategy agreed that it was easy to tell what the solver had done. Two examples of typical exchanges between a student and the teacher are displayed below. In the first example, Sabrina explained what she meant by easy to understand. In the second example, Nathan justified why he was intrigued by the written version of the strategy.

30	Sabrina	If I looked at this now and if I didn't know what they were talking about, I could understand them.
31	FP	You could understand them.
32	Sabrina	In just a few words.

| 40 | Nathan | Cause, we thought it, I thought, it was real interesting. Like to look at it, and you can't figure it out at first, but when if you look at it real closely you can figure it out. |
| 41 | FP | OK. So, you thought it was a very interesting looking one that at first you didn't know what it meant and it was kind of puzzling to you and you like to see puzzles and you like to try and figure things out and this one made you want to do that. OK. So, for Nathan, best means interesting. And for the other people that talked, best means it's easy to see what somebody did. And it's very clear to look at. |

In the first example, Sabrina mentioned the written strategy, herself as the audience, and the unseen author of the strategy; in the second example, Nathan only mentioned two of those components, the written strategy and himself as audience of the strategy. As you can see, the unseen authors and the written strategy could be easily differentiated in Sabrina's and Nathan's speech because the identity of the authors was unknown. This is a situation that was unusual in this classroom in which written strategies by known authors are frequently presented but not evaluated as "best." Thus, the teaching dilemma raised earlier about the need to separate the author from the explanation was resolved for these two students here.

After Mrs. Porter's summary of the explanations from several students, she redirected the class attention to the next strategy (2). The idea of clarity was made problematic by Mrs. Porter and her students during the next segment in which the strategy that used tally marks was discussed. This strategy depicted 18 groups of three tallies, and indicated that one can "count up all the tallies to get 54." The discussion, which began with Benjamin's justification, is illustrated below.

43	FP	OK, now who had one that they chose that was the best that was different from number 1? Benjamin.
44	Benjamin	I had number 2.
45	FP	OK. Do you want to . . .
46	Benjamin	I think it was the best because I thought it was pretty easy to understand and pretty much everyone can like understand it.
47	FP	OK. It was very easy to understand. Did you have another thing, that you said that I didn't hear?
48	Benjamin	Ya uhm, like most pretty much everybody, can understand it because like . . .
49	FP	Like everyone? Who do you mean? Like everyone in this class or?
50	Benjamin	Sorta, like so many people, like can understand it . . .
51	FP	Do you mean the people in this class or other people too?
52	Benjamin	Other people too . . .
53	FP	Like who else?
54	Benjamin	Like if this was like a chart or something
55	FP	Uhhuh.
56	Benjamin	Then they would probably . . . and people would understand it and not just start flat like,
57	FP	Like uhm, grown-ups or little kids or
58	Benjamin	Grown-ups like . . . (mumbling)
59	FP	Second grade and first grade?

60	Benjamin	Ya.
61	FP	OK. So he thinks that number 2, he thinks best is if lots of people, grown-ups all the way down to really little kids can understand it. And he thinks number 2 would fit that.

At the beginning of the discussion of this strategy, Benjamin justified his choice by claiming that "pretty much everyone can like understand it." Notice that Benjamin shifted the focus from himself as the sole audience (as in Sabrina's and Nathan's explanations) to himself and everyone else as the potential audience. Mrs. Porter asked for further clarification of this shift in focus on the potential audience by asking, "Like everyone? Who do you mean? Like everyone in this class or?" As the discussion continued, Mrs. Porter asked for specific information about the audience: older, younger, or same age? Finally, Mrs. Porter summarized Benjamin's justification by highlighting the broad audience that might understand this strategy.

During the segment depicted above, Benjamin suggested that the information displayed in the strategy looked like a chart, which made it easier to understand and perhaps proposed that it provides the background information needed to fully articulate the solution path for a naïve audience (so that people do not "just start flat"). Immediately after the displayed segment, Mrs. Porter asked Benjamin why he thought so many people would find this strategy clear enough to understand: Was it due to the way it was displayed using tally marks? Benjamin agreed with this reason by saying, "Well, just looking at the threes and having the tallies."

Thus, Benjamin's explanation contained two of the three components identified by Sabrina: the written strategy and its audience. Like Nathan, but unlike Sabrina, Benjamin did not mention the unknown author. Unlike either of them, Benjamin expanded the audience from himself to everybody. Mrs. Porter encouraged Benjamin and the class to consider the possible age range of this more general sense of audience and the possibility that different audiences might understand different texts. Benjamin argued (with Mrs. Porter's encouragement) that a strategy that explicitly depicts the solution path is better because it can be interpreted by a broader audience. Thus, for Benjamin, the best explanation was one that can be understood by the most people.

Another reason that this strategy may be seen to communicate its message clearly is that it uses charts of numbers and tally marks to represent the process of counting up the pounds: ways of depicting the strategy that were explicitly mentioned in the discussion of the reading problem from the first week of school. Thus, its selection was consistent with the social norm of explaining yourself clearly so that other members of the class (including the teacher) can understand your thinking from the beginning to end—the whole story.

Commenting on strategy 2, Michael questioned the universal clarity of tally marks when he reflected on the fact that his younger brother did not understand them. Ophrah opposed Michael's position when she argued that tally marks would help younger students keep track while they are using a counting strategy to solve this problem: "They could just count the tally marks and see what the number is." At this point in the discussion, Mrs. Porter suggested an empirical investigation: "it would be interesting, maybe we could show them (kindergarten students) some things and see." In response, Nathan recast his teacher's comment as a teaching experiment, "Maybe we could teach them some things about it." Thus, Nathan showed his awareness of the classroom norm of using communication to guide both assessment and instruction.

The last instrumental strategy (5) was represented in the form of a chart (as was strategy 2); however, it differed from the other two instrumental strategies because it was based on a series of multiplicative equations (e.g., $3 \times 3 = 9$ lbs). Two students, Raj and Ophrah, explained their selection of this strategy in different ways. Raj explained the multiplicative equations in additive terms whereas Ophrah referred to the multiplication tables in her justification. Ophrah also mentioned that this strategy was easy to understand. A portion of that discussion is given below.

147	FP	OK, Raj. Let's all look at number 5 here. And why did you choose number 5, Raj?
148	Raj	I choose to do like, every, every time they did a, a math problem, they were adding 3 to it to uhm, get to 18, and that's how I and that's how they ended up with 54 pounds.
149	FP	OK. You're saying that you can see all the equations and it says at the bottom add 3 each time. Which those people have on their paper. And you could see how they added 3 each time and that's why you think it was the best one. OK, now. Who had two strategies? Which two did you have Ophrah?
150	Ophrah	1 and 5.
151	FP	1 and 5.
152	Ophrah	But I chose 5 first.

153	FP	OK. Did you have the same reason for choosing them
154	Ophrah	No.
155	FP	or different reasons?
156	Ophrah	Different reasons.
157	FP	OK. Tell us the reasons why?
158	Ophrah	I chose number 5 because, uhm, it was really easy to read and understand. And you could see that like, all that, like instead of doing it like 1, then do like 2, you can see the time's tables and the multiplication equations.
159	FP	Uhhuh.
160	Ophrah	And then how many they did. And how many brains there was.
161	FP	OK.
162	Ophrah	And then it was uhm, more easy to understand.
163	FP	So, in a way you're saying, I think what you're saying too is that they put down everything they were thinking.
164	Ophrah	Ya.
165	FP	Three pounds times 2 equals 6, 3 and that is 2 brains. Three times 3 equals 9 pounds and 3 brains. Three times 4 equals 12 pounds and 4 brains. And you're saying EVERYTHING is there. And you know EXACTLY what they were thinking. It was like being right inside their brain, to look at that, right? OK.

Thus, in the discussion of the last instrumental strategy, both Raj and Ophrah justified their choice of the strategy because it laid out the whole solution path from beginning to end. For Raj, this path represented repeated addition; for Ophrah the path depicted a multiplication table. These two students' justifications included additional aspects of the conversational model for explanation by focusing on the process by which unseen authors record their mental processes on paper. In her summary of both of their explanations, Mrs. Porter mentioned the value of recording a strategy that fully describes the solution path. After Raj's explanation, she commented, "And you could see how they added 3 each time." Following Ophrah's explanation, she proposed that: "everything is there. And you know exactly what they were thinking. It was like being right inside their brain, to look at that, right?"

Thus, Mrs. Porter's comments on the justifications of both Raj and Ophrah reiterated the social norm of clarity of explanation while elaborating on the reasons why this norm is useful: It allows one to fully understand the thinking of the speaker or author. This type of clarity is what enables the members of this community to learn from each other due to their shared knowledge of the problem situation—another social norm in this classroom. It is also important to note that Raj's answer echoed Mrs. Porter's comments from her interview about the kinds of background knowledge that students of this age typically bring to a multiplication problem: viewing multiplication as repeated addition.

Discussion of the Abstract Strategy. The discussion changed when one of the abstract strategies (4) was addressed. All of the four male students who selected this strategy argued that they preferred its efficiency. In this strategy the group of 18 brains was symbolically broken into groups of 10 and 8 brains, and each group was multiplied by 3 separately ($3 \times 10 = 30$; $3 \times 8 = 24$) before being combined (30 and 24) to get the total. Bernard started the discussion, saying his choice was "because it was the most efficient way." When Mrs. Porter asked for clarification: "What do you mean by that (efficient)?," Bernard responded by providing the following inference: "if you know your multiplication tables, it's the most efficient." That segment of the discussion is displayed below.

91	FP	Four people chose number 4. (pause) OK. Why did you choose it, Bernard?
92	Bernard	Because it was the most efficient way and for people who, uhm it stands out clearly, 3 times 10 students equals 30 pounds, and 3 times 8 students equals 24, and you add 30 and 24 up, and you get 54.
93	FP	OK. He says it's the most efficient, what do you, efficient, what do you mean by that, Bernard? What's the, let's be clear, I think you kind of know what it means but . . .
94	Bernard	If you know your multiplication tables, it's the most efficient.
95	FP	OK.
96	Bernard	Because it has multiplying in it.
97	FP	So, this is a really good strategy you're saying for people that know their multiplication tables.

Here, another shift in the nature of the discussion took place. Picking up from the previous discussion about the age of the audience (during the discussion of strategy 2, which occurred immediately before the discussion of this strategy), Bernard added to this explication the nature of the author's knowledge base. Thus, not only did the choice of the best strategy change to one that was seen as more efficient (from one that was viewed as easy to understand), but it also changed from a focus on the age of the audience to a stress on the knowledge base of the author and his or her audience. Bernard incorporated all three components of the conversational model of explanation in his justification: the author, the audience, and the written strategy. In addition, he argued that for authors and audiences who share knowledge of the multiplication tables, a compact (e.g., parsimonious) written text can be effective because it can build on that knowledge. Therefore, texts cannot be judged apart from their use in specific community contexts, where a shared knowledge base can be presupposed.

Karl added to Bernard's justification when he said immediately after Bernard's turns at talk, "It's one of the quickest ways and it's easy to understand. And I like it because if someone like from fifth grade looked at it, they'd understand what we're talking about." Therefore, Karl integrated the earlier discussion about the age of the audience with the more recent discussion of the speaker's knowledge to conclude that fifth graders (much older and more sophisticated than mere third graders like them) would find this strategy both more efficient (quick and parsimonious) and easy to understand. Here the best strategy seems to be one that is tailored to the needs and capabilities of both the author or speaker and his or her audience. After three other boys gave their reasons (all efficiency-related), Mrs. Porter summarized and asked her students to react to this controversial notion that strategy 4 could be both the most efficient (fast or parsimonious) *and* the easiest to understand.

| 108 | FP | OK. This group is talking about the fact...(that) it doesn't take up much room. It's fastest, they think. And uhm, they said, most of them said that it's the most efficient and it's the easiest. Do, I think you can see that it doesn't take up much room. That's clear. How many people think it's the easiest? OK. So some people think it's the easiest. |
| 109 | Female student | I don't. |

110	FP	But not everybody thinks it is the easiest. Who would think it was the easiest? I think Bernard kind of gave us a clue about that. Or maybe it was Ethan, I don't remember, but I think it's Bernard. People that know what?
111	Ethan	Their multiplication tables.
112	FP	If you know your multiplication tables well. It's very quick and very efficient. If you don't know your multiplication tables well, then it wouldn't be a quick and efficient strategy for you. Right? So sometimes, it depends on who's doing it. Would it be a good strategy, Karl? You were saying fifth graders were looking at this, they'd really understand it. What about the other kids in this school?
113	Karl	Well, if they don't know their multiplication tables, second grade might not like it.
114	FP	They may not like it. Who, who in this school might have a little trouble understanding this, Karl?
115	Karl	Kindergarten.
116	FP	OK. I think so.
117	Karl	And first.

In the segment displayed above, Mrs. Porter built on students' suggestions to help specify the nature of the audience that might find this strategy the clearest (students who know their multiplication tables) and those who might find another strategy, like the instrumental ones, the easiest to understand.

Discussion of Strategy Comparisons. In the final part of the lesson, the conversation changed for a third time as students shifted from defending their choices to questioning the strategies. Mrs. Porter began this part of the discussion by calling on students who had chosen two strategies and asking them to provide reasons for their choices. Several students abandoned their initial choices and criteria. For example, Nathan began by wondering whether he now preferred the more abstract strategy (4) despite the fact that he had originally chosen one of the instrumental strategies. He mentioned that he now found the abstract strategy "quicker." Although Nathan

switched to the abstract strategy because of its speed, he also criticized it
for its lack of explicitness (no plus sign). Pulak criticized one of the instrumental strategies because it was less efficient (e.g., slow and cumbersome)
than simply multiplying 3 × 18. Thus, Nathan and Pulak felt free to reflect
on and critically evaluate the relative merits of different strategies without worrying about sounding disrespectful of other students' ideas because
those authors were unknown. This was another example of how the teaching
dilemma was resolved by the strategy-choice assignment, at least for these
students.

After Pulak's question, an exchange between Mrs. Porter and several students followed in response to her question: "Why might these students not
have done that (multiply 3 × 18)?" In response to attempts by three students
to answer this question, Mrs. Porter supplied it herself when she connected
this strategy (and the others) to the notion of sense-making. That exchange
is displayed below.

215	FP	Pulak was asking, well, why did they bother going 3 times 2, 3 times 3, 3 times 4? All they had to do, he said, is go 3 times 18. Why might these students not have just said 3 times 18? Pulak probably would have said, I know how I'll do it, I'll just do 3 times 18. Why might these students not have done that, Sabrina?
216	Sabrina	Because they wanted to show what they were thinking, they didn't just want to put it down, just for any old reason.
217	FP	No, if they were really thinking 3 times 18 I think they would have put that down. But they didn't. There must be another reason. Why? Michael.
218	Michael	Uhm, because it's really hard to count three 18 times and once you, if you mess up on the count and you don't remember, you have to go all the way back again. And they don't want the trouble in case they have to go all the way back again because if they don't remember the, the number right.
219	FP	OK. Nathan.
220	Nathan	Well, it will be really, it will, it will be so like, sorta like. If you get 3 times 18 it will be hard to, to see what it was.

221	FP	And some people might find it very hard in third grade, especially early in third grade to know what 3 times 18 is. For some kids who know 3 times 18, that would be an easy way to do it. But if you don't know how to do 3 times 18, then you might need another strategy, which is adding it up, adding 3 each time. And that works. Or by doing 3 times 10 and then 3 times 8 and adding them together. It depends on what you already know and what makes sense to you. Three times 18 is a wonderful strategy if you know how to do 3 times 18. But if you don't, and some day you probably will be able to do that easily, then use a different strategy. And that's why we have so many.

This segment is interesting for several reasons. First, this portion of lesson demonstrated that the strategy-choice task did achieve its desired aim: It enabled Mrs. Porter to resolve the teaching dilemma she had identified. Her students could reflect on and evaluate the relative merits of multiple strategies without violating the social norm of mutual respect. Second, unlike most of the discussions that we have observed, the exchange occurred among Mrs. Porter and more than one student. These three students addressed the advantages and disadvantages of the same strategy ($3 \times 18 = 54$). One student, Sabrina, argued that this strategy disguised the author's thinking processes; another, Michael, suggested that it might enable the author to avoid some of the computational errors inherent in repeated addition; a third, Nathan, proposed that this strategy might be difficult to understand for some audiences. In this instance, although the speakers were known, these three students could reflect on, augment, or disagree with each other's explanations, at least for a brief amount of time. Third, it built on previous discussions of authors, audiences, and their texts because Sabrina and Michael mentioned authors and texts whereas Nathan spoke of audiences and texts. Fourth, it highlighted the importance of the author's knowledge base in interpreting his or her product.

Summary of the Strategy Choice Lessons

The strategy-choice lessons as they were conducted in Mrs. Porter's classroom seemed to offer an opportunity to resolve the teaching dilemma introduced earlier in the chapter. This dilemma arose when the social norms of mutual respect and clarity of communication appeared to contradict the mathematical

norms of valuing increasingly quick, concise, and abstract strategies for solving problems. Our analyses of the discussion that occurred during one of the
two lessons devoted to that task showed that Mrs. Porter's students were able
to reflect on and judge the relative merits of a range of strategies for solving the same multidigit problem. Their criteria for deciding which strategy
was best fell into two basic categories that echoed the two types of norms:
easy to understand (due to the social norm of clear communication) versus efficient (due to the sociomathematical norm). Mrs. Porter's students appeared to find it easier to articulate and compare their decisions for the "best"
strategy because the authors of those strategies were unknown. Thus, they
were able to differentiate the authors from their explanatory texts more easily and with fewer risks than in the more familiar discussions among known
authors.

The discussion of the strategies showed how Mrs. Porter and her students
were also able to reflect on and articulate a model of the nature of explanation that has three components: a written or spoken product, an author,
and an audience. Furthermore, they were able to differentiate between different types of authors and audiences in terms of age and knowledge base.
Finally, they began to reevaluate the original set of strategies in terms of the
degree of congruence between the written product and the shared knowledge
of authors and audiences. Thus, they were beginning to develop a framework
for understanding what counts as an adequate explanation in their classroom
community.

Mrs. Porter and her students explored the issues of clarity of communication and efficiency in greater detail as they discussed specific strategies. For
example, the instrumental strategies were preferred because they told more of
the whole story of the problem-solving process. This whole story was seen (by
students such as Sabrina and Nathan) as necessary for supporting the author's
claim about the problem solution. The whole story was also valued because it
could be understood by the largest audience (both older and younger people),
according to Benjamin. In addition, charts or tally marks were viewed as tools
that can support the author's counting strategies (by Ophrah). Furthermore,
instrumental strategies help everyone in the community learn from each
other and provide clues to effective teaching strategies (according to Mrs.
Porter and Nathan).

In contrast, the more abstract strategies were chosen because they were
quicker, more parsimonious (took up less space), and were easy to understand
if your audience knows their multiplication tables (according to Bernard,
Karl, and Pulak). In this part of the discussion, the students and their teacher

explored the importance of a shared knowledge base among members of a community so that an exchange of a minimum of information could have maximal impact. Throughout the discussion, no clear distinction between the two connotations of efficiency was made. Perhaps this was due to Mrs. Porter's emphasis on sense-making. At this point in the discussion, Nathan became convinced that the more abstract strategies could be better even though important pieces of information (a plus sign) might be missing. Thus, the instrumental strategies seemed to be preferred because they could be understood by the broadest learning community whereas the more abstract strategies were selected because of their power within the confines of a narrower, more mathematically sophisticated community.

DISCUSSION AND CONCLUSIONS

What have we learned about learning to explain in mathematics from our analysis of three lessons in Mrs. Porter's classroom? We found that Mrs. Porter made fostering communication in mathematics a central instructional goal in her classroom by establishing norms that created a climate of mutual respect and personally meaningful solutions to problems. Nevertheless, she discovered a teaching dilemma that has been identified by other researchers also interested in mathematical communication: how to teach students evaluative criteria without threatening the climate of mutual respect (Franke & Carey, 1997; Hatano & Inagaki, 1998; O'Connor, 2001). In order to resolve that dilemma, Mrs. Porter designed the strategy-choice task, which was the focus of our analysis.

We began this chapter with two different goals in mind: a practical aim that addressed the teaching dilemma faced by Mrs. Porter and a theoretical aim of articulating an understanding of the norms of mathematical explanation within this classroom community. In our concluding section we show how these two goals can be merged, beginning with the teaching dilemma. We originally mentioned the distinction between social norms and sociomathematical norms in order to help us understand the teaching dilemma that Franke, Carey, Hatano, Inagaki, and O'Connor have identified. There seemed to be a potential conflict between social norms that fostered mutual respect and clarity of communication and sociomathematical norms that encouraged the critical examination of differentially efficient strategies for solving the same problem. Japanese educators have apparently resolved that dilemma by devoting several years of early childhood education to the creation of a caring community in which errors can be examined without damaging students' sense of self-worth. In contrast, teachers in North American classrooms spend less time nurturing a caring community during the preschool and primary school years before difficult academic content is introduced. Also, the Japanese culture seems to tolerate more public self- and other-scrutiny than would be acceptable in North American classrooms (Hatano & Inagaki, 1998).

Although Mrs. Porter did foster a caring community in her classroom so that students could feel comfortable taking risks and sharing their strategies, she was concerned about their willingness to criticize each other's strategies. The strategy-choice task was designed to support reflection and critical analysis without threatening the climate of mutual respect. During the discussion of the strategy-choice assignment, it became apparent that the original distinction between strategies that are easy to understand and those that are efficient disappeared when one takes into account the author's knowledge base and that of his or her audience. For example, if the author and audience both understand multiplication, then employing symbolic notation that depends upon that shared knowledge will be both efficient and easy to understand. Conversely, if the author and audience both know how to interpret tally marks or a chart that displays the results of repeated addition, then that text will be efficient and easy to understand. Knowing your audience's age may help you anticipate their information needs, but it may not be sufficient because young children who can count may not understand that tally marks represent counting. Thus, it becomes difficult to differentiate between social norms that foster clarity of communication and sociomathematical norms that value efficiency. One is left asking, as Mrs. Porter and her students did: Efficient for whom? Easy to understand for whom? In other words, in a learning community, the distinction between social norms and sociomathematical norms may disappear if one views explaining as a conversational activity. We will articulate this perspective below in light of the results from the discussion of the strategy-choice assignment. How does this new theoretical perspective help us design educational environments that encourage conceptually challenging mathematical communication?

One set of answers comes from the field of discursive psychology (e.g., Billig, 1987, 1996; Harre & Gillett, 1994; Hilton, 1990). Discursive psychology returns to the insights of the late Wittgenstein when it asks us to examine what people actually do when they are communicating rather than to guess what they picture in their minds (Harre & Gillet, 1994). By focusing on communication practices or language games, Wittgenstein proposed that meaning resides in social interaction instead of in internal mental representations.

> (Wittgenstein) came to see that mental activity is not essentially a Cartesian or inner set of processes but a range of moves or techniques defined against a background of human activity and governed by informal rules. These rules, unlike the rules-laws at work in supposed inner, cognitive processes, were the rules that people actually followed. (Harre & Gillet, 1994, p. 19)

Hilton's conversational model of explanation is one of the offshoots of this larger agenda in discursive psychology: He suggests that we analyze what people actually do when they try to explain something to someone else. This model does not refer to mental representations but does suggest that understanding the social context of explanations is crucial for appreciating their adequacy. Hilton's definition of explanation is very similar to the three-part framework for evaluating strategies that emerged during the discussion of the strategy-choice task in Mrs. Porter's classroom. She and her students began to examine the informal rules that govern conversations about strategies and that paid attention to the relationships between authors, texts, and audiences. During that discussion, Mrs. Porter and her students came to recognize that explanations could not be judged as clear or efficient apart from their context of use. They began to explore the power of different kinds of explanations in various important activities such as teaching novices or convincing experts. The issue of different kinds of explanations for different types of purposes also arises in the field of the sociology of science.

Latour (1987), for instance, proposed that communication is a central activity of scientific communities. That is, argumentation about written texts (published articles and books) is used to advance the knowledge claims of one group of investigators over those of their rivals. Different scientific texts are critically evaluated in terms of their relative explanatory adequacy as in the strategy choice-discussion. Furthermore, scientists interested in reaching a broad, general audience (by publishing in *Scientific American*, for example) would need to avoid or explicitly define their technical terms and write with a minimum of assumptions about the audience's specialized knowledge base (Roth & McGinn, 1998). They might have to make their own problem-solving processes explicit for this less knowledgeable audience. In contrast, scientists could write more efficiently, more abstractly, more concisely for a narrow audience of peers when publishing in a more specialized, academic journal. Thus, no one scientific explanation can be evaluated in terms of its adequacy without considering the nature of the authors, the text, and the audience as well as the specific time and place. If scientists are involved in evaluating the communicational adequacy of their explanations, then helping students learn mathematics and science by engaging in a similar activity in their classrooms seems well justified (Lampert, 1990; Roth & McGinn, 1998; Strom, Kemeny, Lehrer, & Forman, 2001). At least one investigation has explored this issue in some detail (Crawford, Chen, & Kelly, 1997).

Therefore, research in discursive psychology and in the sociology of science (e.g., Latour, 1987) has shown that communication in scientific communities shares some similarities with everyday communication: The basic principle of tailoring your explanation to the information needs of your audience applies in both situations. Nevertheless, explanations in science need to be explicit, grounded in warrants and evidence, and addressed toward a skeptical audience more than do explanations in everyday life (Forman, Larreamendy-Joerns, Stein, & Brown, 1998). For scientists, as well as Japanese students, an atmosphere of self- and other-criticism co-occurs with an atmosphere of mutual respect (at least in theory).

A similar issue applies to the field of mathematics. For example, abstract strategies for solving problems are typically preferred over instrumental strategies by professional mathematicians. Yet, at times, mathematicians end up finding value in more everyday instrumental strategies. For example, the history of mathematics shows that important discoveries, such as negative numbers, were first made for instrumental purposes such as bookkeeping (Putnam et al., 1990). Putnam, Lampert, and Peterson asked us to question whether abstract approaches to solving problems should always be preferred in all contexts (cf. Scribner, 1984). They suggest that teachers try to convey an appreciation for a variety of approaches, as we saw in the discussion of the strategy-choice task.

In conclusion, we have found that Mrs. Porter and her students began to articulate a social and discursive framework for explanations in their discussion of the strategy-choice assignment. Like discursive psychologists and scientists, they identified the informational needs of specific audiences and recognized that the best explanations are those that take those needs into account. If the audience is sophisticated, then the best explanations can be abstract, efficient, and concise. If the audience is broader, then the best explanations are often more detailed, instrumental, redundant, and/or process-oriented. In addition, like scientists, they made advancing claims and supporting them with well-articulated evidence and warrants an important part of their classroom practices. Mrs. Porter and her students found it less socially threatening to evaluate different strategies when the authors were unknown (as in the peer review process required by many scientific journals). Yet, her students also found it possible to imagine themselves as assuming the role of author or audience for those explanations. Thus, it appears that asking even young students to imagine the conversational context of explanations, by providing assignments like the strategy-choice task, can allow them to create, with the assistance of their teacher, a learning community that resembles in some respects that of professional scientists and mathematicians.

ACKNOWLEDGMENTS

This research reported herein was supported, in part, by grants to the first author from the Spencer Foundation, from the U.S. Department of Education, Office of Educational Research and Improvement, to the National Center for Improving Student Learning and Achievement in Mathematics and Science (R305A60007-98), and from the School of Education at the University of Pittsburgh. The opinions expressed do not necessarily reflect the position, policy, or endorsement of the supporting agencies. The assistance of Renee Bruckner, Deborah Dobransky-Fasiska, Elizabeth Hughes, Jaime Munoz, Elaine Olds, Martin Packer, Ann Rosebery, Addison Stone, and Beth Warren is gratefully acknowledged.

REFERENCES

Audi, R. (Ed.). (1995). *The Cambridge dictionary of philosophy*. New York, NY: Cambridge University Press.

Bazerman, C. (1988). *Shaping written knowledge: The genre and activity of the experimental article in science*. Madison, WI: University of Wisconsin Press.

Beals, D. E., & Snow, C. E. (1994). "Thunder is when the angels are upstairs bowling": Narratives and explanations at the dinner table. *Journal of Narrative and Life History*, *4*, 331–352.

Billig, M. (1996/1987). *Arguing and thinking: A rhetorical approach to social psychology* (2nd ed.). Cambridge, UK: Cambridge University Press.

Callanan, M. A., Shrager, J., & Moore, J. L. (1995). Parent-child collaborative explanations: Methods of identification and analysis. *The Journal of the Learning Sciences*, *4*(1), 105–129.

Carpenter, T. P., Fennema, E., Franke, M. L., Levi, L., & Empson, S. B. (1999). *Children's mathematics: Cognitively guided instruction*. Portsmouth, NH: Heinemann.

Cazden, C. B. (2001). *Classroom discourse: The language of teaching and learning* (2nd ed.). Portsmouth, NH: Heinemann.

Crawford, T., Chen, C., & Kelly, G. J. (1997). Creating authentic opportunities for presenting science: The influence of audience on student talk. *Journal of Classroom Interaction, 32*, 1–13.

Flavell, J. H., Miller, P. H., & Miller, S. A. (1993). *Cognitive development* (3rd ed.). Englewood Cliffs, NJ: Prentice-Hall.

Forman, E. A., & Ansell, E. (2001). The multiple voices of a mathematics classroom community. *Educational Studies in Mathematics, 46*(1–3), 115–142.

Forman, E. A., & Ansell, E. (2002). Orchestrating the multiple voices and inscriptions of a mathematics classroom. *The Journal of the Learning Sciences, 11*(2–3), 251–274.

Forman, E. A., Larreamendy-Joerns, J., Stein, M. K., & Brown, C. A. (1998). "You're going to want to find out which and prove it": Collective argumentation in a mathematics classroom. *Learning and Instruction, 8*(6), 527–548.

Franke, M. L., & Carey, D. A. (1997). Young children's perceptions of mathematics in problem-solving environments. *Journal for Research in Mathematics Education, 28*(1), 8–25.

Harre, R., & Gillett, G. (1994). *The discursive mind.* London: Sage.

Hatano, G., & Inagaki, K. (1998). Cultural contexts of schooling revisited: A review of *The Learning Gap* from a cultural psychology perspective. In S. G. Paris & H. M. Wellman (Eds.), *Global prospects for education: Development, culture, and schooling* (pp. 79–104). Washington, DC: American Psychological Association.

Hiebert, J. (1992). Reflection and communication: Cognitive considerations in school mathematics reform. *International Journal of Educational Research, 17*, 439–456.

Hiebert, J., Carpenter, T. P., Fennema, E., Fuson, K., Human, P., Murray, H., Olivier, A., & Wearne, D. (1996). Problem solving as a basis for reform in curriculum and instruction: The case of mathematics. *Educational Researcher, 25*(4), 12–21.

Hilton, D. J. (1990). Conversational processes and causal explanation. *Psychological Bulletin, 107*(1), 65–81.

Inagaki, K., Morita, E., & Hatano, G. (1999). Teaching-learning of evaluative criteria for mathematical arguments through classroom discourse: A cross-national study. *Mathematical Thinking and Learning, 1*(2), 93–111.

Lampert, M. (1985). How do teachers manage to teach? Perspectives on problems in practice. *Harvard Educational Review, 55*(2), 178–194.

Lampert, M. (1990). When the problem is not the question and the solution is not the answer: Mathematical knowing and teaching. *American Educational Research Journal, 27*, 29–63.

Lampert, M., & Blunk, M. L. (Eds.). (1998). *Talking mathematics in school: Studies of teaching and learning.* New York: Cambridge University Press.

Latour, B. (1987). *Science in action: How to follow scientists and engineers through society.* Cambridge, MA: Harvard University Press.

Lewis, C. C. (1995). *Educating hearts and minds: Reflections on Japanese preschool and elementary education.* New York: Cambridge University Press.

Linn, M. C., Lewis, C., Tsuchida, I., & Songer, N. B. (2000). Beyond fourth-grade science: Why do U.S. and Japanese students diverge? *Educational Researcher, 29*(3), 4–14.

NCTM. (2000). *Principles and standards for school mathematics.* Reston, VA: National Council of Teachers of Mathematics.

O'Connor, M. C. (2001). Can any fraction be turned into a decimal? A case study of a mathematical group discussion. *Educational Studies in Mathematics, 46*(1–3), 143–185.

Putnam, R., Lampert, M., & Peterson, P. L. (1990). Alternative perspectives on knowing mathematics in elementary schools. In C. B. Cazden (Ed.), *Review of Research in Education* (Vol. 16, pp. 57–150). Washington, D.C.: American Educational Research Association.

Roth, W. M., & McGinn, M. K. (1998). Inscriptions: Toward a theory of representing as social practice. *Review of Educational Research, 68*(1), 35–59.

Scribner, S. (1984). Studying working intelligence. In B. Rogoff & J. Lave (Eds.), *Everyday cognition: Its development in social context* (pp. 13–30). Cambridge, MA: Harvard University Press.

Sfard, A., & Kieran, C. (2001). Cognition as communication: Rethinking learning-by-talking through multi-faceted analysis of students' mathematical interactions. *Mind, Culture, and Activity, 8*(1), 42–76.

Strom, D., Kemeny, V., Lehrer, R., & Forman, E. A. (2001). Visualizing the emergent structure of children's mathematical argument. *Cognitive Science, 25*, 733–773.

Tobin, J. J., Wu, Y. H. D., & Davidson, D. H. (1989). *Preschool in three cultures.* New Haven, CT: Yale University Press.

Yackel, E., & Cobb, P. (1996). Sociomathematical norms, argumentation, and autonomy in mathematics. *Journal for Research in Mathematics Education, 27*(4), 458–477.

7

Instructional Contexts That Support Students' Transition From Arithmetic to Algebraic Reasoning: Elements of Tasks and Culture

Maria L. Blanton
James J. Kaput
University of Massachusetts Dartmouth

If we view learning environments as spaces of contact between students' everyday experiences and the formalisms associated with school mathematics, then our interest in fostering the development of algebraic reasoning in elementary school mathematics prompts us to consider the kind of learning environment teachers should construct in order to facilitate this. In particular, what types of tasks might teachers select or develop to coordinate students' everyday experiences involving number and arithmetic operations with mathematical ideas that the discipline recognizes as "algebraic," and how should these tasks be integrated into the life of the classroom? In addressing these questions, we describe two goals of the work discussed here.

Our first goal is to articulate principles that can inform the design of particular learning environments that will strengthen students' algebraic reasoning skills while integrating the leverage of their everyday experiences with the discipline of mathematics. We derived these principles from examining how certain types of instructional tasks and the classroom culture in which they were embedded served to elicit third-grade students' activity of generalizing and the attendant processes of argumentation and justification, both of which support the integration of arithmetic and algebraic reasoning. Our second goal is to contribute a theoretical framework for analyzing these learning environments, or the *culture of instruction* in which the tasks occurred, as a way to think about how the teacher's instructional decisions might have supported algebraic reasoning. By this designation of culture, we refer to those actions by the teacher, as conveyed through verbal discourse, that supported the algebraic life of the tasks in their implementation. We begin by outlining our framework for analysis and then describing what we view as algebraic reasoning.

VALSINER'S ZONE THEORY AS A FRAMEWORK FOR INTERPRETING THE CULTURE OF INSTRUCTION

Valsiner (1987) extended the notion of a zone of proximal development (ZPD) (Vygotsky, 1986) to include two additional zones of interaction: the zone of free movement (ZFM) and the zone of promoted action (ZPA). He identified the ZFM and ZPA as a way to describe the cognitive aspects of the environment in which a child develops. In particular, he defined the ZFM as an "inhibitory psychological mechanism" (Valsiner, p. 99) that the adult uses to restrict the freedom of the child's choices of thinking and acting by confining the child's access to areas, objects, or ways of acting on such objects (see also Lightfoot, 1988). In essence, the ZFM describes what the adult allows in the child's environment. Moreover, the ZFM is described as "simultaneously a structure of the child's actions within the environment at a given time, and the future thinking of the child" (Valsiner, 1987, p. 98). That is, the idiosyncrasies of the learning environment are internalized by the child and are ultimately reflected in his or her thinking and actions. Thus, we infer that a classroom that regularly cultivates algebraic reasoning skills is creating a habit of mind in students' thinking that, if sufficiently sustained in other contexts, will impact their experiences in later grades.

The ZPA, on the other hand, defines a "set of activities, objects, or areas in the environment" (Valsiner, 1987, pp. 99–100) by which an adult attempts to influence a child's choice in actions. In short, it describes what the adult promotes within the environment. We note that the ZPA is necessarily contained within the ZFM, since one cannot promote what is not at least allowed unless opportunities are falsely advertised by the adult (see Blanton, Westbrook, & Carter, to appear, for a treatment of this). By its very definition, the ZFM/ZPA complex exists between the learner and the environment and hence is observable. Thus, it is a more practical construct than its ontogenetic counterpart, the ZPD, for understanding students' habits of mind, particularly their capacity for algebraic reasoning. In other words, the ZFM and ZPA provide a means by which we can characterize the child's learning environment and thus anticipate his or her ZPD as the idiosyncrasies of that environment are internalized by the child.

ALGEBRAIC REASONING AS A WAY OF THINKING MATHEMATICALLY

Traditionally, the focus of elementary mathematics has been deeply oriented to arithmetic and computation, with little attention given to the relationships and structure underlying simple arithmetic tasks. However, it is now increasingly believed that students' elementary school experiences should extend beyond arithmetic proficiency to cultivate habits of mind that can support the more complex mathematics of the new century (Kaput, 1999; National Council of Teachers of Mathematics [NCTM], 1998, 2000; Romberg & Kaput, 1999). Specifically, there is a growing recognition that algebraic reasoning can simultaneously emerge from and enhance elementary school mathematics (NCTM, 2000) and can consequently build habits of mind that will prepare students for the more abstract mathematics encountered in later grades. In contrast to traditional instructional and curricular elementary school practices that have led to an abrupt, isolated, and largely unsuccessful approach to mathematics from the middle grades onward (U.S. Department of Education, 1997a, 1997b, 1997c), the integration of algebraic reasoning in primary grades is particularly compelling because it can effect a seamless transition for students into more complex mathematics. To appreciate how this transition can occur, we describe here what we mean by algebraic reasoning.

By algebraic reasoning, we refer to students engaging in regular acts of generalizing about data and mathematical relationships and operations, establishing those generalizations through public conjecture and argumentation, and expressing them in increasingly formal ways (Kaput, 1998, 1999; Kaput &

Blanton, 1999a). For example, students are engaged in algebraic reasoning when they are able to identify and describe, with justification, the total number of handshakes for a group of arbitrary size, or the parity of the product of arbitrary even and odd numbers, or the effect of multiplying an arbitrary quantity by zero. From this perspective, algebraic reasoning extends far beyond a traditional view of algebra as an act of syntactically guided symbolic manipulations. Indeed, it can occur in various interrelated forms, including (1) the use of arithmetic as a domain for expressing and formalizing generalizations; (2) generalizing numerical patterns to describe functional relationships (including covariation); and (3) generalizing about mathematical systems abstracted from computations and relations, the domain usually referred to as "abstract algebra" (Kaput, 1998, 1999).

In order to have a complete and coherent view of algebraic reasoning in elementary grades, it is ultimately necessary to consider the instructional and curricular implications arising from all of these forms. Our specific focus in this study, which contributes to a broader, emerging research base on early algebraic thinking (see, e.g., Carpenter, 1999; Carpenter, Franke, & Levi, 2003; Carpenter & Levi, 2000; Carraher, Schliemann, & Brizuela, 2000; Dougherty, 2003; Kieran, 1981; Schifter, 1998), is on the particular process of generalizing from numerical patterns as a context for building functional relationships as either covariation or iteration (Kaput, 1999). In this sense, our study helps identify the kinds of elementary experiences that can support the development of students' early notions of function and thus represents one piece of an "early algebra story."

BACKGROUND FOR THE STUDY

The GEAAR Professional Development Project

Our attention to this particular strand of algebraic reasoning, and the context for the study we report here, is based on our work with elementary teachers in our Generalizing to Extend Arithmetic to Algebraic Reasoning (GEAAR) Project, a districtwide professional development program designed to develop grades PreK–5 teachers' ability to identify and strategically build upon students' attempts to generalize and formalize their thinking and to engineer viable classroom instructional activities to support this. In particular, we conceptualized the project around our "algebrafication" strategy in which we directed teachers' classroom-grounded development along the following dimensions:

1. building algebraic reasoning opportunities, especially generalization and progressive formalization opportunities, from available instructional materials;
2. building teachers' "algebra eyes and ears" so that they can identify classroom opportunities for generalization and systematic expression of that generality and act upon these as they occur;
3. creating classroom practice and culture to support active student generalization and formalization within the context of purposeful conjecture and argumentation, so that algebra opportunities occur frequently and are viable when they occur.

As part of the project, teachers contributed their own "algebrafied"[1] materials that they had developed for use in their own classrooms. During collegial sharing of one of these tasks (see Kaput & Blanton, 1999b), we and the teachers came to value the feature that generalizing a functional relationship between problem variables could be achieved through an analysis of nonexecuted sums generated during the task activity, where the analysis is guided by the *form* of the nonexecuted sums. As a result, we began to focus on a genre of tasks with this characteristic. We have tried here to explicate principles of these tasks and describe how their algebraic character can be supported in instruction.

Jan's Third-Grade Classroom

We based the findings reported here on a one-year case study of a third-grade classroom. At the time of this study, the classroom teacher, Jan (pseudonym), was a second-year participant in our ongoing GEAAR Project. The urban school district in which Jan taught was one of the lowest-achieving school districts in the state based on student performance on a mandatory, statewide assessment of students' critical thinking and problem-solving skills. All of Jan's 18 students, representing diverse socioeconomic and ethnic backgrounds, participated in the project.

---

[1]We use the term "algebrafied" to denote resources and materials that have been transformed from single-numerical-answer arithmetic tasks to include opportunities for algebraic reasoning.

During the academic year in which the study occurred, we observed Jan's 90-minute mathematics class approximately 2 days a week. The data that we report here were taken from one particular visit midway through the academic year, and we focus on a 45-minute classroom episode that occurred on that day. The episode, documented through classroom video, students' written solutions to the problem, Jan's reflections about the implementation of the activity, and our classroom field notes, chronicles students solving our "algebrafied" version of the Handshake Problem. In this version of the problem, the task was extended from a simple arithmetic task comprised of counting handshakes in a group of fixed size to a task requiring students to attend to the structure embedded in the act of determining handshakes for groups of varying sizes:

> The Handshake Problem: If 5 people in a group shake hands with each other once, how many handshakes will there be? What if there are 6 people in the group? 7 people? 8 people? 20 people? Write a number sentence that shows your result. How did you get your solution? Show your solution on paper.

To introduce the task, Jan first discussed with students how to define a handshake, then separated the class into two groups to solve the problem. They worked in groups for about 35 minutes, and then Jan led a 10-minute whole-class discussion on their solutions.

"HOW MANY HANDSHAKES WOULD THERE BE IF WE ALL SHOOK HANDS ONCE?"

We selected the Handshake Problem because it reflects a genre of algebraic problems used by Jan that illustrates our design principles for mathematical tasks. We extracted these principles from tasks that were essentially derivatives of familiar arithmetic problems, that is, tasks that had been "algebrafied" by fluctuating one of the problem variables. For example, the Handshake Problem, as an arithmetic task, might typically be given as "If 5 people in a group shake hands with each other once, how many handshakes will there be altogether?" Our purpose was to understand the potential algebraic character of these tasks, particularly as it relates to generalizing from numerical patterns in order to describe functional relationships, and thereby generate a framework or set of principles that could be used to describe and develop a broader class of problems. In this section, we use transcripts from the classroom episode in which the Handshake Problem occurred to instantiate principles for this type of pattern-eliciting task and to think about how everyday experiences and disciplinary ideas interacted in these tasks.

Principle 1: The Tasks Promoted the Use of Number and Number Sentences as Objects for Reasoning Algebraically

We found a significant feature of the Handshake Problem to be that it advanced the use of nonexecuted sums, or number sentences, as objects for reasoning algebraically. One of the classroom traditions of elementary school mathematics has been to focus on finding "the answer," typically a particular number produced from a particular computation. We argue that this practice disguised the algebraic potential of our tasks by diverting students to an analysis of the data based on finding patterns in a sequence of numbers. That is, rather than looking for a functional relationship between the amount of people in a group of arbitrary size versus the total number of handshakes for that group, students initially looked for differences in the total number of handshakes for various groups and identified patterns such as "the difference in the number of handshakes increases by one each time you add a person to the group" (Fig. 7.1).

Although we appreciate this widely applied type of analysis as an act of pattern-finding, we recognized that the power of functions rests ultimately in their capacity as mathematized objects to allow predictions beyond the scope of known data, and this required an analysis of all problem variables. To this end, we were interested in promoting a deeper, more powerful understanding of mathematics that included an ability to reason with the *forms* of mathematical statements such as number sentences. In contrast, an analysis that considered only patterns in sequences of numbers would limit the scope of predictability to consecutive states and thus would not engage the full algebraic character of the task.

Number of people	Number of Handshakes
2	1
	+2
3	3
	+3
4	6
	+4
5	10
	+5
6	15

FIG. 7.1. Students' single-variable analysis of the "handshake" data.

As the following episodes suggest, we found that students were in fact able to produce a functional relationship between the size of the group and the number of handshakes by analyzing the form in a sequence of number sentences, or arithmetic models, describing the amount of handshakes for particular groups. We refer to these number sentences as arithmetic models because they arithmetically encode the physical act of shaking hands, preserving in their inscriptive forms both the manner in which the physical process was completed and the quantification of this process. The first excerpt opens with students finding the total number of handshakes in a group with eight people. They had negotiated a record-keeping system whereby each person shook hands with those in the group, recorded the amount of handshakes, and then stepped back from the group so as not to be counted again. The act of shaking hands was punctuated by students counting audibly in unison.

1. *Student:* (To Jan) We're making a number sentence.
2. *Teacher:* Oh, are you? You're making a number sentence.
3. *Student:* One, two, three, four, five. . . .
4. *Student:* It's going to keep going down. It's going to go four, three, two, one.
5. *Teacher:* Are you sure?
6. *Student:* It's going to go down until there is no more.
7. *Teacher:* Now what?
8. *Student:* Now put zero.
9. *Teacher:* Why zero?
10. *Student:* Because he's already shook everyone's hand. (Here, the student was referring to the last person remaining in the group.)
11. *Teacher:* Put it (zero) down. So he doesn't get to shake any hands. You've already made your number sentence here?
12. *Student:* It's going seven, six, five, four, three, two, one. It's backwards.
13. *Teacher:* Wait a minute. I'm confused here. O.K., let's see. . . one, two, three, four, five, six, seven, eight (Jan counts the number of people at the table).
14. *Student:* No, because you don't count him. (We infer that the student assumed Jan was counting handshakes, not people.)
15. *Student:* You don't use yourself.

Students then recorded the total number of handshakes in their group of 8 as "7 + 6 + 5 + 4 + 3 + 2 + 1" (some included "0" in their model).

16.	*Teacher:*	If there were 12 people here and they were going to shake hands, what would you do?
17.	*Student:*	You could only shake 11 people's hands. (We infer that the student meant the first round of handshakes would involve 11 shakes.)
18.	*Teacher:*	Why?
19.	*Teacher:*	Because he can't shake his own hand (therefore the number sentence begins with 11 as opposed to 12).
20.	*Teacher:*	So how would your number sentence change if there were 12 people?
21.	*Student:*	Eleven, ten, nine, eight, seven, six, five, four, three, two, one.
22.	*Teacher:*	Do you need a zero in there?
23.	*Student:*	No, 'cause it doesn't count.
24.	*Teacher:*	I would put that zero in, wouldn't you? Because that one person really is not going to be shaking anyone's hand. So isn't that a way of recording that last person saying he's already shaken everybody's hand?

Jan later asked the class to write a number sentence that would give the amount of handshakes in a group of 20 people, without enacting the handshakes. (She had earlier asked individual groups to think about this question.)

25.	*Teacher:*	If there were 20 people, how could we figure out how many handshakes there would be without going around and shaking everybody's hand?
26.	*Student:*	Take 1 from the 20.
27.	*Teacher:*	How many do you want me to start with?
28.	*Student:*	Thirteen.
29.	*Teacher:*	Thirteen?
30.	*Student:*	No. Nineteen, then 18.
31.	*Student:*	Seventeen, 16, 15, 14 ... (student's voice trails off).

In (31),[2] it seems that students' ways of describing the amount of handshakes in a group had progressed to a shared understanding with Jan by which it was enough to imply how the arithmetic model would be constructed without stating all of its addends.

These episodes suggest that students were able to reason with the arithmetic models (e.g., "$7 + 6 + 5 + 4 + 3 + 2 + 1$") as algebraic objects. That is, by using sequences of numerical sums and deliberately not computing them, students were able to attend to the sums for their shapes as inscriptions, rather than as instructions to perform procedures, and thereby use these objects to generalize observed numerical relationships. Jan invited the use of nonexecuted sums as objects for reasoning algebraically when she asked that students shift their focus from a literal enactment of the problem (shaking hands) to the arithmetic models (25). This in turn prompted students to attend to a relationship between the size of the group and the arithmetic model that resulted, leading to the generalization that the number of handshakes in a group of arbitrary size would be the sum of numbers from one (or zero) up to one number less than the size of the group. Thus, while mathematical symbol systems help us compute efficiently, their greater power may be in ways that they express structure. That is, by postponing the computation of these objects, students were ultimately able to use them to find a numerical pattern, *embedded in the structure*, by which they could determine the total number of handshakes for an unknown case (e.g., finding the number of handshakes in a group of 20 people). In essence, treating these nonexecuted sums as algebraic objects allowed for an analysis of covariation in the data by which students were able to describe the total amount of handshakes for an arbitrarily large group without knowing information about immediately prior states.

In the same context of reasoning algebraically with numerical objects, the Handshake Problem enabled what we describe as the algebraic treatment of number. Although there are tasks in elementary mathematics that can support the development of students' symbol sense, we found that these third-grade students' notion of variable as a placeholder for varying quantities was understandably not sophisticated enough to sustain an analysis of a task such as the Handshake Problem for a group of unknown size n. Yet, a mature understanding of the concept of function ultimately requires that students be able to attend to the notion of arbitrariness and not depend exclusively on knowledge about a particular known state in order to describe a future,

---

[2]Numbers refer to lines in the protocol.

unknown state. Thus, we need accessible ways to introduce the notion of arbitrary, or varying, quantities in elementary grades.

Jan effected this through the algebraic use of number in the Handshake Problem. Specifically, we argue that "20" was treated algebraically, that is, as a placeholder or variable, in the task of finding the number of handshakes for a group of size 20 without enacting the handshakes. That is, the use of a large number (such as 20) beyond states that were known required students to analyze the structure embedded in the arithmetic models rather than compute sequences of sums and look for patterns in a sequence of numbers (such as the pattern described in Fig. 7.1). This algebraic use of number would not have occurred if Jan had asked only about a group size for which all prior states were known. However, when she asked students about a group of size 20, her expectation was that students would not determine the amount of handshakes for groups through size 19 and then use that information to find the total handshakes for a group of size 20. Instead, students were expected to analyze the structure of the arithmetic models in order to solve the problem. Thus, we maintain that Jan used number to effect a shift in students' focus from arithmetic processing to algebraic thinking.

What do we learn from this principle about the interface between students' everyday experience and the discipline of mathematics expressed in this setting? In particular, what everyday experiences, as conveyed through what students proposed and discussed, were brought to bear on the mathematics inherent to this task? Our claim is that the attention given to building nonexecuted sums and to understanding what their numerical components represented helped elicit students' everyday experience. This seemed to occur when students argued that, in a group with 12 people, the number sentence describing the amount of handshakes should begin with 11 as opposed to 12 (i.e., "$11 + 10 + 9 + \cdots + 3 + 2 + 1$"). In particular, the claim that "you don't count yourself" (15), that is, a person "could only shake 11 people's hands... because he can't shake his own hand" (17, 19), suggests that students' everyday knowledge of norms about appropriate handshake gestures was invoked to reason about how many handshakes a person might make. There was also occasion for everyday experience to interact with disciplinary ideas in the issue of whether to include "zero" in the models. We maintain that everyday experience was expressed in the argument that zero "doesn't count" and so should not be included in the model (23). In general, students seem to bring to school an intrinsic experience with zero as an expression about the absence of quantity, as "nothing" or "no more" (16), and thus of little mathematical importance. However, when these students had to attend to the mathematics of establishing how many times each person shook hands with the members of the group, zero came to have significance (for some students) as a mathematical quantity. In particular, one student used zero to signify that the last person remaining in the group shook no hands (8, 10) and later argued that "if it was all those people together and then it was me, then I shook nobody's hand." We suggest that the perception of zero as encoding important mathematical information (as opposed to the perception of zero as "nothing") was an expression of disciplinary knowledge that evolved in this task for some students, and it is in part attributable to the significance that nonexecuted sums and the mathematical meanings for their constitutive parts were given here.

Principle 2: The Tasks Involved Sequences of Computations That Could Be Exploited to Engage Students Arithmetically

The dominant role of arithmetic in elementary school mathematics requires that we think about how to embed it in the more complex processes of algebraic thinking. With the Handshake Problem and other similar tasks, students' engagement with arithmetic, particularly number and operation, was deeply integrated into the creation and analysis of patterns. Although arithmetic is certainly not unique to this genre of tasks, we were struck by how deeply these tasks could support arithmetic thinking. For instance, mathematizing the act of shaking hands required students to understand the correspondence between a collection of counted handshakes and the number representing it (e.g., identifying three shakes as "3") and how to operate on consecutive numbers to find a total amount. Although these aspects of the problem did not pose a challenge for students in Jan's classroom, they were significant for teachers in our GEAAR Project who were implementing this task in earlier grades where counting actions were a challenge.

It was also significant that sequences of computations generated from this task could be used to engage students and strengthen their facility with number and operation. We see Jan doing this in the following excerpt, which occurred after she asked students to identify more efficient strategies for finding the total number of handshakes in a group of 12 people. During this portion of the task, students had just predicted an arithmetic model describing the number of handshakes to be "$11 + 10 + 9 + 8 + 7 + 6 + 5 + 4 + 3 + 2 + 1$."

32. *Teacher:*   Did anybody change the order of those numbers in any way when you added them?
33. *Student:*   Yes. You can change them to tens.
34. *Teacher:*   You made tens out of these?

35. *Student:*   We put 11, 10, 9, 8 . . . (voice trails off). You don't need to [add 1 through 7] over again.

36. *Student:*   All you have to do is put 11, 10, 9, 8 on top of all the numbers we had.

37. *Student:*   You don't say 12.

38. *Teacher:*   You don't say 12? Why don't you say 12?

39. *Student:*   Cause you can't shake your own hand.

40. *Teacher:*   Now, wait a minute. You just said . . .

41. *Student:*   . . . that we didn't have to count 7, 6, 5, 4, 3, 2, 1, 0 . . . because we knew they already equaled 28.

42. *Teacher:*   Okay, that's pretty good! . . . Zolan did something that I really liked. . . . What did you do?

43. *Zolan:*   I added the 11 and 10 together. (From the result of 21, he then subtracted 1.) Then I added the extra 1 of the 11 to the 9 and that made a 10.

Zolan had commuted the numbers in such a way that he could add groups of 10. Later in the episode, another conversation occurred about a strategy for computing the sum of the number of handshakes for a group of size 20. At students' suggestion (25–31), Jan had written "$0 + 1 + 2 + 3 + 4 + 5 + 6 + 7 + 8 + 9 + 10 + 11 + 12 + 13 + 14 + 15 + 16 + 17 + 18 + 19$" on the board. She asked, "Is there a way that we can change the order of these numbers and make them easier to add up?"

44. *Student:*   You can take the zero and put it, you can change it around by putting the 19 where the zero was and that would be easier. (We infer that the student meant to add '19 + 0'.)

45. *Teacher:*   Can I do this? If I do this, $19 + 0$. . . .

46. *Student:*   That equals 19.

47. *Teacher:*   What else could I do?

48. *Student:*   You could do $18 + 1$.

49. *Student:*   What about $17 + 2$?

50. *Teacher:*   What about $17 + 2$? Wait a minute. Let me just try this. So I've used those two (19, 18) and these two numbers (0, 1). (Jan drew lines on the board connecting the numbers in each pair.) Let me see $17 + 2$. Okay. These are pairs aren't they? How many pairs of numbers do you think we're going to be able to make out of these 20 numbers? . . . Anthony, how many do you think we are going to make?

51. *Anthony:* Ten.
52. *Teacher:* Why?
53. *Anthony:* Because you need to get 1 from each side.
54. *Teacher:* Let's see if we do make 10 pairs of numbers.
55. *Student:* Each one (pair) is equal to 19.

After they had established that there would be 10 pairs of numbers, the sum of each being 19, Jan said, "Now I've got to add up all these 19's. What is this?"

56. *Student:* Repeated addition. You could do times.
57. *Teacher:* I could do times?
58. *Student:* Nineteen times 10. . . .190.
59. *Teacher:* How did you figure that out so quickly?
60. *Student:* I just changed that to 9 and added a zero.
61. *Teacher:* Why?
62. *Student:* Because the one is a 100 and 9 is 90.
63. *Student:* You could just add a zero.
64. *Teacher:* What did you say? I don't understand what you said.

The student again explained that he made the "one into a 100 and 9 into 90" by using 10 times 10 to get 100 and 9 times 10 to get 90, then finding the sum. Jan acknowledged this and then shifted the conversation to another topic.

We found that when asked to use efficient strategies for computation, students looked for relationships in the arithmetic models in order to organize numbers in ways that exploited productive pairings. For example, recognizing that they could generate a sequence of sums of 19 by adding 0 to 19, 1 to 18, 2 to 17, and so forth, students used this to more effectively "add" by multiplication (56, 58). Moreover, students' proficiency with these maneuvers required an understanding of operation, particularly the generalized commutativity of addition (43, 44, 48), and a sophisticated concept of "counting on" (35, 36, 41). Indeed, although data from observations earlier in the year showed that "counting on" was an emerging part of these students' cognitive schemes, the Handshake Problem seemed to more fully form this concept in their thinking. In particular, students were able to count on from a previously determined sum and operate with that sum as an independent object (35, 36, 41). All of these processes—counting on, commuting numbers, and mathematizing handshakes—occurred in meaningful contexts in which students explored issues of numeracy and increased their facility with number and operation.

Moreover, they were simultaneously engaged in the more complex processes of algebraic thinking about relationships and properties of whole numbers and, especially, attention to forms of the number sentences. As a result, the arithmetic was not neglected but became an integral part of developing algebraic reasoning.

If we think about the ways that everyday and disciplinary ideas encountered each other in the episodes thus far, we find that students' construction of arithmetic models elicited their everyday experiences with number and operation. Tasks such as the Handshake Problem allowed for significant algebraic thinking while using small numbers, numbers with which students already had a depth of experience outside of the discipline of mathematics. We suggest that the Handshake Problem was able to engage students' everyday familiarity with small numbers by drawing upon their capacity for counting and sequencing objects and placing them in correspondence. In this sense, students' everyday experience contributed to the development of the disciplinary knowledge of constructing sequences of arithmetic models (3, 12, 21, 31) and observing the structure of the variation from the layout of the models.

We gain additional perspective on the interaction between everyday and disciplinary ideas if we consider how algorithms for sums of sequences of integers emerged. In particular, students' counting schemes originally involved computing sums of sequences of integers by counting numbers from least to greatest and recounting sequences when they appeared as part of other sums. Building on this, students progressed to schemes by which they identified complex configurations in the sequences that allowed them to simplify the arithmetic (43, 56). Jan contributed to this progression by prompting students to think about different ways of computing sums by regrouping numbers (32) and bringing to the fore students' ideas that illustrated their alternative strategies of addition (42). We maintain that through this guidance, everyday ideas became a springboard from which more sophisticated counting schemes could emerge. In essence, as Jan exploited the arithmetic in this algebraic task, there was opportunity for counting strategies grounded in students' everyday experience to evolve into more refined, discipline-based ways of thinking about number and operation.

Principle 3: The Tasks Allowed for the Enactment of Actions and Situations Familiar to Students

One of the benefits of the Handshake Problem was that it could be sequenced through the physical enactment of a situation familiar to students. By this, we mean that the task allowed students to construct a sequence of arithmetic models from a literal context that accessed students' everyday experiences (e.g., shaking hands), and in such a way that sequential cases could be explicitly examined to see how perturbations in one case affected other cases. For example, students built consecutive arithmetic models, each representing the total number of handshakes for a particular group, by continuing to add people to the original group. Using these cases, students explored how the arithmetic model changed when the size of the group increased by more than one unit. From this, they were able to generalize about the number of handshakes in a group of arbitrary size (e.g., 20 people). We conjecture that to have explicit cases, or models, available as permanent artifacts of the task (i.e., as nonexecuted sums) enabled students to move more easily between the models and the source for interpreting the models, namely, the physical context of the problem. In contrast, reducing a model to a computed sum would have concealed the physical actions embodied by the representation. In essence, we maintain that students' analysis of the relationship between the number of handshakes and the amount of people in the group was facilitated by symbolizing a familiar action and by keeping that action explicit. Moreover, because handshaking is a familiar cultural practice, this particular task drew directly on students' everyday experience to make sense of the problem and, as we described earlier, to reason explicitly about the number of handshakes (17–19). As a result, we claim that the opportunity to enact a familiar situation facilitated the development of arithmetic models that left physical actions explicit and that ultimately enabled students' movement to the abstraction of reasoning with models without physical enactment. To the extent that the sequential nature of these tasks and the explicit number sentences they generated made patterns of number sentences, rather than numbers, more recognizable, we maintain that this principle supported students' opportunity for algebraic reasoning.

THE CULTURE OF INSTRUCTION FOR THE HANDSHAKE PROBLEM

Tasks such as the Handshake Problem did not constitute stand-alone events, but required an appropriate culture in which they could be sustained and, in particular, a classroom teacher who could spontaneously and purposefully exploit the algebraic characteristics of these tasks. One of our goals in using a series of tasks such as the Handshake Problem was to enculturate in those teachers participating in the GEAAR Project a sensitivity to a classroom activity structure in which generalizing and formalizing became habits of mind for students. Thus, to the extent to which this occurred in Jan's classroom, we asked ourselves what observable teacher actions contributed to making the task at hand more fully algebraic. In particular, how would we describe the culture of instruction that made the Handshake Problem work in this case? It is our claim that the zone of free movement (ZFM) and zone of promoted action (ZPA) organized by Jan for her students convey the culture of instruction that supported students' engagement in the algebraic features of the task. In the next section, we use the classroom episode of the Handshake Problem to identify some aspects of what Jan promoted or allowed and describe how these might have facilitated students' algebraic reasoning.

Jan Promoted Students' Active Role in Solving the Task

Once Jan had asked a question that required analysis and conjecture (e.g., 20, 25), she tried to situate students as the problem solvers rather than taking on that role herself. For example, when a student asked if a number sentence could be commuted, Jan responded with a shrug of her shoulders; "Can you? Can you change numbers around when you add?" Or, when students described their goal to make a number sentence (1–4), Jan questioned if they were sure about their result (5). To us, her responses reflected a routine in which Jan sometimes chose not to answer students' questions directly or to offer her immediate assessment of students' work. We maintain that this approach conveyed the expectation that *students* think carefully about their ideas and, as a result, this expectation helped shift the intellectual responsibility in problem solving to students.

Diaz, Neal, and Amaya-Williams (1999) describe that even the teacher's physical withdrawal from the task "places the child at the center of the action and exerts a subtle pressure and demand for the child to take over responsibility for the task" (p. 152). As we observed, instead of presenting herself as the central, authoritative figure, Jan chose primarily to monitor individual groups as they solved the Handshake Problem, asking questions that seemed to scaffold students' thinking about the task (e.g., 9, 20, 25, 32, 38). We maintain that as Jan promoted *students'* engagement in the task, specifically, their activity of analyzing the structure of known cases, conjecturing how an observed pattern extended to an unknown state, and generalizing about a functional relationship between the variables, she was simultaneously "allowing, promoting, and rewarding the child's takeover of the regulatory role" (Diaz et al., p. 129).

In turn, we argue that students' active participation in the act of generalizing allowed them to begin to internalize algebraic reasoning as their *own* way of thinking and acting. In this sense, we maintain that this aspect of the zones Jan organized for her students supported their algebraic reasoning within this task.

Jan Promoted Organizing and Tracking Data in Meaningful Ways

By providing explicit attention to how and if the handshake data were recorded, organized, or represented, Jan promoted the activity of structuring data in meaningful ways before its analysis. She challenged students, "I . . . want to see how you're recording your information . . . so you have to try to find a way to keep track of whose hand you are shaking." In one group, students used symbols such as the initials of a name (e.g., AS represented Alison Smith) as a meaningful way to record a handshake. Another group, rather than symbolize each handshake, counted the number of times one person in the group shook hands with the remaining group members and recorded that amount. In both cases, students systematically kept track of data. During prior observations of Jan's classroom, we noticed that the lack of a sense of how to organize data seemed to hinder students' capacity to solve the problem. They became frustrated when there was no sense of how to manage the data. Thus, we maintain that imposing some sense of structure on the data supported the algebraic reasoning required in these tasks because it helped students develop the arithmetic models, which was fundamental to generalizing about the number of handshakes. In turn, students' idea to use one's initials as a referent for a handshake without a specific directive from Jan suggests that they were beginning to think in their own way about how to track the problem. We infer from this, and know from our long-term observation of Jan's practice, that managing data was an action that Jan promoted with some degree of regularity, the result being that students seemed to be internalizing it as their own way of thinking and acting in the process of algebraic reasoning.

Jan Promoted Students' Acts of Justifying or Establishing Mathematical Statements

Justification in any form is a significant part of algebraic reasoning because it induces a habit of mind whereby one naturally questions and conjectures in order to establish a generalization. We maintain that Jan promoted justification by questioning various aspects of the arithmetic models students constructed in order to focus their thinking on what the particular components represented. For example, she asked that students explain the significance of numbers such as "0" and "11" in the number sentences (e.g., 7–10; 17–19). She had the following conversation with her students about the role of "0":

65. *Teacher:* Why did you put that "0" in?
66. *Student:* Because it would be the last person in the group.
67. *Teacher:* Was that "0" important?
68. *Student:* No.
69. *Student:* Yes.
70. *Teacher:* I think it was.
71. *Student:* If it was all those people together and then it was me, then I shook nobody's hand.

We claim that in conversations like this, Jan promoted, and thus began to enculturate, a habit of mind whereby students looked for and articulated meaning in their mathematical claims (see e.g., 10, 19, 35–36, 39, 41). As Jan validated the notion that "0" was important, at least one student seemed to be contemplating why this might be true, using the situation as a context for interpreting the meaning of "0" (71). Although this practice was perhaps not the case with every individual, it did seem to be emerging as a norm for doing mathematics in Jan's class. We infer from (65) that it was a student's idea to include "0," as it was in an earlier conversation (7–10). Jan's response was to validate the idea (24; 70), at one point revoicing it in a subsequent conversation with another student (22–24). This seems to indicate the coconstruction of an idea between teacher and students, suggesting to us that Jan organized a wide ZFM in which students were allowed and even encouraged to participate in making meaning for the arithmetic models they constructed.

Conversations such as this contributed to students' algebraic reasoning in the task by focusing their attention on unpacking the numerical subtleties of a particular model. That is, Jan seemed to set up the discourse so that students, not Jan, were required to be attentive to mathematical nuances within the models, such as ways the forms of the inscriptions changed when another person was added to the group. Students' facility with the models, specifically, how they represented the physical context, was essential for reasoning with them as algebraic objects. We argue that the attention given to understanding the components of a particular model was a necessary precursor to (correctly) generating other models, all of which could be collectively analyzed algebraically for the purpose of generalizing the number of handshakes in a group of arbitrary size. In contrast, we argue that a discourse in which Jan asked leading or short-answer questions would have excluded students from their *own* acts of reasoning about the models and would have hindered their understanding of the relationship between the models.

Jan Promoted Making Students' Thinking a Part of Public Discourse

We include in this not only students' oral reasoning, but also visual and in-scriptive effects such as acting out and recording handshakes. We see the latter as connected cognitively to the verbalizations that students made by helping them to track their movements and to anticipate subsequent steps. For instance, as students in one group tallied the handshakes, they kept their eyes focused on the physical movements as they counted out loud in unison. We argue that the visual and inscriptive experience of that physical enactment created cognitive markers that informed students' thinking and hence their public comments. The resulting models that students created (e.g., "$7 + 6 + 5 + 4 + 3 + 2 + 1$") became artifacts for public debate from which students could establish the number of handshakes in a group. By encouraging students to externalize their thinking through words, actions, and inscriptions, Jan created the opportunity for all students to begin to make sense of ideas, such as why "0" could be included in the models, and to reason collectively with mathematical information. In our view, this public, or social, side of the task was a critical element in enculturating a habit of algebraic reasoning within the group.

Although we have described some of what Jan promoted, and hence allowed, in the classroom environment (we do not claim that this is an exhaustive list), we note that these aspects of her ZPA could be additionally interpreted as points at which the ZFM coincided with the ZPA. That is, there did not seem to be significant behaviors that she allowed but did not promote. For example, she might have allowed students to collect handshake data in an unsystematic way while she promoted organizing and tracking data in a meaningful way. We did not observe this to be the case; what she promoted she also seemed to require. This may in fact be an important commentary on Jan's practice. In other words, at the algebraic heart of the task, Jan configured the zones so that students were not allowed to operate outside of them. Instead, Jan seemed to require students' attention to analyzing, conjecturing, and generalizing about the data in a context where she gradually worked to shift the regulatory responsibility to them. We argue that this aspect of the ZFM/ZPA complex is a critical component of a culture that can sustain the algebraic character of tasks such as the Handshake Problem, since the activity of analyzing, conjecturing, and generalizing in which they occur build the cognitive structures that facilitate algebraic reasoning.

CONCLUSION

Tasks such as the Handshake Problem represent one (of many) genre of tasks that can enrich elementary school mathematics by infusing algebraic reasoning into the curriculum. We found that tasks which leveraged students' arithmetic knowledge and included some act of mathematizing a phenomenon so that a mathematical abstraction had its representation in an everyday context could help access elementary students' capacity for algebraic reasoning. We have tried to make explicit some of the principles of tasks that support this, as well as aspects of a classroom culture that bring their algebraic character to the fore.

But, given that teachers are constantly struggling with what to include in their curriculum, to what extent do the tasks themselves constitute mathematics worth knowing? We argue that not only do these tasks include an attention to arithmetic, but they are also embedded in a context that requires more complex mathematical thinking and therefore offer critical experiences for elementary students. For instance, students were engaged by the Handshake Problem in (1) knowing to and knowing how to represent data; (2) using arithmetic (number and operations) to model a phenomenon that involved variation; (3) examining how perturbations in a phenomenon affected the model; (4) reasoning algebraically about the forms of sequences of arithmetic models; (5) deepening their arithmetic reasoning to support the appropriate use and choice of operations and to understand relationships between numbers in order to facilitate computation; (6) using numbers and number sentences algebraically; and (7) understanding relationships between operations (e.g., seeing repeated addition as an indicator of multiplication). As such, it is our claim that tasks that reflect the design principles proposed here can offer elementary students a significant mathematical experience, where the arithmetic and algebraic sides of that experience interact symbiotically.

We reiterate that even the most well-designed tasks will be less effective without a supporting culture of instruction. We identified some of the aspects of the ZFM and ZPA Jan organized for her students that we feel supported the algebraic characteristics of the tasks. In particular, Jan promoted (hence allowed) students' activity of analysis, conjecturing, justification, and ultimately generalization, as well as their activity of managing or structuring data and sharing and describing their thinking and strategies. This type of practice points to the need for the professional development of classroom teachers who have (as we describe it) "algebra eyes and ears," or a sensitivity to algebraic opportunities in the classroom that can be exploited as they occur or included as a part of planned instruction. As we have described elsewhere, Jan's class showed great potential for algebraic reasoning as their own way of thinking and acting (Blanton & Kaput, 2000a). We attribute this to Jan's classroom practice and the emphasis she placed on algebraic reasoning throughout the school year (Blanton & Kaput, 2000b), as well as support from the GEAAR Project. However, we recognize that for algebraic reasoning to become a fully established habit of mind for these students will require long-term, sustained effort and an across-grade attention to expressing generalities in increasingly formal ways. Our hope is that students' experiences in Jan's class will not be an isolated occurrence for them, but that it will be included in patterns of practice that exploit the symbiotic relationship between arithmetic and algebra. Among the many prerequisites for these patterns of practice to become the norm across elementary mathematics is a deeper understanding of how to design tasks and instruction that facilitate this symbiosis.

ACKNOWLEDGMENTS

The research reported here was supported in part by a grant from the U.S. Department of Education, Office of Educational Research and Improvement, to the National Center for Improving Student Learning and Achievement in Mathematics and Science (R305A600007-98). The opinions expressed herein do not necessarily reflect the position, policy, or endorsement of the supporting agencies.

REFERENCES

Blanton, M., & Kaput, J. (2000a). Generalizing and progressively formalizing in a third grade mathematics classroom: Conversations about even and odd numbers. In M. Fernández (Ed.), *Proceedings of the XXII Annual Meeting of the North American Chapter of the International Group for the Psychology of Mathematics Education*, Columbus, OH, ERIC Clearinghouse, pp. 115–119.

Blanton, M., & Kaput, J. (2000b). Characterizing generative and self-sustaining teacher change in a classroom practice that promotes students' algebraic thinking. In *Proceedings of the XXIV International Conference for the Psychology of Mathematics Education*, Hiroshima, Japan.

Blanton, M., Westbrook, S., & Carter, G. (to appear). Using Valsiner's zone theory to interpret teaching practices in the classroom: Beyond the zone of proximal development. *Journal of Mathematics Teacher Education*.

Carpenter, T. (1999). *Negotiating the construction and representation of generalization in a primary class*. Paper presented at the American Educational Research Association 1999 Annual Meeting, Montreal, Canada.

Carpenter, T. P., & Levi, L. (2000). Developing conceptions of algebraic reasoning in the primary grades. (Res. Rep. 00-2). Madison, WI: National Center for Improving Student Learning and Achievement in Mathematics and Science [available at www.wcer.wisc.edu/ncisla].

Carpenter, T., Franke, M., & Levi, L. (2003). *Thinking mathematically: Integrating arithmetic and algebra in elementary school*. Portsmouth, NH: Heinemann.

Carraher, D., Schliemann, A. D., & Brizuela, B. (2000). *Early algebra, early arithmetic: Treating operations as functions*. Plenary address. XXII Meeting of the Psychology of Mathematics Education, North American Chapter, Tucson, AZ, October 2000. Available in CD.

Diaz, R., Neal, C., & Amaya-Williams, M. (1999). The social origins of self-regulation. In L. Moll (Ed.), *Vygotsky and education: Instructional implications and applications of sociohistorical psychology* (pp. 127–154). Cambridge, UK: Cambridge University Press.

Dougherty, B. (2003). Voyaging from theory to practice in learning: Measure Up. In N. Pateman, B. Dougherty, & J. Zilliox (Eds.), *Proceedings of the Twenty-seventh International Conference for the Psychology of Mathematics Education* (vol. 1, pp. 17–23). Honolulu, Hawai'i: University of Hawai'i.

Kaput, J. (1998). Transforming algebra from an engine of inequity to an engine of mathematical power by "algebrafying" the K–12 curriculum. In S. Fennel (Ed.), *The nature and role of algebra in the K–14 curriculum: Proceedings of a national symposium* (pp. 25–26). Washington, DC: National Research Council, National Academy Press.

Kaput, J. (1999). Teaching and learning a new algebra. In E. Fennema & T. Romberg (Eds.), *Mathematics classrooms that promote understanding* (pp. 133–155). Mahwah, NJ: Lawrence Erlbaum Associates. Available at http://www.simcalc.umassd.edu/EABook.html.

Kaput, J., & Blanton, M. (1999a). *Algebraic reasoning in the context of elementary mathematics: Making it implementable on a massive scale*. Paper presented at the American Educational Research Association, Montreal, Canada.

Kaput, J., & Blanton, M. (1999b). *Enabling elementary teachers to achieve generalization and progressively systematic expression of generality in their math classrooms: The role of authentic mathematical experience*. Paper presented at the NCISLA Conference on Teacher Change and Professional Development, University of Wisconsin, Madison.

Kieran, C. (1981). Concepts associated with the equality symbol. *Educational Studies in Mathematics, 12*, 317–326.

Lightfoot, C. (1988). The social construction of cognitive conflict: A place for affect. In J. Valsiner (Ed.), *Child development within culturally structured environments*. Norwood, NJ: Ablex.

National Council of Teachers of Mathematics. (1998). *The nature and role of algebra in the K–14 curriculum*. Washington, DC: National Research Council, National Academy Press.

National Council of Teachers of Mathematics. (2000). *Principles and standards for school mathematics*. Reston, VA: Author.

Romberg, T., & Kaput, J. (1999). Mathematics worth teaching, mathematics worth understanding. In E. Fennema, & T. Romberg (Eds.), *Mathematics classrooms that promote understanding* (pp. 3–32). Mahwah, NJ: Lawrence Erlbaum Associates.

Schifter, D. (1998). *Developing operation sense as a foundation for algebra*. Unpublished manuscript.

U.S. Department of Education. Office of Educational Research and Improvement. (1997a). *Introduction to TIMSS: The third international mathematics and science study*. Washington, DC: U.S. Department of Education.

U.S. Department of Education. Office of Educational Research and Improvement. (1997b). *Moderator's guide to eighth-grade mathematics lessons: United States, Japan, and Germany*. Washington, DC: U.S. Department of Education.

U.S. Department of Education. National Center for Education Statistics. (1997c). *Pursuing excellence: A study of U.S. twelfth grade mathematics and science achievement in international context*. Washington, DC: U.S. Government Printing Office.

Valsiner, J. (1987). *Culture and the development of children's actions: A cultural-historical theory of developmental psychology*. New York: Wiley.

Vygotsky, L. (1986). *Thought and language*. (A. Kozulin, Trans.). Cambridge, MA: MIT Press. (Original work published in 1934.).

II
Actions of Teachers as They Participate in the Creation of Classroom Encounters With Everyday Matters of Science and Mathematics

Introduction to Part III

When curriculum designers develop curriculum, and specifically curriculum that attempts to connect with everyday matters, what do they consider?

Curriculum designers consider what the students will bring. What do curriculum designers believe about what students will bring to a lesson both intellectually and experientially? A curriculum begins with a set of assumptions about where the students are academically, about what content knowledge they bring with them. Designers also take into account, whether consciously or not, how they think the students' lives and backgrounds impact the types of everyday experiences they might reasonably have had. What experiences does the curriculum designer count on? Have all the students ridden on a roller coaster or are they at least familiar enough with such a ride that this experience can be taken as common? Can the designer assume that all students are familiar with skiing or riding in a boat? And what about the lives of students the curriculum designer does not or cannot know? What kinds of questions get asked in the stories told in their homes? What practices are they accustomed to in their churches, mosques, or synagogues? How does the designer develop curriculum that can capture and build upon experiences that are not known at first? Finally, and perhaps most importantly, in what ways do designers assume that students bring tools that are disciplinary, whether the students are aware of them or not?

Curriculum designers consider their proximity to the students. Whether the curriculum designer is the students' teacher, working with the students' class on a limited basis, or writing curriculum for unknown teachers and students makes a huge difference in his or her understanding about what students and teacher(s) bring to a lesson. What does the curriculum designer assume about the teacher's everyday and disciplinary knowledge? What does the designer know that the students know, what does the designer know was taught last year (or last week), and what is unknown? Answers to these questions help the designer decide what must be embedded in the curriculum and what can be assumed to be held by the teacher.

Curriculum designers consider their own conception of the discipline. The designer's notions about the nature of the discipline lead her to certain curricular decisions. Must the curriculum guard the discipline and only reveal it in appropriate pieces? Is the discipline such that it can be approached and understood through various entry points and experiences? How does the designer conceive of everyday experiences and their relationships to the discipline?

Curriculum designers consider the limits and possibilities of the classroom. The designer's ideas about and experiences with classroom settings lead to curricular decisions. What kinds of experiences can a designer imagine setting up in a classroom that will likely lead to better understandings of the discipline? What experiences does the designer view as worthwhile with respect to the discipline? How does the designer's understanding of the classroom affect what she can imagine students bringing to the classroom?

The four chapters in this section come at these questions from different perspectives and approach curriculum design on different scales. Yet the authors share a number of concerns and raise a number of common questions:

1. **Hypothetical Learning Trajectories.** What are the likely routes that a student might take through the intended material? The chapters detail the challenges of deciding upon and describing "hypothetical learning trajectories," theorized routes that students may take through the material. Such trajectories are taken up differently, owing in part to the different scope of the curriculum projects under examination.

2. **Control of Direction.** The chapters describe the tension faced by curriculum designers in dictating to what extent students, the teacher, or the curriculum should control the direction of the classroom experience. Should the class follow the directions of the students' questions and ideas, or should the curriculum dictate those decisions? Further, do students pursue disciplines in predictable or patterned ways? What is known about these ways and how can they be described?

3. **The Core of the Discipline.** The chapters delve into questions about what is essential to a discipline and how students gain access to it. In describing this core, the authors agree that it is insufficient to dichotomize skills and content, because both habits of mind and essential skills comprise it.

4. **Appropriate Everyday Contexts.** What is an appropriate "everyday" context within which to base a curriculum? Although there are clearly a vast

number of everyday experiences that students will find familiar or comfortable, some are obviously better suited to particular pieces of content. How does a curriculum designer decide which contexts are appropriate for which subject areas? What makes a context appropriate?

5. **Intended vs. Actual Curriculum.** It goes without saying that designing a curriculum for a certain purpose does not mean the students will experience it that way. What dynamics are at play as the curriculum is enacted by the teacher and students? The dynamics can vary considerably depending on whether a curriculum is being designed for known or unknown students and teachers.

6. **Everyday Habits of Mind.** The notion of "everyday" is associated with contexts and materials, but these chapters also explore the idea that there are everyday habits of mind and ways of thinking that students bring to bear on their explorations of a discipline that these may in fact be seen as part of one discipline.

The chapters in this section make us question the boundaries we draw between "everyday" and "disciplinary" experiences as they explore how curriculum designers understand and engage with such experiences to help students gain greater access to science and mathematics. The chapters paint compelling pictures of curriculum designers developing engaging classroom experiences that match content to students' experiences and ideas, inventing a new language to capture the nature of classroom discussion driven by students' experiences, imagining what it will be like for a particular group of students to wrestle with possible scenarios, and identifying and leveraging everyday practices and habits of mind that are in fact disciplinary. In the final analysis, these chapters lead us back to questions posed in the introduction. If we are to truly build on students' everyday experiences, we must develop tools and language that are equal to the complexity and variability of these experiences as well as appreciative of them.

8

Constructing a Learning Environment That Promotes Reinvention

Els Feijs

Freudenthal Institute, University of Utrecht

RESEARCH FRAMEWORK

The research described in this chapter relates to student materials that were developed for American middle schools as part of the Mathematics in Context (MiC) project. This project was a collaboration between the Wisconsin Center for Education Research, School of Education, University of Wisconsin in Madison, United States, and the Freudenthal Institute at the University of Utrecht, the Netherlands, aimed at the development of a comprehensive mathematics curriculum for Grades 5 through 8.[1] The work was supported by the National Science Foundation. The curriculum as it was developed addresses the recommendations of the National Council of Teachers of Mathematics (NCTM) *Curriculum and Evaluation Standards for School Mathematics* (1989) with regard to philosophy as well as content.

In the collaboration, the development of student materials primarily was the responsibility of the Freudenthal Institute. Both institutes were involved

---

[1] The curriculum materials are published by Encyclopaedia Britannica Educational Corporation, Chicago Il, VS.

241

in classroom experiments, observation, in-service education, assessment, and research. Mathematics in Context, a 5-year project, was completed in 1998. In collaboration with the publisher of the curriculum materials, two more years were spent on the development of teacher guides and other written support to go with the student books.

The complete Mathematics in Context program contains 40 units, 10 at each grade level. The units are organized into four content strands: number, algebra, geometry, and statistics. The research described in this chapter concerns only the geometry strand of the curriculum.

GEOMETRY IN MATHEMATICS
IN CONTEXT: PHILOSOPHY

The geometry strand in the Mathematics in Context curriculum was developed by the Freudenthal Institute according to the principles of Realistic Mathematics Education (RME). Geometrical aspects of daily life contexts are used as a starting point; the education builds on students' informal experiences with such contexts. Students are expected to play an active role in the learning process; they construct their own knowledge, triggered among other things by classroom activities and manipulatives. Students are enabled to actually reinvent geometrical concepts by solving problems offered by teacher-guided reinvention (Freudenthal, 1973, 1991). Reflection plays an important role in the learning process; students are urged to become conscious of their experiences and to describe and understand these in mathematical terms, for example, by making their own productions (Streefland, 1990). In order for students to learn from interaction, there is ample room for students to interact with other students. And, finally, there are many connections within the curriculum, not only within the geometry strand but also across strands, in which knowledge is built on units students have done earlier. For example, number skills are frequently required in the geometry strand, and there are many connections of geometry with algebra and statistics as well.

The overall goal for the geometry curriculum that was developed for American middle schools is Freudenthal's idea of "grasping space" "geometry is grasping space. . . . it is that space in which the child lives, breathes and moves. The space that the child must learn to know, explore, conquer, in order to live, breathe and move better in it" (1973, p. 403). Activities aimed at "grasping space" are abundant in the student materials. As for the content of the geometry strand, more traditional subjects are embedded in a way that suits realistic mathematics education, and a very important role is given to what we call "vision geometry." Vision geometry deals with the relationship between representations of reality and reality itself, and the role of vision in this relationship (Team W12-16, 1992, p. 27). This emphasis on vision geometry follows a long Dutch tradition rooted in the innovation of geometry education, which was initiated in the early seventies by the Institute for Development of Mathematics Education (IOWO). Besides Freudenthal, as a source of inspiration we should name especially the pioneering work of Schoenmaker, Goddijn, De Lange, and Kindt (1981). For American schools, where the standard Euclidian geometry curriculum is still prevailing, this approach is totally new. In our opinion, this justifies the choice of geometry as a research subject.

Finally, we should remark that within the boundaries of the Mathematics in Context project, there was a certain amount of freedom for the Freudenthal Institute regarding the development of the curriculum, albeit limited in certain respects. The curriculum had to be in accordance with both the NCTM standards and with a blueprint document (Romberg, 1992) written by the advisory committee of the project, and the development took place in a dialogue with the American staff on the project team.

GEOMETRY IN MATHEMATICS IN CONTEXT: THE CURRICULUM

Three themes run through the geometry curriculum: (1) orientation and navigation; (2) shape and construction; and (3) visualization and representation. These themes determine the focus and direction of the geometry strand. Although individual units may emphasize one theme over the others, no theme is completely absent in any unit.

The first theme, orientation and navigation, is of a dynamic character. The student is placed at the center of space, and geometry is considered to be the study of the student moving through space. One aspect of orientation has to do with realizing your position relative to other objects and the consequences for seeing those objects. Another aspect of orientation is realizing your position relative to a certain direction and distance to a certain point and the possibilities to use coordinates and vectors. Navigation includes the use of coordinate systems to represent positions, the use of directions and distances to design routes and to locate places, and the use of changes in direction to define angles and turns.

The second theme is of a more static nature, the focus being on characteristics of objects in the student's space. Topics include shape identification and classification, shape in design and building, two- and three-dimensional shapes and their relationships with each other, similarity and congruence, abstract models of shape that highlight important features like edges, vertices and faces, lines with special properties, and transformations.

Construction involves the active manipulation of shapes by the student. Some related topics are constructibility of triangles, tiling, constructing solids, and design and construction of maps. The more traditional subjects in geometry are primarily found in this second theme.

The final theme, visualization and representation, is pervasive in the geometry strand. It can be found not only in geometry but in many other subject

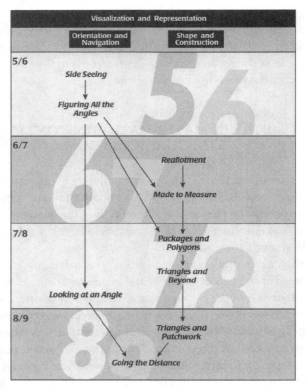

FIG. 8.1. The geometry curriculum in Mathematics in Context.

areas in mathematics as well. Visualization and representation have to do with what you see, how you see it, and how you can communicate that to other people. Example topics are two-dimensional representations of three-dimensional objects, projections, side/front/top views, maps, nets, cross-sections, contour lines, vision lines, networks, and graphs.

The geometry curriculum is organized into 10 units for 4 grade levels. Each of the units concentrates on a more or less confined subject. It is structured by mathematical subject rather than by the context in which the mathematics is presented. All 10 units are interconnected. The unit titles are listed in Fig. 8.1; arrows show the connections between units.

The research described in this chapter is restricted to the unit "Looking at an Angle," which was designed for Grade 7 (12- through 13-year-olds) (Feijs, De Lange, Van Reeuwijk, Spence, & Brendefur, 1998).

RESEARCH PROBLEM

The initial research question was, in general terms: Is it possible to translate the philosophy of realistic geometry education described earlier into student materials?; how to develop such curriculum materials?; and how effectively can these materials be taught in American schools? Because it was impossible to answer this research question in relation to all of the geometry curriculum materials, a selection had to be made. After a small-scale pilot in several American classrooms, the unit "Looking at an Angle" was chosen, as it seemed most suitable for the following reasons. The developers of "Looking at an Angle" have tried to incorporate all significant characteristics of realistic geometry education in the design of this unit. The unit is characterized by a large variety of learning settings, a broad mathematical content, and a rather complex structure of this mathematical content. A large degree of student input is required, so it was to be expected that this unit would generate a considerable amount of student materials for analysis. The mathematical content is for the most part completely new to American mathematics teachers in the middle grades, which would justify a study into their experiences. And, last but not least, early experiences with this unit in classrooms showed that the resulting students' learning processes were interesting from a developmental perspective. In other words, there was plenty of room for improvement in the sense that the original design should be subjected to a cyclic process of design and research.

The initial research question now is focused on the unit "Looking at an Angle." Several more specific research questions have arisen as a result of classroom experience with this unit, such as: (1) To what extent does reinvention actually take place and how can reinvention be promoted? (2) What are the effects of the chosen realistic contexts on students' learning processes? (3) What is the role played in the learning process by hands-on experience and hands-on materials? (4) To what extent are mathematical connections that are implicit in the materials visible to students? and (5) In what way does the student material elicit student reasoning and the making of connections by students? This chapter focuses on the first research question, that is, the feasibility of reinvention as a designer's goal.

RESEARCH METHODOLOGY

This study can be characterized as developmental research. The goal, as described by Freudenthal, is to "consciously experience, describe and justify the cyclic process of development and research so that it can be passed on to others in such a way that they can witness and relive the experience."[2] In this process the thought experiment[3] plays an important role: It is at the base of the curriculum design. The designer of the curriculum tries to envision how a teaching–learning process will proceed and uses classroom experiments to search for indications whether or not the expectations were correct. This will lead to new thought experiments that will induce an iterative process of development and research.[4]

In this research the design principles and the goals of the pilot version of the unit "Looking at an Angle" were made explicit as much as possible, the design was piloted in classrooms, observation reports were analyzed, and the materials were revised and piloted again in an iterative process. During each stage of the design, student learning processes were analyzed in order to find indications for the revision of the materials. Learning processes that were not anticipated proved especially interesting in the sense that they often indicated the need for revision.

---

[2]Freudenthal, H. (1988). Ontwikkelingsonderzoek. In: K. Gravemeijer en K. Koster (eds.). *Onderzoek, ontwikkeling en ontwikkelingsonderzoek.* Utrecht: OW&OC. 52.

[3]Freudenthal, H. (1973). *Mathematics as an Educational Task.* Dordrecht: Reidel. 100.

[4]Gravemeijer, K. (1994). *Developing Realistic Mathematics Education.* Utrecht: CD β Press. 112.

There are two main sources of data collection in this research study. First is the curriculum materials themselves in all different stages of the development process. Data collection is focused on making the implied local instruction theory[5] explicit and describing it. Second is the data collected through classroom experiments. The unit "Looking at an Angle" was piloted at a number of American middle schools, and after revision tried again, not only at American schools but also at a school in the Netherlands. Lessons were audio- and video-taped and classes were observed extensively, with emphasis on students' thought processes that were generated by the student materials and influenced by the teaching methods chosen by the teacher. Observation notes were worked up to detailed lesson reports. Video- and audio-tapes were transcribed. Transcripts include conversations between students and the researcher, who sometimes acted as a participant observer with small groups of students. Data collection also included written student materials and answers to questionnaires that were developed for students for research purposes. Finally, interviews with teachers who taught the unit are used as background materials to evaluate and validate research findings. All data mentioned above were analyzed in an iterative process that is to a large extent similar to the "constant comparative method" described by Glaser and Strauss (1967).[6]

STRUCTURE AND CONTENT OF THE UNIT

In the Mathematics in Context curriculum, the concept of angle was introduced 2 years earlier in a unit called "Figuring All the Angles." In the dynamic context of navigation, students discovered that an angle can be perceived as a turn, that is, a change of direction.[7] Next they learned how to measure angles using a compass card, also in the more static context of geometric shapes. In Grade 7, "Looking at an Angle" is meant as a follow-up unit. The focus now is on a special angle: the angle of elevation. In connection to this angle, the concept of tangent is introduced. Through several other units in the geometry and other strands, students supposedly have developed a number of skills and

[5]Gravemeijer, K. (1994). *Developing Realistic Mathematics Education*. Utrecht: CD β Press. 113.
[6]Glaser, B. G., & Strauss, A. L. (1967). *The Discovery of Grounded Theory: Strategies for Qualitative Research*. New York: Aldine. 101–115.
[7]Feijs, E., & De Lange, J. (1994). Een andere koers in het Amerikaanse meetkundeonderwijs. *Tijdschrift voor nascholing en onderzoek van het reken-wiskundeonderwijs*, 12(4). 25–32.
De Lange, J., & Feijs, E. (1994). Verschillende koersen leiden tot een hoek. *Tijdschrift voor nascholing en onderzoek van het reken-wiskundeonderwijs*, 13(2). 10–15.

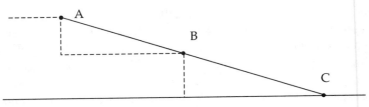

FIG. 8.2. Vision line in the Grand Canyon.

concepts that can now be considered to be basic knowledge to them. These skills and concepts are related to views (front, side, top), triangles (also right triangles), altitude, area, graphs, ratio and proportion, fractions, percents, and decimals.

The backbone of the unit "Looking at an Angle" consists of five different contexts that all have the same mathematical structure, that is, the right triangle. The unit starts with the concept of vision lines (or lines of sight) in the context of the Grand Canyon. How can vision lines be used to determine whether or not the river at the bottom of the canyon can be seen from the rim? In this situation it is important to consider the steepness of the vision line and the presence of objects that might block the view. Figure 8.2 shows a side view of the situation. The eye of the person looking toward the river is at point A, point B shows a ledge of the canyon wall, and at point C the vision line touches the ground.

The concept of vision line is further explored in a second context, that of boats, in order to investigate the concept of steepness and to discover regularities in the ratio between the height of the object blocking the view and the length of the resulting blind area. This situation can again be pictured as in Fig. 8.2, provided that now point A represents the eye of the captain on the boat, point B represents the bow of the boat, and point C indicates the borderline between the area that can be seen and the area that cannot be seen by the captain.

A third context makes a connection with shadows. If the eye of a person looking at an object is replaced by a light source, the blind area becomes visible as a shadow. Students may now use construction drawings to investigate the direction, the shape, and the length of shadows. Also, they discover differences between shadows caused by a nearby light source and shadows caused by the sun. Similarly, in this context the right triangle as a representation is used to grasp the situation, provided that now the vision line is replaced by a light ray.

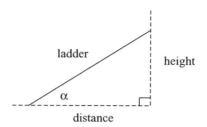

FIG. 8.3. The steepness of a ladder.

A fourth context concerns the steepness of ladders. Students come to understand that steepness can be expressed by means of the size of the angle between the ladder and the ground and by means of the ratio between the height the ladder reaches on the wall and the distance between the wall and the foot of the ladder. This ratio can be expressed as either a fraction or a decimal. Again, the right triangle can be used to represent the situation, as shown in Fig. 8.3.

Finally, the context of hang gliding is introduced in order to further develop and formalize students' concepts of steepness into the concept of tangent. The performances of different hang gliders are compared by means of the so-called glide angle and by means of the ratio between the height the glider is launched from and the distance it flies measured along the ground. (Or, by means of the tangent of the glide angle.)

The situation can again be visualized as shown in Fig. 8.3. So far we have presented a short description of the structure of the unit design as it eventually crystallized. However, before the unit got its definite shape, it underwent a long and extensive process of design, experiment, and revision. The following section describes this process in detail.

GUIDED REINVENTION AND DIDACTICAL PHENOMENOLOGICAL ANALYSIS

As indicated previously, one of the leading principles in the design process was that of "guided reinvention." According to this reinvention principle, students should be given the opportunity to experience a process similar to the process by which mathematics was invented. It implies that by solving a carefully designed "real" problem, students develop "new" mathematical concepts. This solving can be done in a very informal way with very informal language as well, but quite often during the process students sharpen both the concept and the language to describe it.

In the case of this particular unit, "Looking at an Angle," it was indeed the intention that students themselves would reinvent mathematical concepts. At a macro level the mathematical content involves ratios in a right triangle related to an angle, in connection to the concept of steepness, and on an abstract level resulting in the concept of tangent. But also on a micro level this is the leading principle as to contexts in which the concept of tangent may come up, such as contexts in which vision lines or shadows play a role.

It is the task of the developer to design a learning trajectory that will enable students to reinvent the mathematical concepts, in doing so finding inspiration in the history of mathematics and/or in informal strategies used by students. It is crucial to select contextual problems that offer a wide array of solution strategies and that hopefully give an indication of a possible learning trajectory through progressive mathematization as a starting point for the learning process.

The didactical phenomenological analysis as described by Freudenthal[8] plays an important role in the design process. This analysis considers situations in which the mathematical concept concerned is applied, in the first place because it has to be made clear in education where the concept is applied and, in the second place, because their suitability to promote the process of progressive mathematization has to be evaluated. In other words, a selection has to be made of situations that will elicit the development of paradigmatic solution strategies that can be generalized.

A didactical phenomenological analysis was indeed carried out in the early stages of the development of "Looking at an Angle." As far as the mathematical content is concerned, a preset goal of the unit was the development of the abstract concept of tangent and the concept of steepness. It already was common knowledge that the context of hang gliding was very suitable for this purpose, based on the successful experiences with a previous unit ("Vlieg er eens in"[9])—developed by the predecessor of the Freudenthal Institute, the IOWO—which was the primary source of inspiration. As in that earlier unit, the concept of tangent was to be developed by investigating the relationship

[8]Freudenthal, H. (1983). *Didactical Phenomenology of Mathematical Structures*. Dordrecht, Reidel.
[9]De Lange, J. de. (1980). *Vlieg er eens in*. Utrecht: IOWO. Or:
De Lange, J. de (1991). *Flying Through Math: Trigonometry, Vectors, and Flying*. Scotts Valley: Wings for Learning.
The mathematical content of this unit involves vectors, sine, cosine and tangent. "Looking at an Angle" is inspired by the first chapter only.

between the glide ratio (the ratio between the height a glider is launched from and the distance it flies measured along the ground) and the glide angle. However, it was the aim of the developers to include several other fields of application in the unit and to let students reinvent the concept of tangent more gradually in a broader context, namely that of ratios in a right triangle in connection to an angle. For that purpose several contexts were selected in which steepness or angle of elevation were key concepts. From a first collection of possible contexts, a selection was made on the basis of the didactical experience of the designers. The main criterion for the selection was the variety of phenomena of the mathematical concept of steepness. Eventually the designers chose for the following phenomena: steepness of vision lines, steepness of light rays, steepness of objects, and steepness of roads. A more or less simultaneous step in the design process was the search for everyday contextual situations that would fit these phenomena, in other words, the translation of mathematical phenomena into concrete situations. Now the main criteria were the familiarity and appeal for students. This selection process resulted in the following choices: Steepness of vision lines is elaborated in the context of the Grand Canyon and that of boats; steepness of light rays is investigated in the context of a searchlight shining from a fort onto tree stumps behind which people are trying to hide; steepness of objects is translated into the context of ladders; and, finally, the steepness of roads is translated into the context of hang gliders. The order in which these contexts are presented is not random but is based on an imaginary learning trajectory in which progressive mathematization is to take place.

One of the first goals in "Looking at an Angle" is reinvention of the vision line. This concept seemed most suitable as a starting point because all students are familiar with situations in which you can or cannot see objects or persons (think of games such as peek-a-boo or hide-and-seek) and because it allows for a broad exploration. All students know by experience that sometimes your view is blocked by an object or person. To determine whether or not something is visible, it may be necessary to make a sketch of the situation. After exploring several situations, students are stimulated to make such a sketch, which will look like a right triangle with the vision line being the hypotenuse (Fig. 8.2). Having discovered this, students have a model on which they can build throughout the remainder of the unit. In the context of vision lines, students have found a model that at the beginning is still closely connected to the context but which later on in the unit may be used for mathematical reasoning. In other words, as described by Gravemeijer (1994), a model *of* a situation can become a model *for* that situation through an ongoing process of generalization and formalization. In this approach the model is used as a mediating tool to bridge the gap between situated knowledge and formal mathematics.[10]

At the beginning of the unit, the term "vision line" may remain unnamed. Students first implicitly explore the concept of steepness by investigating what happens in case the location of the person looking changes, or in case the object blocking the view is moved to a different location. However, in the context of boats it becomes necessary to name the vision line as well as the area that cannot be seen ("blind spot" or "blind area"). The reason is that in this context questions are asked which focus on the relationship between the angle of the vision line and the water surface on the one hand and the dimensions of the area that cannot be seen by the captain of the boat on the other. Such questions demand a precise construction of vision lines (again using the right triangle as a model of the situation), the measuring of the angle of elevation (without being named as such), and the measuring of the length of the blind area. In doing so students will discover that if the angle of elevation is small, the blind area will be long and as a consequence the captain's view will be poor. The context of boats is used not only to refine students' terminology and ability to make precise drawings, but it also offers splendid opportunities to explore the relationship between height, distance, and angle of elevation.

At first such an exploration takes place by means of toy boats, the captain's vision line being materialized by a piece of string. Then, by using a model of a tugboat made of cubes and skewers to model vision lines, it becomes possible to make a precise construction of the blind area and to discover numeric relationships between the exact height of the captain and the length of the blind area. Also, the relationship between the shape of the blind area and the shape of the bow of the boat is clarified. Figure 8.4 shows how the blind area of the captain of a tugboat can be constructed by drawing vision lines.

As the context of the fort and the tree stumps is introduced, we move away from the subject of vision lines. However, the contexts involved are isomorphic. Sketching or constructing vision lines and blind areas is done in the same basic way as sketching or constructing light rays and shadows. The reason to introduce this new context is that it very well suits a deeper exploration of the concept of steepness. For example, in dealing with shadows

---

[10]Gravemeijer, K. (1994). *Developing Realistic Mathematics Education*. Utrecht: CD β Press. 100–102.

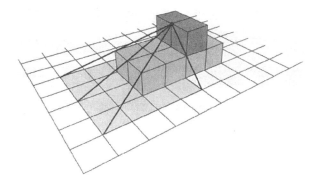

FIG. 8.4. Vision lines of the captain of a tugboat.

caused by the sun it may be determined that at a certain moment and at a certain place there is a constant ratio between the height of an object and the length of the shadow of that object, because all sun rays are equally steep and the angles between the sun rays and the earth's surface are all the same size. There are plenty of discoveries related to the concept of steepness to be made by students investigating shadows caused by the sun. Also, they may compare their observations with what happens if shadows are caused by a nearby light source. Certainly not all of the mathematics in this shadows chapter is necessary for the core learning trajectory of this unit. Along the way students reinvent other mathematical concepts that fit into the MiC curriculum.

With the introduction of the context of ladders, an important step is made in the process of progressive mathematization. The context in itself is fairly bare. A ladder leaning against a wall in a side view looks like a right triangle. There are no more objects blocking the view or casting shadows. There is only height (where the ladder touches the wall it is leaning against), distance (between the wall and the foot of the ladder), hypotenuse (the ladder itself), and the angle between the ladder and the ground. The context itself provokes a discussion of steepness, as this is relevant in thinking about a safe positioning of ladders. As a consequence, in this stage of the learning trajectory it is natural to start focusing on the construction of right triangles in order to investigate the relationship between height, distance, and angle of elevation. Formal notation is introduced, and for the first time in the unit the term steepness is mentioned.

Toward the end of the unit, the context of comparing the performances of different hang gliders is used to make the step to the formal concept of tangent. As mentioned previously, the context in earlier experiments had proven to be very suitable as "model for." As soon as students discover that the performance of a hang glider can be expressed by means of the "glide ratio" (the ratio between the height the glider is launched from and the distance it flies measured along the ground) or by means of the glide angle, the step toward the formal concept of tangent is merely a matter of terminology and notation.

In its original form the unit looked quite simple, meaning that before and during the initial development the designers did not yet have a very clear and detailed picture of how the unit was going to be structured. In the initial design phase, a refinement of the learning process as envisioned took place. However, there was a constant danger of following side paths that were touched upon, thus neglecting the larger structure. For instance, it would have been possible to dedicate a complete unit to the subject of shadows. Also, during the design process there were moments of doubt about the structure of the unit and the order in which contexts were to appear. For example, it was discussed whether or not it would be better to precede the reinvention of vision lines with the exploration of shadows. A number of context situations in which mathematical concepts on side tracks are applied had to be left out of the unit because there simply were too many and because they would obscure the flow of the unit.

The final product was created through a long process of deliberation in which classroom experiments, observations, and analysis played a crucial role. However, this has not only led to a final product but also offered possibilities for an ongoing refinement of the hypothetical learning trajectory. In other words, the designers/researchers through this process became more and more able to describe and justify the underlying structure of the unit under design. Or, it would be more accurate to say the many structures and connections, considering that classroom experiments have shown that students saw connections and structures that were not consciously brought into the unit but that nevertheless fit in very well. We may conclude that from being simple in its original form, the curriculum design has turned out to be rather complex.

The original structure of the unit has survived. It was not affected by all the changes that have been made. Based on classroom experiments, we can conclude that at a macro level the goal of reinvention can indeed be attained. The chosen contexts attribute to a gradual reinvention of the concept of steepness and eventually the concept of tangent. Note, however, that not all students reach the highest level as far as tangent is concerned. For some students, the step toward working with tangent on a formal level is too big. They feel more comfortable thinking at a level on which the model of the right triangle refers to a well-known situation, such as that of a glide ratio in the context of hang gliders.

The development process has shown that the structure as described in the hypothetical learning trajectory at times remained obscure to students. As a result, in the final product connections between the various contexts featuring in succession in the unit were made more explicit to students. Mind that the word "guided" in "guided reinvention" does not only apply to curriculum designers. It is also the teacher's duty to regularly hold discussions with students aimed at reflection on the ongoing learning process in order to keep the main ideas and the flow of the unit in mind. The following examples of students' written reflections on the first two chapters of the unit suggest that students are indeed highly capable of puting into words the connections they see between different contexts.

"They (are) all related because they all use mathematical figurations to get an answer. They all have something to do with a view point and where you can or cannot see. All form right triangles and all use ratios."

"I think the activities we've done are related because they all had to do with blind spots and lines of vision or light."

"All of the activities thus far are related because they all show vision lines and blind areas. Each activity showed a person's view of something from where they were standing. It also showed what they could see and what they couldn't see."

"All of them have to do with vision lines. Someone's blind spot if they are in a certain spot. How you can see more or less if your position or height is moved. (. . .) All blind spots form a right triangle. The larger the angle the smaller the blind spot."

Next, in order to draw some conclusions about reinvention on a micro level, we now refer to the beginning of the unit "Looking at an Angle," when students are put on the track to reinvent the vision line.

GUIDED REINVENTION OF THE VISION LINE

After it was decided to use situations in which vision lines are important as an introduction to the unit, the question was how to put students on the track to reinvent the concept of vision line. The developers thought this could be

FIG. 8.5. Hiker on the rim of the Grand Canyon: Can the hiker see the river below?

accomplished by presenting photographs. The first version of the unit started with a photograph of a hiker on the rim of the Grand Canyon looking down trying to see the Colorado River at the bottom of the canyon. The question that accompanied the photograph was: Can the hiker see the river below? The photograph is shown in Fig. 8.5. It was meant to stimulate students to think about how to determine what you can or cannot see. It was followed by three more photographs as well as questions concerning the reason that the river cannot be seen on parts of the photographs.

Students were expected to naturally start talking about the view being blocked by protruding rock, implicitly discussing vision lines. Because most students probably would never have visited the Grand Canyon, it seemed likely that some would have trouble interpreting the photographs. The developers considered it desirable to have students experience a three-dimensional representation of the situation, and therefore the unit offers nets that could be used to make a paper model of the Grand Canyon with a curve in it. The assembled model is shown in Fig. 8.6.

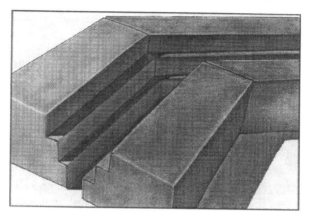

FIG. 8.6. Paper model of the Grand Canyon.

The model was intended to have students investigate from which places on the rim of the canyon the river would be visible. The student unit also showed side views of the model in which students could draw vision lines if they wished to do so. As soon as students discovered the vision line, they could, based on the model, investigate ratios between heights and widths of the ledges of the canyon walls. Just in case students would not have invented vision lines by themselves, after a couple pages it was suggested to use knitting needles or skewers with the paper model to determine whether or not the river was visible from the canyon rim. The text said that knitting needles or skewers may serve as a model of vision lines: imaginary straight lines from the eye to an object. And from that moment on, vision lines would be a concept understood by students, whether or not they reinvented it by themselves.

Reinvention of the vision line did not take place during the first tryout of the unit. This may be attributed to the fact that the pilot teachers, who regretfully as a result of circumstances had not been well-informed about the goals of the unit, gave away the idea of a vision line right at the beginning of the unit on the first page. As teachers noticed that students were not able to give a conclusive answer to the first question (Can the hiker see the river below?) they suggested drawing vision lines in the photograph. However, it is inappropriate to draw vision lines in a photograph that does not show an exact side view of the situation. Also, the student work shows that many students did not know how to draw vision lines nor had the faintest idea how drawing a vision line would help to answer the question. Some students drew a line from the eye of the hiker who seemed to stare straight ahead. Other students drew a seemingly random line going straight through rock. Of course the use of a paper model of the Grand Canyon in this situation could no more contribute to any kind of reinvention.

This experience clearly indicated some issues that are very important for the curriculum development process. First of all, even if students are familiar with situations involving a blocked view, in no way does this imply they are familiar with the concept of vision line. Second, the choice of photographs was very unfortunate if the aim is reinvention of the vision line, because photographs give a perspective representation of the situation and they are not suited to draw vision lines. At best, photographs are only suited to elicit thinking about ways to determine what you can or cannot see. Third, it is not at all obvious that there is only one specific vision line that is crucial in order to determine what you can or cannot see, that is, the vision line that goes from the eye exactly along the ledge of the rocks. The hiker on the rim of the canyon wall may look in all different directions. There are in fact numerous vision lines. And, finally, the wording of the questions was not precise enough. It was not clear to students that the hiker was not looking straight ahead but downward, in an attempt to see the river at the bottom of the canyon.

These conclusions called for a revision of the design of the beginning of the unit.

In collaboration with a teacher, a new introduction was developed and tried in the classroom. The new introduction is as follows. The teacher discusses with his class that he is going to leave the room. While he is gone, the door will remain open. Of course students will start doing all sorts of things they are not supposed to be doing, and therefore it will be desirable to appoint a student as a lookout to announce the return of the teacher. Now the question to the class is which student's position is most suited to be the lookout post, and why. After the students have written their prediction, the teacher will actually leave the classroom and come back after a while, so that students may check whether or not their prediction was right.

This introduction was chosen because it was supposed to be close to students' implicit experiences with vision lines. Also, the intention was to make students aware of their implicit notions of vision lines through reflection. The classroom experiment that followed made clear that the first supposition proved correct: The situation was appealing and familiar to students. However, the question is also, did the context elicit a discussion about vision lines? In the class discussion students did talk about, for example, "he does not see the door from the right angle" or "she looks straight through the door into the corridor," but on the other hand many of their suggestions obscured the issue. For instance, students suggested that they could get out of their seats and walk to the door, in which case students closer to the door could be back in their seats more quickly, or that students who are seated closer to the door can better hear the teacher coming back. In short, the situation was so recognizable to students and they got so involved in it that it was too hard for them to stick to the rules as described by the teacher. If it were for real they would, for example, not stay in their seats.

The fact that the situation proved to be overfamiliar had the effect that mathematical notions remained implicit in the class discussion. There was no reason whatsoever for students to put into words what everybody knows, that is, that people look in a straight line and cannot look around a corner or through a wall.

The situation with the teacher leaving the room did fulfill a role in the sense that the students became aware of a phenomenon they had often experienced but had never reflected upon. The learning effect was limited, however, because students handled the "problem" as a real and relevant problem, which solution consisted of a series of very practical and effective strategies—none of them necessitating the vision line. Therefore further rethinking on the part of the designers became necessary. But the experiment did give certain indications for a different revision of the unit.

The starting point for revision was that students had to be enabled to explore a three-dimensional situation involving vision lines, for it was clear that photographs were not suited for this purpose. This situation had to call for some sort of materializing of vision lines, and questions would have to urge students to put into words how they determine what you can or cannot see from a certain position. If possible we would like to keep the context of the Grand Canyon in order not to break the flow of the rest of the unit that had already been developed.

In fact, the paper model of the Grand Canyon that was already in the unit was well-suited to investigate vision lines after they had been reinvented. However, the model was much too small to enable students to imagine themselves standing on the rim of the canyon wall, so to speak. The developers actually were looking for some sort of life-size canyon with walls in the shape of ledges like in the model, so that students with their own eyes could determine whether or not they could see the river below. Besides, the situation had to be such that students would feel the urge to grab a stick or piece of string in order to "prove" what can or cannot be seen by the person looking down. It that case there would be some sort of tangible vision line, and all that was left was the need to find an appropriate word for it.

FIG. 8.7. Table model of the Grand Canyon.

This process, during which the demands became more and more explicit and detailed, helped the developers in finding the solution that eventually presented itself: canyon tables.

The new version of "Looking at an Angle" started with the photograph of the hiker on the rim of the Grand Canyon, just like in the old version, but now with the sole intention of making students think about ways to determine for sure what can or cannot be seen from the rim. The latter was now to be investigated through an activity in which students build a model of the Grand Canyon using two tables placed parallel to each other with a gap in between. Figure 8.7 shows two students seated behind a table looking down and trying to see the imaginary river (the floor between the two tables) below. They tell each other what they see when looking over the edge of the table. A third student puts marks for each of the two viewers on the canyon walls (paper hanging down form the tables) across from them, indicating how far down they can see on each of the canyon walls.

Students are then asked to compare the marks on both canyon walls. How is it possible that these are further down for one of the viewers? What could you do in order to see the river? One of the tables is moved backward so that one student can barely see the bank of the river below. Can the other student see the river as well? A fourth student lies down on the floor pretending to be swimming in the river, in such a position that she can be seen by one of the viewers but not by the other. In the latter case we say that the "swimmer" is in the "blind spot."

The canyon table activity turned out to hit the bull's eye. Right during the first tryout, a beautiful lesson evolved with a class discussion that in a nutshell revealed the core of the whole unit. Students discovered, guided by the teacher, that the vision of the person being in a higher position is better; that the vision line of that person is steeper; that in that case the blind area is smaller; that the angle between that person's vision line and the floor is larger; that the vision angle of that person is smaller; and that moving a table will move the location of the blind area and broaden the river so that more of it becomes visible. This can be clarified by some quotations from students:

"One person is taller than the other one so they can probably see further down than the other, the shorter person could."

"It's like, if your [sic] gonna be on the top looking down, you should be able to see almost straight down. If you were 10 feet back from the sides of the wall you wouldn't be able to see anything straight down."

"If you're leaning further, then you can see further down than when you're leaning back, because of the side. . . ."

Note that the way students put their notions into words is informal. They show their understanding of the factors influencing the view but struggle in finding the right words. In this case it was the teacher who introduced the term "vision line" as students were making movements with their hands to indicate how the person sitting behind the canyon table looks downward along the edge of the table. At that point one student used the words, "from her eyes to the edge of the desk and then down." Also, it was the teacher who proposed using a stick in order to model the vision line. When one of the students mentioned looking at a certain angle, it was again the teacher who required a precise indication of the angle that was meant. And when one student described the blind area (without naming it this way) as "there where you cannot see," the teacher indicated that he wanted this area to be named the "blind spot."

However, for the developers this did not imply that the design does not meet its expectations. The intention is to stimulate students to reinvent mathematical concepts and to make these concepts explicit using their own words, and according to the transcripts this is precisely what happened. It is fine if a teacher wants students to use mathematically correct terms to describe these findings, but less commendable if a teacher starts fishing for one particular word he wants to hear.

Students quite often grasp a new mathematical concept before they actually "discover" the appropriate language to describe it. The present example shows that students did indeed understand the mathematical concept in a very convincing way. They were also able to explain their "inventions" in appropriate terms, but not (of course) in the appropriate mathematical language. In the case of the vision line, the students used gestures and descriptions in their own words, and when the teacher felt that it was appropriate he introduced the appropriate term. In the case of the blind spot, students themselves came very close again: "There where you cannot see." This kind of mathematization process closely fits our definition of reinvention.

Incidentally, the first tryout of the canyon tables activity brought up an interesting issue the developers had not considered. The teacher asked students to mark on each of the canyon walls three points that were on the boundary of what could still be seen and what could not. Then he asked the class to make a prediction of what these three marks on a canyon wall would look like. This resulted in three different "theories" being brought up by students in the class discussion that followed. One theory was that all marks would be on a straight line at the same level; a second theory was that the mark in the middle would be further down than the marks on the sides; and the third theory was that it would be exactly the other way around, the mark in the middle being higher than the other two. For each of these theories there are possible implicit assumptions, such as the assumption that the vision line is shorter if you look straight ahead, and therefore you will see further down if compared to looking to the sides. Students may also have reasoned that you will see more if you look to the sides, for in the photograph of the hiker on the canyon rim it seemed likely that the hiker would see the river when looking aside instead of straight ahead, missing the fact that this was due to a curve in the river. In the tryout of the activity, the teacher offered students the opportunity to find out for themselves which of these theories was correct. The students had to come to the conclusion that all marks had to be on a straight line, on the same level, if only the canyon walls were parallel to each other, no matter how long the canyon walls are.

As a result of these observations, in the next version of the unit it was suggested to have students investigate this issue about the three marks on a canyon wall. But later experience tells us that such an investigation is only successful if students are really fascinated to find an explanation why these marks are on a straight line at the same level.

The canyon tables activity has proven to be very succesful in all subsequent classroom experiments, both in classroom settings where the activity was carried out with the whole class and in settings where students carried out the activity in groups of three or four. The canyon tables are a rich source for student exploration in which they can reinvent concepts worded in more or less explicit ways. From the most successful of the classroom experiments, we may even state that the activity foreshadows all core concepts of the whole unit. As a consequence, throughout the learning processes that occur later on in the unit references can be made to students' experiences with the canyon tables. For example, the vision lines of the captain of the tugboat looking over the (straight!) bow all end on one line; in other words, the shape of the captain's blind area is the same as that of the bow of the tugboat. This is basically the same issue as the marks on the canyon wall across all being on the same level, on a straight line, an issue that will come up again in the context of shadows later on in the unit, when the endpoints of the shadows of the tree trunks that are on a straight line all form a straight line as well.

Finally, there is one more observation related to the reinvention of vision lines that we want to mention at this point. It shows that it is not only possible for students to reinvent the concept of vision line but also that a student may also come up with that particular name for the mathematical phenomenon all by himself. This is what happened at a school in the Netherlands where a tryout of the unit eventually took place.

The students were seated in groups of four, two by two behind "canyon tables," ready to do the canyon tables activity described above. They first discussed the question concerning the photograph of the hiker on the rim of the canyon. In one of the groups the students spontaneously started to make drawings of the situation, some trying to draw perspective representations and others drawing side views. One student in his side view drew a line in order to determine that the hiker cannot see the river. Next to it, he had written "vision line." The observer asked him where that word came from, whether he himself had brought it up. The student answered that the teacher had just walked by asking him what that line was supposed to be, "and then I said, well, that is how he looks, and then I, well, then I call it vision line. A new word: vision line." Now this same student came to class very disappointed the next day, because in looking through the unit at home he saw the word "vision line" everywhere, so after all he had not invented a new word. But in fact he really had invented it all by himself: a prototype of reinvention.

This completes the description of the developmental research into reinvention of the vision line at the beginning stage of students' learning process in the unit "Looking at an Angle." A deeper understanding of what vision lines are, how they can be used to determine what can or cannot be seen by a person, and how to make a precise drawing of vision lines requires many more student reinventions that have to be elicited during the learning process. The developmental research has resulted in many indications for further student reinventions. Especially telling are moments when students did or said unexpected things indicating where the hypothetical learning trajectory needs to be refined. At such moments it becomes clear that the developers' assumptions were incorrect or incomplete.

CONCLUSIONS

In this chapter we described how a learning environment that promotes reinvention of the concept of vision line was constructed. Based on the developmental research, we can conclude that the final product indeed enables students to reinvent this concept. According to the observations, it is clear, however, that we may not expect the same level of success in all circumstances. Success to a large extent depends on the knowledge and teaching qualities of the teacher; on students' previous learning experiences; and on facilities offered by the school, such as time, materials, and room. Implemention issues require a great deal of attention.

As far as the final product is concerned, the developmental research was successful. Equally important is the process through which this goal was accomplished and the knowledge that accumulated. We conclude that the developmental research was of enormous value to the creation of the final design. Additionally, the cyclic process of design, data collection and analysis, and revision has resulted in a large amount of experience that may be utilized for further developmental research in the area of realistic geometry education.

Designing a hypothetical learning trajectory appears to be a first and most important step. Thanks to the students and the teachers involved in the research who have offered the researchers the opportunity to analyze their learning and teaching processes, it was possible to put the thought experiment to the test and to continually refine and improve the learning trajectory.

REFERENCES

De Lange, J. (1980). *Vlieg er eens in*. Utrecht: IOWO.

De Lange, J. (1991). *Flying through math: Trigonometry, vectors, and flying*. Scotts Valley: Wings for Learning.

De Lange, J., & Feijs, E. (1994). Verschillende koersen leiden tot een hoek. *Tijdschrift voor nascholing en onderzoek van het reken-wiskundeonderwijs, 13*(2), 10–15.

Feijs, E., & De Lange, J. (1994). Een andere koers in het Amerikaanse meetkundeonderwijs. *Tijdschrift voor nascholing en onderzoek van het reken-wiskundeonderwijs, 12*(4), 25–32.

Feijs, E., De Lange, J., Van Reeuwijk, M., Spence, M. S., & Brendefur, J. (1998). Looking at an Angle. National Center for Research in Mathematical Sciences Education & Freudenthal Institute (Eds.), *Mathematics in context, a connected curriculum for grades 5-8.* Chicago: Encyclopaedia Britannica.

Freudenthal, H. (1973). *Mathematics as an educational task.* Dordrecht: Reidel.

Freudenthal, H. (1983). *Didactical phenomenology of mathematical structures.* Dordrecht: Reidel.

Freudenthal, H. (1988). Ontwikkelingsonderzoek. In K. Gravemeijer & K. Koster (Eds.), *Onderzoek, ontwikkeling en ontwikkelingsonderzoek* (pp. 49–55). Utrecht: OW&OC.

Freudenthal, H. (1991). *Revisiting mathematics education.* Dordrecht: Kluwer Academic.

Glaser, B. G., & Strauss, A. L. (1967). *The discovery of grounded theory: Strategies for qualitative research.* New York: Aldine.

Gravemeijer, K. (1994). *Developing realistic mathematics education.* Utrecht: CD β Press.

National Council of Teachers of Mathematics. (1989). *Curriculum and evaluation standards for school mathematics.* Reston, VA: NCTM.

Romberg, T. A. (Ed.). (1992). *A blueprint for mathematics in context: A connected curriculum for grades 5-8.* Madison, WI: NCRMSE.

Schoenmaker, G., Goddijn, A., De Lange, J., & Kindt, M. (1981). Neuer geometrieunderricht auf der sekundarstufe. In H. G. Steiner & B. Winkelman (Eds.), *Fragen des geometrieunderrichts* (pp. 99–156). Köln: Aulis Verlag Deubner.

Streefland, L. (1990). Free productions in teaching and learning mathematics. In K. Gravemeijer, M. van den Heuvel, & L. Streefland, *Contexts, free productions, tests and geometry in realistic mathematics education* (pp. 33–52). Utrecht: OW&OC.

Team W12-16. (1992). *Achtergronden van het nieuwe leerplan wiskunde 12-16. Band 2.* Utrecht: Freudenthal Instituut; Enschede: SLO.

9

Involving Students in Realistic Scientific Practice: Strategies for Laying Epistemological Groundwork

Jennifer L. Cartier
University of Pittsburgh

Jim Stewart
University of Wisconsin-Madison

Cynthia M. Passmore
University of California-Davis

John P. Willauer
Monona Grove High School

DESIGNING CLASSROOMS THAT PROMOTE UNDERSTANDING

Teaching for, and learning with, understanding are clearly desirable educational goals. As such, they have been the centerpiece of significant reform efforts in science education in the United States (National Research Council, 1995; American Association for the Advancement of Science, 1993). Although the positions in these national documents are not always explicit about what is to count as understanding, they do lay out broad classes of target learning outcomes. Included in these are the expectations that students will

- understand central concepts in various scientific disciplines;
- learn how to use those concepts to conduct their own inquiries; and

267

Cognitive Tasks

1) Constructing relationships.

2) Extending and applying [scientific] knowledge.

3) Reflecting about [scientific] experience.

4) Articulating what one knows.

5) Making [scientific] knowledge one's own.

FIG. 9.1. **Cognitive tasks that promote understanding.** These five interrelated forms of mental activity support student achievement of understanding in science (after Carpenter & Lehrer, 1996).

- understand how those concepts were developed through disciplinary practices and the role that they have played as guides to inquiry.

Thus, student learning outcomes include those of a "content" nature as well as those of an epistemological nature. Put more plainly, it is desirable for students to have knowledge of specific scientific endeavors as well as the knowledge claims that resulted from such inquiries. We, and others, have argued elsewhere that scientific *inquiry* is a process of developing explanations about the natural world through participation in the complex activities of *discipline-specific practice* (Cartier, Passmore, & Stewart, 2001; see also AAAS, 1990; Toumey, 1996; Kitcher, 1984, 1993). Thus, scientific knowledge is inextricably bound up with its generation and use. We further assert that to engage in scientific practice is both to demonstrate and to achieve understanding.

To promote the acquisition of understanding so conceived, the National Center for Improving Student Learning & Achievement in Mathematics & Science (NCISLA) has begun by describing cognitive tasks that enable understanding to develop (after Carpenter & Lehrer, 1996; Fig. 9.1). However, even with these general perspectives on how scientific understanding develops, the creation of intellectually rigorous science curricula is not a trivial undertaking! NCISLA researchers have also formulated a set of design principles to facilitate the development of curricula in which students' understanding of (and often participation in) the practices of particular scientific disciplines is the goal (Lehrer, Carpenter, Schauble, & Putz, 1998; Fig. 9.2). Yet, we feel that there is a need for more specific strategies to serve as a bridge between general guidelines and design principles on the one hand and actual curriculum development on the other. In this chapter we highlight two such

---

Design Principles

1) Students should be afforded access to complex ideas in science at every grade.

2) Disciplines have characteristic forms of argument, and students should learn to participate in these forms. To achieve means to comprehend and participate in scientific argument.

3) Assessment of student achievement must be designed in ways that provide teachers with greater access to student thinking.

4) Invention and revision of models affords students at all grades the opportunity to learn about important ideas in science by engaging in practices that capture important aspects of the activity of scientists.

5) Modeling tasks for classroom instruction should be designed so that that students develop insights about central conceptual structures in the discipline.

6) Classrooms should exploit important connections between everyday reasoning and arguments in disciplines.

7) Classroom instruction must be grounded in experience.

8) Classroom instruction should be grounded in a history of learning. Long-term views of the development of student thinking must underlie attempts to improve student achievement.

FIG. 9.2. **Design principles for science classrooms.** Lehrer, Carpenter, Schauble, & Putz (1998) described several general characteristics of science classrooms that support students' achieving understanding through inquiry.

intermediate guidelines (or *implementation strategies*) that have been used with success in the curriculum development work of Project MUSE (Modeling for Understanding in Science Education):

- Introduce students to foundational ideas about scientific inquiry early in instruction by engaging them in tasks where developing insights about the reasoning involved in practice—and not any particular science content—is the focus.
- Return to this foundation (or framework) as science content is studied in the context of particular disciplinary practices.

The primary context for illustrating these implementation strategies is a 9-week unit on Earth–Moon–Sun astronomy (EMS) that is a part of an introductory science course for high school students. In addition, we describe their use in a high school evolutionary biology course and point to ways in which the same basic strategies can be used to introduce students to scientific practice in significantly different disciplinary contexts. As a prelude to illustrating the implementation strategies, we discuss more fully our perspective on understanding in science—a perspective that blurs distinctions between content, process, and nature of science learning outcomes. This perspective has emerged from a consideration of practice in various science disciplines and has culminated in the recognition of both the common purposes that underlie scientific inquiry generally and the uniqueness of practice within specific disciplines (Cartier, Passmore, et al., 2001).

UNDERSTANDING AND SCIENTIFIC PRACTICES

Understanding in science involves a set of interrelated components that form the basis for ways of knowing about and interacting with the world. Included is what is typically referred to as conceptual knowledge (a discipline's concepts, theories, and models), an understanding of how knowledge is generated and justified (methodological and epistemological concerns), as well as the ability to engage in inquiry. Yet, when thought of as distinct categories of learning outcomes (content, nature of science, and process), the potential exists for instruction to misrepresent the complex and highly integrated nature of scientific practice. It is clear that scientists do not carve up their intellectual lives along the lines of this triad so common in science education. One would never find biology courses that bear the title "The Method of Biological Observation" or "The Process of Generating Hypotheses in Biology." The reason why no such listings are found can be understood by listening to biologists (including geneticists, ecologists, physiologists, etc.) interact with one another about their research. Their talk is holistic, integrative, and messy, with the distinctions between content and process constantly blurred. The conceptual structures of a discipline, the problems deemed worth pursuing, the means by which they are to be pursued, and so on are completely intermixed in the conversations, benchwork, and conceptualizing of scientists (see Latour & Woolgar, 1986). Thus, scientific knowledge is inseparable from its generation and use, and scientists (and, we argue, students) achieve understanding through participation in the messiness of practice.

Further complicating the scientific landscape we are painting here is the recognition that although there is no meaningful distinction between content and process in inquiry, there are important distinctions between disciplinary practices in terms of methodology, argument structure, and cognitive goals (Rudolph, 2000; Rouse, 1996; Fine, 1986). Philip Kitcher (1993), a philosopher of science, defined scientific practice as "a multidimensional entity whose components are the language used in the scientist's research, the statements made about nature that the scientist accepts, the questions that are counted as important . . . the methodological views that are specific to the research of the field of science, the canons of good observation and experiment, and the standards for assessing the reliability of others" (p. 31). There are two points worth emphasizing here: (1) because each discipline has its own specific research methods, hypothetical course offerings such as "*The* Scientific Method" are unthinkable; and (2) not only do disciplines have distinct methodologies, but they also may be underpinned by significantly different epistemological assumptions. This last point has been forcefully made by Ernst Mayr (1982) in his distinction between explanations that invoke proximate causation (*how* explanations) versus ultimate causation (*why* explanations). Mayr argued (as have other biologists and philosophers of biology) that evolutionary biology differs from other biology subdisciplines in its reliance on ultimate causation, the historical contingency of evolutionary events, and the nature of the data at the heart of evolutionary inquiry (also see Kitcher, 1993; O'Hara, 1988; Richards, 1992). The centrality of explanation, rather than prediction, to the discipline's argument structure also sets evolutionary biology apart from more traditional biology subdisciplines (see Gould, 1990, for a popular treatment of this idea). In summary, the forms of argumentation and even the underlying cognitive goals of evolutionary practice differ from those in many other biology practices (physiology, for example) where the nature of inquiry and claim making is realized by drawing on causal explanations of a proximate nature. This is but one example of the ways in which scientific disciplines and subdisciplines differ from one another—an example we perhaps belabor in our attempt to argue for the importance of attending to such differences in designing curricula. To create opportunities for students to learn about and participate in authentic scientific practice, one must take into account the specific ways that disciplines create, justify, and talk about knowledge.

THE ROLE OF MODELS IN PRACTICE

Acknowledging that scientific practice varies depending upon disciplinary constraints is only a starting point for curriculum developers. In fact, abandoning the notion of a single "scientific method" actually complicates the task of curriculum design considerably. What is needed is a view of scientific practice that recognizes discipline-specificity while being general enough to provide a framework for curriculum work and instructional design. Simplifying practice to make it pedagogically useful begins by identifying elements of practice that are common across disciplines and making those the central focus of an educational framework. Although the constraints that determine the nature of data, forms of evidentiary arguments, and range of questions pursued are determined within individual scientific disciplines, modeling plays a central role in scientific inquiry regardless of discipline. The development of models that can be used to explain phenomena may be the primary goal of inquiry or, alternatively, scientists may utilize key models (such as natural selection) as they endeavor to reconstruct historical events through inquiry (Richards, 1992; Donovan, 2001). Given its ubiquity, modeling—the construction and/or use of causal models—provides a useful inroad into the complexities of disciplinary practices. By focusing on the development, use, and revision of causal models, as well as the justification of explanations that utilize those models, we believe we have created a framework that recognizes essential elements of scientific practices and yet is general enough to be useful in classrooms. The Practice Framework (Cartier, Passmore, et al., 2001; Fig. 9.3) focuses on the central role of models in asking questions, recognizing data patterns, and constructing explanations, as well as the criteria for judging knowledge claims.

Data collection, pattern recognition, proposing causal models, and defending explanations in science is, in reality, both a highly discipline-specific process and a seamlessly integrated one; that is, data collection and analysis proceeds concurrently with the use and production of causal models. Nevertheless, the simplification represented in the Practice Framework has proven to be a powerful pedagogical tool. The MUSE team employed this framework to design science instruction in genetics, evolutionary biology, and astronomy (Cartier & Stewart, 2000; Passmore & Stewart, 2002; Barton, 2001). Disciplinary constraints guided the selection of phenomena and the types of patterns sought and also provided the basis for framing specific research questions with an eye toward central causal models necessary to formulate acceptable explanations. The specificity of disciplinary practice became *explicit* for *students* when they began to discuss and defend their models with one another in MUSE classrooms. The structure of their explanations, as well as the body of scientific ideas in relation to which their models were judged, was discipline-specific.

Given the importance of models and modeling in our classrooms (and in science), it is essential that students learn *about* scientific models (in addition to learning the concepts relevant to *particular* models) and how to communicate with one another regarding the use and evaluation of such models. In

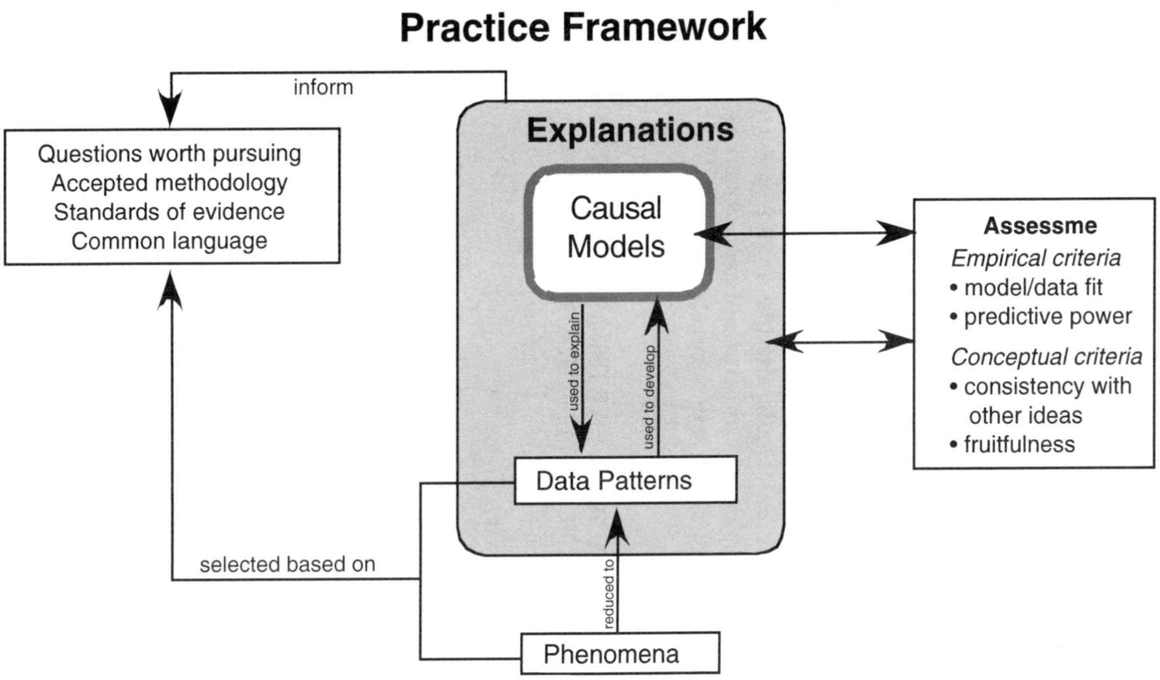

FIG. 9.3. **The Practice Framework.** This view of scientific practice is grounded in science studies literature but is simplified to be pedagogically useful (see Kitcher, 1993; Giere, 1988; Finley & Pocoví, 2000). The framework reflects a view of inquiry as a process of making sense of phenomena in the natural word. Thus, scientific practice necessarily begins with the recognition (mediated by conceptual lenses provided by explanatory models) of some phenomena warranting explanation. From data about natural phenomena, scientists then strive to establish patterns related to the data. A goal, nearly universal in the sciences, is to create, revise, or use explanatory models to account for these data. Explanations for phenomena are rhetorical structures containing specific reference to data patterns and elements of models that are brought to bear in accounting for those patterns. Scientific explanations are judged based on whether all of the specified data are adequately explained and whether the causal model brought to bear in the explanation is consistent with accepted knowledge in science. In some disciplines, modeles are also judged based on whether they can be used to predict new data, but this is not always a criterion for acceptance (see Rudolph, 2000).

the remainder of this chapter we illustrate how "content-free" introductory activities have been used to help students learn about models in general, about particular models (celestial motion and natural selection), and about using models to construct explanations for phenomena. We draw on our experiences in a 9-week EMS (Earth–Moon–Sun) astronomy unit for ninth-grade students and describe how teachers introduced students to important ideas about models and argumentation (assessment of explanations) using a "black box" activity. We emphasize ways in which MUSE teachers returned to the ideas developed with the black box activity in the context of astronomy instruction. Finally, we provide a brief look at a unique activity designed to introduce students to important aspects of practice in evolutionary biology. We have chosen the EMS and evolutionary biology units in order to emphasize unique elements of practice within these two disciplines. As mentioned above, although models play a significant role in evolution, practitioners also devote considerable attention to reconstructing the history of past events. Consequently, the practices and explanatory structures of evolutionary biology differ from those within other disciplines, including astronomy.

"BLACK BOX" SCIENCE AND EARTH–MOON–SUN ASTRONOMY FOR NINTH GRADERS

Developing the Black Box Activity

During the summer of 1998, high school teachers and university researchers collaborated to design a 9-week unit that would introduce all incoming ninth graders to inquiry in science.[1] Paying attention to the MUSE practice framework (Fig. 9.3), we created a unit where students could systematically develop a Celestial Motion Model (CMM) that could explain patterns associated with Sun rise/set, Moon rise/set, Moon phases, eclipses, and seasons. The focus of student work within the unit was to become familiar with various celestial phenomena, identify data patterns associated with those phenomena, and develop or refine a causal model (CMM) to explain those patterns.

For the EMS unit to work the way we hoped, students needed to share ideas in very public ways: They worked in small groups to develop the CMM and craft explanations for various phenomena and shared those explanations with the entire class in a critical forum mimicking that of a scientific community.

---

[1]The EMS unit is described in detail in Barton (2001) and is available electronically through the MUSE Web site at: http://www.wcer.wisc.edu/ncisla/muse.

While designing the unit, the MUSE team anticipated that students would find participation in such a community to be challenging, at least initially, because it bore little resemblance to the more traditional learning environments within which they had experience. Students would need to learn the "rules" of participation in this community, which included valid criteria for evaluating ideas and explanations. Thus, we chose to begin the unit with an activity that would make key aspects of the practice framework transparent and afford teachers the opportunity to make explicit connections between this activity and scientific practice. We adapted an activity that had regularly been used in the ninth-grade introductory science course in the past, the black box activity.

Originally (prior to the MUSE collaboration), the black box activity encompassed one or two days of instruction and was intended to provide a concrete analogy between scientific inquiry and the process of discovering the mechanism within a black box. Students viewed a wooden box that had a funnel at the top and an outlet tube at the bottom. They poured various amounts of water into the box and found that water emerged only after a certain amount was put in. So for example, a student might add 200 milliliters of water and nothing would come out. After adding 200 milliliters more, all 400 milliliters would emerge. The task was for students to imagine a mechanism within the box that might account for this pattern and to share their ideas with their peers.

The black box activity as it was originally taught was problematic in that students were focused on *discovering* the *correct* answer to the problem (i.e., discovering the actual mechanism within the box). By analogy, they were led to believe that the goal of scientific inquiry is to discover truth. Moreover, the inductive view of scientific inquiry that underscored the original black box activity is incompatible with the MUSE practice framework, in that it fails to acknowledge both the importance of identifying empirical patterns and, more significantly, the role of explanatory models in recognizing and making sense of such patterns in the first place.

Despite shortcomings in its original form, the black box activity had several characteristics that the teachers in our team valued. In particular, it was engaging for the students and immediately set the tone in a science class that focused on students' own ideas and explanations. Moreover, students were not expected to learn any particular science concepts as a result of participating in the activity, so it tended to be inviting to students who were intimidated by science in the first place. Thus, rather than discard the activity, we decided to adapt it to provide explicit opportunities for students to justify scientific explanations derived through inquiry. We brainstormed a list of characteristics we

Water In (milliliters)	Water Out (milliliters)
*400	0
400	400
400	600
400	400
400	0
400	1000
*400	0
400	400

FIG. 9.4. **The black box.** The photograph shows the black box used during the EMS unit. A typical data pattern is shown in the adjacent table. Note that this pattern is cyclical, with an asterisk (*) marking the beginning of each new cycle.

wanted the new box to have in order to make various connections to inquiry. Then, we designed a box that would

1. be sturdy and contain no expensive or particularly delicate parts. Students could manipulate it without destroying it.
2. afford students an opportunity to collect data and make predictions.
3. be able to be flexibly manipulated. Students could add water in any reasonable amount while testing their models about how the box works. They could also add food coloring to the water, etc.
4. give rise to empirical patterns that students might not expect.

In its new form, the data pattern associated with the more complex box was typically that shown in Fig. 9.4.

Implementing the Black Box Activity

Students worked on the black box activity during the first 11 days of the EMS unit and engaged in what was actually a series of several related "activities" including informal presentations, critical discussions, written assessment of working models, and formal presentations of final models. For detailed instructional notes about the black box activity, the reader is referred to the MUSE Web site (http://wcer.wisc.edu/ncisla/muse).

Recall that the black box activity was designed to provide an introduction to scientific practice for students. We intended that they would use their skills of data gathering, pattern recognition, and argumentation as they proposed a variety of models to describe how the inner workings of the box led to particular empirical results. In the words of one EMS teacher, the purpose of the black box was

> the idea of collecting data and being able—having [students] realize what data is, the observations. And then looking for a pattern in the data. So being able to take seemingly disconnected pieces of information and trying to look at a larger picture and trying to find a trend or a pattern through that is an important part in that. . . . The main goal is to then have them come up with an idea, a model, that fits their data. To have them actually practice the process of science as we're trying to teach them. (John Willauer, interview, October 23, 2000)

Consequently, the activity was an ideal time to make elements of the practice framework explicit with students and the teachers' instruction reflected this goal.

On the first day of instruction, teachers[2] demonstrated the use of the black box by pouring various amounts of water into it and noting the volume that emerged. Because water emerged from the box in what appeared to be "random" ways, the students were immediately intrigued and eager to collect more data the next day. However, before allowing small groups of students to begin work on their own boxes on Day 2, the teachers began class by asking their students to evaluate two ideas that might explain their data from Day 1. First, they drew a picture of a box with a straight tube running from the funnel to the outlet. Second, the teachers drew a picture of a tiny person within the box manipulating a container of water and tipping it to expel water from the box. Focusing on these representations, the teachers led a discussion about whether the students thought their models were "good" ones or not. In John Willauer's class, the students were engaged in this discussion, often

---

[2]"Teachers" refers to the four members of the ninth-grade teaching team. Because the teachers had a common planning period during the day, it was possible to determine that they were adopting similar instructional practices while implementing the MUSE curriculum. Researchers observed all four teachers at various times, but collected classroom transcripts only in John Willauer's class. Thus, the examples we offer within this chapter occurred in John's class.

responding with humor, but in the end, developing consensus about how to evaluate a scientific model:

John: I went home last night, as I do most nights, and I was thinking about our black boxes. . . . And I wanted to come up with an idea, *an idea*, for how this would work. I am going to share it with you, okay? Follow along and see if you can understand my drawing . . . [*draws a box with a single, straight tube*] So this is the idea that I had—

Students: That's not what it's like.

John: Now let me explain how this works so we're all clear. I take the water and I pour the water in like so and the water flows through the tube and it comes out here and I collect it. Now, don't yell out. Anybody want to make a comment on my idea here? Chris?

Chris: I don't think it was right.

John: Why? What don't you like about this, Chris? Why don't you like it?

Chris: If the water was to go all the way down, if the water was to go through that tube and go straight down, it wouldn't stop.

John: Okay. So what are you addressing? There's something here on this side [*referring to the board, where students have summarized their data from yesterday*], that you're looking at right here. What is it? You're on the right track. Maybe you can't say it out loud. You're exactly right. I just want you to say it again. Um, Doug?

Doug: If you poured water down the tube that went at that oblique angle, then there's no reason why the water shouldn't come out the first time or the second time.

John: Okay. Now you see what Chris and Doug did? The first thing they did was they looked at my model and then what did they use to decide if this model would work?

Student 1:   Their brain.

Student 2:   Information.

John: What do we call this stuff?

Students: Data!

John: Data or observations. That was the first thing they went to. They looked at the model, they thought "Okay, I see how it works. Now I'm going to take the data that we generated. I am going to apply it to that idea and see if it works." And I

| | think we can all agree that the way I have it set up here, I pour water in and what's going to happen? |

Student 3:   Water is going to come out.

John: Like a second later? Less than a second later it's going to come dripping out the other end. Is that what we experienced?

Student 2:   No.

John: No, so some problems with this model. I'd like you to get a sheet of paper out and write this down at the top of the sheet of paper: Model Judgment. [John writes this on the board.] We're going to be doing a lot of that. Okay? And actually you all did that a second ago. Chris and Doug were the ones that actually spoke up and did the judging for us. Most people were doing that. What's the first thing you want to do when you're trying to judge whether or not an idea or a model is working?

Chris: Observe it.

John: You want to use the observations, to see if the observations are explained with the model. Right? So, we want to make sure that the model *explains* the observations. [writes this on board] And those observations can also be called data. And that's the first thing that Chris and Doug did. . . . Well, I thought you might not like that model, so I thought about a second model and this one I think you might like. So I will draw another one for you. [John draws the little man or "Martian" model] All right, now . . .

Peter: Told you there was a little guy in there!

Keith: Peter was right!

John: Okay. Let me explain how this one works. I pour water in the top and my little purple Martian guy collects the water in this container until it gets to a certain point that I talked about and then he dumps out the water I just poured in, he dumps that out, along with this water that's saved up inside and then the water comes out here. So raise your hand to comment on this one. . . . How does this model do in terms of this, explain the observations or the data? [points to board where this model judgement criterion is written]

Student 4:   Pretty good.

Student 5:   Yeah.

John: Does that explain the data?

Students: Yeah.

Keith: No.

John:	No. Why, Keith?
Keith:	Cause it's not real.
John:	Does it explain the data though?
Keith:	No.
John:	It doesn't?
Students:	Yeah it does!
Keith:	Yes it does. [laughter]
John:	Okay, but now go ahead, Keith, what are you going to say.
Keith:	Nothin'.
John:	All right. So it seems to explain the data, but do you have any problems with it?
Keith:	Yeah, there's something wrong with it. He's purple. He's supposed to be green. What's going on?
John:	Well, I used green for my containers. What's the problem with it?
Elizabeth:	It's not realistic.
John:	It's not realistic. Is there anything in your experience that tells you a little person, be it Martian or not, could squeeze inside one of these boxes and do that? So, this is not something that our experiences have allowed us to say, "yeah, this could happen." . . . Everybody disregards this model when judging it because you say there aren't little purple men from Mars inside all these boxes at [our high school]. Does that make sense? So the second thing we want to put up here [on the board] is "Is the model consistent with the way the world is?" With the way we know the world to be. That's the second criterion we want to use to judge models. Does that make sense? Ask yourself, "Based on all the personal experience, all the personal knowledge that I have, does it make sense?" Well, this one here [straight tube model], nobody had a problem with that. You all have experience with water and tubes and things of that nature. And you look at this and you're like, well, that could actually happen, but it doesn't match the data here. Does that make sense? This one [Martian model] seemed to match the data just fine but it's certainly not consistent with the way you know the world to be. We're not going to have little beings in these boxes pouring buckets of water for us. Okay? It just doesn't seem logical. With that in mind, I want you guys to start developing your own ideas about what's going on here, how these things work.

Like John, the rest of the EMS teachers used these specific examples to establish some language for talking about how ideas are judged in science. Students described how the first model (the straight tube model) had been rejected because it failed to "*explain*" the data pattern that they had identified—if the box contained only that tube, then each addition of water would result in an immediate output of equal volume, a pattern they had not seen the day before. The second model (the tiny person model) was clearly "*unrealistic*," or inconsistent with their knowledge about the world. At the end of this discussion, the teachers explicitly stated that the students' task was to propose a model, *an idea*, that might account for their data pattern and *not* to identify what was *actually* within the box.

Subsequently, each student model was judged according to the assessment criteria established within the context of evaluating the teachers' initial models. Initially, the teachers led by example with respect to judging models and explanations. As one group presented their final black box model, John demonstrated through questioning how to assess a model based upon how well it fit the data:

Brian: For our black box project, we were given a wooden box and told to put water in it and find out how it works. So we made a model of our idea and are going to try and show you how it works.

The group of three students then showed the class a chart of their data. The chart was too small to see, however, so they read several data points aloud. They noted their pattern: after 600 milliliters were added, between 550 and 700 milliliters would emerge. Their representation showed two containers connected by tubing. Weight-sensitive suction cup/spring mechanisms controlled the outflow of water from each of the containers. After describing the model, one group member defended it by saying,

Gina: It matches our data because it explains how sometimes we have a little bit coming out and sometimes we have more.

John: I know your data isn't big enough for me to see, but I would like if you could follow through there some of the data just so I can . . . I'm trying to clarify just how it's working.

Gina: After a while, we started with between 200 and 400 . . . First we put in 400 and that would push it down a little but not enough to engage the suction cups.

John: Okay. In your model it has to hit the suction cups and when it's touching the suction cups, then the water can come down the tube, right? . . . So now we have 400 in there—

Gina: Chris put in another 200 so the suction cups bring it down and it goes over here [*points to second container*]. And there's already a little bit in here from last time.

        Gina went on to explain how this matched their data which showed an output of about 700 milliliters.

Throughout the black box activity, students had practice proposing models and defending explanations according to the practice framework. The link between this activity and scientific inquiry was explicit, and several students were able to discuss the similarities between their work on the boxes and scientific inquiry more generally:

Interviewer: Okay. Why do you think your [introductory science] teachers wanted you to spend so much time doing this kind of work?

Staci: So we would get an idea of how much time it actually takes to get a decent model that explains the data. Scientists usually don't figure out too much stuff in a couple of days.

Interviewer: Would you say that you have been doing science these past couple of weeks?

Staci: I guess in a way we are. Yeah. Yeah. That is what scientists, yeah.

Interviewer: That is what scientists?

Staci: Well, the scientists like to, well, I shouldn't say like to, I mean, scientists like experiment and observe and take data.

Interviewer: And then what do they do?

Staci: They try to come up with a reasonable explanation for the observations and data.

Interviewer: You guys spent over two weeks working on these boxes, collecting data . . .

Peter: That was two weeks?!

Interviewer: You look surprised! Yeah. And talking with each other and is this what you were expecting to be doing in science class?

Peter: No! Not at all. Last year was the teacher would write formulas on the board, we'd write them down in our notes and have a test like a week later or something. This is a lot more, it's a lot funner [sic] with the group work and figuring things out.

Interviewer: Why do you think your [introductory science] teachers thought that this was such an important thing for you to be spending time doing?

Peter: Well one, it kind of got us on the right foot, you know working with groups. And talking to people. And also it helped with now what we're doing, the astrology [sic] kind of thing, the looking at patterns and all that, so it got us ready for that too.

Interviewer: Do you think that you've been doing science?

Peter: Yeah! Pretty much, well, yeah. The thinking, figuring things out, why they work, how they work. Making models. Explaining why and how they work to others. Yeah, it's pretty much science.

Building on the Foundation: EMS Instruction

The practice framework was reinforced through the instruction about EMS topics. Using this framework allowed teachers to address student ideas in a variety of ways. For example, some of the teachers encountered student models in their classrooms that were unable to explain data patterns or were inconsistent with other knowledge. At times teachers were able to use the assessment criteria within the practice framework to refute such models in ways that furthered students' understanding. Even when there were no competing models to judge, teachers relied on the framework to help focus student work on using the CMM to create coherent explanations for complex data patterns such as those associated with seasons.

Making Sense of Complex Phenomena.   Teachers used the MUSE practice framework to guide interactions with students throughout the EMS unit. Early in the unit, the teachers took the lead in prompting students to support their knowledge claims by drawing specific connections between data and their model. Thus, teachers explicitly framed class discussions around the assessment criteria established during the black box activity:

> *Kenny, Mark, and Susan are standing in front of the classroom explaining Moon rise and set using an inflatable globe and Styrofoam ball. Following their explanation, Kenny asks if the students have any questions. Before anyone can ask a question, John interrupts:*

John: As we're listening to these, we have to make sure we have to do three things as we're listening to these explanations. What's one of them, Ed?

Ed: See if their model makes sense.

John: See if their model makes sense with how we know the world works.

           John points to a student whose hand is raised.

Jason: If it fits their data.

John: If it fits our data.

           He points to another student.

Kelly: Predict.

John: And does it predict. Okay.

Beth: [*to Kenny's group*] If you have solar eclipses and the moon stays in the same place, how would you explain that?

Kenny: Solar eclipses we haven't gotten to yet.

Beth: Yeah, I know. You're saying it will predict. It has to predict a solar eclipse—

Kenny: It has to predict why it [the Moon] rises and sets.

Beth: I know that but I'm just saying—

John: Okay. Hang on. Hang on! Great point there [*to Beth*] and excellent way of defending what you're talking about [*to Kenny's group*]. You're absolutely right, that's something that we're eventually going to talk about . . .

Beth was attempting to use the criterion of "prediction" as she assessed her classmates' explanation in the preceding example. In this case, the students were getting ahead of where John wanted them to be, and he acknowledged that they were doing a good job discussing their ideas even though they were not ready to discuss eclipses yet. With practice the students became quite skilled at using this framework themselves as they shared and critiqued explanations for astronomical phenomena.

One of the more complicated phenomena the students attempted to explain was that of seasons. They identified several seasonal data patterns including midday angular height of the Sun, average temperature, maximum shadow length, and average day length. The students found that all these patterns were dependent on both time of year and global location. They were able to make sense of this complicated data set by falling back on the practice framework. In particular, John reminded them that answering the question,

"What causes seasons?" was not the objective. Rather, the students needed to *use* their CMM and their knowledge of what causes seasons to *explain* various data patterns:

> *John asks the students what causes seasons. Greg volunteers to go the board and draw a picture of his idea. Greg's drawing shows the Earth and Sun with the Earth tilted on its axis such that the Northern Hemisphere is tipped toward the Sun. He identifies this "tilt" as the cause of seasons.*

John: All right. So, how many people have actually heard this before in terms of seasons? So, yeah, almost everybody. Now the question comes in, "How do we *explain* the *data* based on that model?"

> *Kenny goes to the board and draws a series of diagrams that show the maximum height of the Sun during different seasons. A few students ask him to clarify his drawings and he explains how the Sun appears higher in our sky when the Northern Hemisphere is tilted toward the Sun, during summer. Later, John asks the students to explain temperature patterns in different seasons.*

John: OK, we're close here.

Ed: We're trying to explain why it's colder in winter.

John: Yes, I would like to convince people—

Ed: —well, one of the reasons is that when you're in the winter we've obviously found out that the days are shorter, right?

John: What do you mean "the days are shorter"?

Ed: Daylight shines less.

John: Daylight. Thank you.

Ed: And, ah, well when the Sun, the longer the Sun shines on your part of the Earth, or like Madison, let's say, the warmer it's gonna keep getting. And if you have a shorter day, shorter daylight period, there's not enough time for the Sun to heat up you as much. And at night it gets cold and stays cold.

Moira: [*standing up, holding a globe next to a light source*] Like what Kenny said, direct sunlight. Like if my hand—

John: Well, hang on a second. I want to go back to what Ed is saying. Does that seem to make sense. Would everybody—is that something that you can say "yeah, that's kinda how I think things work." The longer I am exposed to a light source or something like that the hotter I will get.

Students: Yes.

John: Hmm, maybe that seems like a reasonable thing. Moira is going to add something else here, she wanted to.

Moira: Like if my fist were a ray of sunlight and you hit it like this [extends her arm to the globe, parallel to the floor], it's hitting a smaller area than if it were like this [extends her arm at an angle].

After this exchange, John used an overhead projector and a transparency grid to demonstrate how light hitting a curved surface directly is concentrated in a smaller area compared to light that hits that surface at an indirect angle. Thus, the amount of energy in the latter case is dispersed over a greater area and is analogous to light energy hitting some location during winter.

Judging Models.   The practice framework also played a role in teachers' interactions with students when competing models were being discussed. On one occasion, John was discussing his students' explanations for eclipse phenomena. One of his students proposed that eclipses occur approximately every 6 months because the Moon, Earth, and Sun are aligned only twice in a year. For most of the year, the Moon's orbit is tipped at an angle relative to the Earth/Sun plane. However, the angle of the Moon's orbit (its "tip") gradually flattens over a period of 6 months until it aligns with the Sun/Earth plane. Thus, the angle of the Moon's orbit is in a state of constant flux.

John's students liked this model quite a bit. It was relatively simple and was able to account for the pattern in their data (i.e., that eclipses occur every 6 months). John then had a dilemma: How should he refute this model, which he knew to be unacceptable? Rather than simply *present* the accepted explanation to his students, John wanted to identify some data or previously accepted model that he could use to enable his class to determine for themselves that this model was unacceptable based on already established assessment criteria. John agreed with his students that this model was very good at explaining the data. He then stated that he had a problem with it, however:

John: It goes back and forth. All right. That's an interesting idea. Let's look at this for a second. Let's listen. Gary says that the Earth's orbit and if I use, I thought we'd end up talking about orbits, so that's why I have my hula hoops here. So if I put the Earth in the center, Gary's saying that the Moon's orbit kind of does this and then tilts back and forth. Is that what you're saying?

Gary: Yes.

John: Does everybody see that? Okay. Now if you think about this for a second, I have one question. How many of you guys have ever talked about Newton's laws of motion before? Anybody? Can you name a law of motion?

Elizabeth: Isn't something like if something is moving it needs another force to make it move different?

John: Okay, that's one of Newton's laws that says an object in motion will remain in motion unless acted upon by another force. So I like Gary's idea except for if the Moon's orbit is tilting this way, why would it stop and go back that way? Something would actually have to act on the Moon in order to cause that to happen. It would have to be a constant force always being applied to redirect the direction of the orbit. Does that make sense?

Students: Yeah.

John: I like your idea. Don't get me wrong. But we want to try not to violate any of the things we know. Remember one of our criteria for a good model, well it's got to explain the data and I think that Gary's model would actually explain the data and we'll go into that in a second. But it also has to be within realistic terms. It has to be within the way we know the world works. The laws of nature and things like that. While I like what Gary suggested, in order for that to happen, something would have to act on the Moon every so often to stop it from going in this direction and cause it to go back in the other direction. Okay?

John's reasoning made sense to his students, and they were able to recognize where the model fell short. John's instruction in this instance was compatible with the goals and methods set forth in our framework and provides an example of how one teacher used the framework successfully in his classroom practice.

SUMMARY

The black box activity provided teachers with a context in which to introduce foundational ideas about modeling in scientific inquiry and begin to practice public assessment and justification of explanations with students. Teachers deliberately and explicitly used these ideas to frame discussions throughout the

EMS unit as students engaged in practice similar to that of astronomers (albeit, early astronomers whose inquires centered on Earth–Moon–Sun phenomena and relied on data collected with simple instruments). Such practice in the EMS unit involved the identification of empirical patterns using both quantitative (ex: Moon rise times) and qualitative (ex: the appearance and sequence of Moon phases) data. Students relied on data they collected themselves as well as archived data from other sources. At the heart of acceptable explanations in this context was the ability to pinpoint and demonstrate the exact motions (of particular celestial bodies) that gave rise to observed phenomena. Public demonstration involved some physical replica of phenomena—the use of props such as globes and Styrofoam balls and/or two-dimensional drawings were not only common, but also became expected within the community of student-scientists in these classrooms. Ultimately, students became skilled at offering and demanding evidence for knowledge claims according to the criteria established at the outset of the unit.[3] Using these criteria, sometimes with coaching by teachers, enabled them to choose among competing models and form coherent explanations for complex sets of data.

Here we have provided one example of how the general strategy of introducing modeling and argumentation through a "content-free" activity can enable teachers to create an epistemological foundation that supports learning in a specific disciplinary context. We conclude this chapter with a brief description of how this same strategy can be used to lay the groundwork for inquiry and argumentation in a very different context: evolutionary biology. In near-Earth astronomy, causal models and explanations are both created and defended through the use of tools (props and two-dimensional representations, and, for more complex phenomena, mathematical algorithms and computer programs) that enable practitioners to enact the motions of particular celestial bodies and observe phenomenological consequences. Persuasive argument relies on a clear match between empirical observations and causal models brought to bear in accounting for those patterns. Thus, in the EMS unit, the emphasis of student work is the creation or modification of a causal model (the CMM) that can account for celestial phenomena and demonstration of model-data fit.

A primary goal of evolutionary biologists is to create explanations for data using the natural selection model (originally proposed, without an explicit

---

[3]In addition to the learning achievements mentioned here, instruction enabled the majority of students to describe empirical patterns (such as the frequency and type of solar eclipses typically seen on Earth in a year) and to provide comprehensive explanations for a variety of celestial phenomena. These results are reported in Cartier, Barton, and Mesmer (2001).

mechanism for inheritance, by Charles Darwin). Unlike the demonstrative nature of explanations in near-Earth astronomy, explanations in evolutionary biology possess a specific narrative structure. Phillip Kitcher (1993) called such explanations "Darwinian histories" and noted how they trace "the successive modifications of a lineage of organisms from generation to generation in terms of various factors, most notably that of natural selection" (pp. 20–21). Not only are explanations narrative in form, but they also rely specifically on the use of historical reasoning: "Narratives fix events along a temporal dimension, so that prior events are understood to have given rise to subsequent events and thereby explain them" (Richards, 1992, p. 23). Thus, an acceptable Darwinian explanation draws together the components of the natural selection model (variation in populations, heritability, selective advantage, etc.) with a narrative structure that demands attention to historical contingency (O'Hara, 1988; also see Passmore & Stewart, 2002, for a longer description of Darwinian explanations in MUSE classrooms). In the section below, we describe an introductory activity that invites students into the unique practices of evolutionary biologists.

THE THREE LITTLE PIGS AND EVOLUTION BY NATURAL SELECTION

Introducing Evolutionary Thinking Through the Cartoon Activity

Using the Practice Framework as a guide, we constructed a unit in evolutionary biology that enabled twelfth-grade students to become familiar with the components and the structure of Darwin's model of natural selection through examination of phenomena such as the prevalence of cryptic coloration in nature and the effects of selective breeding on pigeons. The focus of the unit was for students to use the natural selection model to develop Darwinian explanations for real or realistic phenomena that they explored through data-rich case studies.[4]

We sought to develop an introductory activity that would serve as an analog to the historical reasoning that is so prevalent in the practice of evolutionary biology. Unlike highly experimental fields where knowledge claims are judged based on their ability to explain or predict data patterns from empirical

---

[4]See Passmore and Stewart (2002), for a longer description of the evolutionary biology unit. Unit materials are also available on our Web site at http://www.wcer.wisc.edu/ncisla/muse.

investigations, evolutionary biologists seek to first chronicle and then explain past events that are not available for experimental manipulation. Thus, as discussed above, historical reasoning plays a central role in much of the intellectual work of evolutionary biologists (Richards, 1992; O'Hara, 1988). In designing an introductory activity for the evolution unit, it seemed important to introduce students to this type of reasoning. However, as this was to be the first experience in the unit, the activity also needed to be readily accessible to students and not rely on a great deal of specific scientific knowledge.

Early on, we discussed the possibility of using a family photo album as an analogy for the fossil record. Michael Crichton (1986) captured this basic idea in his novel *The Lost World*:

> When you think about it, the fossil record is like a series of photographs: frozen moments from what is really a moving, ongoing reality. Looking at the fossil record is like thumbing through a family photo album. You know that the album isn't complete. You know life happens in between, you only have the pictures. So you study them, and study them. And pretty soon, you begin to think of the album not as a series of moments, but as reality itself. (p. 192)

Upon further reflection, however, it seemed that pictures of strangers might not be very engaging for students and that developing a life story from them would be quite difficult. Eventually, we struck on the idea of giving students individual frames from an animated story in random order and asking them to construct a sequence and a narrative to share with their classmates using only information they could glean from the images. Many people participated in the brainstorming around this introductory experience, the "Cartoon Activity," but two very creative women, Sue Johnson and Patti Soderberg, brought it to life. They spent a great deal of time watching cartoons and contemplating the desirable characteristics of chosen snapshots and of the set of snapshots as a whole. Such characteristics included

1. characters that were familiar to students such that they could rely on some background information to form inferences about the story.
2. involvement of characters in unanticipated actions/events. That is, we wanted students to use their prior knowledge of characters in their sense-making. However, we also wanted to provide evidence (images) such that prior knowledge alone was insufficient for students to make inferences. (For example, we created a story that included Little Red Riding Hood and the Three Little Pigs, familiar characters to our students. However, their prior knowledge was insufficient for

FIG. 9.5. **Example of cards from the Cartoon Activity**. The full set includes 13 cards. These images are available at http://www.wcer.wisc.edu/ncisla/muse/naturalselection/ materials/section1/lesson1B/handouts/handout2/index.html

the students to predict what kind of interactions these characters, not normally found together in a single story, might have. Thus, their inferences were based on both prior knowledge and specific aspects of the data/evidence.)

3. sufficient "gaps" in the photo record to allow for many interpretations or stories to emerge.

4. colorful, interesting images that would motivate students to participate in the work.

5. at least one underlying story that "held together" the images in a logically defensible way. Even though the students were never privy to this story, we felt it was important that some rational story did exist in order to avoid introducing contradictory evidence inadvertently.

Eventually, the team worked with artist Steve Scoville to develop a series of 13 cards depicting Little Red Riding Hood, her grandmother, the Big Bad Wolf, and the Three Little Pigs. Several cards are shown in Fig. 9.5.

During the inception of the Cartoon Activity, the primary goal was to provide a context in which students could engage in historical reasoning and construct a narrative explanation. However, during the first year that this activity was implemented with students, it became apparent that it could also be used to think about and analyze the structure of scientific arguments. As students worked with the cards, they created a wide variety of stories. Explicit discussions about the differences from group to group provided an excellent opportunity to consider how individual students' prior knowledge and beliefs, as well as their observations of the cards themselves, led to a wide range of inferences related to story sequence. For example, on the second day of the Cartoon Activity in Ms. Johnson's class, she gave the students a few minutes at the beginning of the period to gather with their group members and display their cards on large whiteboards. She then invited each group to share their story with one other group. After this she called the whole class together for discussion. She had two groups present their stories to the whole class and then directed a discussion about why the stories were not all the same:

Ms. Johnson:	You all said something that really sparked me to ask a question. How many groups noticed that the pig was looking up?
	Some students say they did while others say they did not.
Ms. Johnson:	All of you? It looks like not all of you. And how many of you noticed that the dress was different?
	Several students say they did; others say they did not.
Ms. Johnson:	Again, not all of you. So one of the reasons for the differences in the stories is that some people make slightly different observations than others which tended to have them decide that X card might go before Y. Why else might you have different stories?
Nick:	We might have a different prior experience.
Ms. Johnson:	For example . . . ?

. . .[transcript break]. . .

Kathy:	We have heard of these stories with the three little pigs and red riding hood.
Ms. Johnson:	Okay, prior knowledge of this story about the three little pigs. . . . We can extrapolate from that and say that not everyone would know those stories or know them equally well and therefore make some different inferences.

She wrapped up this discussion by asking them to think about some of the inferences they made about particular cards and to write about those as a homework assignment. Figure 9.6 shows two of the responses. By the end of the Cartoon Activity, students showed that they could analyze individual inferences in an argument by examining the data and prior knowledge upon which they were based. Furthermore, Ms. Johnson explained that in critiquing an argument they should be critical of both the data and the possible prior knowledge used to make inferences. This approach to examining arguments

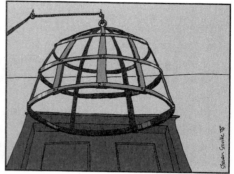

Our group decided to put the picture of the wolf laying in the grandma's bed, and the picture of just the steel trap together because we noticed that there was a rope tied to a ledge in the upper left portion of the page with the wolf on it. We also noticed that the rope in the wall picture and the rope holing in up the trap were very similar, almost identical, from that we inferred that the two pictures belonged together, one way or another.

We put the wolf-stomping-on-the-flower-bed picture first because it just made the rest of our story fall into place. The wolf angers granny so she develops a plan to "get him". Thus we cut to the scene with her, little red, and momma red looking at construction plans because it's all part of this big plan to get the annoying wolf. Our prior knowledge of the "Litle Red Riding Hood'' story led us to believe that Granny and the wolf are feuding enemies. It seemed logical that the 2 would be in some sort of dispute and then they would be plotting against one another.

FIG. 9.6. **Students' Cartoon Activity homework.** Two students wrote about how their groups used their prior knowledge as well as data from the images to make specific inferences about the underlying story.

became important in subsequent classroom discussions within the context of evolutionary biology.

The second major section of the evolutionary biology unit engaged students in examining the arguments of three men who proposed explanations for species adaptation and diversity. Students read original writing by William Paley, Jean Baptiste de Lamarck, and Charles Darwin. During this portion of the course, Ms. Johnson and the students returned repeatedly to the argument analysis approach developed during the Cartoon Activity. For example, when learning about Paley's ideas of intelligent design, the students had explicit discussions about how his prior knowledge and beliefs about supernatural forces influenced the inferences he made regarding the origin of adaptive traits (i.e., Paley proposed that adaptive traits were designed by a divine creator). This idea emerged during one discussion in which the students were grappling with the question of whether Paley viewed species as fixed or malleable:

Ms. Johnson:	Within a species, would Paley say that that species was fixed or that it might change over time?
Students:	Fixed.
Ms. Johnson:	What is your evidence for that? Corey?
Corey:	We were saying, kind of along the lines that everyone was saying. Paley brought his strong theology to it. That influences what he is saying a lot you can tell throughout it [the reading]. So he is saying that there is a creator like God which is to him most likely infallible and he creates the Earth and the animals and other living things according to their niche or whatever. So, he creates everything just how it is going to be you know. He wouldn't make mistakes so it wouldn't have to change.
Ms. Johnson:	So saying something changed is almost like saying that there was a problem in the first place. According to Paley it is perfectly designed to begin with?
Corey:	Yeah.

The groundwork laid during the Cartoon Activity was instrumental in engaging students in discussion about the three models of Paley, Lamarck, and Darwin. By parsing the arguments into the data, prior knowledge and beliefs, and inferences drawn, students were able to make comparisons across all three models. This both supported a deeper understanding of the models themselves and provided clear dimensions along which to compare them. In the end, students were able to see why Darwin's model of natural selection is the dominant model in science today. They determined that the naturalistic prior knowledge and beliefs of Darwin are more consistent with contemporary science than Paley's theistic views. They also noted that Darwin's data on heritability and variation was more compelling than Lamarck's on acquired characteristics. Later in the unit, the students demonstrated their ability to use the framework to critique one another's explanations for phenomena such as brightly colored plumage in male ringed-neck pheasants and the similar coloration of monarch and viceroy butterflies—phenomena that they explored through complex case studies (see Passmore & Stewart, 2002).

Summary

At the beginning of the evolution course, students spent three class periods working with the cartoon cards, presenting their stories, and discussing their reasoning around the cards. By the end of instruction on these three days, the students had a concrete experience with historical reconstruction and had developed and practiced an approach for analyzing arguments that required them to pay explicit attention to the role of observations and prior knowledge and beliefs in developing inferences. This introductory activity enabled Ms. Johnson to emphasize unique aspects of practice in evolutionary biology (including the reliance on historical reasoning and the narrative structure of explanation) and to invite students into that practice in a fun and effective way.

CONCLUSIONS AND IMPLICATIONS: UNDERSTANDING SCIENTIFIC PRACTICE

Throughout this chapter we have described our perspective on scientific inquiry—particularly the centrality of models and explanations within a variety of unique disciplinary practices—and how that perspective has been instantiated in two high school science classes. We have described instances where students in these classes developed sophisticated understanding of aspects of scientific practice in addition to an understanding of central explanatory models such as the celestial motion model and Darwin's model of natural selection.[5] Key to students' achievement of understanding in these classes was their participation in introductory activities that laid bare the foundations for developing and using models and judging explanations within the scientific disciplines in question. Subsequently, students utilized these epistemological principles as they explored various phenomena in astronomy and biology, ultimately coming to understand disciplinary content within the context of realistic practice.

As the examples within this chapter show, instruction that takes full advantage of appropriate introductory activities (and the design of such activities in the first place) is challenging and time-consuming. Without a well-articulated view of the scientific discipline in question, clear goals related to reasoning in that discipline, professional development support, appropriate curricular materials and assessments, and a willingness to establish classroom norms of argumentation and participation, even the most engaging "black box" activity will fall far short of helping students *understand* scientific practice. The teachers within the MUSE team have successfully used the black box and cartoon activities to help students learn about scientific practice in the disciplines of astronomy and evolutionary biology. Their success has been due in large part to the fact that teaching *about* inquiry, as well as *through* inquiry, is a goal to which they are fully committed. Our multiyear collaboration has shown that quality introductory activities coupled with skillful instruction can open the door for students to participate in and learn about scientific practice.

ACKNOWLEDGMENTS

This manuscript and the research described herein are supported by the National Science Foundation (Grant # REC-9972963) and the Educational Research and Development Centers Program (PR/Award Number R305A600007), as administered by the Office of Educational Research and Improvement, U.S. Department of Education, and by the Wisconsin Center for Education Research, School of Education, University of Wisconsin-Madison. The opinions, findings, and conclusions do not necessarily reflect the views of the supporting agencies.

---

[5]Due to space limitations, we have provided succinct evidence of students' learning gains. For more detailed discussion and empirical studies of student learning in these contexts, see Cartier, Barton, et al. (2001) and Passmore and Stewart (2002), or Passmore and Stewart (2000), available at http://www.wcer.wisc.edu/ncisla/publications/reports/RR00-1.PDF.

REFERENCES

American Association for the Advancement of Science. (1990). *Science for all Americans*. New York: Oxford University Press.

American Association for the Advancement of Science. (1993). *Benchmarks for science literacy: Project 2061*. New York: Oxford University Press.

Barton, A. M. (2001). A "MUSE"ing look at inquiry: Ninth grade students and Earth-Moon-Sun astronomy. *The Science Teacher, 68*, 34–39.

Carpenter, T. P., & Lehrer, R. (1996). Teaching and learning mathematics with understanding. In E. Fennema and T. A. Romberg (Eds.), *Mathematics classrooms that promote understanding* (pp. 19–32). Mahwah, NJ: Lawrence Erbaum Associates.

Cartier, J. L., & Stewart, J. (2000). Teaching the nature of inquiry: Further developments in a high school genetics curriculum. *Science & Education, 9*, 247–267.

Cartier, J. L., Barton, A. M., & Mesmer, K. (2001). Learning through and about inquiry in a 9th grade earth-based astronomy unit. Paper presented at the annual meeting of the National Association of Research in Science Teaching, St. Louis, March 25–28.

Cartier, J. L., Passmore, C. M., & Stewart, J. (2001). Balancing generality and authenticity: A framework for science inquiry in education. Paper presented at the 6th International Conference of the International History, Philosophy, and Science Teaching Society, Denver, November 7–11.

Crichton, M. (1986). *The lost world*. New York: Ballantine.

Donovan, S. (2001). Using the nature of evolutionary inquiry as a guide for curriculum development. Paper presented at the 6th International Conference of the International History, Philosophy, and Science Teaching Society, Denver, November 7–11.

Fine, A. (1986). *The shaky game: Einstein, realism, and quantum theory*. Chicago: University of Chicago Press.

Finley, F., & Pocoví, M. C. (2000). Considering the scientific method of inquiry. In J. Minstrell and E. H. van Zee (Eds.), *Inquiring into inquiry learning and teaching in science* (pp. 47–62). Washington, D.C.: American Association for the Advancement of Science.

Giere, R. N. (1988). *Explaining science: A cognitive approach*. Chicago: University of Chicago Press.

Gould, S. J. (1990). *Wonderful life: The Burgess shale and the nature of history*. New York: Norton.

Kitcher, P. (1984). 1953 and all that. A tale of two sciences. *The Philosophical Review, 93*, 335–373.

Kitcher, P. (1993). *The advancement of science: Science without legend, objectivity without illusions*. New York: Oxford University Press.

Latour, B. W., & Woolgar, S. (1986). *Laboratory life: The construction of scientific facts*. Princeton, NJ: Princeton University Press.

Lehrer, R., Carpenter, S., Schauble, L., & Putz, A. (1998). Designing classrooms that support inquiry. Unpublished manuscript available through the National Center for Improving Student Learning and Achievement in Mathematics and Science.

Mayr, E. (1982). *The growth of biological thought: Diversity, evolution, and inheritance*. Cambridge, MA: Belknap Press of Harvard University Press.

National Research Council. (1995). *National science education standards*. Washington, DC: National Academy Press.

O'Hara, R. J. (1988). Homage to Clio, or, toward a historical philosophy for evolutionary biology. *Systematic Zoology, 37*, 142–155.

Passmore, C. M., & Stewart, J. (2000). A course in evolutionary biology: Engaging students in the "practice" of evolution. Research report 00-1 for the National Center for Improving Student Learning & Achievement in Mathematics & Science. [available at: http://www.wcer.wisc.edu/ncisla/publications/reports/RR00-1.pdf]

Passmore, C. M., & Stewart, J. (2002). A modeling approach to teaching evolutionary biology in high schools. *Journal of Research in Science Teaching, 39,* 185–204.

Richards, R. J. (1992). The structure of narrative explanation in history and biology. In M. H. Nitecki & D. V. Nitecki (Eds.), *History and evolution* (pp. 19–53). Albany, NY: State University of New York Press.

Rouse. (1996). *Engaging science: How to understand its practices philosophically.* Ithaca, NY: Cornell University Press.

Rudolph, J. L. (2000). Reconsidering the nature of science as a curriculum component. *Journal of Curriculum Studies, 32,* 403–419.

Toumey, C. (1996). *Conjuring science: Scientific symbols and cultural meanings in American life.* New Brunswick, NJ: Rutgers University Press.

10

"What Are We Going to Do Next?": Lesson Planning as a Resource for Teaching

Ann S. Rosebery
Chèche Konnen Center, TERC

Imagine that you are teaching a class of third and fourth graders about the relationships among distance, time, and speed. Up until now, the children's work has primarily focused on taking walking trips of different speeds down a 9-meter line affixed to the floor of your classroom. The children have worked in pairs to create stories of their trips in both words and pictures, and exchanged them with classmates to see if someone else can recreate their trip using only the representation. One of the goals of the unit is for students to be able to communicate with one another about motion using a range of representations (e.g., stories, pictures, tables, and graphs). It is the end of class and you decide to introduce the children to a new representation that will allow them to measure the speed of their trips. You tell them a version of the "Hansel and Gretel" fairy tale in which Hansel and Gretel run and the witch walks, and each drops a rock every 10 minutes. You ask the children, "Which set of rocks would be closer together, the witch's or Hansel and Gretel's?"

Hands shoot up. About half the class is ready to answer your question. You are surprised. You had expected to leave the children thinking about it until next time. Instead, in the face of this unexpected response, you extend the lesson and give everyone a turn who wants one. Sitting in a circle on the rug, many children use their fingers to "walk" on the floor, their legs, or their shoes to show what they think the pattern of Hansel and Gretel's rocks and the witch's rocks would look like. Sonja says, "The witch is going so slow that every 10 minutes she won't be as far as Hansel and Gretel. The witch would place a rock right here and right here (a distance of about 2 inches) and Hansel and Gretel would place a rock right here (a distance of about 6 inches)." Leann explains, "Since

Hansel and Gretel were going faster, they had more time—they had more space between each rock because they were going faster and if you go really fast then you're like a half-mile away or something." Other children say things you don't understand in the blur of the moment. Bernard asks, "Were they running in a circle?" Karen explains that she thinks Hansel and Gretel's rocks would be farther apart "because if they were running 10 minutes would go fast for them."

When the children have finished, you tell them that they have done good thinking and that next time they'll think more about the trips of Hansel and Gretel and the witch. As you bring the lesson to a close, you wonder, "What are we going to do next? What will help my students continue to deepen their understanding of the relative speeds of two trips?"

How do teachers answer these and other questions related to planning lessons and carrying out a course of instruction for their students? According to recent research (Ball, 1997; Ball & Bass, 2002; Rosebery & Warren, 1998; Wilson & Berne, 1999), to develop a lesson a teacher should take into account what her students know and what she wants them to learn. She should pull together materials (e.g., manipulatives, problems, explanations, questions, representations, etc.) that will support her students' learning, and make decisions about the course of action she and they will take. When done seriously, none of these activities is trivial. Each requires teachers to draw on their experience and expertise and to think creatively and deliberately about "what to do next."

Sometimes teachers teach from units they have developed themselves. Creating such lessons requires significant expertise, thought, time, and effort on the part of the teacher. Increasingly, and especially in the areas of science and mathematics, teachers are being required by school- and district-level administrators to teach from commercially published curricula. This is in part because these curricula have been developed by experts and in part because they are viewed as keystones to districtwide efforts to meet state and local standards. The teacher's guides associated with these curricula typically describe lessons in detail, specifying instructional objectives, hands-on materials and texts, activities, and the like. Some even go so far as to specify what teachers are to say to students, scripting explanations, directions, and so on.

At their best, curriculum guides support a teacher's planning by providing a number of important resources, for example, new perspectives on content, thoughtfully designed activities, and innovative materials. Whether a teacher develops her own curriculum or uses a commercially available one, however, one of her primary responsibilities is to figure out how her students, given their backgrounds and experiences, are likely to take it up. Experienced teachers do not implement curricula wholesale. They modify content, activities, and materials so that these resources make contact with the meanings they see their students grappling with. Sometimes this means tweaking a lesson; at other times it means completely revamping it. Tailoring a lesson to what students know is what Ball and Bass (2000) called a "core activity of teaching." It is part of what all teachers must do, but it is of singular importance for teachers who work with students from diverse socioeconomic, racial, cultural, or linguistic backgrounds because the life experiences of their students are far from those of the middle-class, "mainstream" students for whom most curricula are developed.

Regardless of how much a lesson is changed during planning, one assumption that typically underlies the process is that if a plan is developed carefully and implemented well, the lesson will unfold pretty much as anticipated and achieve the expected outcomes. Following in the footsteps of Suchman (1987), I argue that this view of lesson planning is misconceived and ignores the true potential generated in the activity of planning. Using data from a planning session with an experienced teacher, I show that lesson planning can be a situated, imaginative and lived experience, one in which a teacher calls on her theory of learning and teaching, her knowledge of her students, her knowledge of the subject matter, and her instructional objectives to create a scenario that she can use in situ to respond creatively to her students' spontaneous talk and activity while at the same time keeping her instructional objectives in focus.

THEORETICAL BACKGROUND

What is it that experienced teachers do as they plan and teach a lesson? What aspects of content, students, learning, and teaching do they consider? What do they do with what they know as a lesson unfolds? The answers to these questions speak directly to concerns current in educational reform in science and mathematics. As school districts, professional organizations, and government agencies take on the challenges associated with implementing and supporting standards-based reform (NCTM, 1989; AAAS, 1993; NRC, 1996), they must address the demands for higher standards for teachers that are part and parcel of demands for higher standards for students. If educational reform is to succeed, we need to know what it is that experienced teachers do when they teach (Wilson & Berne, 1999).

Perspectives on Teachers' Knowledge

Approximately 15 years ago, Lee Shulman and his colleagues put forward a paradigm that enabled the field to begin to address questions about growth in teachers' knowledge (Lampert, 1990; Grossman, Wilson, & Shulman, 1989; Shulman, 1986, 1987; Wilson, Shulman, & Richert, 1987). In his well-known essay, Shulman (1987) elaborated the notion of pedagogical content knowledge and asked how teachers actually go about teaching a particular discipline. His questions focused on teachers' knowledge—what do teachers know that enables them to be effective? what analogies and explanations do they find most useful? what makes the learning of a particular idea difficult? Attention to the kinds of knowledge that teachers use has provided the field with ways to think about how the disciplinary ideas that they are teaching are tied to the pedagogy and the curriculum they are using and creating through their teaching.

A focus on teachers' knowledge continues to be productive (Wilson, 1992; Wilson & Berne, 1999). This focus has recently been enlarged to include questions about what teachers *do* when they teach and how they *use* their professional knowledge. In essence, this marks a shift from focusing solely on what's inside a teacher's head to include the site of lived practice. Deborah Ball, among others (Ballenger, 1999; Chazan & Ball, 1999; DiSchino, 1998; Gallas, 1995, 2001; Lampert, 1990; Paley, 1986), was at the forefront of this examination, offering her own experiences teaching elementary mathematics as the subject of analysis (Ball, 1993, 1997). In a recent article, Ball and Bass (2000) explored the core activities of mathematics teaching, which for them include, "figuring out what students know, choosing and managing representations of mathematical ideas, appraising, selecting and modifying textbooks, deciding among alternative courses of action, [and] steering a productive discussion" (p. 12). They are concerned with ways experienced teachers respond to the dilemmas, questions, and myriad unanticipated events that happen day in and day out in a mathematics classroom. In this chapter, I explore the role that the core instructional activity of lesson planning can play in preparing teachers to respond creatively and thoughtfully in the moment-by-moment activity that is teaching.

Perspectives on Planning

To begin, I briefly consider the familiar human activity we call planning. What is planning? What do people do when they plan, and what is the relationship of their plans to what actually happens? In her book *Plans and Situated Actions*, Lucy Suchman (1987) described the view of planning that is prevalent in Western society:

> A plan [is] a sequence of actions designed to accomplish some preconceived end. The model posits that action is a form of problem solving, where the actor's problem is to find a path from

some initial state to a desired goal state, given certain conditions along the way. Actions are described, at whatever level of detail, by their preconditions and their consequences. (pp. 28–29)

This view underlies traditional Western philosophies of rational action and many of the behavioral sciences, including the fields of artificial intelligence, cognitive science, and information processing psychology.

Drawing on work in anthropology and sociology, Suchman critiqued this perspective. Her book opened with a contrastive description by Gladwin (cited in Berreman, 1966) of European and Trukese navigation methods that highlights an alternative notion of planning. According to Gladwin, the European navigator charts his course "according to certain universal principles" and "carries out his voyage by relating his every move to that plan." By contrast, the Trukese navigator "begins with an objective rather than a plan," and utilizes a host of information available in the situation (e.g., the wind, the waves, the tide and currents, the clouds, the stars, etc.) to reach his destination. "His effort is directed to doing whatever is necessary to reach the objective. If asked, he can point to his objective at any moment, but he cannot describe his course" (quoted in Suchman, 1987, p. vii).

Suchman argues that, in action, human planning more closely resembles Trukese than European navigation, that the view of a plan as a set of actions that achieve a preconceived end is simply not true of human experience. Purposeful actions, however planned they may be, are really situated actions—that is, they happen in the context of contingent, concrete circumstances. "In this sense one could argue that we all act like the Trukese, however much some of us may talk like Europeans. We act like the Trukese because the circumstances of our actions are never fully anticipated and are continuously changing around us. As a consequence our actions, while systematic, are never planned in the strong sense that cognitive science would have it" (Suchman, 1987, pp. viii–ix). Conceived in this way, "common-sense notions of planning are not inadequate versions of scientific models of action, but rather are resources for people's practical deliberations about action" (Suchman, 1987, p. 49).

Not surprisingly, teachers' lesson planning has been conceptualized within this general framework. For the most part, lesson planning has been characterized and treated as a process of prescribing instructional steps that, if all goes well, lead to specific learning outcomes. Programs of teacher preparation, schools, and educational researchers have, for the most part, conceptualized it as "a set of psychological processes in which a person visualizes the future, inventories means and ends, and constructs a framework to guide his or her future action" (Clark & Peterson, 1986, p. 260; see also Leinhardt &

Greeno, 1986). Based on their review of the literature, Clark and Peterson (1986) found that the lesson planning of experienced teachers is recursive and cyclical, typically beginning with a general idea and moving through phases of successive elaboration until a "final" plan emerges (Clark & Yinger, 1979; Neale, Pace, & Case, 1983; Yinger, 1977). Although this finding is significant because it showed that lesson planning is more complicated than originally conceived, most models of lesson planning continue to characterize it as an a priori process. The relationship between a plan and its outcome is viewed as predictable and causal: If a plan is developed carefully and executed well, the lesson will unfold as anticipated and achieve the desired outcomes. Inversely, if a lesson does not go as anticipated, it is generally assumed that the plan was faulty or not fully developed. Viewed from this perspective, the focus is on the goodness of fit of the plan as opposed to the vitality, generativity, and usefulness of the planning process itself. The question of how the activity of lesson planning can function as a resource during teaching remains unaddressed.

Perspectives on Constructing Human Experience

To characterize how teachers actually use lesson planning, I draw on two bodies of work, Nemirovsky, Tierney, and Wright (1998) and Casey (1976), that aim to describe how humans experience and make sense of the world. Nemirovsky et al. (1998) posited the metaphor of "lived-in space," an experience or way of being that is forged on an ongoing basis by one's actions, expectations, life history, and so on to "do things and accomplish practical purposes" (p. 153). Far from being an inert structure, a lived-in space is continually re-created as one acts, explores possibilities, and practices ways of doing things within it. It is a place into which and from which to project, enact, and evaluate intentions; to explore possibilities; to juxtapose past, present, and future time; and so on. It is a space in which abstractions emerge as the recognition of patterns fully embedded in the idiosyncrasies of a lived situation (Arnheim, 1971), rather than as entities detached from the complexities of a situation. In other words, it is a place in which to make sense of our past, present, and future experiences.

To understand in some detail the potential power of the planning process, I use the work of Casey (1976) to flesh out the notion of lived-in space. The phenomenologist Edward Casey (1976) described the role of imagination in making sense of human experience. Casey sought to alter a tendency on the part of Western philosophers to belittle or, worse from his point of view, neglect the role of imagination in thinking. His goal was twofold: to demonstrate that imagination is an autonomous mental act, comprehensible and significant in its own right, and to acknowledge its amplitude and intrinsic power in our everyday lives.

According to Casey, imagination can involve at least three modes of thinking. First, it can involve entertaining sensory-based entities or events such as "visualizing, audializing, smelling in the mind's nose, feeling in the mind's muscles, tasting with the mind's tongue," and so on (1976, p. 41). Second, it can involve constructing relationships that link objects and events together, for example, "temporal precedence, spatial contiguity, causal connection, and modification or qualifications of various kinds" (1976, p. 42). Finally, imagining can involve anticipating how an event will unfold or a task will be performed, "imagining how to do, think, or feel certain things, as well as how to move, behave, or speak in certain ways" (1976, p. 44). Casey emphasized that "while distinguishable for the sake of analysis," these aspects jointly structure the activity of imagining and should be considered "co-essential instead of being regarded as strictly separate items" (1976, pp. 39 and 38, respectively).

Using Nemirovsky et al.'s construct of lived-in space and Casey's notion of imagination, I examine the intellectual activity of an experienced teacher as she plans a lesson on distance, time, and speed. I explore how she creates and uses a lived-in space, in her case a richly imagined version of her classroom, to plan her next lesson. Specifically, I address the following questions: What does an experienced teacher do as she plans? What does she bring to bear as she considers what to do next? How do her knowledge and experience shape her planning? And how does her planning shape her subsequent action?

CONTEXT OF THE STUDY

Design Study: Mathematics of Motion

During the 1997–1998 school year, research staff of the Chèche Konnen Center[1] collaborated on a design study with Mary DiSchino, an elementary classroom teacher, to investigate what third and fourth graders could learn

---

[1]The Chèche Konnen Center is dedicated to improving science and science-related mathematics for low-income, linguistic, racial, and cultural minority students. Chèche Konnen means "search for knowledge" in Haitian Creole.

about the relationships among distance, time, and speed, an intersection of physics and mathematics that is often referred to as the Mathematics of Motion. "Imagine an object (a person, a car, an atomic particle) moving along a straight line at a varying speed. As this happens, there are three important quantities that vary as time goes by: the distance the object covered since the beginning of the trip, the object's speed (or velocity) as it moves along, and its acceleration, which is the rate of change of velocity. The Mathematics of Motion is the systematic study of the relationships among these three quantities, as they vary in time" (Monk, 2000, p. 4). The Mathematics of Motion is typically taught to middle and high school students, eventually linking to calculus through the study of formal representations such as tables, graphs, and equations. Some reform mathematics curricula introduce students to aspects of the Mathematics of Motion as early as fifth grade, for example, the *Patterns of Change: Tables and Graphs* unit in the Investigations into Number, Data and Space curriculum (Tierney, Nemirovsky, Noble, & Clements, 1998).

One of our hypotheses in the design study was that young children have enormous experiential resources to bring to bear in understanding motion: knowledge and experiences gained through their own bodily movements as they run, walk, hop, ride in cars and on bikes, skate, and so on. We were interested in studying whether these resources could be used as a foundation for working with informal representations of motion, and the extent to which understanding of informal representations could in turn become a resource from which to build an understanding of standard representations such as tables and graphs. (For a detailed analysis of what the children learned in the design study, see Monk, this volume; Wright, 2001.)

As part of the design study, researchers[2] collaborated with Mary DiSchino, a third–fourth-grade teacher, to design a series of 19 lessons to introduce students to various aspects of the relationship among distance, time, and speed. The team met each week for approximately 1.5 hours to develop the subsequent lesson. In addition, researchers were present in the classroom, documenting what happened in video and field notes. To design the lessons, the team drew on a rich set of resources, including their own understandings of the content; the *Patterns of Change* unit from the Investigations curriculum; and their interpretations of the students' talk and activity based on videotapes of each lesson.

---

[2]In addition to the author, researchers participating in planning meetings included Cindy Ballenger, G. S. (Steve) Monk, and Beth Warren.

The Teacher

Mary DiSchino is an experienced educator. She has been teaching for 30 years. She describes herself as a former "A" student who feels she learned little in school. Mary likes to distinguish her experience of going to school from her experience learning—she describes the latter as "coming to own" an idea. One of the first times that Mary came to own a scientific idea was in a professional development project with Eleanor Duckworth (DiSchino, 1987; Duckworth, 1987). She was part of what has come to be known as "the Moon Group" because of their long-term investigation of the phases of the moon. Mary feels that the learning context that Duckworth established enabled her to learn to trust her own questions, confusions, and ideas about scientific phenomena and to develop a sense of what it means to really understand something. This sense of ownership, of trust in and probing of one's own understanding, is a foundation of Mary's theory of learning and is central to her teaching. It is what she strives to foster in her students. One consequence of this is that for Mary "curriculum" is an emergent phenomenon constituted by interactions among her understanding of the discipline, materials, and her students' ideas, questions, and activity.

The Classroom

The design study took place in Mary's combined third- and fourth-grade classroom in a public elementary school in an ethnically and socioeconomically diverse city. Mary's class reflects the city's diversity. In the 1997–1998 school year, there were 24 children in her class: 14 girls and 10 boys; 13 children of color; 12 children who received free or reduced lunch; and 5 children who spoke a language other than English at home and had previously been in a bilingual program. We deliberately conducted our design study in a classroom with a diverse population because we wanted to investigate what third- and fourth-grade children from a range of socioeconomic, linguistic, racial, and cultural backgrounds could learn about the Mathematics of Motion when their knowledge and varied experiential resources were put at the center of their learning (see also Rosebery, Warren, Ballenger, & Ogonowski, in press, for a further discussion of these and related issues).

Mary's students engaged with the Mathematics of Motion once a week for approximately 50 minutes during a time they call "Sherlock." Sherlock has been a regular part of Mary's academic program for over 10 years; it takes place in addition to and separate from the students' regular, ongoing mathematics and science programs. During Sherlock, Mary and the children conduct an investigation into a question they have about the natural world; the investigation often lasts 3 to 4 months (DiSchino, 1998). Mary, sometimes in collaboration with researchers, designs activity contexts that support her students in learning to think, talk, and act in scientific and mathematical ways. For example, as part of their Mathematics of Motion investigation, the students learned different ways to tell someone about a trip down a straight line, including written narratives, representations of roads that showed speed, charts, tables, and graphs. This was the first time that Mary had taught the Mathematics of Motion; the previous year, she had engaged with it as a learner in the Chèche Konnen Teacher Researcher Seminar (for more on the role of inquiry in science and inquiry in students' ideas in professional development, see Rosebery & Puttick, 1998; Rosebery & Warren, 1998).

As in any classroom, not all of Mary's students took up and learned the same things. In the motion study, all of Mary's children engaged with and learned about important ideas and practices associated with the mathematics of motion, including the concepts of speed, acceleration, and interval and cumulative distance; and various informal and formal representations such as trip narratives, beanbag roads, tables, and distance versus time and speed versus time graphs. Not unexpectedly, some children gained greater mastery over some of the more formal representations, such as speed versus time graphs, than did others. At the end of the unit, all of Mary's students understood and could interpret patterns of change of speed using a beanbag representation, a notion closely related to acceleration. All of the children could complete and interpret a standard speed table. And approximately half of the children could read and interpret standard distance versus time and speed versus time graphs (see Monk, this volume; Wright, 2001).

METHOD

In this chapter, I examine the talk and activity that took place during a meeting that took place on May 1, 1998 in which Mary, in collaboration with Chèche Konnen researchers, developed a plan for "what to do next."[3] This planning meeting was one of approximately 15 that occurred during the course of the design study; audiotapes and field notes were recorded for 7 of these.

---

[3]It is important to note that although these meetings were a collaboration among Mary and the researchers, the researchers were participating in Mary's process, not vice versa. The process described here is one that Mary has used routinely throughout her career as a teacher.

Examination of all seven tapes revealed that the work and talk that occurred during the May 1 meeting were similar to that of the other six meetings. I have chosen to analyze the data from the May 1 meeting because it occurred directly after a lesson that was central to the Mathematics of Motion unit.

To conduct the analysis, I transcribed the audiotape of the planning meeting and studied the transcript[4] to determine how the session unfolded, what was accomplished, and how it was accomplished. Field notes were used to augment and support interpretation of the transcript. In general, I used an iterative process that combined several cycles of analysis and interpretation of the audiotape, transcript, and field notes (Erickson & Shultz, 1977; Mishler, 1990), focusing on the mathematical and pedagogical ideas and thinking practices in which Mary engaged. I presented my interpretations along with transcripts to the Chèche Konnen group, subjecting the analysis to rounds of comment, critique, and elaboration. Mary's own views were solicited on an ongoing basis and incorporated into the analysis. This chapter is the result of many such rounds of comment and criticism.

Working within a situative framework (Bahktin, 1981; Greeno, 1997; Hymes, 1996; Labov, 1972; Lave & Wenger, 1991; Suchman, 1987; Vygotsky, 1978), my aim was to analyze Mary's talk in order to describe what she did; the challenges she encountered; the ways she took up and transformed particular ideas, experiences, and tools as she went along; and how she used these varied resources to plan the next lesson in the motion unit. By varied resources, I refer to Mary's life history, knowledge and experiences (i.e., in relation to science, mathematics, learning, teaching, and the students in her classroom), the material and symbolic artifacts present and envisioned (e.g., tools, data, children's work), and her activity with others (e.g., to plan the lessons, in the Moon Group, etc.).

CONTEXT OF THE PLANNING SESSION

Before turning to the analysis itself, I want to situate the May 1 planning session in the context of the larger, ongoing unit. At this point in time, Mary and the children had completed nine lessons on linear motion and

---

[4]The following transcription conventions have been used: [] contains explanatory information inserted by the author; (. . .) indicates deleted utterances; dashes (like—this) indicate self-interruptions; (to say) indicates a best guess at the identity of a phrase that is difficult to hear; commas refer to pauses within sentence units; (spe:::d) indicates lengthened syllables, each : = one "beat"; conventional punctuation marks indicate ends of utterances.

distance, time, and speed relationships. The purpose of these sessions was to help the children focus on particular features of linear motion (e.g., that, in this context, how many times a traveler stopped during a trip and the duration of each stop was more important than why she stopped). To do this, they spent several sessions taking and describing trips down a 9-meter ribbon taped to their classroom floor. Then they worked on building a shared understanding of some basic conventions associated with distance, time, and speed tables (e.g., whether what we might call interval or cumulative distance was expected in the "distance" column of the table).

As previewed in the opening vignette, in the final 10 minutes of the preceding class, Mary told the children a version of the "Hansel and Gretel" fairy tale, in which she highlighted the difference in the speed of the children and the speed of the witch. She had created the story to introduce them to an activity she had adapted from the *Patterns of Change: Tables and Graphs*, a fifth-grade unit (Tierney et al., 1998). She hoped that the adapted activity would give the children a way to measure and compare the speed of their trips down the ribbon. The *Patterns of Change* unit describes the beanbag activity in this way:

> Students record their trips along a track by dropping beanbags at two-second intervals. They make tables and diagrams showing where the beanbags landed. [. . .] [The teacher should] explain to two volunteers that when you say "start," they will both move along the track, starting at the same end, one on each side of the track, but at different speeds. Every time you say "drop," they will both drop a beanbag. Both stop when they reach the end of the tape.

> Because there will be a delay in the students' reaction time, the interval from the start to the first beanbag drop will be longer than the other intervals, which should be quite regular. The fast walker's intervals (space between beanbags) will be longer than the slow walker's intervals.

> Some students may find it confusing that the person moving fast dropped fewer beanbags with larger spaces in between (●   ●   ●   ●) than the person moving slowly (● ● ● ● ●). One way to make sense of this is to note that the number of beanbags is a measure of time. The greater number for the slower trips shows that it took *more* time for the slower person to go the whole length; that person's time was more multiples of 2 seconds. (pp. 47–48)

Here is the Hansel and Gretel story that Mary told her students:

Mary: What we're going to do next time is use the ribbon to figure out if a trip is fast or slow. So next time we'll put a ribbon on the floor and we'll have you take a fast trip and a slow trip and see if there is any way we can mark the ribbon to see if the trip was fast or slow. Think of Hansel and Gretel. When they were running they left behind bread. Instead of leaving bread let's pretend they left rocks behind and they were running really fast. And they left a rock behind every 10 minutes. The witch took all the time in the world and she left rocks behind too. And she walked really really slowly. And she dropped a rock behind every 10 minutes. I want you to think about this as a challenge and a puzzle. Which rocks would be closer together? The witch's or Hansel and Gretel's?

As suggested in the introduction, Mary expected to leave the children think-ing about the story until next week's Sherlock. To her surprise, however, more than half the class was eager to answer her question there and then. Mary gave each child a chance to illustrate and explain what he or she thought would happen. Most used their fingers to walk along the floor, their legs, or their shoes to show what they thought the patterns of Hansel and Gretel's rocks and the witch's rocks would look like. The children's thinking and activity during these last 10 minutes of class were the subject of discussion in the planning session.

ANALYSIS

The planning session itself lasted approximately 90 minutes. We spent ap-proximately 20 minutes reviewing a videotape of the children's response to the Hansel and Gretel story, and then Mary asked, "So, what do you think? What are we going to do next?" We spent the next 70 minutes exploring possible answers to this question.

For clarity, I have organized the analysis around three aspects of Mary's thinking during the planning session, her consideration of: (1) the mathemat-ical ideas and practices she wanted her students to learn; (2) the mathematical ideas that particular children expressed during the previous class and how they might take up various aspects of the activity she was planning; and (3) her own past and current understandings of distance, time, and speed and how these might inform her teaching and her students' learning. These foci are widely recognized as central to teachers' thinking (Ball, 1993, 1997; Gallas, 1995, 2001; Rosebery & Warren, 1998).

Disciplinary Goals for Students' Learning

Prior to beginning the motion unit, Mary was clear about her overall goal for her students' learning. She wanted them to learn to communicate with one another about motion using a variety of representations, including stories and various mathematical representations like tables and graphs. While Mary was not sure how far she and the children would get in learning about any given representation, she knew that she wanted them to understand that there were several different ways to describe and represent linear motion. One of her subgoals was for her students to learn how to "interpret when [a trip] is fast and when it is slow." A central question for Mary in this planning session was how best to engage her students in learning this—what particular content focus, activities, and materials would best support their learning? As we will see, Mary grappled with this on an ongoing basis throughout the planning meeting.

At the beginning of the meeting, Mary introduced the idea of having the children reenact the Hansel and Gretel story outside during the next class. She was thinking of drawing a "ribbon" on the playground with chalk based on the activity from the Investigations curriculum and asking the children to take trips along it at different speeds, dropping beanbags every 5 seconds, and using a stopwatch to measure time. As we considered the possibilities afforded by this activity, she expressed a concern that it would not allow the children to reflect on or analyze the beanbag patterns associated with different trips:

> *Mary:* See my worry is about the beanbags—is that they [the children] need to be on top to see down. Do you know what I mean? If they—if we did the story and they were in a helicopter then they could see the pattern. But if we go outside and we do the stopwatch stuff and it's down there it's going to be difficult to get—(...) it would be hard for them to see the whole thing.

Mary wanted to be sure the activity would give her students the visual perspective they needed to recognize and probe the beanbag patterns of the trips. This concern led her to revise the developing lesson. Instead of going outdoors and asking the children to run down a chalk ribbon, Mary proposed to:

> *Mary:* do something in the classroom, like we could have them sit on either side of the [ribbon] and do a reenactment and just have me or somebody be the witch and somebody be Hansel and Gretel. (...) What I was thinking was—OK we've got the ribbon on the floor, and they—they have the—somebody has a Hansel puppet and somebody has a Gretel puppet and they're running and somebody else is dropping something. Somebody

else is the witch. That person is walking and they drop when I say "Drop." OK, and we would look at it. Then we would go to the board and I would hang [the ribbon] up and we would look at it. And label one "the witch" and one "Hansel and Gretel." (. . .) And I think I need to relate [their activity] to communication, to the different ways we've had of communicating [about motion trips] and when we read the ribbons from Hansel and Gretel's trip I am going to say, "We're going to read these ribbons now. This is a way we've had—we're communicating in a different way so we're going to look at these marks and read them and see what they tell us."

In this excerpt, Mary imagined in her mind's eye (to paraphrase Casey, 1976) how her initial idea for the next lesson might bring her students into contact with the mathematical ideas and practices she wanted them to learn. As she realized that "go[ing] outside and do[ing] the stopwatch stuff" wouldn't allow them to create shared, public knowledge of what the rocks represented, she began to visualize activities and materials that would afford such an opportunity. In short, Mary created a lived-in space (Nemirovsky et al., 1998), an imagined classroom, which she inhabited with possible events, materials, and actions. She scaled down the children's activity and moved it indoors. She envisioned specific activities and materials ("we could have them sit on either side of the [ribbon]"). She projected a possible sequence of events as her students reenacted the Hansel and Gretel story on a smaller scale ("somebody has a Gretel puppet and they're running and somebody else is dropping something. And somebody else is the witch. That person is walking and they drop when I say 'Drop.'"). And perhaps most importantly, she imagined the children viewing, handling, hanging up, juxtaposing, and inspecting ribbons of Hansel and Gretel's and the witch's trips. By working within the walls of the lived-in space of her imagined classroom, Mary began to get a handle on what exactly she wanted the children to learn and how they might learn it.

Children's Mathematical Ideas

The ideas of particular children significantly shaped Mary's planning process. At the beginning of the meeting, she expressed concern that "there were lots of kids who were still quiet, like Scott and casts of thousands" during the previous week's Hansel and Gretel discussion. This concerned her because she routinely used her interpretations of children's thinking to assess "where they are and where they need to go next." Following each Sherlock class, Mary studied her children's ideas and sense-making practices by watching a videotape of the lesson. At Mary's suggestion, the planning group viewed parts of the tape during the planning meeting to examine what the children had said and done.

Mary then used her interpretations of her children's talk and activity in two ways: (1) to assess their understanding of particular ideas and practices, how students had taken these up, and how she might continue to best support their learning of distance, time, and speed relationships; and (2) to imagine how particular children might enter into and take up particular aspects of the lesson being designed. As she thought about what they were understanding, she considered many children, both those she was worried about and those she was not. She engaged in this kind of thinking throughout the meeting.

In the following example, Mary examined what she thought one student, Karen, might have understood about the Hansel and Gretel story during the previous lesson. She was interested in how Karen had interpreted the rock patterns of Hansel and Gretel and the witch. Karen participated in the class's discussion twice; she volunteered a response at the beginning and Mary solicited her thinking a second time toward the end of the discussion.

In her initial response, Karen said that Hansel and Gretel's rocks would be closer together than the witch's rocks, which was not correct. (Because Hansel and Gretel were moving faster than the witch, their rocks would be farther apart—not closer together—than the witch's because they would cover more distance in the same amount of time.) In her second response, Karen showed—demonstrating with her hands—that she had reconsidered her earlier response and now thought that the witch's rocks would be closer together than Hansel and Gretel's. Thus, Mary thought that delving deeper into Karen's talk might give her some insight into what she and other children might be understanding about the rock patterns:

Mary: I guess my question is, OK, the relationship between, I mentioned
        40 miles an hour, 10 minutes. Twenty miles an hour, 50 minutes.
        Let's just keep the numbers—as the speed number gets smaller,
        the time number gets bigger, right? That's the relationship.

Steve: For a given distance.

Mary: So if that's the relationship, 10 miles an hour would take 80
        minutes, OK? I'm just trying to show it. Do they [the students]
        need to understand that relationship?

Steve: Not necessarily.

Mary: OK. So that was what was happening for all of us. It was happening for Karen. At the end, she said, "Well, the rocks would be closer" but she started to—her word was—what was it?

Cindy: Time goes faster when you are running.

Ann: When you are running 10 minutes goes faster.

Mary: Yeah, your 10 minutes go faster. There are two ways of looking at that. She could be thinking that it feels like it's gone faster or she wanted to say you've gone more distance. I don't know. [At the end of the discussion] when she figured out the rocks of the witch did this [holds her fists up in front of her chest, approximately 4 inches apart, mimicking Karen's gesture on the videotape to show the distance the witch would have gone in the 10 minutes between rock drops] I think she understood that the witch's rocks would be closer together [than Hansel and Gretel's]. So wait a minute. What is the confusion? What am I confusing?

In this example, Mary began by articulating the distance, time, and speed relationship she wanted the children to work with. As she did this, she became aware that she herself was having some difficulty keeping the relationships straight. Steve clarified that in the first case distance was being held constant while speed and time were varying. As she thought about this, Mary realized that the same kind of confusion might have been "happening for all of us" during the lesson. This led her to focus on what Karen had said and done. Followed by Cindy and Ann, Mary reviewed Karen's second utterance and tried to think about what she might have meant. Mary saw Karen's words "your 10 minutes goes faster" as data that could potentially help her understand the meanings she and the children had been working with during class. Mary offered two possible interpretations: that Karen was suggesting that (1) it *feels* like time has gone faster, or (2) you've gone more distance. By considering what Karen might have meant—instead of simply ignoring her remark as confused—Mary broadened her own understanding of the ways the children might have been thinking about the relationship of the distance between rocks and relative speed (see Wright, 2001). And she started to get a feel for what might be confusing about this relationship for the children and for herself.

After studying Karen's talk, Mary again revised the emerging lesson plan, this time to include an additional activity in which the children would work in pairs to mark strips of adding machine paper to create separate representations of the trips that Hansel and Gretel and the witch might take:

> Mary: So we need to go and do the ribbon together and we'll sit on either side and do it. So we should start with the ribbon. And then we'll have the witch on one side and the kids on the other—Hansel and Gretel. And then we'll have them [the children] look at the two ribbons—two pieces of adding machine tape. You brought me some, didn't you? And then we'll give them each two strips of paper where they write their own—OK—now wait a minute—spee::d trips [for Hansel and Gretel and the witch]. [She writes the word "speed" in her notebook and underlines it twice as she says the word aloud.]

To evaluate this potential move and to consider what it would entail, Mary continued to work within the lived-in space of her imagined classroom. She visualized the children's actions from their perspective, seeing them "look at the two ribbons" and even noting that the ribbons would be replaced by "pieces of adding machine tape." As she enacted the lesson in her mind, she saw that this modification had the potential to engage the children in probing Hansel and Gretel's and the witch's trips separately; moreover, it would allow the children to "write their own (. . .) spee::d trips."

During this excerpt Mary not only worked out her own momentary confusion about the relationships among distance, time, and speed, but also began to see connections between her students' ideas and the mathematics that she could draw on to achieve her instructional goals. Let us consider her final utterance, "And then we'll give them each two strips of paper where they write their own—OK—now wait a minute—spee::d trips." Her emphasis on "spee::d" in this statement, in combination with the act of writing and underlining the words "speed trip" in her notebook, suggests that Mary has resolved the confusion she expressed earlier about the relationships among distance, time, and speed. Her words suggest that she deliberately slowed herself down ("OK—now wait a minute") in order to be clear about how she was thinking about distance, time, and speed and how she wanted her students to think about them. Her elongation of the "e" in speed ("spee::d") and the underlines she drew in her notebook indicate that, in this moment, she thought she was coming to an important understanding. Finally, the verbal and written emphasis she gives this utterance suggests that as she reviewed Karen's words and as she imagined various possibilities for the next lesson she began to see how a focus on "spee:d trips" (i.e., keeping time constant and letting distance vary as a function of speed) might help her students delve more deeply into the Mathematics of Motion.

The Teacher's Understanding

As we saw in the previous episode, Mary scrutinized her own understanding of distance, time, and speed during her planning process. In this section, we examine the role of her knowledge in planning in greater detail.

Just prior to the following excerpt, Cindy, one of the researchers, told Mary that when she interviewed several of Mary's students who were speakers of English as a second language she noticed that they talked a lot about "feeling" speed and motion with their bodies. She wondered if there might be a way to incorporate this into the developing lesson plan. Mary responded:

> Mary: As you were talking I was thinking that maybe this Hansel and Gretel trip needs to be with fingers on the ribbon because there is no way we can have two people running and the witch going slowly because they'll be at the end of the trip [before the witch starts] so it might need to be—and this always brings me back to my—my confusion a million—well 20 years ago when the ball was going down the ramp and I thought that it would—the spots would be left closer together as it went down the ramp. See there was a mark on the ball. OK? OK? Everything—it rotates—it's going to leave a mark on the ramp, OK? And because the ball speeds up as it goes down [the ramp] initially I assumed that the marks would be closer together. So I'm always careful when I'm thinking of this—of their footsteps, OK? You really can't tell from Hansel and Gretel's footsteps that they are running and the witch is walking after them, you know? So there is something else. It has to be outside of you. The mark can't come from your body. It needs to come from outside of you, the measure that indicates what the speed was. (...) So maybe we need two ribbons, one for the witch and one for Hansel and Gretel and maybe we need someone else with a marker to mark the ribbon [where the rocks will fall].

To respond to Cindy's question, Mary invoked memories of her own experiences exploring motion 20 years ago in the Moon Group with Eleanor Duckworth. Apparently, her memory was prompted by Cindy's description of the children "feeling" speed with their bodies. Mary explained that at one point during her own investigation, she hypothesized that as a ball accelerated down a ramp, it would leave a trail of marks that would get increasingly closer together as the speed of the ball increased. Upon experimenting, however, she found that as the ball rotated down the ramp, the distance it traveled with each rotation was constant. Instead, what changed was the number of rotations that occurred within a given period of *time*. Mary called on aspects of this 20-year-old memory to re-view the Hansel and Gretel problem. She speculated that, like the motion of the rolling ball, the length of Hansel's and Gretel's and the witch's strides would be more or less constant and therefore her students would not be able to detect rates of speed from their "footsteps" ("You can't really tell from Hansel and Gretel's footsteps that they are running and the witch is walking after them, you know?"). This insight prompted Mary to respond negatively, albeit implicitly, to her understanding of Cindy's question about incorporating the students' bodily feeling of movement. "The mark can't come from your body. It needs to come from outside of you, the measure that indicates what the speed was." This episode in turn motivated her to revise the lesson plan one last time to include an outside measure of time: "we need someone else with a marker to mark the ribbon" where the rocks would fall (i.e., the relative locations of Hansel and Gretel and the witch at 5-second intervals, harking back to Mary's idea that she would tell the students to "drop" a rock every 5 seconds of a given trip).

This example illustrates how, in considering Cindy's suggestion, Mary once again entered the lived-in space of her imagined classroom. She called on and probed relationships between her past and present understandings of distance, time, and speed purposefully, using her own experiences to inform her teaching and possibilities for her students' learning. In doing so, her understandings of both the content and the instructional situation took on new meaning. For example, her understanding of speed and its relationship to distance and time, formed by her earlier work with a ball and ramp, was expanded by considering it in the context of her students' walking trips and their bodily experience. By literally "thinking through" her earlier experience, Mary came to understand that if distance is held constant another frame of reference, that is, time, is needed to detect the relative speeds of two bodies or acceleration by a single body. As a direct consequence of her expanded understanding, Mary's view of what her students needed to do and think about came sharply into focus. She realized that records of footsteps would not help her students learn how to "interpret when [a trip] is fast and when it is slow," her express goal at the beginning of the planning session. Instead, to help them get a handle on this, they would need to create trip records that incorporated both time and distance. Only in this way could they begin to see how the relationship between these two variables determines speed.

Summary

Mary came to the planning session with the goal of helping her students learn how to "interpret when [a trip] is fast and when it is slow." During the session, she explored what this might mean through the lived-in space of her planning activity, in which she brought together her own and her students' experiences and understandings to project and try out possible combinations of activities in her classroom. At the beginning of the session, she thought that she would take the children outside and have them walk down a chalk line, dropping beanbags as they went. As she and the researchers considered this activity, however, she grew concerned that it would not allow the children to step back from and reflect on the patterns of speed represented by the beanbags. This led her to revise her plan: The children would line up along a single ribbon and reenact the Hansel and Gretel and witch trips. As she considered how students like Karen had talked about the rock representation in the previous class, Mary started to probe her own understanding of the relationship among distance, time, and speed, and as a consequence she made additional revisions to the emerging lesson. She added an activity in which the children would work in pairs to recreate Hansel and Gretel's and the witch's trips on separate pieces of adding machine tape. She felt that this would enable them to compare and contrast "spee:d trips" and would give each child firsthand experience with the variables of distance and time, that is, by "walking" the trips and dropping the rocks, respectively. Finally, in response to Cindy's question about having the children "feel" speed, Mary drew on memories of her own experiences with a ball and a ramp to re-view her understanding of distance, time, and speed and to rethink her emerging lesson plan once again. She ultimately revised the plan so that someone other than the child taking the trip would mark the rock drops (i.e., the distance covered in 5-second intervals) on the ribbon. She imagined the children creating a representation that would enable them to see and explore how speed varies according to the relationship between distance and time. Thus, by the end of the session, Mary had achieved her goal of designing a lesson that would engage her children in "interpreting when a trip is fast and when it is slow."

Toward the end of the planning session, Ann asked Mary to summarize the plan for the next class. Not surprisingly, to explain her plan, Mary once again invoked the lived-in space of her imagined classroom, this time going so far as to populate it with broad projections of what she and the children might say and do:

> Mary: We're going to meet on the rug. I'm going to say, "There are two ribbons out this morning and we'll use the tape—paper stuff instead of the nice ribbons. And we're going to line up on either side of these ribbons and we're going to have different people be Hansel and Gretel and different people—someone else be the witch and someone else be the dropper and someone be the timekeeper." Because if they're busy doing their fingers, if this is Hansel and Gretel doing this [walking her fingers on the table], how are they going to drop it at the same time? So I was going to have them do finger trips as opposed to real walking trips. (. . .) The paper is going to be on the floor like we've had the ribbons before from one end of the room to the other. The kids are going to be on either side and then they're going to be the actors who are going to be doing this (walking her fingers across table). And someone is going to say "drop." [. . .] So then someone drops the beanbag or marks the paper. I haven't decided which it should be. At the same time on the other side is going to be the witch and she's going to be going "ahh, ahh, ahh" (walking her fingers slowly across table). And then we're going to pick up the ribbons and look at them and say, "OK, what do you see here?" And we'll say, "Oh, the beanbags or stickers are far apart and that means Hansel and Gretel's tape because they ran fast. And these marks are close together and that's the witch's tape because she's slow." "So now I'm going to give you a ribbon and I'm going to give you six stickers and you're going to put these stickers on the tape and you're going to let—OK, so now, OK—and then we're going to look at your tapes and decide whether"—what? It's Hansel and Gretel's or the witch's? Right? And then I'll say, "Make your own trip tapes and let's see" and then we'll look at them. And maybe we can reenact them.

This then was the "final" plan that emerged from the May 1, 1998 session.

Throughout the analysis I have tried to give the reader a feel for the *ongoing* way in which Mary wove together the thematic threads of her planning—her goals for her students' learning, her attention to the children's mathematical understandings, and her examination of her own understanding. Thus, although I presented the themes episodically for the purposes of analysis and discussion, the boundaries between these themes are artificial. In reality, Mary experienced them—and the session itself—as a seamless whole.

The Lesson

Mary taught the lesson the following week, on May 7, 1998. Some of it went as planned, but Mary also found herself improvising in response to what her students said and did as they took up the lesson. As planned, children were asked one by one to fingerwalk the trips of either Hansel and Gretel or the witch on a ribbon that had been taped to the classroom floor. A second child accompanied the fingerwalker, dropping beanbags to mark constant time intervals of 5 seconds (i.e., the "outside" measure). All the children participated eagerly, volunteering their interpretations of the placement of the beanbags and the relative speeds of the trips. Mary was pleased and a little surprised by the students' quick responses to this first activity.

Given their evident understanding, Mary changed the lesson in midstream, something she had not anticipated during the planning session. On the spot, she generated a variation of the fingerwalking activity that engaged the children in thinking about the beanbag representation from a different point of view. She placed beanbags for a single trip at various places on the ribbon and asked the children to "tell a story that goes with it." Again, the children responded with enthusiasm, telling increasingly outlandish and mostly accurate motion stories. When each child who wanted a turn had had one, Mary adapted her plan on-line a final time. She put beanbags on the ribbon to show two simultaneous trips, one slower than the other, each reflecting internal changes in speed (i.e., acceleration). She told the children to spend the rest of the session in pairs writing a story about these trips.

It is interesting to see how the lesson plan actually functioned during the session. As planned, Mary started with the fingerwalking activity. At first, it went pretty much as planned. However, as the children engaged with it, they demonstrated a level of understanding that Mary had not anticipated. In response, she improvised and instead of moving forward with the plan, she used it as a resource for generating a novel lesson. For example, she spontaneously created a new activity, asking the children to interpret a beanbag representation that she made up. This activity, essentially the inverse of the one discussed during the planning session, forced the children to take a new perspective on the Hansel and Gretel task and the beanbag representation.

Although novel, Mary's move had clear conceptual roots in her planning and was grounded in her ongoing interpretation of the children's developing understanding. In short, Mary's lesson plan functioned in different ways as the session unfolded. Initially it functioned as a detailed and specific design for what actually unfolded. As the children responded to the activity in ways not anticipated during the planning process, however, the plan also functioned as a powerful resource that enabled Mary to respond generatively to the children's understanding while at the same time maintaining her instructional focus.

CONCLUSION

This case study builds on and extends the work of others (Ball, 1993, 1997; Ball & Bass, 2000; Shulman, 1986, 1987; Wilson, 1992; Wilson & Berne, 1999; Wilson et al., 1987) by examining the activity of an experienced elementary classroom teacher, Mary DiSchino, as she planned "what to do next" in an open-ended investigation of the Mathematics of Motion and then how that plan actually functioned in her teaching. Following Nemirovsky et al. (1998), I characterized Mary's planning as a process of creating a lived-in space. According to Nemirovsky et al., a lived-in space is a place into which and from which to project, enact, and evaluate intentions and to explore possibilities. It is a fully contextualized experience that allows abstractions to emerge as the recognition of patterns embedded in the particulars of a lived situation. Mary planned her lesson by envisioning her classroom in future time, populating it with specific ideas, questions, activities, personalities, materials, experiences, and memories. In this space, she assessed the potential pedagogical value of her evolving ideas and plans.

To describe some of the unique features of this lived-in space, I also drew on Casey's (1976) modes of imagining. Like Casey's modes, Mary's planning had vivid sensory qualities, a sense of immediacy, and a feeling of intimacy. These qualities played a critical role in her planning, allowing her to "see" the world she was creating in detail. In her mind's eye, Mary's classroom was replete with objects that had color and texture (a chalk line on a playground, adding machine tape, beanbags), events both projected and remembered (students enacting "finger trips" along a ribbon, her memory of her own work with a ball and a ramp), and embodied enactments (dropping beanbags, walking motion trips, comparing ribbons) that allowed her to project how an activity might unfold, what it would look like in one configuration or another from the children's point of view, and how she and the children might experience it.

As we saw, Mary's planning process continued to be generative as she taught the lesson the following week. Not only did it provide her with a clear starting point, but it also enabled her to be responsive to her evolving assessment of what her students were understanding and what they seemed ready to learn as the lesson unfolded.

This view of lesson planning stands in some tension with the view common in programs of teacher preparation, in schools, and among curriculum developers and educational researchers: that of a plan determined a priori by preconditions and goals. Like Suchman's (1987) analysis of models of human planning, this study shows that one important function of lesson planning is as a powerful, on-line resource for informing the contingent, multidimensional, situated activities that comprise teaching. During the planning session, Mary thought through what had happened in the previous lesson and carefully considered what she wanted her students to learn. As a result, when she found herself in unexpected circumstances, she could adapt her teaching to her students' developing understanding in ways that supported her goals for their learning. In short, Mary's planning prepared her to be, in Ball's (1997) words, both "responsive to students and responsible to the discipline."

As I think about how lesson planning functioned for Mary, what stands out for me is how deeply rooted it was in her theory of learning and teaching. As discussed earlier, Mary believes that learners come to "own" an idea when they are allowed to question and probe connections among their own understandings and the ideas and practices they are learning. From Mary's perspective, what the students bring to the learning situation is as important to learning as are the ideas she wants them to learn. Thus, for Mary, planning is a process in which to consider what students may potentially understand, how they might take up and interact with the ideas, materials and activities she is considering, and how this relates to her instructional goals. It is a time to think through and prepare herself for the moment-by-moment negotiations of meaning that she believes make up learning and teaching.

Equally as important to planning is Mary's own understanding of the content she is teaching. As discussed at the beginning of this chapter, Mary conceptualizes her own learning in terms similar to those she uses to think about her students' learning. She expects to examine what she knows from a variety of perspectives, including past and present experience, "official" meanings (e.g., from teachers' manuals, textbooks, and in this case, what Steve, a mathematician with special interest in the Mathematics of Motion, had to say), and her students' understandings. As we saw here, Mary is not satisfied with her own understanding until she has integrated these potentially disparate points of view into a coherent whole. Nor is she ready to make decisions about teaching until she has achieved this. Thus for Mary lesson planning is as much a process of learning as it is of teaching.

What emerges from this case study is a view of lesson planning as a process of learning as much as it a process of preparing for the contingent activity of teaching. How often are pre- and inservice teachers encouraged to think about planning in this way? To reflect on the relationship between lesson planning and their theories of learning and teaching? To view lesson planning as a time to prepare themselves, as best they can, to be on the one hand responsive to the diverse experiences and knowledge their students will bring to the lesson and on the other responsible for representing the ideas and practices of the discipline with clarity and depth? To explore how their disciplinary understanding fits with what the teacher's manual says or with what their students may be thinking? Or to envision in specific, detailed, and grounded ways how their students are likely to take up the materials and activities at hand and how this might support their developing understanding?

In my experience, teachers are most often encouraged to think of lesson planning as a process of familiarizing themselves with the content, objectives, materials, and activities for a lesson, usually a lesson that someone else has authored. This has been the prevailing view of planning for years. It was dominant when I taught 20 years ago, and it is ubiquitous in today's educational climate, with its emphasis on standards-based learning. Beneath this stance, I would suggest, lies a view of lesson planning as an a priori process, one that leads to predictable outcomes. Thus the message that teachers receive, both implicitly and explicitly, is that they should be able to define their lessons in advance based on their instructional goals, independent of the contingencies of the lived situations of their classrooms.

As this case study suggests, it is simply not possible for teachers to anticipate how the particulars of any given lesson will play out. To suggest otherwise is to do them, and perhaps more importantly, their students, a disservice. The professional practice of at least one experienced teacher suggests an alternative: that teachers learn to experience planning as the creation of a lived-in space, a space in which to envision how individual students might take up specific activities, problems, or materials and in which to consider how these imagined events might relate to their instructional goals. In this way, they can develop richly detailed scenarios to work from as they teach, resources they can call on as they engage with their students in the necessary negotiation of meaning that constitutes learning and teaching.

ACKNOWLEDGMENTS

The research reported in this chapter is the result of a collaboration with Mary DiSchino and her students; I am grateful for the opportunity to have worked with and learned from them. This chapter was shaped by the thoughts of the following individuals: Cindy Ballenger, Mary DiSchino, Paula Hooper, Josiane Hudicourt-Barnes, Steve Monk, Tracy Noble, Mark Ogonowski, Gillian Puttick, Ricardo Nemirovsky, Jesse Solomon, Beth Warren, and Tracey Wright.

The research reported herein was supported by the U.S. Department of Education, Office of Educational Research and Improvement, Cooperative Agreement No. R305A60007-98 to the National Center for Improving Student Learning and Achievement in Mathematics and Science, University of Wisconsin, Madison, the National Science Foundation, ESI 9555712, and the Spencer Foundation. The data presented, the statements made, and the views expressed are solely the responsibility of the author. No endorsement by the funding agencies should be inferred.

REFERENCES

AAAS/Project 2061. (1993). *Benchmarks for science literacy.* New York: Oxford University Press.

Arnheim, R. (1971). *Visual thinking.* Berkeley: University of California Press.

Bakhtin, M. (1981). *The dialogic imagination: Four essays.* Austin: University of Texas Press.

Ball, D. L. (1993). With an eye on the mathematical horizon: Dilemmas of teaching elementary school mathematics. *Elementary School Journal, 93,* 373–397.

Ball, D. L. (1997). What do students know? Facing challenges of distance, context, and desire in trying to hear children. In T. Biddle, T. Good, & I. Goodson (Eds.), *International handbook on teachers and teaching* (pp. 769–817). Dordrecht, Netherlands: Kluwer Press.

Ball, D. L., & Bass, H. (2000). Interweaving content and pedagogy in teaching and learning to teach: Knowing and using mathematics. In J. Boaler (Ed.), *Multiple perspectives on the teaching and learning of mathematics* (pp. 83–104). West Port, CT: Ablex.

Ballenger, C. (1999). *Teaching other people's children: Literacy and learning in a bilingual classroom.* New York: Teachers College Press.

Berreman, G. (1966). Anemic and emetic analyses in social anthropology. *American Anthropologist, 68*(2) 1, 346–354.

Casey, E. (1976). *Imagining: A phenomenological study.* Bloomington and London: Indiana University Press.

Chazan, D., & Ball, D. (1999). Beyond being told not to tell. *For the Learning of Mathematics, 19*(2), 2–10.

Clark, C., & Peterson, P. (1986). Teachers' thought processes. In M. C. Whitrock (Ed.), *Handbook of research on teaching* (3rd ed., pp. 255–296). New York: Macmillan.

Clark, C., & Yinger, R. (1979). Teachers' thinking. In P. L. Peterson & H. J. Walberg (Eds.), *Research on teaching* (pp. 279–394). Berkeley, CA: McCutchan.

DiSchino, M. (1987). The many phases of growth: One teacher's experience of learning. *Journal of Teaching and Learning, 1*(3), 12–28.

DiSchino, M. (1998). "Why do bees sting and why do they die afterward?" In A. Rosebery & B. Warren (Eds.), *Boats, balloons, and classroom video: Science teaching as inquiry* (pp. 109–133). Portsmouth, NH: Heinemann.

Duckworth, E. (1987). *The having of wonderful ideas.* New York: Teachers College Press.

Erickson, F., & Shultz, J. (1977). When is a context? Some issues and methods in the analysis of social competence. In J. Green & C. Wallat (Eds.), *Ethnography and language in educational settings* (pp. 147–160). Norwood, NJ: Ablex.

Gallas, K. (1995). *Talking their way into science. Hearing children's questions and theories, responding with curricula.* New York: Teachers College Press.

Gallas, K. (2001). Look Karen, I'm running like Jello": Imagination as a question, a topic, a tool for literacy research and learning. *Research in the Teaching of English, 35*(4), 457–492.

Greeno, J. (1997). On claims that answer the wrong questions. *Educational Researcher, 26*(1), 5–17.

Grossman, P. L., Wilson, S. M., & Shulman, L. S. (1989). Teachers of substance: The subject matter knowledge of teachers. In M. Reynolds (Ed.), *The knowledge base for the beginning teacher* (pp. 23–36). New York: Pergamon.

Hymes, D. (1996). *Ethnography, linguistics, narrative inequality: Toward an understanding of voice.* Bristol, PA: Taylor & Francis.

Labov, W. (1972). *Language in the inner city: Studies in the Black English Vernacular.* Philadelphia: University of Pennsylvania Press.

Lampert, M. (1990). When the problem is not the question and the solution is not the answer: Mathematical knowing and teaching. *American Educational Research Journal, 27*, 29–63.

Lave, J., & Wenger, E. (1991). *Situated learning: Legitimate peripheral participation.* New York: Cambridge University Press.

Leinhardt, G., & Greeno, J. G. (1986). The cognitive skill of teaching. *Journal of Educational Psychology, 78*, 75–95.

Mishler, E. (1990). Validation in inquiry-guided research: The role of exemplars in narrative studies. *Harvard Educational Review, 60*(4), 415–442.

Monk, G. S. (2000). "Why is run a speed?": Negotiating meaning within classroom representational practices. Paper presented at the Annual Meeting of the American Educational Research Association, New Orleans, LA.

National Council of Teachers of Mathematics. (1989). *Curriculum and evaluation standards for school mathematics.* Reston, VA: NCTM.

National Research Council. (1996). *National science education standards.* Washington, DC: National Academy Press.

Neale, D. C., Pace, A. J., & Case, A. B. (1983, April). *The influence of training, experience and organizational environment on teachers' use of the systematic planning model.* Paper presented at the annual meeting of the American Education Research Association, Montreal.

Nemirovsky, R., Tierney, C., & Wright, T. (1998). Body motion and graphing. *Cognition and Instruction, 16*(2), 119–172.

Paley, V. (1986). On listening to what the children say. *Harvard Educational Review, 56*(2), 122–131.

Rosebery, A. S., & Puttick, G. M. (1998). Teacher professional development as situated sense-making: A case study in science education. *Science Education, 82*, 649–677.

Rosebery, A., Warren, B., Ballenger, C., & Ognonowski, M. (in press). The generative potential of students' everyday knowledge in learning science. In T. Carpenter & T. Romberg (Eds.), *Improving student learning in mathematics and science.*

Rosebery, A. S., & Warren, B. (Eds.). (1998). *Boats, balloons and classroom video: Science teaching as inquiry.* Portsmouth, NH: Heinemann.

Shulman, L. (1986). Those who understand: Knowledge growth in teaching. *Educational Researcher, 15*(2), 4–14.

Shulman, L. (1987). Knowledge and teaching: Foundations of the new reform. *Harvard Educational Review, 57*(1), 1–22.

Suchman, L. (1987). *Plans and situated actions.* New York: Cambridge University Press.

Tierney, C., Nemirovsky, R., Noble, T., & Clements, D. (1998). *Patterns of change: tables and graphs: A unit of investigations in number, data, and space.* White Plains, NY: Dale Seymour Publications.

Vygotsky, L. (1978). *Mind in society: The development of higher psychological processes.* Cambridge, MA: Harvard University Press.

Wilson, S. M. (1992). A case concerning content: Using case studies to teach about subject matter. In J. Shulman (Ed.), *Case methods in teacher education* (pp. 64–89). New York: Teachers College Press.

Wilson, S., & Berne, J. (1999). Teacher learning and the acquisition of professional knowledge: An examination of research on contemporary professional development. In A. Iran-Nejad & D. P. Pearson (Eds.), *Review of research in education* (pp. 173–210). Washington, DC: AERA.

Wilson, S., Shulman, L., & Richert, A. (1987). 150 different ways of knowing: Representations of knowledge in teaching. In J. Calderhead (Ed.), *Exploring teachers' thinking* (pp. 104–124). Eastbourne, UK: Cassell.

Wright, T. (2001). Karen in motion: The role of physical enactment in developing an understanding of distance, time and speed. *Journal of Mathematical Behavior, 20*, 145–162.

Yinger, R. J. (1977). A study of teacher planning: Description and the development using ethnographic and information processing methods. Unpublished Ph.D. dissertation. Michigan State University, East Lansing.

11

Exploration Zones: A Framework for Describing the Emergent Structure of Learning Activities

Bruce L. Sherin
Northwestern University

Flávio S. Azevedo
Andrea A. diSessa
University of California

The theme of this book—learning environments as spaces of contact between students' and disciplinary perspectives—implies a general orientation toward instruction in which the perspectives of students are taken seriously. This orientation has some important entailments. If students' perspectives are to be well-represented in the classroom, students must take an active role in shaping and guiding ongoing classroom activity. Teachers must relinquish to students some control over the classroom explorations, actively incorporating students' questions and products into the classroom inquiry. We call this kind of classroom practice *student-directed*.

The design of student-directed activities poses specific challenges. On the one hand, our job as instructional designers is to specify classroom activities. On the other hand, if our activities are to be truly student-directed, our designs must not fully define the course of classroom events. We want to leave enough space for students' ideas, interests, and perspectives to drive the activity.

The difficulty of this challenge is mitigated by an important observation. Even when we allow an activity to be directed largely by the students involved, we often have a reasonably good idea of how events will proceed. We may not know exactly what will happen, but we frequently have a good idea of the space of possibilities or the territory that students are likely to explore in a given activity. This knowledge may be based on previous trials of similar activities or on a more general understanding of the knowledge, capabilities, and experiences of our students.

The task that we take up in this chapter is to develop a way to capture wisdom of this sort; we want to develop a way to talk about this "space of possibilities" and, based on this understanding, to design more engaging and effective student-directed activities. To reach these ends, we develop a framework and terminology around a notion that we call *exploration zones*. The phrase "exploration zone" is meant to describe the territory that students might explore in a student-directed activity. In using a spatial metaphor such as "territory," we do not mean to imply that an exploration zone exists as a well-defined space of possibilities; instead, we believe this territory is constructed in, or emerges from, the joint action of teacher and students. But this construction process may exhibit regularities across contexts and trials, and it is these regularities that we wish to understand and capture.

To illustrate the idea of exploration zones, consider a teacher-led classroom discussion in which the teacher proposes a question for students' consideration. In a unit on the physics of motion, a teacher might ask students to predict the path that a tethered ball might follow if the rope is cut while the ball is spun around on the end of the rope. The teacher might have anticipated a few answers that students might give initially, such as: (1) the ball continues to move in a circular path; (2) the ball moves in a direction tangent to its trajectory at the time the string is cut; (3) the ball moves inward in relation to its original trajectory; or (4) the ball continues to move along a curved trajectory, but the path gradually straightens.

Furthermore, the teacher might have a reasonably good idea about the directions the discussion might take when one of these initial answers is examined, including conceptual hurdles students might encounter. The teacher might even have planned additional subtasks that are based on some of the possible answers or expected student reactions to such answers. For example, the teacher might propose that students enact some experiments that add empirical evidence pointing to the plausibility or implausibility of one particular answer. Additionally, she might deploy a number of props, collected prior to the task, to help students better visualize and work through the problem.

Because the teacher has a relatively good idea of how the discussion might proceed, she can plan for a manageable set of contingencies.[1]

In sum, a map of the exploration zone for a discussion of this sort might be comprised of anticipated initial answers and several paths of exploration, including those that students naturally follow, those that provide important conceptual leverage, and those that should be avoided. The map might also contain techniques and props that nudge students into or out of certain areas of the exploration, thus providing a means for managing movement through the exploration zone. Other map parameters, such as established norms and values that support collaborative inquiry, are equally important because they make up an important part of the substrate in which the exploration zone exists.

In advancing the notion of exploration zones, our goal is to develop a framework that is general enough to support the analysis and design of a broad range of student-directed activities, from reasonably constrained ones (such as the example above) to radically open-ended tasks. As a way to organize this endeavor, we divide it into four complementary subgoals:

1. *Devising a terminology and methodology for describing the structure of exploration zones.* If we think of an exploration zone as a landscape that students move through, our first goal is to find a means of describing the structure of this landscape. We will do so by crafting a language that captures general classroom phenomena and dynamics. Many of these phenomena are familiar to us in our experimental work, and we believe they are likely familiar to teachers, curriculum designers, and researchers more generally.

2. *Explaining how the structure of an exploration zone depends on various factors, such as student capabilities and contextual constraints.* We want to understand what factors determine the structure of an exploration zone as well as how those factors act to determine this structure. This item defines a long-term research agenda, and our goals for this chapter are modest.

3. *Describing the trajectories that students take through exploration zones and developing techniques for guiding students as they move through an exploration zone.* As a pedagogical concern, we want to be able to

---

[1]"Benchmark lessons," as described by diSessa and Minstrell (1998), rely heavily on this kind of cumulative teacher knowledge.

describe how students may move through an exploration zone, taking various possible trajectories, and understand how to guide students along trajectories without destroying the student-directed nature of the activity.

4. *Describing desirable properties of an exploration zone.* Finally, we want to articulate desirable properties of an exploration zone in terms of the terminology developed in meeting the above goals. In this regard, we are particularly interested in understanding what properties of an exploration zone make for engaging explorations and generate commitment on the part of students.

SITUATING THE EXPLORATION ZONES FRAMEWORK

Before proceeding with our main presentation, we briefly situate this work within the larger body of educational research. The work we present in this chapter fills an unusual niche, one that has been only thinly populated with prior research. Thus, our purpose in this section is not to describe competing approaches. Rather, we seek only to describe this niche and to give a sense of its relation to other educational research.

Broadly speaking, our goal is to contribute to attempts to develop principles and frameworks that guide the design of learning environments (e.g., Brown & Campione, 1996; Collins, 1995). More specifically, our intention is to contribute to theories of *classroom activity*. We want to provide a framework for describing and understanding the unfolding of classroom events, particularly for student-directed activity.

Our analysis of the unfolding of classroom events is targeted at a particular timescale. Our intent is to describe specific patterns in *moderate* timescale activity, on the order of a few minutes to a few hours. On the low end in timescale, our work nearly reaches the grain size of analyses of the structure of classroom dialogue, which look at patterns in the utterances of participants such as turn-taking structure in classroom discourse (e.g., Lemke, 1990; Mehan, 1979). However, unlike our own work, these small timescale analyses have tended to be content-independent, in the sense that they are not focused on the semantic content of utterances.

At the high end in timescale, our work is bounded by analyses of the month- and year-long evolution of such things as classroom norms (e.g., Yackel & Cobb, 1996), and the roles that individuals play within the classroom culture (see, for example, Lave & Wenger, 1991, on legitimate peripheral participation).

Attempts to describe and design *activity structures* address the same timescale as our own work. In defining activity structures, researchers specify formats for the organization of interaction within the classroom. These formats include, for example, small group discussion, whole-class discussion, recipro-cal teaching, and jigsaw classrooms (Brown & Campione, 1994). However, like the discourse analyses described above, activity structures are generally defined in a manner that is content-independent. An activity structure de-scribes the roles played by individuals in a classroom and the rules that govern how those individuals interact, such as who can talk and at what time. In contrast, we are concerned with structure in an epistemic space—the space of ideas that the group can explore. In addition, most treatments of activity structures focus on prescriptions that are more or less enforced, as opposed to fluid, spontaneous organization of activity, which is more our focus.

Attempts to understand classroom progress and learning in terms of the zone of proximal development (ZPD) (Newman, Griffin, & Cole, 1989) are a close match to this work in timescale. Indeed, the notion of a ZPD is grounded on a similar metaphor to our own: Ideas and activities are located within a larger space. Furthermore, like our exploration zone, the structure associated with a ZPD analysis is seen to emerge from the capabilities of participants and the resources that are available to them. However, the original purpose for ZPD-based analyses was measurement of competence—what things a person can do, with and without help. Hence use of the spatial metaphor is limited, essentially, to "in or out." We aim for a more-refined description of structure. By the same token, analyses of sequences of elements of activity forming a larger whole ("exploring a zone") are emphasized in our analysis, but not in ZPD-oriented work.

Finally, one part of our orientation deserves particular mention, our fo-cus on *engagement*. There have been almost no modern cognitive analyses of learning that deal with engagement in a central and principled manner. Furthermore, where issues of engagement are addressed, they are addressed in a very different manner than we propose. As we discuss later, prior analyses have tended to focus on such things as the intrinsic interest of the subject matter or "motivation" viewed as a trait possessed by individuals. In contrast, an exploration zone analysis targets the *structural* features that make an activ-ity engaging. In this regard, some of the closest prior work to ours was done by Csikszentmihalyi (e.g., Csikszentmihalyi, 1988), as we elaborate later in this chapter. Also related are diSessa's (2000) arguments concerning engagement and the structure of activities, especially as they relate to individuals' capacities and interests for participating in certain activities and the long-term development of these capacities. In the present analysis, these would count as background factors that influence the smaller-scale exploration structure that is examined here.

A Plan for the Chapter

In the next section we consider two open-ended, student-directed activities in which students design representations of natural phenomena. For each of these activities we present the work students produce and some of the activity dynamics, including places in which impasses are encountered and aspects of the activity that are more or less engaging to students. Following that we tackle, in order, each of the four subgoals previously listed, using the example activities to illustrate our points. Finally, we review the contributions of the chapter and reflect on the limitations inherent in our use of a spatial metaphor. In addition, we propose further work to advance the general research program.

REPRESENTATIONAL DESIGN ACTIVITIES: TWO EXAMPLES

Since 1991, we have been engaged in the investigation of students' metarepresentational competence (MRC)—the ability to design, critique, and use representations of natural phenomena. These natural phenomena include motion, landscapes (i.e., the varying altitude of some terrain), and wind information (Azevedo, 2000; diSessa & Sherin, 2000; diSessa, 2002; diSessa, Hammer, Sherin, & Kolpakowski, 1991; Sherin, 2000). The theoretical goal of this research is to uncover what students know about representations in general rather than their knowledge of particular scientific representational forms. Consonant with this orientation, our approach has been to involve students in a creative process through which they design novel representations. Pedagogically, we want to devise ways to engage students' "natural" abilities and knowledge about representations while helping them construct more canonical understandings of the representations of science.

Of all representational design activities we have tried with students, two have received particular attention: *Inventing Graphing* (IG) and *Inventing*

Mapping (IM). Inventing Graphing refers to a set of activities in which students design representations of motion. Inventing Mapping consists of activities in which students design representations of landscapes.

We believe that Inventing Graphing and Inventing Mapping are good examples of student-directed activities, and they are ones that we know quite well. We have run several IG sessions in a number of contexts, including "real-world" classroom situations and miniclasses with volunteer students from a public high school. In addition, IG sessions were carried out during two 6-week courses that we taught on the subject of representational design. These courses were part of the Berkeley Academic Talented Development Program (ATDP), a K–12 summer enrichment program intended for students who wish to engage with nontraditional or advanced subject matter. In a nutshell, we have extensively tested the activity with students in Grades 6 to 11, and thus far we have amassed a total of roughly 20 hours of IG video data.

Inventing Mapping is relatively less tested, but the results we obtained from session to session, and across contexts, are quite consistent. Thus far, we have enacted IM with students Grades 7 to 11 in the context of open-ended, 1 hour-long group interviews with students from a local public school as well as during the 6-week ATDP summer courses. Overall, we have collected about 6 hours of IM video data.

Given this history with IG and IM, we feel we have developed a good understanding of how these activities tend to unfold—what designs students are likely to create, what criteria they generally apply in assessing the merits of their designs, and the pitfalls students encounter. In addition, we have collected pedagogical moves that are effective in guiding students in these design activities without wresting undue control from them (Madanes, 1997), and we have described how students and teachers negotiate a common understanding of such design tasks (Granados, 2000).

In what follows, we present a synthesis of our findings about IG and IM activities. For details regarding Inventing Graphing, readers are referred to diSessa et al. (1991) and Sherin (1997, 2000). A full description of Inventing Mapping is found in Azevedo (1998, 2000).

When we present IG and IM examples in the sections that follow, we will refer to these different classroom settings by our pseudonyms for their respective schools. Our regular classroom situations were in Benson Middle School and City High School. Students in our after-school miniclasses were from Trenton High School. Our summer course will be referred to as the ATDP course.

Designing Representations of Motion

Originally, Inventing Graphing was conceived as an activity in a larger curriculum aimed at teaching the physics of motion to Grade 6 students at Benson Middle School (diSessa et al., 1991). In particular, IG was to serve as a 1-day prelude to focused work on Cartesian graphing. Somewhat unexpectedly, however, by the end of that day students had created an impressive array of representational forms. Because students had much to say about their representations and because they appeared so deeply invested in the activity, we decided to extend Inventing Graphing to a full week of activities (a total of 5 days).

During the next 4 days students created many more representational forms. As a group, they argued cogently for the positive qualities of their representations and also discussed limits and how one might overcome them. Throughout the 5 days of activity, students maintained a level of engagement that made the activity nearly self-sustaining. In fact, the students were so enthusiastic that, for long stretches, the only role of the teacher was to guarantee an orderly voicing of opinions. Near the end of the week, students seemed to arrive at a consensus that Cartesian graphing of speed versus time was, indeed, the best among the representations they generated.

The Activity and Its Organization.   The Inventing Graphing activity typically proceeds through repeated cycles. Each cycle begins with the teacher briefly describing a motion or enacting it for students. A common starting point for the activity has been "the desert motion": A motorist is speeding across the desert and she is very thirsty. When she sees a cactus, she stops short to get a drink from it. Then she gets back in her car and drives away slowly.

Following the description of the motion by the teacher, students work alone or in groups for about 5 or 10 minutes using paper, pencil, and colored markers. Students then present their work to the class. During these presentations, the teacher helps the class as a whole to critically compare and evaluate the qualities of their representations. As is appropriate for a design task, the emphasis of these evaluations is not to achieve a correct answer; rather, students are encouraged to discuss the trade-offs involved in the design of each representation in light of the uses the representation is to fulfill.

Thus, in idealized form, the IG activity consists of a series of rounds in which: (1) The teacher describes a motion, (2) the students represent the motion, and (3) the class discusses the various representations produced.

Occasionally, the teachers do deviate from this formula. For example, sometimes groups are asked to practice using the representations of other groups. On other occasions, problems are couched as challenges in which each group represents a particular motion pattern not known to the others. Then, during the presentation and discussion phase, groups read each other's representations in an attempt to figure out the original motion. On occasion, a teacher may also instigate the comparison of representations by involving the class in sorting representations, grouping together those that appear similar. This pedagogical strategy may serve conceptual and pragmatic goals.[2] Conceptually, working on comparing and categorizing representations may focus students attention on issues such as clarity (which representations show motion patterns cleanly), quantitative precision (which representations allow for precise readings of relevant parameters), and consistency (which representations adopt a consistent set of conventions). Pragmatically, comparing and categorizing often functions to narrow the existing pool of representations, thus making the exploration more manageable for students.

Students' Designs.   From the very beginning of the activity, students produce a variety of representational forms. We have argued in prior work that students' designs fall roughly into three broad categories of representations: drawings, temporal sequences, and graph-like depictions (Sherin, 1997, 2000).

Drawings refer to depictions that are based on a set of conventions and techniques for portraying 3 dimensional scenes on paper. As an illustration of a drawing, consider Damon's representation of the desert motion (Fig. 11.1).[3] In the figure, one can see many elements of the desert motion story, including a side view of the road (represented as a single line), some cacti, snapshots of the car, and the driver. To a large extent, Fig. 11.1 can be understood as an assemblage of conventional drawing elements. These conventional elements, such as the stick figure of a human and cars portrayed from a side view, are part of the standard repertoire of elements possessed by students in U.S. schools (e.g., Willats, 1985).

Two points about drawings are worth noting here. First, drawing techniques are very flexible and can be adapted in many ways. Indeed, Damon has somewhat "bent" strict drawing conventions when making his representation.

---

[2] See diSessa et al. (1991) for more details on what we mean by "conceptual" and "pragmatic."
[3] All names are pseudonyms.

FIG. 11.1. Damon's representation of the desert motion. Trenton, Session 1. Scanned from original.

FIG. 11.2. Representation of a person who stops twice during his daily jog. Trenton, Session 2. Scanned from original.

Although the desert motion describes the movement of a single car, Damon used several renditions of a car to represent snapshots of its movement. Damon is not alone in adapting drawing elements; most students readily capitalize on drawing's flexibility to produce a wide range of representations.

The second notable point about drawing is that essentially all individuals in our culture have some experience with it. Although individuals are certainly not equally proficient, most can produce recognizable drawings and virtually all have the ability to understand drawings produced by others.

A second class of representations that prominently appears in IG sessions is what we refer to as *temporal sequences*. A temporal sequence is a linear array of representational elements, each of which refers to a specific part of the motion being represented. As with written text, temporal sequences are read one element at a time in an order defined by the designer (e.g., left to right, top to bottom).

In the temporal sequence in Fig. 11.2, each element tells us something about the speed of a jogger at a given moment in time; the length of the arrows

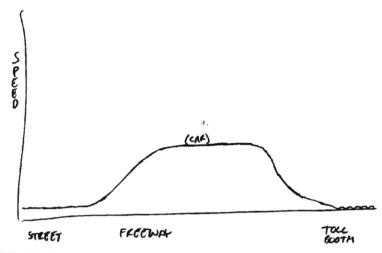

FIG. 11.3. Ryan's graphing representation. Trenton, Session 1. Scanned from original.

represent the speed at which the person is moving, and a circle indicates that the person is stopped. Thus, the representation in Fig. 11.2 shows a person moving fast (a long arrow), stopping for a short period of time (one circle), then gradually increasing his speed (arrows increasing in length), stopping for a longer period of time (two circles), and finally speeding up again.

As might be evident, the nature of the elements in a temporal sequence can vary widely. Students have represented speed by using the size of an icon (such as a triangle) as well as the slant, thickness, height, and color of a line segment. The variability of elements in temporal sequences makes for a very flexible class of representations, which can support quite a range of exploration.

The third and final class of representations students generate in IG is *graph-like* depictions. Graph-like representations include standard Cartesian graphs of a situation as well as adaptations that overlay drawings or other representational elements onto graphs. As an example of a graph-like depiction, consider Ryan's representation, shown in Fig. 11.3. In the figure, we can identify many elements from standard graphs, including labeled axes and a curved line whose height represents an object's speed. Ryan's graph shows speed as a function of position. In some cases, however, the quantities graphed by students are nonstandard and idiosyncratic.

Elsewhere we have argued that the appearance of graph-like depictions in IG sessions is almost always a gradual accomplishment of the students

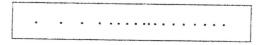

FIG. 11.4. Dots representation of the desert motion.

involved (Sherin, 2000). Furthermore, the appearance of the first graphs does not constitute the end of an IG session; much work typically remains to be done even when graphs are suggested. For instance, most students are not immediately convinced of the advantages of graphing, and many prefer to continue making temporal sequences instead of graphs.

"Getting Stuck" and Moving Beyond It.   Our many trials of IG have convinced us that students are capable of engaging competently in the activity. However, IG activities do not always unfold smoothly. To exemplify this point, we recount an episode that occurred at City High School.

On that occasion, students had largely committed to representing motions through a subclass of drawing representations they called "Dots." Essentially, Dots representations are depictions in which a trail of dots is laid out along the path of the moving object, with dots dropped at equal intervals of time. The separation between successive dots allows one to infer the speed of motion (the farther apart the dots appear, the faster the object is moving), whereas the dots themselves show spatial displacement. Fig. 11.4 shows a rendition of the desert motion using the Dots representation.

Although the Dots representation is extremely schematic, it is still strongly tied to drawing conventions. In particular, Dots implicitly works according to a drawing convention in which displacements on the page correspond to displacements in the real world of the motion. As discussed in Sherin (2000), this strict correspondence makes this class of representations inherently limited. For example, attempting to show backward motion with a Dots representation leads to solutions that are difficult to read because dots may overlap or intersperse.

For a significant part of two class periods, the students at City High School focused only on creating versions of Dots representations. Although the teacher regarded Dots-based representations as acceptable, she had hoped to foster a richer discussion in which students discussed the merits of multiple representational forms. In an attempt to break the logjam, the teacher asked students whether the representation in Fig. 11.4 showed the *duration* of the stop at the cactus. Students were quick to respond that it did not. The teacher then asked students to revise the representation in Fig. 11.4 so that it showed the duration of the stop. The intervention was effective; students struggled with this question briefly and then began creating new representations in which the vertical dimension had various meanings. Some of these representations were temporal sequences.

Designing Representations of Landscapes

Following the success of our investigations of Inventing Graphing, we decided to explore students' meta-representational competence in a number of domains. Given the prominence and importance of mapping practices in Western cultures (Wood & Fels, 1992), Inventing Mapping was a natural direction to explore.

The Activity and Its Organization. In Inventing Mapping sessions, students are shown a number of props that stand for elements of a landscape. These props are made of Styrofoam or similar material and have many different shapes—elliptical mounds, hemispherical domes of various sizes, domes with the top portion cut off, washboards, and ramps.

In a typical IM activity, the teacher/researcher places props inside an empty cardboard box and asks students to represent the assembled landscape. Students then work individually or in groups for 10 minutes or more, depending on the complexity of the landscape. Work is carried out with paper, pencil, and colored markers.

Following the initial round of designs, students present their work to the class and, as in IG, all engage in critically examining the existing pool of representations. After all students have presented their work, a new landscape is presented. In general, IM activities progress from simple to more complex landscapes, which include a larger number of landscape elements and more irregular objects. Every IM activity thus far has included representing a fairly complex landscape, which we sculpted out of hardened sand poured into a $25'' \times 18'' \times 3''$ cardboard container (Fig. 11.5).

Students' Designs. In prior work, we argued that students' designs in Inventing Mapping fall into two broad classes of representations: drawings and quasi-topographic maps (Azevedo, 2000).

Drawings are a prominent class of representations in Inventing Mapping. As in Inventing Graphing, drawings produced in IM are based on a flexible set of techniques that are commonly learned by children in our culture. Although the IM task context may seem to require significant drawing abilities,

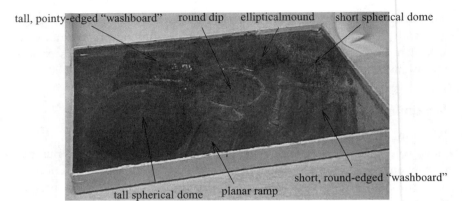

FIG. 11.5. A complex landscape made of hardened sand.

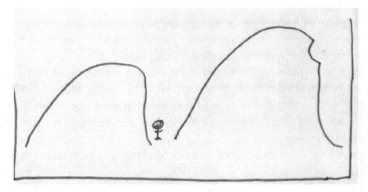

FIG. 11.6. Nina's representation of two domes of different sizes, one of which has a dent. Trenton, Session 1. Scanned from original.

in practice we have observed that most students can produce drawings that others accept as representationally effective.

Roughly speaking, the drawings students produce in IM may be said to occupy a continuum from "simple" to more "sophisticated" drawings. Simple drawings are renditions that portray the main elements of the proposed landscape from a single point of view. Figure 11.6 shows one such representation. In it, Nina has drawn two domes of different sizes, the larger of which has a dent. Between the domes, a human figure, not present in the original landscape, has been used to index the height of the domes. As Nina explained, "if you were walking in this landscape, everything around you would look really big." Nina's strategy again illustrates the flexibility with which students

FIG. 11.7. Lisa's representation of two domes of different sizes: (a) side view, (b) top view, and (c) oblique view. Trenton, Session 2. Scanned from original.

adapt drawing conventions and elements in order to achieve certain representational effects.

More-sophisticated drawings include depictions that coordinate several renditions of the landscape, each drawn from a different point of view. When showing complementary views of the landscape, students usually remark that their intention was to portray all aspects of the given landscape. This rationale drove Lisa's production of Fig. 11.7. In the figure, we see a front, top, and oblique renditions of a two-dome landscape.

Quasi-topographic maps form the second class of representations that students create in IM. Although these representations share many elements with common topographic maps, they also depart from the standard in important ways. For example, in Fig. 11.8, Tamara has used colored lines inside landscape objects to serve a function akin to contour lines. Furthermore, the height represented by each color is shown on a legend, another element appearing in topographic maps.

Contrary to canonical contours, however, Tamara's "contour lines" do not generally connect points of the same height in the landscape. Instead, the drawings seem to be based, in a more impressionistic manner on the wavy contours she has probably seen in topographic maps. Although other students' use of contour lines was more in accordance with standard conventions, virtually all such representations deviated from the standard conventions in important respects.

Colors as Representational Devices. Although students can proficiently participate in Inventing Mapping, the activity does not appear to engage students as much as one might hope (and in the way IG generally did). When comparing the representations produced in a round of design, students frequently offer minimal comments. And, from round to round, students often stick to their original representational techniques without attempting any

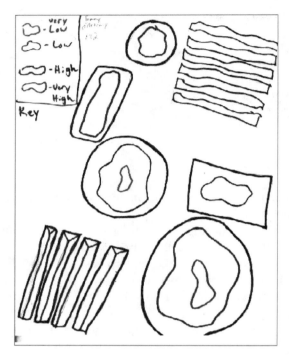

FIG. 11.8. Tamara's representation of the large sand landscape. ATDP '97. Scanned from original.

significant innovations. Compared to the frenzy of activity that IG seems to inspire, IM seems generally a bit dull.

However, there is one subtopic within IM that creates very different dynamics of engagement: the use of colors to represent altitude information. Using colors as representational devices is a strategy that surfaces almost exclusively when students work with quasi-topographic maps. In that context, students consider the coloring of contour lines, contour intervals, or both. Design solutions are often based on coloring schemes such as light-to-dark or dark-to-light sequences of colors, and students suggest many such sequences. Students also cogently consider the benefits and drawbacks of adopting schemes based on varying saturation of a single hue.

Discussions around the uses of colors in quasi-topographic maps are usually quite lively. Within any single IM session, these discussions are the ones in which students articulate the greatest number of design criteria. In this regard, students' concerns relate mainly to the ease of reading and interpreting map information.

THE EXPLORATION ZONES FRAMEWORK

We now tackle the main elements of the exploration zones framework. In our presentation, we proceed, one by one, through the components of our program listed in the introduction: (1) devising a terminology and methodology for describing the structure of exploration zones, (2) explaining how the structure of an exploration zone depends on various factors, (3) describing the trajectories that students take through exploration zones and developing techniques for guiding students, and (4) describing desirable properties of an exploration zone. Throughout this presentation, we draw primarily on examples from IG and IM to illustrate our points.

Characterizing Exploration Zones

We begin by introducing terminology for describing exploration zones, to capture their phenomenological structure. For instance, one familiar phenomenon is that some tasks or discussions provide richer grounds for students' explorations than others. Another familiar phenomenon is that students sometimes limit themselves to small areas of the exploration; they "get stuck," so to speak, and seem unable to consider alternative solutions or arguments. Our terminology should be suited to describing such phenomena. We first identify three basic structural components of exploration zones: *pockets*, *pathways*, and *landmarks*. Then we introduce a typology of pockets.

Pockets.   The first basic structural component of exploration zones is the pocket. A pocket is a collection of specific moves in the exploration that tend to be mutually activating and reinforcing in discourse and action. For example, two responses—call them Response A and Response B—are within the same pocket if mentioning Response A tends to lead to mentioning Response B. Moves can include any of a large number of action types, including responses, explanations, questions, arguments, examples, hypotheses, and proposals.

For an illustration, let us return to the tethered ball scenario discussed earlier. As a starting point, suppose a student argues that the ball will move in the direction of its original trajectory (around in a circle) on the grounds that moving objects tend to continue their current motion. That answer, together with the set of relevant considerations (including at least, we see, an argument in favor of the proposal based on persistence of action), constitutes a pocket. A second student might then counter this idea by arguing that this is only true in a vacuum; in the real world, the ball will continue in a curved path, but that curved path will gradually straighten. (Both of these arguments are common, yet fallacious.) The second answer defines a second pocket ("gradually straightening"), and the rationale "only in a vacuum" may be considered part of both pockets, tending to validate one and undermine the other contention. Yet a third student might support the "gradually straightening" conjecture by volunteering an example; he might claim he has seen racing cars skidding forward and outwards as they try to round a curve. The example belongs to the second pocket.

The central point is that the set of mutually cuing and supporting moves in the exploration characterize a unique portion of the exploration zone—a pocket within that zone. Repeated observations of the activity in a number of contexts informs us about the number of pockets typical of the activity and, furthermore, the characteristic features of each pocket. Thus, we might find that our hypothetical tethered ball exploration zone has four pockets, as discussed previously.

Within the IG activity, we can imagine several ways that moves may be mutually cuing and supporting:

1. The description of a motion phenomenon associated with any representation will, by necessity, attend to some features of the motion phenomena and not others. Such a description may lead to further moves that attend to these same features. For instance, if some student starts attending to speed, other students are likely to do so.

2. A representational form proposed by one student may possess a certain structure that can be appropriated and used, in new ways, by other students. For example, if one student makes a temporal sequence representation, this can lead to the production of similar representations by other students.

3. Finally, the pragmatics of discourse may naturally lead from one move in the discussion to another. For example, a proposal for a representational form may lead naturally to a move that is a justification for the proposal. Widespread aesthetics of judgment of representations may determine whether justifications or critiques are more common and whether agreement in the group tends to be quick or involve extended debate.

Empirically, the type of cuing and support in case (2) seems to us responsible for the primary top-level structure in the IG activity. Thus, the main pockets in IG correspond to the categories of representational forms students create: drawings, temporal sequences, and graph-like representations. These categories of representations appear to strongly define the character of IG explorations, although a very large number of issues cut across the exploration of individual IG pockets.

These categories of representations, however, only describe the top-level pocket structure in the IG activity. In the IG exploration zone—and all other exploration zones—pockets may nest, one inside the other, thus forming a hierarchy. This nesting may be of two distinct types. In the first type of nesting, we may see pockets within pockets, simply because we look at the activity at a finer grain-size. For example, within any of the three main pockets of the IG exploration zone, we can imagine a description in terms of pockets that captures the relatedness of some moves within the larger pocket. For instance, while considering a category of representations, students might start listing all the negative characteristics of the category. (This is mutual cuing of Type 3.) When pockets nest in this manner, we have our choice as to what level we want to consider. If subpockets flow easily into one another, the higher-level pocket is likely the most natural level of consideration. If distinctions among subpockets align with important conceptual issues, we may want to consider both levels.

The second type of nesting is subtler. In some cases, an activity may tend to spawn a new exploration, with its own integrity. For example, in the IG activity, students have sometimes fallen into a discussion of whether an object, when reversing its direction of motion, must necessarily stop (diSessa & Minstrell, 1998). Within this little bubble in the IG activity, the very currency of the discussion has changed. The students are no longer proposing new representational forms and debating their merits; rather, they are having a debate about the physics of motion. The nature of the likely or allowed moves is thus profoundly different.

Pathways. The second structural element of exploration zones is the pathway. A pathway is a transition that takes students from one pocket to another pocket. To exemplify pathways, let us recount in greater detail the Dots representation episode as it played out at City High School. In our prior discussion we noted that, early in the activity, the students became stuck in using Dots. Up to that point no other pocket had been explored, and the exploratory moves were becoming repetitive. Then the teacher made a crucial intervention. She began by asking students to represent the desert motion with their existing versions of Dots. The pool of representations resulting from this

FIG. 11.9. Using a vertical row of dots to show duration of a stop. City High School. Our rendition.

activity consisted mostly of drawings, with dots placed over the trajectory of the car. Next, the teacher suggested that students erase the "unnecessary" features of the representations, such as the car, cactus, and road. By stripping off extraneous details from the representations, the teacher simplified the display, making it easier for students to recognize the unused vertical dimension in Dots.

Focusing on the resulting picture, shown in Fig. 11.4, the teacher then queried students about whether the representation showed the duration of the stop at the cactus. Students recognized that it did not and, following the teacher's suggestion, they attempted to amend the representation. Eventually, students proposed adding a vertical row of dots to represent the duration of the stop, with each dot standing for a unit of time (Fig. 11.9). Following this proposal, the space of inventiveness opened up and students began creating a variety of temporal sequences. The progression observed in the Dots episode indicates that there is a pathway leading from a certain class of drawings into the temporal sequences pocket.

The teacher's intervention may have facilitated, in multiple ways, movement along this pathway. First, she highlighted common features of the existing pocket, helping students see elements of it as the same. Second, she highlighted features unused in the current pocket (the vertical dimension) that could be used in a new pocket. Third, she motivated the need for a new class of designs by eliciting a critique that would be difficult to accommodate inside the current pocket.

As a further example, consider Inventing Mapping activities. Our repeated observations of IM show that students readily create landscape drawings that are orthographic projections made from a top view. However, the production of quasi-topographic maps is more spotty. This suggests the need to find pedagogically accessible pathways between orthographic projections and topographic maps. Our observations suggest that such pathways exist. Suppose, that a class of students has failed to create any quasi-topographic maps. The teacher might explicitly guide the class by asking students to first draw orthographic renditions of a given landscape. Then, resorting to another idea with which students are fluent, the teacher might ask them to represent height information by "color-coding" their representations.

Landmarks. Landmarks are specific contributions to an exploration that, for one reason or another, are particularly prominent to participants. For example, in a simple class discussion, a landmark can be a specific answer or argument proposed by one of the participants. In a representational design activity, a landmark can be a specific representational form and (possibly) some of the arguments surrounding its design rationale.

Landmarks may play important roles in organizing classroom activity. For instance, references to a landmark might have the effect of invoking the larger context of the pocket within which the landmark lies, effectively returning the exploration to that pocket. Additionally, invoking a landmark might bring to attention some conceptual issues that were investigated when the landmark/pocket was first considered. In the hands of teachers and students, then, landmarks might function pragmatically (i.e., by transferring an exploration back to a particular pocket) or conceptually (i.e., by highlighting particular key issues in the exploration). Teachers might productively think about the properties of landmarks—for example, their proximity to a pathway and/or their relations to important conceptual issues—and then use them instrumentally. A teacher has less control over how students use landmarks, although she might subtly encourage productive landmarks and discourage those that have little productive function.

During enactments of the IG activity at Benson Middle School, the "Slants" representation (Fig. 11.10) played the role of a landmark. Slants is a temporal sequence in which the slope of each line represents the speed of the object at a given moment. According to the convention established by Mitchell, the inventor of Slants, a horizontal line depicts "as fast as it (the car) can go" whereas a vertical line indicates the object is stopped.

FIG. 11.10. The "Slants" representation.

Slants was often referenced, both by teacher and students, and these references seemed to have a range of felicitous effects. In some instances, invoking Slants worked to raise for consideration general issues concerning the task as a whole. For instance, on the second day of activities, Mitchell compared Slants to other representations in an attempt to decide which representation showed *all* aspects of the desert motion. The issue of completeness was thus linked to Slants and could, on other occasions, be invoked by considering if a representation was "like Slants."

On another occasion, invoking Slants caused the initiation of an extremely productive line of exploration, essentially making movement along a new pathway possible. On the third day of activities, Mitchell suggested hooking Slants end-to-end, as a means of representing continuous motion. Another student, Steve, then quickly proposed adding a grid to the resulting representation, essentially transforming it into a graph. A teacher, understanding the proximity of Slants to graphing and what final steps might accomplish the transition (in this case, introducing continuity to Slants), could nudge the exploration forward by invoking Slants. This could be accomplished immediately or further upstream, by reintroducing Slants or helping to solidify its landmark status.

Landmarks can gain their prominence for many reasons. Although we cannot pinpoint the reasons why Slants functioned as a landmark at Benson, we conjecture that at least four factors were influential. First, Slants contrasted significantly with the existing representational forms when it was first introduced. Second, it made substantial contact with a number of issues that were central to many discussions, leading it to be considered on several occasions.[4] Teachers and students thus variously returned to Slants throughout the activity in order to make important points. Third, the Slants creator was outspoken and articulate. Although he sometimes argued in favor of other representations, he often acted as an advocate for Slants and other representational forms that were inspired by Slants. Finally, the fact that the representation was given a name by the class—"Slants"—likely helped to solidify it as a landmark. In fact, the teacher at Benson encouraged students to name invented representations that she deemed to be particularly novel or noteworthy, illustrating the strategic facilitation of the creation of landmarks by teachers.

A Typology of Pockets.   Inspired partly by our data and partly by observations of other activity types, we begin developing a typology of pockets. The first pocket of significance is the *pit*. Pits are pockets with "deep topography," which results in students being stuck in a narrow region of the exploration zone. For instance, the episode in which students at City High School could not create alternatives to Dots representations may illustrate a pit.

---

[4]Thus, in the best of circumstances, things become landmarks for the good reason that they embody many important issues.

Pits can exist for various reasons, such as students' attraction to particular types of solutions, perceived authority, or the nature of the intellectual leap needed to escape the pit. As an example where perceived authority could have resulted in a pit, consider an episode that took place at the first IG session in one of our summer courses. On that occasion, soon after the teacher had proposed the desert motion task to the class, Tamara declared that "obviously, graphing is the best way to show it." The teacher deflected Tamara's assertion by stating: "I'm suspicious of single best answers." He then stated that although Cartesian graphs could well solve the problem, he wanted the class to explore more broadly, and briefly suggested that different representations work better or worse depending on context. The class took the teacher's suggestion and generated a variety of representational forms. But it is conceivable that students might have focused on Tamara's idea, particularly since it is known by students to be an officially sanctioned school representation. Had they focused quickly on graphing, they might have missed a lot of learning about the advantages of other representations and a gradual appreciation of the diversity of criteria that are possible. Although we worried initially about this dangerous pit, our experience has been that graphing is seldom introduced early on. Even students quite familiar with graphing do not immediately associate it with the function of conveying information about motion.

The second significant type of pocket is the *plain*—pockets in which a large number of solutions are perceived to be equally good and thus progress, in the form of the production of perceived-to-be improved representations, is hard to obtain. For example, the drawing pocket within IM may be plain-like. There are many ways to draw a landscape, each with its own merits. So choosing among them is likely to be difficult and would likely not provide grounds for a productive exploration.

The characteristics of pits and plains combine naturally. If a broad range of accessible representations are perceived to be equally good and, in addition, there is some conceptual or other barrier to escaping the pocket, we have a *crater*.

The Factors That Shape the Structure of an Exploration Zone

We understand exploration zones as emergent patterns in activity that arise from a complex conjunction of multiple influences, including individual, social, and environmental factors. Building an account of how an exploration zone emerges from these factors is beyond the scope of the present chapter. In fact, the complexity of this problem is one of the motivations for introducing the notion of exploration zone in the first place. By introducing exploration zones, we have reified a level of consideration of emergent patterns in student-directed activities. This level of consideration, we believe, provides the basis for a useful and empirically tractable research program, while stopping short of a complete analysis of underlying influences. Here, we restrict ourselves to two brief points that pertain to the factors that shape the structure of an exploration zone.

Stability of exploration zones and the time-scale of classroom explorations. Implicit in our discussion thus far is the assumption that the topography of an exploration zone (i.e., the collection of pockets and pathways and their characteristics) remains stable over timescales that are characteristic of classroom explorations. Essentially, the metaphor we have adopted presumes a stable landscape over which the exploration proceeds. Thus, we have been implicitly assuming that the factors that are shaping an exploration zone, especially student knowledge, remain largely stable over the course of classroom events. However, the structure of an exploration zone might well change during an exploration, particularly as students acquire new knowledge.

Cases in which one factor is particularly important in shaping an exploration zone. Note that the enactment of the IG activities requires no special-purpose props beyond pencil and paper. The exploration zone of IG is thus not primarily defined by physical resources that are particular to these activities. Instead, most of the defining resources for IG are embodied within the participants, particularly the students. Once the teacher has given the simple specification of the task, students propose and discuss alternatives with only some simple guidance from the teacher. Indeed, we have essentially been arguing that the structure of the IG exploration zone can be identified with families of representational forms and that these, in turn, substantially mirror the representational capacities that students bring to the task. For example, all of the (speculative) features we identified for the existence of pockets—common perceived features, shared form, and relatedness via familiar rhetorical strategies—are purely conceptual.

This conceptual basis for the structure of IG's exploration zone is highlighted if we contrast IG with a quite different set of curricular activities. A curriculum called "Struggle for Survival" was developed by researchers at Northwestern University in collaboration with Chicago Public Schools (Reiser et al., 2001). In this curriculum, students investigate why, on one of the Galapagos Islands, the population of finches declined sharply during the late 1970s. To support this investigation, students are given a specially designed computer database and tools for exploring this database. The database contains a variety of kinds of information, including field notes made by fictional biologists. Students can browse these field notes and read about observations of individual finches. The database also includes quantitative data concerning environmental conditions during the years in question (e.g., rainfall) as well as data concerning characteristics of the finches (e.g., wing length and beak length). For the data concerning finches, the software allows the students to produce a number of kinds of data plots, which they can use to form and support their hypotheses. All of this work is supported by a set of curricular activities that include tasks both on and off the computer.

The factors that give the exploration zone its structure are very different in Struggle for Survival compared to IG. In IG, the exploration zone is generated largely by what students know about representations and does not depend on supporting materials. In contrast, the exploration in Struggle for Survival would be impossible without the computer database, and the exploration zone takes its structure, in large measure, from this database. In a sense, the exploration in Struggle for Survival is *over* the data and the queries permitted in the database, rather than over a space defined mainly by ideas available to students. For example, the software has data concerning the beak length and wing length of individual finches. The students can thus entertain hypotheses such as "the finches with large wings were more likely to survive."

This contrast suggests a possible simplification in our attempts to understand how an exploration zone is shaped by various factors. Although an exploration zone will always emerge from a complex conjunction of factors, there may be some interesting prototypical cases we can think about in which we can understand the exploration zone as principally defined by one type of factor. For example, IG may be an example of a *brainstorming* exploration, a prototypical type of exploration in which the exploration zone is principally defined by the ideas of student participants. And Struggle for Survival may be an example of another prototypical type, a *data-based* exploration, in which the exploration is over a collection of data or other reference materials provided for students. Understanding such prototypical types may be a more manageable task than attempting a full description of how different factors contribute to the topography of an exploration zone.

Describing and Guiding Movement Through an Exploration Zone

As designers of learning environments interested in helping students to acquire scientific and mathematical competence, it is not enough that we understand the space of possibilities that students can explore. We have an agenda: We usually want students to move through an exploration zone in a specific direction or, at least, to have them visit certain locations. This requires an understanding of trajectories through an exploration zone and how to guide students along those trajectories.

In discussing the structure of exploration zones above, we have done much of the preliminary work necessary to understand trajectories; a trajectory can be thought of as movement through an exploration zone, within pockets and from pocket-to-pocket along pathways. The movement within pockets occurs because of the natural chaining of moves that results from the mutual activation and reinforcement of ideas, arguments, and products within a pocket. By definition, then, movement within a pocket is relatively easy to accomplish.

In contrast, movement between pockets can be difficult and may require intervention by the instructor. We have partially addressed this point in the preceding discussion of pathways. In this section, we want to expand on that discussion to consider the instructional techniques that guide students along various trajectories, including interventions that facilitate transitions across pockets and those that are used as a means to organize the activity as a whole.

As a starting point, it is important to note that trajectories through a given exploration zone will certainly differ across enactments of an activity. For example, in the enactments of IG at Benson Middle School and City High School, students began the exploration within the drawing pocket. City High students got stuck there, whereas Benson Middle students did not. With the progression of the activity, both Benson's and City's students eventually explored drawings, temporal sequences, and graphing pockets. In Trenton High's trials of IG, we witnessed explorations of drawing and temporal sequences pockets right from the beginning, with the graph-like pocket appearing later.

In spite of the differences in the activity dynamics that will always exist across trials of an activity, it is sometimes helpful to speak in terms of *canonical trajectories* that are followed through an exploration zone. For example, in the case of IG, there is a canonical trajectory from drawing to temporal sequences to graph-like representations. Likewise, in IM there is a canonical trajectory from drawings to quasi-topographic maps.

Identifying one or more canonical trajectories can help teachers to understand and guide exploration in their classrooms. Moving students along a canonical trajectory can be an explicit initial goal for a teacher, and perhaps one that is most achievable by a novice teacher unfamiliar with details of the exploration zone. Still, reacting to unforeseen contingencies along the canonical trajectory may require high-level expertise of the sort only more expert teachers—who would be more prone to improvise rather than try to force a canonical trajectory—would possess. Once a canonical trajectory is identified, we can collect instructional techniques that can guide students along this trajectory and that help ameliorate exploratory difficulties. Here we list a few categories of instructional techniques, illustrated with examples from our experiences with IG and IM.

Socratic Questioning. One technique for moving students through an exploration zone is an old standby, Socratic dialogue. Socratic dialogue helps students progress by asking them questions and posing challenges. In the IG activity this questioning takes a particular form: Students are presented with a sequence of motions to represent that are devised to test their current representational techniques. For instance, after students create their first representations of the desert motion, the class is asked to represent a motion with an extended stop. Students are thus faced with the task of adjusting some of the conventions deployed in their original representations. Students are then asked to represent a motion with stops of different time lengths, followed by one in which an object reverses its direction.

Sequences such as the one just mentioned do double duty. First, they foster extended exploration within already-discovered pockets because many of the proposed motions can be realized (more or less successfully) within the pockets we have identified. Conceptually, fostering exploration of individual pockets is important because it allows students to investigate the limits and strengths of particular classes of representational forms. Second, toward the end of the sequence of motion problems, one finds more complicated motion patterns that pose difficulties that eventually force students to consider alternative representational schemes. In other words, the sequence of problems may motivate a spontaneous transition to other pockets.[5]

It is worth mentioning that within a student-directed perspective, Socratic questioning and other intervention strategies are intended mainly to move students from pocket to pocket rather than to get them to produce some particular answer or insight, as might be the case in other contexts.

Locating, Consolidating, Reifying. When an exploration is long and complex, the participants in the exploration need techniques for keeping track of the territory that has been explored and for consolidating gains that have been made. In the context of IG, we have identified a number of techniques

---

[5]In addition, introducing challenges can obviously "unflatten" plains and craters by shaping and sharpening the evaluation criteria that distinguish proposed representations.

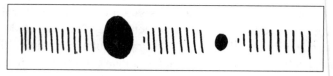

FIG. 11.11a. Sonar representation, as drawn by students at Trenton.

FIG. 11.11b. Sonar representation with an envelope added.

that have proven effective. For example, after several rounds of design have been carried out, the existing set of representations may be quite large. At this point, it is sometimes productive to engage students in a whole-class effort to sort representations according to some community-established criteria. As previously stated, this exercise may be used to narrow the working pool of representations and to focus students' attention on particular attributes of classes of representational forms.

A related pedagogical strategy is to involve students in collectively naming individual representations and, depending on the teacher's goals and style, this exercise may follow the sorting task. Naming representations facilitates future references to representational forms, and it gives students a sense of ownership over the products they generate (Madanes, 1997). As discussed above, naming individual representations may function as a strategy for establishing landmarks.

Transforming.   In some cases, it might not be enough to ask questions and consolidate gains. One additional possible class of instructional techniques involves the transformation of pocket-specific ideas into products that belong to a new (target) pocket. For example, using the Sonar representation (Fig. 11.11a) as a departing point, one may draw envelopes over each part of the temporal sequence to suggest plots akin to those found in graphs (Fig. 11.11b).

Similarly, in the Dots episode discussed earlier we saw that erasing features of a representation simplified the display so that students could more easily attend to unused dimensions of the paper. More generally, erasing features

FIG. 11.12. Adam's representation of a motion that includes a reversal in direction. City, Session 1. From video capture.

of a representation may suggest representational approaches that motivate exploration of a new pocket. As an example, consider annotated drawings— drawings with diverse elements added to suggest specific motion information— such as the one in Fig. 11.12. In the figure, Adam has represented the moving object as a small circle and marks that stand for the object's speed emanate from the object's rear. In Adam's scheme, the greater the speed of the object, the more marks appear behind it. Now, if we erase the object and the road (the single line at the bottom of the representation), we are left with the essential elements of a temporal sequence: an array of discrete representational elements (i.e., the marks), each conveying a particular piece of the motion story, which should be read from left to right. It is even possible that students could pick up "erasing extraneous elements" as a common spontaneous move. Doing so would establish a new line of affinity among moves, altering the structure of the exploration zone.

What Makes an Exploration Zone Engaging?

Student engagement has received increasing attention in the literature (e.g., Hidi & Harackiewicz, 2000; Lepper & Cordova, 1992; Marks, 2000; Newmann, 1992). These researchers generally proposed models of engagement based on factors such as students' intrinsic motivation toward academic achievement and students' interest in particular topics. Thus, for example, students interested in science tend to engage in science-related subjects for longer periods of time and to persist in the face of complex problems. Similarly, academically oriented students are more likely to engage and participate in classroom activities.

Our approach here departs from this usual treatment of engagement in the sense that we are concerned with describing how structural features of an exploration zone—its configuration of pockets and pathways—might heighten the opportunities for student participation and engagement. Hence, the assumption underlying our arguments is that the structure of the exploration zone is largely orthogonal to variables such as students' interests and motivation. With that in mind, let us consider how activities differentially engage students by drawing upon a comparison between the two representational design activities we reviewed earlier.

As stated previously, our experiences with Inventing Graphing convinced us that the activity is generally very successful in engaging students. Our perceptions of student participation are that they feel strongly engaged and committed to the ideas being generated. At each design round, students demonstrate a strong ability to refine their previous designs, to appropriate ideas proposed by others, and to create new products. In addition, students actively engage in the classroom discussions, generating a number of comments and design criteria that are then used to feed overall design improvements.

In contrast, Inventing Mapping has proved to be a less-engaging activity. In their initial attempts to represent a given landscape, students promptly create a number of drawings and quasi-topographic maps of the landscape. But the discussions that follow this initial round of designs have tended to be terse and uninspired. Subsequent rounds of design present a similar picture: brief, slow-paced discussions and few or no class-generated design innovations. Overall, our perception is that in IM students do not feel very engaged or committed to the ideas they put forth. The exception to these dynamics occurs when the theme of using colors as representational devices in quasi-topographic maps arises. This theme elicits increased response from students, both in terms of the number of products and in terms of the quality and quantity of comments on each other's designs.

A Hypothesis.   In terms of our framework, then, how can we explain this noticeable difference in engagement fostered by IG and IM activities? In an initial formulation of our hypothesis, we follow Csikszentmihalyi (1988). Like us, Csikszentmihalyi has been concerned with identifying the structural features that make for engaging activity, although his emphasis has been on individual activity rather than group design. In particular, he proposes that more clearly structured activities are best suited to sustaining extended engagement (Csikszentmihalyi, 1988, p. 30). Among the many properties he lists for clearly structured activities, three are particularly relevant for our purposes here: (1) Opportunities for self-expression must be abundant, yet (2) such opportunities must be constrained by a relatively clear set of rules for action, and (3) individuals must be able easily to assess their progress in achieving the activity's goals. An engaging exploration zone thus maintains a balance between clear structure and room for self-expression. To use one of Csikszentmihalyi's examples, a game of chess offers good grounds for extended engagement because play variations are nearly infinite. Yet, action in the domain of chess playing is guided by rules that constrain moving options at each point. Furthermore, many moves are clearly improvements in positioning or, after an opponent's response, can easily be evaluated as failed attempts at improvement.

The Hypothesis Applied to IM and IG. We can now look at our analysis of IM and IG in terms of our framework, and we can see where and how the balance between creativity and constraint is maintained in the two activities. As a first analysis, we look at the major pockets in each activity. We saw in our analysis that IG has three major pockets and IM has two major pockets. Crudely speaking, two pockets may simply not provide enough room for exploration to make for an engaging activity.[6]

We can also apply Csikszentmihalyi's hypothesis to the within-pocket structure of the exploration zones of IG and IM. In IG we find extended-class activity in the temporal sequences pocket, more so than in the other two pockets in that zone. Recall that temporal sequences are linear arrays of elements strung together, each conveying a piece of the story being told. In practice, this specification constitutes a template that loosely defines what needs to be done at each round of IG design. The temporal sequences template thus can be seen as providing a clear structure for action (Property 2), productively constraining possible design solutions. At the same time, such a template allows for enormous personal expression because so many of its parameters can be tweaked (Property 1). The tweaking of elements in temporal sequences can be more or less significant, and we have observed a very wide range of inventiveness in students' works (from idiosyncratic signs to "vectors"). Importantly, because these elements can be systematically varied and compared to previous solutions, the crafting of temporal sequences allows students to gauge their progress and to decide on future design improvements (Property 3).[7]

---

[6] Our considerations in this section should not be taken as dismissing the potential of IM activities. Rather, our arguments point to the fact that, in practice—with the insights we currently have and the interventions we have considered—IM activities profitably sustain engagement systematically for a shorter period of time relative to IG.

[7] For example, some students complained that certain temporal sequences contained too many kinds of signs, which were unrelated to each other. These establish goals for improved design.

No other pocket in the IG exploration zone seems to us to do so well with the conditions listed above as the temporal sequences pocket. For example, the drawings pocket allows for a lot of individual self-expression (Property 1). On the other hand, drawing conventions are so plastic that almost anything goes. To use our terminology, this pocket is too much of a *plain*, as we discussed earlier. This makes it hard for students to assess progress and to choose relevant aspects for design refinement. In fact, students appear less able to comment on the limits and strengths of drawing representations, an observation that may reflect the lack of clear parameters for judging such representations (Property 3).

The graph-like depictions pocket also suffers from problems when measured against our criteria. To be sure, there are clear rules governing the making of graphs (Property 2). But because such rules are strict, the possibilities for self-expression are reduced in relation to those offered by the temporal sequences pocket (Property 1).[8]

Finally, we can apply the same reasoning to explain the lower levels of student engagement observed in IM. As in IG, the drawing pocket in IM offers a much too broad space of possibilities and makes it hard for students to evaluate progress (Properties 2 and 3). Quasi-topographic maps offer a relatively clear set of rules for action, but these rules allow for very little variation and creative expression (Property 1). The theme of using colors as representational devices overlays onto quasi-topographic maps the possibility for individual expression while keeping the structured rules for the making of quasi-topographic maps. This may explain why activity within that theme elicits heightened engagement from students. Still, students seem to exhaust the possibilities for creating coloring schemes relatively quickly.

Pathways and Engagement. Our considerations of the engaging nature of exploration zones thus far have revolved exclusively around the number and character of pockets. Pathways, however, also play an important part in sustaining engagement. If there are too few pathways or the pathways are too difficult to traverse, then some pockets may remain largely unexplored (effectively decreasing the amount of room for exploration). For example, in demonstrating pathways between temporal sequences and graph-like depictions, we listed three pathways, some of which have appeared in more than

---

[8] As an added problem, students are not fluent with graphing, which drives them away from strong engagement with graphs, at least initially.

one edition of the activity. This fact, once again, helps us to understand why IG is so engaging.

Variations in Engagement During an Activity. Regardless of the structure of an exploration zone, student engagement is almost never constantly high. Even in activities that are generally highly engaging, such as Inventing Graphing, engagement fluctuates, increasing or decreasing depending on the nature of classroom events. Certain conditions are notably detrimental to engagement. For example, when students find themselves inside a pit, engagement suffers a marked drop. The Dots representations episode at City High School empirically illustrates this point, and it is also in accordance with Csikszentmihalyi's (1988, pp. 32) observation that engagement suffers when one has difficulty making progress.

Incidentally, the observation that overall difficulties reduce engagement levels leads us to postulate that engaging exploration zones must have one or more pockets within easy initial reach. In practical terms, this means that students can get to work rather quickly. To understand this idea, it helps to consider its opposite: An activity that makes it hard for students to get started is equivalent to putting students in a pit right from the start. Empirically, we have observed that IM and IG are equally engaging in their initial moments because, in both activities, there is at least one pocket that is immediately within reach. Difficulties may systematically be less of a problem later in explorations. Students may develop a strong commitment to succeeding (or improving) and may have faith, borne of prior success, that they can succeed.

CONCLUSION

Review

The goal of this chapter has been to propose a way to think about the nature of open-ended, student-directed activities. This way of thinking should synthesize and explain (at some level) regularities in the conduct of such activities, such as repeated patterns we perceive when "running an activity again" (e.g., with different students). We are not focusing on conceptual development or learning per se, but on things like engagement, the flow of ideas, and interventions teachers make to move the activity along or change its direction without wresting control from students. In our case, we use group design of representations as an inspiration and testing ground for these ideas.

Our analysis is based on a systematic use of a spatial metaphor, of students being *at a particular place* at a given time and *moving around in a landscape* of known properties. One of the principle regularities we observe is that certain moves (proposals for design, comments, criticisms, etc.) seem to come in clumps. This gives rise to the concept of a *pocket*, a collection of "places" that allow relatively easy movement among them. Pockets come in different forms, which have systematically different properties. *Pits* are narrow pockets that are difficult to escape. Generally, one wants to avoid pits or to design ways to escape them. *Plains* are relatively rich pockets, yet which do not allow significant differentiation among places. Plains may be as boring as pits.

Pathways are viable transitions between pockets. Knowing about pathways and ways to scaffold their associated transitions can be highly strategic in a teacher's promotion of an active, effective exploration. We described several fairly general strategies for facilitating transitions across pathways. *Landmarks* are particularly interesting and memorable "points" in an exploration zone. Like pathways, teachers and students can use existing landmarks (or foster the development of new, useful landmarks) for many purposes.

We discussed features of exploration zones that promote active engagement. One needs good starter pockets and a sufficient number of pockets to keep the exploration going. In addition, we found that our framework and observations mesh well with some of Csikszentmihalyi's (1988) ideas, in particular, in our observation of the need for (1) room for expressive diversity, (2) constraints on possible moves, and (3) the possibility of effective judgment.

Limits of the Spatial Metaphor

We are under no illusion that the level of consideration contemplated in exploration zone analysis will prove to be complete. The complex dynamics and many influential parameters underlying engagement in activities will eventually surface in scientific study, in one way or another. Here, we mention two loci in which we expect difficulties to surface.

The spatial metaphor presumes a collection of "places," and a sense of "nearby." Implicitly one should be able to visit the same places on multiple occasions. In contrast, "going back to identical places" in an activity is at least implausible, if not impossible. For example, once students have thought about other things, the context for a revisited thought will be different and "being back there" will have different consequences. Furthermore, if a student tries literally to make the same move again, its repetition will be interpreted as a message, making the repeated move distinct from its original. So, ironically, the spatial metaphor may work best when one does not attempt to return to the same place, but only to nearby places.

"Nearby," of course, is subject to the same contextual variation. Having learned and experienced other things, returning to the vicinity of a certain place may find different moves selected as "easy to make." Thus, "nearby" will be different the second time.

Moving to our second locus of difficulty, the spatial metaphor works well in part because we have vivid imaginations and descriptive capabilities for the 3-dimensional landscapes that populate our physical world. In principle, even if the spatial metaphor were perfect, we have no reason to believe engagement dynamics can be adequately described in only two or three dimensions. If it takes many dimensions to capture regularities in activities, then as a practical matter we may need other metaphors to help us think about these regularities.

FUTURE WORK

What do we take to be the most profitable and interesting future developments in a theory of exploration zones? First, we need to be more articulate about our methodology. What are the criteria by which one determines whether one or another analysis of the structure of an exploration zone is better or more accurate? Our exposition here has been suggestive, but how would we fend off truly competing analyses? Along similar lines, at what grain size should we describe pockets and pathways?

One way to operationalize good or bad exploration zone analyses might be to ask whether our analyses help teachers conduct effective, engaging explorations. However, we must be careful to recognize that science and practical help do not necessarily align. Still, it will probably be productive for us to see this enterprise as, in part, guided by a desire to give relatively practical help to teachers.

Theoretically, we would like to be clearer on what elements of what is happening in an activity at a particular time define its "place" and how they do so. So far, we have been somewhat vague and inclusive, taking essentially any "move" (proposal, comment, critique, etc.) as an element whose properties define (by principles about which we have been fairly mute) "where we are." In this vein, it is very likely that the perceptions of participants are critical to the definition of places and pockets. For example, ideas that are perceived as different will provoke surprise and the energy of novelty, even if they are not objectively very different from what has come before.

A major issue is the relation of exploration zones to a more fine-grained theory of activities. We broached this transition in several places. For example, we suggested that (1) ideas that involve similar descriptive terms, (2) ideas that fit into a common framework (such as all temporal sequences), and (3) ideas that follow regular rhetorical patterns (like justifications and explanations) frequently go together, thus helping to define pockets. Of course, one could try to remain at a purely empirical level, using, for example, statistical correlations of kinds of happenings across editions of an activity. But speculations about underlying mechanisms are at least heuristically helpful in identifying pockets. The danger, as we mentioned early on, is that a careful and accountable consideration of the dynamics of activities might blow apart the spatial metaphor and the tractable simplicity of an exploration zone analysis and throw us into an arena that we are, as yet, not ready to pursue responsibly.

To what extent do exploration zone analyses cover different kinds of activities? Our main examples have been about design, which has different properties compared to other activities, like scientific investigation or purely artistic activities. We have no reason to be deeply suspicious that the framework will fail in other arenas, and yet creativity and "design proposals" play such a central role in design and in our analyses of example exploration zones that their ubiquity begs the display of equivalent features in different activities. Quite possibly this could turn into a cogent argument about the ways in which design and scientific activity are closely related.[9]

Finally, we believe our treatment of interest and engagement is still relatively crude. It bears a lot of empirical and analytical scrutiny. This we feel reflects the state of the art in the study of these features of activity rather than a particular lack of exploration zone theory.

REFERENCES

Azevedo, F. S. (1998). *Inventing mapping: Meta-representational competence for spatially distributed data*. Paper presented at the Annual Meeting of the American Education Research Association, San Diego, CA.

Azevedo, F. S. (2000). Designing representations of terrain: A study in meta-representational competence. *Journal of Mathematical Behavior, 19*(4), 443–480.

---

[9]In this regard, consider the arguments about the relation of design to learning science in diSessa (1992).

Brown, A. L., & Campione, J. C. (1994). Guided discovery in a community of learners. In K. McGilly (Ed.), *Classroom lessons: Integrating cognitive theory and classroom practice* (pp. 229–270). Cambridge, MA: MIT Press.

Brown, A. L., & Campione, J. C. (1996). Psychological theory and the design of innovative learning environments: On procedures, principles, and systems. In L. Schauble & R. Glaser (Eds.), *Innovations in learning: New environments for education* (pp. 289–325). Mahwah, NJ: Lawrence Erlbaum Associates.

Collins, A. (1995). Design issues for learning environments. In S. Vosniadou, E. de Corte, & H. Mandl (Eds.), *International perspectives on the psychological foundations of technology-based learning environments* (pp. 347–361). Hillsdale, NJ: Lawrence Erlbaum Associates.

Csikszentmihalyi, M. (1988). The flow experience and its significance for human psychology. In M. Csikszentmihalyi & I. S. Csikszentmihalyi (Eds.), *Optimal experience: Psychological studies of flow in consciousness* (pp. 15–35). New York: Cambridge University Press.

diSessa, A., & Sherin, B. (2000). Meta-representation: An introduction. *Journal of Mathematical Behavior, 19*(4), 385–398.

diSessa, A. A. (1992). Images of learning. In E. De Corte, M. C. Linn, H. Mandl, & L. Verschaffel (Eds.), *Computer-based learning environments and problem solving* (pp. 19–40). Berlin: Springer.

diSessa, A. A. (2000). *Changing minds: Computers, learning, and literacy.* Cambridge, MA: MIT Press.

diSessa, A. A. (2002). Students' criteria for representational adequacy. In K. Gravemeijer, R. Lehrer, B. van Oers, & L. Verschaffel (Eds.), *Symbolizing, modeling, and tool use in mathematics education* (pp. 105–129). Dordrecht: Kluwer.

diSessa, A. A., Hammer, D., Sherin, B., & Kolpakowski, T. (1991). Inventing graphing: Meta-representational expertise in children. *Journal of Mathematical Behavior, 10,* 117–160.

diSessa, A. A., & Minstrell, J. (1998). Cultivating conceptual change with benchmark lessons. In J. G. Greeno (Ed.), *Thinking practices* (pp. 155–187). Hillsdale, NJ: Lawrence Erlbaum Associates.

Granados, R. (2000). Constructing intersubjectivity in representational design activities. *Journal of Mathematical Behavior, 19*(4), 503–530.

Hidi, S., & Harackiewicz, J. M. (2000). Motivating the academically unmotivated: A critical issue for the 21st century. *Review of Educational Research, 70*(2), 151–179.

Lave, J., & Wenger, E. (1991). *Situated learning: Legitimate peripheral participation.* New York: Cambridge University Press.

Lemke, J. L. (1990). *Talking science: Language, learning, and values.* Norwood, NJ: Ablex.

Lepper, M. R., & Cordova, D. I. (1992). A desire to be taught: Instructional consequences of intrinsic motivation. *Motivation & Emotion, 16*(3), 187–208.

Madanes, R. (1997). *Teaching through discussion: Using critical moves and support moves.* Paper presented at the Annual Meeting of the American Eductional Research Association, Chicago, IL.

Marks, H. M. (2000). Student engagement in instructional activity: Patterns in the elementary, middle, and high school years. *American Educational Research Journal, 37*(1), 153–184.

Mehan, H. (1979). *Learning lessons: Social organization in the classroom.* Cambridge, MA: Harvard University Press.

Newman, D., Griffin, P., & Cole, M. (1989). *The construction zone: Working for cognitive change in school.* New York: Cambridge University Press.

Newmann, F. M. (1992). *Student engagement and achievement in American secondary schools.* New York: Teachers College Press.

Reiser, B., Tabak, I., Sandoval, W. A., Smith, B. K., Steinmuller, F., & Leone, A. J. (2001). BGuILE: Strategic and conceptual scaffolds for scientific inquiry in biology classrooms. In S. M. Carver & D. Klahr (Eds.), *Cognition and instruction: Twenty-five years of progress* (pp. 263–305). Mahwah, NJ: Lawrence Erlbaum Associates.

Sherin, B. (1997). *The elements of representational design.* Paper presented at the Annual Meeting of the American Association for Educational Research., Chicago, IL.

Sherin, B. (2000). How students invent representations of motion: A genetic account. *Journal of Mathematical Behavior, 19*(4), 399–441.

Willats, J. (1985). Drawing systems revisited: The role of denotation systems in children's figure drawings. In N. H. Freeman & M. V. Cox (Eds.), *Visual Order: The nature and development of pictorial representation* (pp. 374–384). New York: Cambridge University Press.

Wood, D., & Fels, J. (1992). *The power of maps.* New York: Guilford Press.

Yackel, E., & Cobb, P. (1996). Sociomathematical Norms, argumentation, and autonomy in mathematics. *Journal for Research in Mathematics Education, 27*(4), 458–477.

Author Index

Numbers in *italics* indicate pages with complete bibliographic information.

A

American Association for the Advancement of Science/Project, 301, *325*

Amaya-Williams, M., 227–228, *233*

American Association for the Advancement of Science, 267, 268, *297*

American Association for the Advancement of Science/Project 2061, 4, 5

Anderson, J., 2, 5

Ansell, E., 100, *117*, 178, 179, *208*

Arnheim, R., 304, *325*

Audi, 179n1

Azevedo, F. S., 334, 335, 341, *364*

B

Bakhtin, M., 309, *325*

Balacheff, N., 97, *117*

Ball, D. L., 96, *117*, 151, *152*, 153, 171, *173*, 300, 301, 302, 311, 322, 323, *325*

Ballenger, C., 302, 307, *325*, *327*

Barton, A. M., 272, 274n1, 288n3, 296n6, *297*

Bass, H., 96, *117*, 300, 301, 302, 322, *325*

Bastable, B., 99, *117*

Bauersfeld, H., 12, 23, *44*

Bazerman, C., 179, *207*

Bazzini, L., 46, *92*

Beals, D. E., 177, *207*

Bednarz, N., 45, *92*

Belanger, M., 45, *92*

Bereiter, C., 97, *117*

Berne, J., 300, 301, 302, 322, *327*

Berreman, G., 303, *325*

Biagioli, M., 3, 5

Biehler, R., 158, *173*

Billig, M., 204, *207*

Blanton, M., 107, *117*, 213–214, 215, 232, *232*, *233*

Blumer, H., 12, *44*

Blunk, M. L., 178, *208*

Boufi, A., 13, *44*

Brendefur, J., 245, *265*

Brizuela, B., 214, *233*

Brown, A. L., 332, 333, *365*

Brown, C. A., 206, *208*

367

Subject Index